THE IRISH MEDIA DIRECTORY AND GUIDE 2006

A comprehensive guide to all media
on the island of Ireland

Helen Shaw
Editor

Produced by Athena Media

Gill & Macmillan

Gill & Macmillan Ltd
Hume Avenue, Park West, Dublin 12
with associated companies throughout the world
www.gillmacmillan.ie
© Athena Media Limited 2005
0 7171 3910 7
Index compiled by Cover To Cover
Design and print origination by Carole Lynch
Printed by MPG Books, Cornwall

This book is typeset in MBembo 11pt on 14 pt, and Meta 10pt on 14pt.

The paper used in this book comes from the wood pulp of managed forests.
For every tree felled, at least one tree is planted, thereby renewing natural resources.

A CIP catalogue record for this book is available from the British Library.

5 4 3 2 1

CONTENTS

Foreword   viii

JOHN HORGAN

1. The Irish Media Landscape: Information Island   1
    An overview of the Irish media landscape and an introduction to the book
    HELEN SHAW
    Irish media in Irish DONNCHA Ó CRÓINÍN   4
    Media facts, Ireland   12

2. Newspapers: Pressing Times   13
    The newspaper industry: dailies, weeklies, regional and local press
    MARK O'BRIEN
    Regional papers: Making a killing CARIONA NEARY   18
    ■ Directory   21

3. Television: Ireland on the Box   60
    Television stations—national, regional and community
    HELEN SHAW
    ■ Directory   67

4. Radio: The Audio Boom   75
    *Radio stations—national, local, regional, community, hospitals and
    institutions*
    HELEN SHAW
    ■ Directory   81

5. New Media: Riding the Technology Wave   104
    *The internet, mobile telephones, digital culture, games and the
    digital media business*
    APHRA KERR
    Faster and smaller: Moore's Law and the gadget NEIL LEYDEN   109
    ■ Directory   112

6. Books: Reading the Future 121
The book publishing industry and bookselling
MARK O'BRIEN
■ Directory 127

7. Magazines and Periodicals: Off the Shelf 139
Magazines and periodicals sector
MARK O'BRIEN
■ Directory 144

8. Film and Audio-visual Production: Cinema Hibernia 189
Production companies, studios, equipment
HELEN SHAW
■ Directory 195

9. Education, Careers and Training: Working in the Media 236
Universities, colleges, third-level institutions and evening courses
MARK O'BRIEN
■ Directory 240

10. Advertising, Public Relations and Marketing: The Hard Sell 257
*Agencies, branding, corporate communications, marketing strategists
and public relations*
CARIONA NEARY
PR and marketing: The professional soft sell! 262
■ Directory 264

11. Media Institutions, Services and Professional Organisations:
Regulating for Choice 289
*Regulation and accountability mechanisms, state departments and
state agencies; Lawyers, agents, financial services, unions, professional
organisations, media research (e.g. media monitoring) and services*
HELEN SHAW
■ Directory 294

12. Global Media: Fewer Owners, More Choice?   300
Key contact list of relevant media beyond Ireland for anyone working in, using or studying the sector
HELEN SHAW
Around the world in 80 minutes: Murdoch's global empire   303
■ Directory   307

13. Media Awards, Festivals and Competitions: One for
Everyone in the Audience!   321
Media-related awards, festivals and competitions
HELEN SHAW
■ Directory   327

Index   334

FOREWORD

John Horgan, Professor of Journalism,
Dublin City University

The relationship between Irish media and the society of which they form a part is, and has been for centuries, a fluid—even a volatile—one. Not least because of our history as a former British colony, the relationship between media and politics has been a close and occasionally symbiotic one. As a community increasingly influenced by the British (and latterly Anglo-American) communications ecology in which we participate willy-nilly, for linguistic and other reasons, we import and use foreign media as readily as we import foreign oil. This, inevitably, helps to define the field in which media studies will pitch its tent as we go forward into the twenty-first century.

In a globalised world, can there be, any longer, such an entity as 'national media' or, if there is, how is it to be defined? Until very recently, one of our 'national' newspapers (the *Sunday Business Post*) was owned by a British company and physically produced—although not edited—outside the physical boundaries of the state. Another (the *Irish Daily Star*) is 50% owned by British press interests. A third (*Ireland on Sunday*) is wholly owned by the Daily Mail conglomerate. Our privately owned television station and our only national radio competitor to RTÉ are both owned by non-Irish companies, as are a number of important regional radio stations and regional newspapers. Under EU law, in any case, any EU-based company can, within the parameters formed by anti-monopoly legislation and the content regulations laid down by the Broadcasting Commission of Ireland, walk in our front door and buy any print or broadcast medium it can afford. What are the implications of this state of affairs for our self-understanding, and for the way in which we talk to ourselves and forge our own identities?

As the barriers against external ownership and control crumble, the question of regulation assumes a new and higher place on the agenda. There are two sets of issues here. One of them is connected with the issues of monopoly generally and the belief, held by policy-makers in many liberal democratic societies but legislated for by far fewer, that it is important to maximise the number of outlets for news, public opinion and democratic self-expression generally. The problem about this is that it is an area in which high ideals often come to a shuddering halt when faced with the brute realities of the market place. All media, like all other businesses, strive to protect their market position against competitors and, generally speaking, operate on the belief that the fewer competitors there are, the better.

In this context, the role of public media assumes an ever-greater importance, even where it is partly commercial, as in Ireland. Forty years ago the reality for most television viewers in Ireland was rather like that offered by Henry Ford to the early purchasers of his Model T machines: they could have any colour they liked, as long as it was black. In the early years of television, national public broadcasters in Ireland and elsewhere were a monopoly, which could, and did, operate almost insulated from competition and from the harsh imperatives later dictated by a huge spectrum of digital, satellite-delivered rivals. Today, there is almost a sense in which the wheel has turned full circle. Commercial broadcasting, dependent wholly on the market place for its revenues, is showing a tendency to fragment in myriad directions but with its content increasingly narrowly based on infotainment. In this context, can public broadcasting, derided twenty years ago as a grey monolith, enter an era in which it will be able, perhaps, to develop new strengths (or re-develop its old ones) as a source of diversity and pluralism in social, cultural and political terms? How should this be paid for, who should determine its content, and how should its performance be assessed?

The second area of regulation relates less to ownership and control than to content and accountability. Print and broadcast media alike have been exercised for many years, and often with some justice, about the restrictions placed on legitimate journalistic activity by antiquated libel laws. These obviously can and should be changed, although in what way and to what extent will be a matter for keen political argument. At the same time, the image of the media as striving heroically against the overpowering might of church and state is, to put it mildly, now a bit overblown. The media are a powerful force in their own right, whatever restrictions they labour under.

As an institution that—quite rightly—holds those in power in society to account, how and to whom should the media become accountable for the use of their own power? Is journalism a profession, like medicine or accountancy, and should it be regulated as these professions are regulated—or is there some other, more appropriate model?

And how will the new media be regulated, if they can be regulated at all? As the bloggers trample on the toes of the more traditional media and manage, on occasion, even to be first with the news, a whole series of new challenges arises for traditional print and broadcast media that they will ignore at their peril. Although the death of the newspaper has been predicted for many decades now, as radio, television and the web came along, it has proved a remarkably resilient form of expression. But the ways in which not just newspapers but all media will have to continually re-invent themselves in order to maintain a meaningful role in today's world are, as yet, only faintly visible.

1

THE IRISH MEDIA LANDSCAPE: INFORMATION ISLAND

Helen Shaw

It's hard to imagine, but in 1970 when Dana won the Eurovision Song Contest, most people watched on a tiny black-and-white television set if they were lucky enough to have a television. Reception was poor and choice was non-existent. The rabbit ears were replaced by clutters of aerials on the roofs, and in the 1970s those lucky enough to get the UK channels along the east coast watched HTV and got used to hearing Welsh.

To an information-saturated media age in which the internet is now available on mobile phones and half the country has digital television, the hazy monotone images of early RTÉ seem an ancient memory. Today's student generation has grown up in a post-computer age in which instant messaging, iPods, digital games, 3G phones and interactive media are part of everyday life. One of the biggest challenges as technology races ahead is not just the digital divide between rich and poor countries but the digital information and skills gap between the generations, as many people over forty-five struggle to keep up in a world where video recorders have become obsolete and e-communications have taken hold.

While our access to broadband internet has been slow to happen (there were only 150,000 broadband connections by March 2005[1]), our take-up of mobile phones and digital television is high. By June 2005, there was 96% mobile phone penetration, and 38% of television homes were digital.[2] Mobile phone usage in Ireland is amongst the largest in Europe per head

1. Department of Communications, Marine and Natural Resources, DCMNR, response 12 January 2005.
2. ComReg's Quarter 1 commentary and survey, issued June 2005 (*www.comreg.ie*).

1

of population according to the Irish Commission for Communications Regulation (ComReg). Average mobile phone spending is €45 per month, compared with the European average of €30. The sectoral revenue is €3.6 billion per annum for services and charges on mobile phones, with nearly €600 million being paid in VAT to the government (2004).

In the UK, broadband rollout accelerated up to 2004, with 11 million people using fast internet connections by the end of 2004—50% of all internet connections according to AC Nielsen. With Ofcom, the UK regulator, pushing the price for broadband down, it reported six million broadband connections and some 120,000 in Northern Ireland at the end of 2004. Ironically, the problems facing fixed broadband internet in Ireland have meant that mobile broadband solutions are racing ahead.

In order to accelerate the broadband market the Irish Government is spending an extra €35 million in 2005, and in each of the next two years building fibre optic networks in a regional broadband programme along with a cross-border network between Derry and Letterkenny. This involves building high-speed fibre optic trunks and metropolitan networks in up to 120 towns and cities. However, it would be fair to say that Ireland's lacklustre entry into broadband internet is largely the result of poor state planning and policy in the late 1990s. Everything that has happened in the past two to three years is part of a fire-brigade effort to get Ireland into the high-speed loop in order to protect our high-tech industry and economic development. The sale of the state-sector cable network to NTL in 1998 and NTL's subsequent inability to invest heavily in the cable network played a part in Ireland's slow broadband development.[3] NTL's recent sale to UnitedGlobalCom, for €329 million, may pave the way for future investment and growth.

Irish media profile

In Ireland the media landscape is rich. Irish people listen more to radio, read more newspapers, watch more films and buy more books than most of their European neighbours. This handbook reflects the rich diversity of the media, from newspapers, magazines and books to the electronic broadcast media of radio and television and the new media forms of online and interactive digital media. Each sector of the media is editorially spanned and a full directory of media outlets and contacts is given. The guide also

3. See chapter 3, Television: Ireland on the Box. Telecom Éireann at that stage owned 85% of Cablelink, with RTÉ holding 25%.

includes the film and audio-visual production sector, one of the fastest-growing media sectors in the country, which is, as we describe, being transformed by new technology.

We also give a profile of media institutions, from state to voluntary, and the range of media services that support the industry. Most importantly, we have listed all the training and educational resources relating to the media, from traditional media courses and degrees in journalism to the wide range of multimedia and new media courses now available, which reflect the new roles and careers open to Irish students today.

In 1982, Dublin City University started the first year of its then postgraduate degree in journalism. The concept of professional courses for journalism, let alone the media, was so unusual that many leading professionals mocked the idea that someone would want or need a degree.

Today DCU's postgraduate degree in journalism has become a two-year master's degree, while its range of degree courses now includes multimedia. A host of other universities have also developed media, communications and journalism degrees and it has become, as one university head remarked recently, one of the most popular growth areas in academia. Traditional universities such as Trinity College, Dublin, and Queen's University have entered into the sphere with well-respected film courses, while a host of private colleges also offer alternatives to the main established media participants at DCU, Dublin Institute of Technology, NUI Galway, the University of Limerick and the University of Ulster.

Some grumble about where all these students are going. But few graduates from the established degree courses have much difficulty in finding employment, as the range of media players has expanded dramatically since 1990.

Until 1989, anyone interested in broadcasting in Ireland had two options, RTÉ or BBC Northern Ireland. With the growth of local radio and the development, from 1997 to 1999, of national independent radio (Today FM) and national independent television (TV3) as well as the birth of a new public service radio (RTÉ Lyric FM) and television channel (TG4), the range of both career and production opportunities expanded. While RTÉ and the BBC still remain the big players in broadcasting and news, anyone coming out of college today has a range of choices, from Newstalk 106, the Dublin talk radio station, to regional television and the digital radio and television channels in Northern Ireland and the UK.

Twenty years ago, few students would consider film or independent television production as a career, yet today there are more than 200 independent production companies in the Republic and a further 30 in

Northern Ireland, which are part of a UK–wide base of a thousand companies. While many complain that the market is too limited to support that level of activity, some of the more successful companies are becoming international players in broadcast, animation, film and new media content.

In print, while there have been notable casualties, such as the loss of the Irish Press Group, others have opened, such as the *Sunday Business Post*. In addition, the range of UK titles has meant jobs and opportunities for Irish people as Irish editions have developed. New ventures, like *Daily Ireland*, are still unproven businesses, but new television and radio services are expected to be launched in the coming years.

Irish media in Irish

Donncha Ó Cróinín

Despite census figures indicating that over 1 million people in Ireland can speak Irish, the actual number of speakers is considerably lower. Current estimates are that 15,000 within the recognised Irish-speaking areas (Gaeltacht) use Irish as an everyday language, while 30,000 others use it regularly within the English-speaking areas. This latter figure is increasing, mainly because of the widespread establishment of all-Irish pre-schools (naíonraí) and all-Irish primary schools.

The actual boundaries of the Gaeltacht are currently being reviewed in order to present a more realistic picture of the state of the language. While the importance of these regions cannot be overestimated, it is recognised by many that, with such a small target group, the media must attempt to serve all Irish-speakers. This is reflected by some of the main players: Raidió na Gaeltachta was set up to cater for the Gaeltacht regions but has since commenced broadcasting nationally, while the original name for TG4 ('Teilifís na Gaeilge' rather than 'Teilifís na Gaeltachta') indicated a national service.

Television

TG4, the national Irish-language television station, which commenced broadcasting in October 1996, sources its programmes from the independent production sector and from RTÉ. Its establishment in Co. Galway has led to the development of a cluster of independent production and postproduction companies in the region, sustaining an estimated 350 jobs. A sizeable subtitling and dubbing industry has developed, as well as a thriving animation sector, which has had considerable international critical and financial success.

The station has had some success in certain areas, including sports programming and programming for children and young teens. Its programmes for children have been particularly successful, reflecting the demand for such programming throughout the country as a result of the all-Irish education expansion.

While its soap ('Ros na Rún') has a loyal audience, the amount of drama commissioned and broadcast is not high.

Some additional Irish-language programming is broadcast on RTÉ 1 and 2 and on BBC Northern Ireland.

The Government is now in the process of legally separating TG4 from RTÉ and establishing it as an independent public media body.

Radio
RTÉ Raidió na Gaeltachta, which provides a national Irish-language radio service, commenced broadcasting in 1972. It is also available online. The station broadcasts a full range of programming 24 hours a day from studios in Cos. Galway, Kerry, Donegal and Mayo. It manages to combine a strong local focus with excellent coverage of national and international affairs.

Raidió na Life is an independent all-Irish community radio station, which has been broadcasting to the greater Dublin area since 1993. The station broadcasts mostly in the evenings and nights and is principally operated by volunteers. Programming includes news and current affairs, community affairs, and special interests. Its special-interest music programmes are of high quality.

Other independent radio stations provide smaller amounts of Irish-language programming (generally only 1 or 2 hours per week), as do RTÉ Radio 1 and BBC Radio Ulster.

A Broadcasting Commission of Ireland survey on Irish language radio, in January 2005, showed clear support for Irish language radio, with about a quarter of all listeners dipping in occasionally.

Newspapers and periodicals
Foinse is the Irish-language national weekly newspaper, published every Saturday. Based in Co. Galway, it covers national and international news,

current affairs, sport, travel, business, education and reviews. While concentrating on issues relating to Gaeltacht and Irish-language affairs, it also provides strong coverage of national and international affairs. In addition, it publishes regular educational and literary supplements aimed principally at second-level pupils.

Lá is an Irish-language newspaper published in Belfast four days a week, covering current affairs and topical stories. As might be expected, it is particularly strong in its coverage of politics in Northern Ireland.

The *Irish Times* publishes several articles in Irish. As well as regular opinion pieces, the half-page 'Tuarascáil' column, published each Wednesday, contains news and reviews.

Comhar and *Feasta*, which are both published monthly with circulations of between 2,000 and 2,500, offer literary criticism, creative writing and current affairs.

Books

Approximately 450 Irish-language books are published each year. The publishers receive financial support from a number of sources. In addition, a national book distribution network, Áis, has been established. The principal publishers in Irish are Coiscéim, Cló Iar-Chonnachta, Cois Life and An Gúm (which was formerly the Irish-language publications branch of the Department of Education and Science but now forms part of Foras na Gaeilge).

Trends

While considerable support is expressed for the Irish language within Ireland, the circulation of Irish-language print media is alarmingly low. A study of much that has been printed in Irish over the last twenty years indicates an obsession with the state of the language itself: many commentators have observed that if we wrote more in Irish about other topics, maybe more people would read it!

Irish-language newspapers could not survive without the continued heavy subsidies provided by the state. There are no monolingual Irish-speakers in the country; Irish-speakers are more likely to read an English-language newspaper, so the Irish-language newspapers must compete with national and British titles. The recent decision of *Lá* to cut one of its editions indicates the difficulties faced.

While still a small player in the overall market, the success of TG4 in certain areas, such as children's programming and sports programming, indicates potential for expansion and growth.

Probably one of the most interesting developments in the Irish language media sector in the past year has been the launch of the Irish Language Broadcast Fund under the Northern Ireland Film and Television Commission in November 2004. The £12 million fund is intended to support the development of an independent Irish-language production sector in Northern Ireland over the next five years. Submissions to the fund began in March 2005 with the intention that programmes may be on air by 2006. The fund initiative grew from the Belfast Agreement, and it will support programmes that are at least 60% in Irish, with subtitling in English. With TG4 now being carried throughout Northern Ireland, viewers in that region now have a lot more access to Irish-language content, and BBC Northern Ireland has also increased its commitments to the language in its commissioning and scheduling promises. The fund is likely to increase production in Irish in both the Republic and Northern Ireland, since many of the funded programmes will be received throughout Ireland, particularly on TG4, and many of the companies bidding for the fund are partnerships between the Gaeltacht production companies in Co. Galway and the independent sector in Northern Ireland.

Irish media policy

In Ireland, freedom of expression stems from the Constitution, which, under article 40, guarantees the 'right of the citizens to express freely their convictions and opinions' but equally gives the state the right to control mass media, in that 'the State shall endeavour to ensure that organs of public opinion, such as the radio, the press, the cinema, while preserving their rightful liberty of expression, including criticism of Government policy, shall not be used to undermine public order or morality or the authority of the State.'

The legislative framework creating RTÉ as a public body dates from 1960. It set out RTÉ's obligations and responsibilities and also the state's ability to control RTÉ's output in the public's interest. The concept of public order as the basis for censorship obviously draws legitimacy from the

Constitution but was extended in the RTÉ legislation and eventually was used in section 31 of that Act, from 1972 to 1994, to censor the broadcasting of members of banned organisations, such as the IRA, and of Sinn Féin.

The Radio and Television Act (1988) established both an independent broadcasting regulator and independent commercial radio and television. Local radio grew rapidly in Ireland, assisted in no small part by an RTÉ strike in 1992, and in less than ten years the local radio market took 50% of the radio share from RTÉ and offered choice not just to listeners but also to advertisers and broadcasters. Independent television had a slower and more fragile start, and it took ten years for TV3 to enter the market. At present, the UK company Granada Media Group and CanWest each have a 45% share in TV3, and the Granada interest has ensured TV3's ability to deliver strong and popular content like 'Coronation Street' and reality block-busters like 'I'm a Celebrity, Get Me Out of Here'.

In 1997 the Freedom of Information Act was introduced to provide more governmental and state accountability to the public, and while Irish citizens now have to pay a few euros for access to information, the FOI Act itself has greatly enriched the public's right to information. RTÉ as a public body comes under the FOI requirements and therefore is the only medium that has to provide open and accountable access to its operational information, including editorial decision-making. However, since the government's decision to impose charges on FOI queries there has been a 70% reduction in the number of FOI queries to RTÉ. According to RTÉ, in the six months before the introduction of the charges in July 2003 there were 100 FOI requests, while there were only 25 in the following six months.

The digital transition has dominated recent media debate and indeed policy since the late 1990s, but the attempt of the Broadcasting Act (2001) to create a framework for digital television in Ireland (digital terrestrial television) failed, and in recent years the gap has been filled by BSkyB's rollout of satellite television, which is now the primary delivery platform of both satellite and digital television services to Irish people. The BBC's Freeview satellite offering is available in Northern Ireland and the BBC has, through the UK, developed both DTT and digital radio (digital audio broadcasting) networks. The lack of coordination on digital policy between Ireland and the UK has exacerbated the media divide within the island, so that, while all-island broadcasting was an ideal from the All-Ireland Forum report in 1984, the reality of having easy access to all the indigenous broadcasters throughout the island remains a challenge today.

The 2001 Act created a new regulator—the Broadcasting Commission of Ireland (BCI)—and paved the way for community television, which is now beginning to happen. However, the DTT framework of that Act has since become obsolete and will be replaced by new legislation in late 2005. That legislation is expected to create a new regulator, merging the duties of the BCI and the RTÉ Authority, the government-appointed body that regulates RTÉ. This new regulator is expected to be called the Broadcasting Authority of Ireland, although RTÉ has objected to the BCI becoming the new body.

From 2001, RTÉ was in financial crisis, with declining public licence revenues and a production base that was two-thirds dependent on commercial advertising. When its application for an increase in the television licence fee was rejected by the Government, a range of external consultants were tasked to look at the financial base of RTÉ. By 2002 an ad hoc body, the Forum on Broadcasting, was appointed by the Irish Government to explore key issues relating to Irish broadcasting. In a short, intensive review, which included public consultations and open hearings at Dublin Castle, many core policy issues were raised. The resulting report and the Government response to it have shaped broadcasting policy since, leading directly to a licence fee increase for RTÉ by the end of 2002 and a Government decision to create a combined or integrated broadcasting regulator. That decision, and the need to address digital broadcasting, has underlined the drafting of the new legislation.

Other policy decisions that flowed from that process were the RTÉ Charter, published by the Government in mid-2004, and the Government's decision to create the Broadcasting Funding Scheme, in December 2003. This fund siphons off 5% of the television licence fee to a central broadcasting fund, administered by the broadcasting regulator, to support quality programme-making in defined genres, such as culture, heritage, language and arts, in both public and independent broadcasting, and from commercial to community operators. The Broadcasting Funding Scheme, which is worth over €8 million a year, was launched in late July 2005 with an accumulated value of nearly €25 million by the end of 2005.

The media market and media players

Media are big business on the island of Ireland. Tony O'Reilly's Independent Media Group dominates the print media with a 48% market share of the newspaper business—three weekday dailies, three Sunday newspapers and twelve regional papers. In broadcasting, RTÉ remains the key player on the island, but in the commercial and private business world Scottish Radio Holdings (now owned by Emap) has a significant presence in both the radio and newspaper market. UTV, the Belfast-based broadcasting company, is also a key player in the radio world and is now hitting the current ownership cap of 17.9% imposed by the BCI in December 2004.[4] UTV owns the Dublin radio station Q102 and the highly successful 96FM in Cork and at the beginning of 2005 bought LMFM, the Louth local station. It is shortly set to launch a new station in Belfast to challenge BBC Radio Ulster's lion's share of that market. Denis O'Brien's company Communicorp Group has major radio interests in the Republic (98FM, Spin FM, East Coast and Newstalk 106) and is extending that broadcasting business interest across Europe.[5] The major share of the digital television satellite distribution market is held by BskyB, which launched its services in Ireland in 1998 and had 355,000 digital television subscribers in Ireland by May 2005—over a quarter of all television homes. Rupert Murdoch's global media empire News Corporation owns 37% of BskyB, and BSkyB is headed by Murdoch's son James Murdoch, with Mark Deering, formerly of TV3, heading Sky Ireland.

The global advertising market keeps the media circus on the road. The worldwide $1 trillion advertising and marketing industry pumped more than $343 billion into media—newspapers, magazines, television, radio, cinema, outdoor and the internet—in 2004. But media fragmentation and new technologies, including devices that allow users to block or skip advertisements, are challenging the traditional advertising business, and in the US, where residential broadband is well established, internet advertising is the growth zone. Not surprisingly, US surveys show that up to 70% of people would pay to avoid advertisements and marketing pitches, so the ad industry is increasingly looking for new ways of influencing consumers, rather than using direct media advertisements. In Ireland, the advertising industry is worth about €1.1 billion, with newspapers still getting nearly half the media spending. Advertisers now have a choice of 14 television stations, 4 terrestrial and 10 external channels, with which to reach consumers, and that choice is set to grow, with more of the UK digital channels providing Irish advertising space and at least three more Irish commercial TV channels launching in the coming year.

4. *Irish Times*, 22 December 2004, p. 17.
5. 'Communicorp Buys Metromedia', followthemedia.com 1 September 2004.

Future trends

New broadcasting legislation is expected in late 2005, which may see the establishment of a new combined broadcasting regulator and may set the stage for the future of digital broadcasting. While digital television is available through satellite, the lack of a digital terrestrial framework blocks the development of new Irish television services and fails to guarantee the delivery of Irish television services in the future. However, as the majority of television homes have already switched to a digital option through BSkyB, NTL or Chorus, and are paying for additional channels through those providers, the business plan for the roll out of digital terrestrial television is weak.[6] Expect major changes too with the changed merger of NTL and Chorus following NTL's sale to the international cable conglomerate UGC, a subsidiary of US magnate John Malone's Liberty Media empire.

The digital radio plans for Ireland are also embryonic, and, unlike the UK, which has the most successful rollout of digital audio broadcasting (DAB) in Europe, Ireland does not have a DAB network or an agreed policy decision on an alternative digital future for radio. ComReg, the Irish communications regulator, has recommended that DVB, digital video broadcasting, a technology originally devised for the transmission of television be used. So a technology debate still continues over whether DAB has a future for radio or whether countries like Ireland, which has so far not adopted any digital audio technologies, should leap-frog to the next phase, bypassing DAB, and adopt a newer technological solution that may be more suited to mobile multimedia.

3G phones went on sale in Ireland before Christmas 2004 and mobile phones are now seen as a vehicle for delivering both audio and visual content in the future. Nokia, one of the biggest international operators in the mobile phone market, predicts a growth of 10% in 2005 in the mobile phone market, largely through the impact of high-end mobile devices and new media content. Television on the mobile phone is already a reality in trials throughout Europe, and mobile digital technologies will be the future drivers in delivering content.

---

6. Comreg, Market Survey, Quarter 1 2005; subscribers to digital television represented 57% of all pay-television households.

Media facts, Ireland

- There is 96% mobile phone penetration in the Republic of Ireland
- By the end of 2004, mobile phones outnumbered fixed land lines
- 59% of pay-television subscribers have digital television
- There are 1.35 million television homes in Ireland
- 38% of Irish people have internet access
- Over half of fixed land lines are online
- More than 14,000 people are employed in the telecommunications industry
- 4 billion text messages are sent in Ireland every year
- The mobile ringtone business in Ireland is worth over €16 million annually
- Approximately 25% of newspapers sold in Ireland every day are British
- Independent Newspapers has a 48% daily newspaper market share
- Irish people listen to the radio for more than four hours every day
- The most popular radio show in Ireland is RTÉ Radio 1's 'Morning Ireland'
- Ireland has the second-highest cinema-going rate in Europe
- UK television commands on average over 45% of Irish viewing
- Two-thirds of Irish homes have more than one television set
- 15 to 24-year-olds value their mobile phone above any other technology
- Nearly a million people watched the 'Late Late Toy Show' in 2004
- RTÉ 1 is the most watched television station in Ireland, with a 33% share

(*Sources*: ComReg survey 1, 2005, Amárach, RTÉ, Department of Communications, European Institute for the Media.)

2

NEWSPAPERS: PRESSING TIMES

Dr Mark O'Brien

Ireland has one of the highest newspaper readership rates in Europe. Over half the population (2.1 million) buy a newspaper every week and 92% of the population read a newspaper during the same period. For a country of approximately four million people the volume of newspapers produced is staggering. There are 6 daily titles, 2 evening titles, 10 Sunday titles, 58 regional titles, 13 local titles and 40 free local titles published within the Republic alone. On top of all that there is the voluminous newspaper market north of the border and a plethora of non-national titles also available.

The Irish newspaper market is unique on several fronts. It has the highest rate of VAT (13.5%) on newspapers in Europe, is characterised by a high degree of concentration in ownership, and its close proximity to (and shared language with) Britain ensures that it faces extraordinary transnational competition. In the past, English newspaper titles were merely dumped on the Irish market, but in recent years local versions of these titles have begun publication within the state and have proved very successful. This development has considerably upped the ante in the battle for circulation and the competition for both readers and advertisers.

The newspaper landscape

The newspaper industry is not for the faint-hearted. The acrimonious collapse of the Irish Press Group in 1995 and the overnight disappearance of three national titles demonstrated that having a prominent historical heritage and a highly respected reputation for news-gathering are no longer enough to survive in a highly competitive market. Since then, several titles—*Evening News, Dublin Daily, Stars on Sunday*—have come and gone, indicating the precarious nature of the industry and the difficulty new titles face in establishing themselves in the market place. Nonetheless, Ireland looks forward to the launch of a new national daily title from the Andersonstown News stable of newspapers—the *Daily Ireland*. This stable also publishes the Irish-language daily *Lá*, which has a circulation of approximately 4,500. Other successful special-interest titles include the weekly *Irish Farmer's Journal* (with a circulation of 69,000) and the weekly Irish-language paper *Foinse*.

The success (or otherwise) of a newspaper is calculated in two ways. Firstly, circulation—the number of copies sold every day or week—is measured every six months by the Audit Bureau of Circulation. These figures allow six-monthly or yearly comparisons to be made by newspaper proprietors and advertisers as to the sales performance of a particular title. Secondly, readership—the number of people who look at or read a title for a minimum of two minutes—is measured every six months by the Joint National Readership Survey (JNRS). The two measurements are very distinct from one another. While newspaper sales are of concern to news-paper proprietors, because of circulation revenue, the readership results are of paramount importance, because of advertising revenue.

The JNRS is a comprehensive readership survey that provides a wealth of detail about the demographics—age, sex, geographical location—of each newspaper's regular readership. It also examines the typical socio-economic background of a newspaper's readership: its earning potential, its disposable income, its ownership of luxury goods and so on. It is, essentially, the spending power of a newspaper's readership. So the JNRS not only measures the quantity of a paper's readership but also qualifies the life-style pursued by that readership. This has obvious effects on the amount a newspaper can charge for its advertising space. The more high-earners a newspaper has among its readership, the more it can charge for advertising space. These highly sought-after readers are typically referred to as the A, B and C1 readership categories.

This detailed information makes the JNRS the bible for advertisers who buy advertising space in the print media in Ireland. Indeed, newspaper advertising remains a firm favourite among advertising agencies. Given the detailed information contained within the JNRS, newspapers offer advertisers the ability to target their desired segment of the population. In addition, production costs for newspaper advertisements are among the lowest of any advertising medium.

The newspaper market

The biggest operator in the newspaper market is Independent News and Media, which has a stake in 48% of all newspaper sales. Its size and its controlling interest in several sectors of the newspaper market have prompted questions about the appropriateness of such a high degree of concentration in ownership in such a small country. Nonetheless, it owns the best-selling title in the daily (*Irish Independent*), evening (*Evening Herald*) and Sunday (*Sunday Independent*) categories. It also owns or part-owns several other successful daily and Sunday titles, including the *Irish Daily Star*, the *Sunday World*, the *Irish Sunday Star* and the *Sunday Tribune*, and is a significant player in the regional press also. Recently, it has turned its attention northwards with its purchase of the *Belfast Telegraph*. North of the border, the biggest newspaper group is the Alpha Group. It has combined sales of over 120,000 for its various weekly titles, which include the *Roscommon Champion* and the *Coleraine Chronicle*.

The best-selling daily newspaper is the *Irish Independent*. In 2004 the paper became available in both broadsheet and compact (tabloid) format—a move that increased its total circulation by 19,000 to 181,000 copies per day. It has a readership rate of 19% of the adult population, or 607,000 readers per day. In comparison, the *Irish Times* has a daily circulation of 116,000, a readership rate of 10.9%, or 347,000 readers per day. Subsequent to the demise of the Irish Press Group in 1995, the newspaper market has been characterised by the growing presence of local editions of English tabloids. The *Irish Sun*, for example, has a daily circulation of 114,000, a readership rate of 9.3%, or 296,000 readers. In contrast, the *Irish Daily Star* has a lower circulation (108,000) but a greater readership rate of 14.3%, or 456,000 readers. This indicates that the paper has a greater 'pass-on' rate, making it the second-most-read daily paper.

Despite the similarities in circulation, the readerships of broadsheet and tabloid titles are distinctly different. While the *Irish Independent* and the *Irish Times* have ABC1 ratings of 24.6% and 23.0%, respectively, the comparative figures for the *Irish Sun* and the *Irish Daily Star* are 5.5% and 9.8%. In addition, while the readerships of the broadsheets have a near-even distribution of male and female readers, the readerships of the various tabloids are heavily skewed towards males.

Circulation and readership of national daily titles, January–June 2004 ('ooo)

	Circulation	Readership	Readership (%)	ABC1 (%)	Male (%)	Female (%)
Irish Independent	181	607	19.0	24.6	19.3	18.7
Irish Times	116	347	10.9	23.0	10.4	11.3
Irish Sun	114	296	9.3	5.5	11.0	7.6
Irish Daily Star	108	456	14.3	9.8	16.8	11.8
Irish Daily Mirror	80	239	7.5	4.8	8.1	6.9
Irish Examiner	58	207	6.5	6.6	6.8	6.2

Note: The *Irish Independent* circulation figures can be separated into broadsheet (129,000) and compact (52,000).
Source: JNRS.

The evening market is less crowded, with just one national evening title, the *Evening Herald*. It has a circulation of 93,000 copies per day, but this dips to 59,000 on Saturdays, reflecting perhaps the commuter readership of the paper. Although the Examiner Group publishes the *Evening Echo* (circulation 28,341), its circulation is confined to Munster.

In contrast, the Sunday market is the most crowded of all newspaper markets. Independent News and Media again leads with the best-selling broadsheet (*Sunday Independent*) and tabloid (*Sunday World*). The market is again characterised by locally produced versions of English papers, both tabloid and broadsheet. In 2004 the *Irish Daily Star* launched a Sunday version, hoping to translate some of its daily sales into Sunday sales. It has so far been modestly successful, attracting roughly half its weekday readership on Sundays. In total, the readership of Sunday newspapers is higher than daily newspapers. While 59.2% of the population read a daily paper, 78.3% of the population read a Sunday title. The competition for these readers is particularly intense, with many titles periodically including a free CD or book to entice new readers and to keep regular readers from straying. While the inclusion of such 'freebies' usually results in extra sales, this effect is usually short-lived.

Circulation and readership of national Sunday titles, January–June 2004 ('000)

	Circulation	Readership	Readership (%)	ABC1 (%)	Male (%)	Female
Sunday Independent	292	1093	34.2	41.5	32.5	35.9
Sunday World	268	841	26.4	17.1	28.5	24.3
News of the World	166	531	16.6	10.2	16.6	16.7
Ireland on Sunday	152	481	15.1	14.9	14.5	15.7
Sunday Times	104	315	9.9	18.3	10.4	9.4
Sunday Tribune	87	219	6.9	12.0	6.7	7.0
Irish Sunday Star	57	N/A	N/A	N/A	N/A	N/A
Sunday Business Post	52	168	5.3	10.1	5.5	5.1
Irish People	51	151	4.7	3.9	4.9	4.5
Irish Sunday Mirror	45	198	6.2	4.7	5.9	6.5

Source: JNRS.

North of the border, the best-selling locally produced title is the *Belfast Telegraph*, which has a circulation of 94,602 (readership of 295,000 or 22% market share). The *Belfast News* and the *News Letter* have a combined circulation of 79,281, while the *Irish News* has a circulation of 50,080 (with a readership of 186,000 or 14% market share). The best-selling locally produced Sunday title is the *Sunday Life*, with a circulation of 83,766 (readership 274,000 or 20% market share).

Future trends

In general, while the Irish newspaper market remains buoyant, there are a number of issues that will affect its future. Three of the main concerns of the newspaper industry are the high rate of VAT on newspapers, the archaic libel laws that date back to 1961 and the threat of below-cost selling from non-indigenous media operators. On the positive, national newspaper advertising revenue jumped by more than 13% in 2004 and was valued at €287 million by the National Newspapers of Ireland (NNI). Reform of the defamation law has been promised in return for the creation of a Press Council.

Likewise, below-cost selling to gain competitive advantage remains a live issue. While most newspapers would engage in this tactic at one time or another, the circulation wars of the 1990s, in which some non-indigenous titles were selling for a mere 20p, were viewed as damaging to indigenous titles. In 1996 the Newspaper Commission recommended to the Government that legislation to outlaw below-average marginal-cost selling of newspapers be introduced as a matter of urgency. No action has yet been taken on this recommendation. The issue of ownership will continue to be a topic of debate and concern, with newspaper proprietors here anxious to avoid the fate that befell the Scottish indigenous newspaper industry. Nowadays, Scottish editions of English newspapers account for almost 80% per cent of the market.

Circulation figures for Irish titles remain buoyant. So is advertising revenue. Advertising revenue for indigenous national titles increased by 12.6% in the first half of 2004—rising to €143 million from €123 million in the same period of 2003. The Official Languages Act (2003) may provide a boon for Irish-language newspapers, as under the act, state and state-sponsored bodies are obliged to place a certain amount of advertising space in Irish-language media. The continuing development of e-communications will also influence future trends. The advent of the internet has seen most national and regional titles investing in web-based editions of their papers. The quality of these sites varies from title to title, but the demise of the printed version of newspapers, so often heralded in the early days of the internet, is still a long way off.

Regional papers: Making a killing

Cariona Neary

In recent years regional newspaper titles have been snapped up by Irish and international media groups, paying anything from €5 to €30 million per title. The price is generally calculated at fifteen times the current level of profitability. Buyers expect a ten-year payback period. There are only eleven private or family-owned newspapers remaining, and these papers are likely to be bought up in the coming years.

At fifty-eight titles, the regional market is a vibrant one, with approximate sales of 700,000 papers per week. The popularity of the regional press is demonstrated by the fact that more than 1.6 million people read a regional title each week. The regional market has been characterised by considerable consolidation in ownership in recent years, as small family-owned titles have been taken over by larger media organisations, many of which are not Irish-owned. The acquisition of a regional title by an established media group brings benefits in areas such as printing capacity, technology back-up, staff training, marketing and advertising sales. A small number of players now dominate the regional press.

Independent News and Media plays a prominent role, with an interest in twenty-five regional titles, including the *Kerryman*, the *Drogheda Independent* and the *Meath Chronicle*. The arrival of Scottish Radio Holdings in the market upped the ante considerably. It outbid Thomas Crosbie Holdings (publisher of the *Examiner* and the *Sunday Business Post*) for the well-known *Longford Leader* in 2002, paying €9 million for the title. It also owns the *Kilkenny People* and the *Tipperary Star*. In June 2005, SRH's Irish regional press businesses were sold to the UK media group Johnston Press which now owns all five papers: *The Kilkenny People, Longford Leader, Leitrim Observer, Nationalist & Munster Advertiser* and the *Tipperary Star*. In recent years, Dunfermline Press and its Irish subsidiary, Celtic News Group, have become prominent participants in the regional newspaper market. In December 2002, Dunfermline Press bought the *Meath Chronicle* and its printing facility for €30.5 million. In January 2004, Celtic News Group paid €15 million for the *Anglo Celt*, one of the Republic's oldest papers, and in mid-2004 it acquired the three titles of the Westmeath Examiner Group for €20 million.

Other prominent players in the regional market are Thomas Crosbie Holdings, which owns several high-profile regional titles, including the *Newry Democrat*, the *Carlow Nationalist*, the *Western People* and the *Kingdom*; the Leader Group, which owns the *Leinster Leader*, the *Dundalk Democrat* and the *Offaly Express*; and the Alpha Group, mentioned above. The *Limerick Leader* and the *Connacht Tribune* are two of the largest regional titles still operating as independents. The regional newspaper advertising network offers access to all or some of its members' titles to advertising agencies for national and regional advertising campaigns.

Regional papers are considered to be an important medium by advertisers for a number of reasons. According to the Regional Newspapers Association of Ireland (RNAI), 64% of readers read their local newspaper from cover to cover and each paper may be kept in the home for up to a week. Not surprisingly, 80% of advertisements are sourced locally. However, with better printing processes and consolidation among regional papers, local papers also want to attract national advertisers.

National advertisers, such as the drinks companies, are critical of the fact that a sizeable percentage of newspapers are not audited by the Audit Bureau of Circulation (ABC). While local advertisers are unconcerned about ABC ratings, national advertisers feel very differently. In 2003 Mediaforce, a UK company specialising in media representation, was brought in by the RNAI to represent the interests of regional papers to media buyers and advertising agencies. An important objective of Mediaforce is to push all the newspapers to be audited by the ABC.

Mediaforce has been successful in working with the retail sector, and regional papers are running advertising from shops such as Centra, Super Valu, Dunne's Stores and Superquinn. Lidl advertise all year round in the regional papers in those localities where they have a presence. In fact Lidl kick-started the trend of retailers advertising heavily in their local paper.

The regional papers deal with the local news. Readers want 'sports and courts', local news about sports and court sittings. While in the past, local papers ran heavy, long stories, today's regionals carry short human-interest snippets and up to 100 photographs per newspaper.

According to research carried out by Joint National Readership Survey/Lansdowne in 2003, regional papers are successful at reaching the youth market, with approximately 50% of people between the ages of 15 and 24 reading regional papers weekly.

Republic of Ireland

Anglo-Celt, The
Station House, Cavan
Managing Editor: Johnny O'Hanlon
  t. +353 49 433 1100
  f. +353 49 433 2280
  e. johnny_ohanlon@anglocelt.ie
Advertising Manager:
Barbara Fortune
  t. +353 49 433 1100
  f. +353 49 433 2280
  w. www.anglocelt.ie
■ *This weekly regional newspaper has a circulation of more than 15,000 in Co. Cavan and border areas. It is published by the Celtic Media Group, a subdivision of the Dunfermline Press Group.*

An Phoblacht/Republican News
58 Parnell Square, Dublin 1
Editor: Martin Spain
  t. +353 1 873 3611
  f. +353 1 873 3074
  e. editor@anphoblacht.com
  w. www.anphoblacht.com
■ *This is a weekly newspaper for Republican readers with a circulation of about 20,000.*

Argus, The
Park Street, Dundalk, Co. Louth
News Editor: John Mulligan
  t. +353 42 933 4632
  f. +353 42 933 1643
  e. johnmulligan@argus.ie
  w. www.argus.ie
■ *Weekly regional newspaper for Co. Louth with a circulation of 10,000.*

Athlone Observer
Station Road, Athlone, Co. Westmeath
Editor: Jason Gill
  t. +353 9064 74975
  f. +353 9064 78668
  e. jasonathloneobserver@eircom.net
  w. www.athloneobserver.itgo.com
■ *This freesheet circulates in the Athlone area.*

Athlone Topic
Arcade Buildings, Barrack Street,
Athlone, Co. Westmeath
Editor: Eugene Deering
  t. +353 9064 94433
  m. +353 86 601 3536
  f. +353 9064 94964
  e. athlonetopic@eircom.net
■ *Weekly regional newspaper circulating in Athlone and surrounding areas.*

Athlone Voice
14 Seán Costello Street, Athlone, Co. Westmeath
Chief Executive: Deirdre Hughes
  t. +353 90 64 20610
  m. +353 86 248 8504
  f. +353 90 64 20632
  e. dhughes@athlonevoice.ie
■ *Weekly regional paper circulating in Athlone and surrounding areas. Owned by Alpha Newspaper Group.*
Managing Editor: Jim Farrelly

The Avondhu
18 Lower Cork Street, Mitchelstown, Co. Cork
Editor: Liam Howard
  t. +353 25 24451
  f. +353 25 84463
  e. info@avondhupress.ie
  w. www.avondhupress.ie
■ *The regional weekly newspaper, established in 1978, covers north-east Cork, west Waterford, south Limerick and south Tipperary. It is published each Thursday.*

Ballincollig Newsletter, The
DC Graphics, Parknamore Lodge, West Village, Ballincollig, Co. Cork
Editor: Derry Costello
  t. +353 21 487 7665
  f. +353 21 487 1404
  e. dcgraph@indigo.ie

Blanch Gazette

8 The Mall, Main Street, Lucan,
Co. Dublin
Editor: Kevin MacDermot
t. +353 1 601 0240
f. +353 1 601 0251
e. info@gazettegroup.com
■ *Local newspaper for north-west Dublin launched in May 2004. It is owned by the Andersonstown News Group.*

Bray People

25 Main Street, Bray, Co. Wicklow
Editor: Michael Ryan
t. +353 1 286 7393
f. +353 1 286 0879
e. michael.ryan@peoplenews.ie
■ *This weekly regional paper circulates in the Bray area. It is owned by the People Group of newspapers.*

Buy and Sell (Dublin Office)

Argyle Square, Dublin 4
Managing Director: John Whelan
t. +353 1 608 0700
f. +353 1 608 0770
e. tradeads@buyandsell.ie
w. www.buyandsell.ie
■ *Published three times a week, this newspaper provides free classified advertisements for private advertisers. Also provides business and international advertising and personal ads. The Republic of Ireland paper edition is published on Wednesdays. A web edition is available.*

Carlow Advertiser

Strawhall Industrial Estate, Carlow
Editor: Barry Duggan
t. +353 59 913 1512
f. +353 59 914 0016
e. carlowadvertiser@eircom.net
■ *This weekly freesheet circulates in Carlow and surrounding areas.*

Carlow Nationalist

42 Tullow Street, Carlow
Editor: Eddie Coffey
t. +353 59 913 1731
f. +353 59 913 1442

e. news@carlow-nationalist.ie
w. www.carlow-nationalist.ie
■ *Weekly regional paper circulating in Co. Carlow.*

Carlow People

Lismard House, Tullow Street,
Carlow
Editor: Michael Ryan
t. +353 59 913 1877
f. +353 59 913 4185
e. michael.ryan@peoplenews.ie
■ *This weekly regional paper circulates in Co. Carlow. It is part of the People newspaper group.*

Carlow Times

37 Dublin Street, Carlow
Senior Editor: Shay Fitzmaurice
t. +353 59 913 7111
f. +353 59 917 6886
e. carlowed@localtimes.ie
■ *A freesheet distributed in the Carlow area.*

Carrigdhoun Newspaper

Wylie House, Main Street, Carrigaline,
Co. Cork
Editor: Vincent O'Donovan
t. +353 21 437 3557
f. +353 21 437 3559
e. carrigdhoun@eircom.net
w. www.carrigdhounnews.ie

Celtic Media Group

Market Square, Navan, Co. Meath
Managing Director: Deirdre Romanes
t. +353 46 907 9600
f. +353 46 902 3565
e. info@meath-chronicle.ie
w. www.meath-chronicle.ie
■ *This media group publishes the **Meath Chronicle**, the **Offaly Independent**, the **Westmeath Independent**, the **Westmeath Examiner**, and the **Anglo-Celt**. It is a division of the Scottish media company **Dunfermline Press**.*
Operations Director: David Sheehan

City Tribune
15 Market Street, Galway
Editor: Mike Glynn
t. +353 91 536 222
f. +353 91 567 242
e. news@connacht-tribune.ie
w. www.connacht-tribune.ie

Citywide News
26A Phibsborough Place, Dublin 7
Editor: Trish Coogan
t. +353 1 830 6667
f. +353 1 830 6833
e. lifetimes@dna.ie
■ *This is a Dublin freesheet with editions for the west, north-west and north-east of the city.*

Clare Champion
Barrack Street, Ennis, Co. Clare
Acting Editor: Tony Mulvey
t. +353 65 686 4140
f. +353 65 682 0374
e. editor@clarechampion.ie
w. www.clarechampion.ie
■ *This weekly regional newspaper for Co. Clare has a circulation of 21,900.*
Advertising Manager: Ollie O'Regan

Clare County Express
Clonakilla, Ballynacally, Ennis,
Co. Clare
Editor: Seamus O'Reilly
t. +353 65 682 4726
f. +353 65 686 4508
e. patcosgrove@eircom.net
■ *This is a freesheet circulating in Co. Clare.*

Connacht Sentinel
15 Market Street, Galway
Editor: Brendan Carroll
t. +353 91 536 222
f. +353 91 567 242
e. news@connacht-tribune.ie
w. www.connacht-tribune.ie

Connacht Tribune
15 Market Street, Galway
Editor: John Cunningham
t. +353 91 536 222
f. +353 91 567 242
e. news@connacht-tribune.ie
w. www.connacht-tribune.ie
Sales Manager: Sabina Sheppard

Connaught Telegraph
Cavendish Lane, Ellison Street,
Castlebar, Co. Mayo
Editor: Tom Gillespie
t. +353 94 90 21711
f. +353 94 90 217 11
e. news@con-telegraph.ie and
tgillespie@con-telegraph.ie
w. www.con-telegraph.ie
Advertising Executive: Bernard Hughes

The Corkman
The Spa, Mallow, Co. Cork
t. +353 22 42394
f. +353 22 43183
e. newsdesk@thecorkman.ie
w. www.thecorkman.ie

Donegal Democrat
Larkin House, Oldtown Road,
Letterkenny, Co. Donegal
Editor-in-Chief: Michael Daly
t. +353 74 91 28 000
f. +353 72 91 28 001
e. editorial@donegaldemocrat.com
■ *This bi-weekly regional paper has a circulation of more than 15,000. It publishes each Tuesday and Thursday. Its Tuesday edition is combined with the* **Donegal People's Press** *title.*
Editor: Paddy Walsh
Advertising Manager: Deirdre McEnaney
e. advertising@donegalonsunday.com

Donegal News

St Anne's Court, High Road,
Letterkenny, Co. Donegal
t. +353 74 91 21014
f. +353 74 91 22881
w. www.donegalnews.com
Editor: Columba Gill
e. editor@donegalnews.com
Advertising Manager: Eunan McGlynn
e. advertising@donegalnews.com

Donegal on Sunday

Larkin House, Old Town Road,
Letterkenny, Co. Donegal
Editor-in-Chief: Michael Daly
t. +353 74 91 28000
f. +353 72 91 28001
e. editorial@donegalonsunday.com
Editor: Connie Duffy
■ *This regional Sunday title is part of the Derry Journal Newspapers Group, owned by Local Press Ltd.*
Advertising: +353 74 91 28000
e. advertising@donegalonsunday.com

Drogheda Independent

Independent House, 9 Shop Street,
Drogheda, Co. Louth
Group Editor: Darren Hughes
t. +353 41 983 8658
f. +353 41 984 2753
e. editorial@drogheda-independent.ie
w. www.drogheda-independent.ie
■ *Weekly regional paper for Drogheda and Co. Louth, with a circulation of more than 10,000. It is owned by Independent News and Media.*
News Editor: Joanne Little
Advertising Manager: Pat Gough

Drogheda Leader

10–11 Laurence's Street, Drogheda,
Co. Louth
Editor: Anthony Murphy
t. +353 41 984 3606
f. +353 41 984 1517
e. anthonymurphy@droghedaleader.ie
w. www.droghedaleader.net
Advertising Manager
t. +353 41 983 5700

Dundalk Democrat

11 Crowe Street, Dundalk, Co. Louth
Editor: Dolan O'Hagan
t. +353 42 933 4058
f. +353 42 933 1399
e. editor@dundalkdemocrat.ie
■ *Weekly regional paper with a circulation of 9,500 in Dundalk and surrounding areas.*

Dungarvan Leader

78 O'Connell Street, Dungarvan,
Co. Waterford
Editor and General Manager: Colm Nagle
t. +353 58 41203
f. +353 58 45301
e. dungarvanleader@cablesurf.com
■ *This weekly regional newspaper has a circulation of more than 12,000 in the south Co. Waterford area. The editor, Colm Nagle, is also the paper's publisher.*

Dungarvan Observer

Shandon, Dungarvan, Co. Waterford
Editor: James Lynch
t. +353 58 41205
f. +353 58 41559
e. new@dungarvanobserver.com
■ *This weekly regional paper has a circulation of 10,500 in the south Co. Waterford area.*

Echo, The

Village Green, Tallaght, Dublin 24
Editor: David Kennedy
t. +353 1 466 4500
f. +353 1 466 4555
e. editor@echo.ie
■ *Local weekly paper for the west Dublin area. It has two separate editions for different areas.*
News Editor: Robert Kennedy-Cochrane
f. +353 1 466 4555
e. news@echo.ie

Echo Group

Mill Park Road, Enniscorthy,
Co. Wexford
Editor-in-Chief: Tom Mooney
t. +353 54 33231
f. +353 54 33506

e. editor@theecho.ie
w. www.theecho.ie

■ *This Co. Wexford newspaper group pub-lishes the* Echo, *the* Farming Echo, *which is published monthly, the* Gorey Echo, *the* New Ross Echo, *the* Property Echo *and the* Wexford Echo.

Managing Director: Norman Buttle

Evening Echo
Academy Street, Cork
t. +353 21 427 2722
f. (News room) +353 21 480 2135
w. www.eecho.ie

■ *The* Evening Echo *is one of two Irish evening papers; the other is the* Evening Herald. *Its circulation is about 28,800, mostly in the Cork and Munster region. The paper also has a Limerick edition. Since 1894 it has been published by the Examiner Group in Cork, which also publishes the* Irish Examiner.

Chief Executive: Dan Linehan
t. +353 21 427 2722
e. dan.linehan@eecho.ie
Editor: Maurice Gubbins
e. maurice.gubbins@eecho.ie
Circulation Manager: Diarmuid O'Donovan
e. diarmuid@eecho.ie
Production Editor: Eoghan Dinan
e. eoghan.dinan@eecho.ie
Advertising Manager: Valerie Deane
t. +353 21 427 2722
e. valerie.deane@eecho.ie
Features Editor: John Dolan
t. +353 21 427 2722
e. john.dolan@eecho.ie
Entertainment Editor: Eoghan Dinan
t. +353 21 427 2722
e. john.dolan@eecho.ie
Picturers Editor: Brian Lougheed
t. +353 21 427 2722
e. picturedesk@eecho.ie
Deputy Editor: Vincent Kelly
t. +353 21 4802317
e. vincent.kelly@eecho.ie

News Editor: Emma Connolly
e. emma.connolly@eecho.ie
Chief Correspondent: Vincent Power
e. vincent.power@eecho.ie
Marketing Manager: Orla Keane
e. orla.keane@eecho.ie
Sports Editor: John McHale
e. john.mchale@eecho.ie

Evening Echo (Dublin Office)
80 Harcourt Street, Dublin 2
Dublin Correspondent: Brian Winders
t. +353 1 605 6300
e. brian.winders@eecho.ie
w. www.eveningecho.ie

Evening Herald
Independent News and Media, 27–32 Talbot Street, Dublin 1
General Enquiries
t. +353 1 705 5333
f. +353 1 705 5784
e. (News room)
hnews@unison.independent.ie
w. www.unison.independent.ie

■ *Dublin evening paper published by Independent News and Media, the only evening paper in the capital. It contains a large classified section. It has been a tabloid since the 1980s.*

Editor: Gerard O'Regan
t. +353 1 705 5640/03
f. +353 1 705 5597/84
e. goregan@unison.independent.ie
News Editor: Martin Brennan
t. +353 1 705 5720
f. +353 1 872 0304
e. mbrennan@unison.independent.ie
Assistant Editor: David Kenny
t. +353 1 705 5627
e. dkenny@unison.independent.ie
Picture Editor: Declan Cahill
t. +353 1 705 5609
e. dcahill@unison.independent.ie
Deputy News Editor: Ian Mallon
t. +353 1 705 5721
f. +353 1 872 0304
e. imallon@unison.independent.ie

Assistant Editor (Business and
Technology): Ronan Price
t. +353 1 705 5617
e. rprice@unison.independent.ie
Sports Editor: David Courtney
t. +353 1 705 5651
e. dcourtney@unison.independent.ie
Assistant News Editor: Bairbre Power
t. +353 1 705 5721
f. +353 1 872 0304
e. bpower@unison.independent.ie
Deputy Editor: Stephen Rae
t. +353 1 705 5722
f. +353 1 872 0304
e. srae@unison.independent.ie

Fingal Independent

4 Main Street, Swords, Co. Dublin
Group Editor: Darren Hughes
t. +353 1 840 7107/8
f. +353 1 840 7022
e. editorial@fingal-independent.ie
w. www.unison.ie
■ *Weekly local newspaper with a circulation of 4,900 in the north Dublin area.*
Advertising Manager: Patricia Caffrey
News Editor: Fergal Maddock

Foinse

An Cheathrú Rua, Co. na Gaillimhe
Editor: Seán Tadhg Ó Gairbhí
t. +353 91 595 520
f. +353 91 595 524
e. nuacht@foinse.ie
w. www.foinse.ie
■ *This is a weekly Irish-language newspaper, published each Saturday in Connemara, with a circulation of almost 10,000.*
Political Editor: Áine Ní Chiaráin
t. +353 1 618 3254
m. +353 87 258 7821
e. oharaj@eircom.net
Advertising Manager: Seán Clancy
e. sean@foinse.ie
Arts Editor: Sorcha Ní Chéilleachair
e. sorchanic@foinse.ie
Sports Editor: Mártan Ó Ciardha

Galway Advertiser

41–42 Eyre Square, Galway
Managing Director: Peter Timmins
t. +353 91 530 900
f. +353 91 565 627
e. newsroom@galwayadvertiser.ie
w. www.galwayadvertiser.ie
■ *Weekly freesheet published every Thursday in Galway, with a circulation of 29,000.*
Editor: Declan Varley

Galway Independent

Prospect House, Prospect Hill,
Galway
Editor: Hilary Martyn
t. +353 91 569000
f. +353 91 569 333
e. info@galwayindependent.com
w. www.galwayindependent.com
■ *Freesheet circulating in the Galway area.*
Sales Manager: Rory Tyson

Gazeta

55 Lower O'Connell Street, Dublin 1
Editor: Sergei Garugin
t. +353 1 874 0004
f. +353 1 874 0404
e. gazeta@russianireland.com
w. www.russianireland.com
■ *This is a weekly Russian newspaper in Ireland.*

Guardian, The

Castle Hill, Enniscorthy, Co. Wexford
Editor: Michael Ryan
t. +353 54 33642
f. +353 54 35910
e. michael.ryan@peoplenews.ie
■ *This weekly regional newspaper circulates in Co. Wexford. It is part of the People group of newspapers.*

Guardian, The (Gorey Office)

Thomas Street, Gorey, Co. Wexford
Editor: Michael Ryan
t. +353 55 21091
f. +353 55 20273
e. michael.ryan@peoplenews.ie

■ *This weekly regional newspaper circulates in Co. Wexford. It is part of the People group of newspapers.*

Imokilly People
Tattan House, 34 Main Street,
Midleton, Co. Cork
Editor: Patrick O'Connor
t. +353 21 461 3333
f. +353 21 463 2500
e. news@imokillypeople.ie
w. www.imokillypeople.ie
■ *This full-colour weekly regional newspaper circulates in parts of Cos. Cork and Waterford*

Independent News and Media
Independent House, 2023 Bianconi
Avenue, Citywest Business Campus,
Naas Road, Dublin 24
Reception
t. +353 1 466 3200
f. +353 1 466 3222
e. mail@inplc.com
w. www.inmplc.com
■ *Independent News and Media is the largest newspaper group in Ireland, as well as being a leading international media conglomerate with interests in Australia, New Zealand, South Africa and the UK. The group's Irish national titles are the* Irish Independent, *the* Sunday Independent, *the* Evening Herald *and the* Sunday World. *It also owns 50 per cent of the* Star, *which it publishes jointly with Express Newspapers, and has a 29.9 per cent share in the* Sunday Tribune. *The group is also the largest publisher of provincial titles. Titles controlled by the group account for 80 per cent of national newspaper circulation or close to 60 per cent of total newspaper circulation. Its head is Dr Anthony O'Reilly.*
Chief Operating Officer: Gavin O'Reilly
Chairman: Brian Hillery
Company Secretary: Andrew Donagher

Inis Times, The
St Mary's Road, Buncrana, Co. Donegal
Editor: Liam Porter
t. +353 74 93 41055
f. +353 74 93 41059
e. info@inishtimes.com
w. www.inishtimes.com

Ireland on Sunday
3rd Floor, Embassy House, Herbert
Park Lane, Dublin 4
General Enquiries
t. +353 1 637 5800
f. +353 1 637 5880
■ *This Sunday newspaper is owned by Associated Newspapers, publishers of the* Daily Mail *and the* Mail on Sunday. *It originally started as a sports paper, the* Title, *before merging with* Ireland on Sunday *in 1997. It shares some content with the UK* Mail on Sunday.
Editor-in Chief: Ted Verity
t. +353 1 637 5800
e. news@irelandonsunday.com
Editor: Paul Drury
t. +353 1 637 5802
m. +353 86 605 9562
e. paul.drury@irelandonsunday.com
Assistant Editor (news and features):
John Cooper
t. +353 1 637 5862
e. john.cooper@irelandonsunday.com
Editorial Manager: Grace Murray
t. +353 1 637 5821
e. grace.murray@irelandonsunday.com
Deputy Features Editor: Georgina
Heffernan
t. +353 1 637 5843
e. georgina.heffernan@irelandonsunday.com
Political Correspondent: John Lee
t. +353 1 637 5845 and
+353 1 618 3620 (Leinster House)
m. +353 87 251 8568
e. john.lee@irelandonsunday.com
Picture Editor: James Meehan
t. +353 1 637 5862
e. pictures@irelandonsunday.com
Deputy Pictures Editor: Garrett Brennan
t. +353 1 637 5863
m. +353 87 679 1166
e. pictures@irelandonsunday.com

Sports Editor: Jack White
t. +353 1 637 5881
m. +353 87 221 8830
e. jack.white@irelandonsunday.com

Irish Catholic, The
55 Lower Gardiner Street, Dublin 1
Editor: Garry O'Sullivan
t. +353 1 855 5619
f. +353 1 836 4805
e. news@irishcatholic.ie
w. www.irishcatholic.ie
■ *This weekly Catholic newspaper covers church news and issues with an Irish perspective. It has a circulation of 31,000.*
Advertising Manager: Ger Crowley

Irish Daily Mirror
4th Floor, Park House, 191–197 North Circular Road, Dublin 7
Editor: John Kierans
t. +353 1 868 8600
f. +353 1 868 8626
e. jkierans@mgn.co.uk
w. www.mirror.co.uk
■ *This is the Irish edition of the UK Daily Mirror, combining Irish and UK content for separate editions in the North and the Republic. News and sports staff are based in the Republic, while production is carried out in the paper's Belfast office. Web edition contains content from the UK edition only.*
Deputy Editor: Michael McNiffe
t. +353 1 868 8602
f. +353 1 868 8626
e. news@irishmirror.ie
Assistant Editor: Geoff Frazer
t: +44 2890 568000
e. gfrazer@mgn.co.uk
Assistant Editor: Kevan Furbank
t: +44 2890 568000
e. kfurbank@mgn.co.uk
News Editor: Paul Clarkson
t. +353 1 868 8603
f. +353 1 868 8626
e. news@irishmirror.ie (newsdesk);
paul.clarkson@irishmirror.ie

Investigations Editor: Damien Lane
t. +353 1 868 8603
f. +353 1 868 8626
e. damien.lane@irishmirror.ie
Circulation Manager: Alan Kelly
t: +353 1 868 8600
f: +353 1 868 8626
e: alan.kelly@mgn.ie
Advertising Controller: Michael Savage
t: +353 1 868 8600
f: +353 1 868 8612
e: michael.savage@mgn.ie
Advertising Manager: Gavin Deans
t: +353 1 868 8615
f: +353 1 868 8612
e: gavin.deans@mgn.ie

Irish Daily Star
Star House, 62a Terenure Road North, Dublin 6W
General Enquiries
t. +353 1 490 1228
f. (News desk) +353 1 490 2193;
(Advertising) +353 1 490 7425;
e. news@thestar.ie
Managing Director: Paul Cooke
Personal Assistant to Managing Director: Lorraine Worth
t. +353 1 499 3404
f. +353 1 490 7425
e. lorraine.worth@thestar.ie
Financial Controller: Colm Davitt
t. +353 1 499 3481
f. +353 1 490 7425
e. colm.davitt@thestar.ie
Editor: Gerard Colleran
Editor's Personal Assistant: Geraldine D'Cruz
t. +353 1 499 3445
f. +353 1 490 2193
e. geraldine.d'cruz@thestar.ie
Senior Deputy Editor and Features Editor: Danny Smyth
t. +353 1 499 3452
m. +353 87 267 7222
e. danny.smyth@thestar.ie

Senior Assistant Editor: Phil Mason
t. +353 1 499 3440
f. +353 1 490 2193
e. phil.mason@thestar.ie
News Editor: Michael O'Kane
t. +353 1 499 3458
f. +353 1 490 2193
e. news@the-star.ie
Deputy News Editor: Cormac Burke
t. +353 1 499 3512
f. +353 1 490 2193
e. news@thestar.ie
Assistant News Editor: Shane Doran
t. +353 1 499 3434
f. +353 1 490 2193
e. news@thestar.ie
Assistant News Editor: Catherine
Halloran
t. +353 1 499 3462
m. +353 87 821 8060
f. +353 1 490 2193
e. news@thestar.ie
Pictures Editor: Brian Dowling
t. +353 1 499 3420
f. +353 1 490 2193
e. brian.dowling@thestar.ie
Deputy Pictures Editor: Mark Rice
t. +353 1 499 3420
f. +353 1 490 2193
e. mark.rice@thestar.ie
Sports Editor: Eoghan Brannigan
t. +353 1 499 3432
f. +353 1 490 2193
e. eoghan.brannigan@thestar.ie
Deputy Sports Editor: Brian Flanagan
t. +353 1 499 3457
f. +353 1 490 2193
e. brian.flanagan@thestar.ie
Assistant Sports Editor: Jackie Hennessy
t. +353 1 499 3426
f. +353 1 490 2193
e. jackie.hennessy@thestar.ie
Financial Pages: Edel Kennedy
t. +353 1 499 3476
f. +353 1 490 2193
e. edel.kennedy@thestar.ie

Features Editor: Moira Hannon
t. +353 1 499 3518
f. +353 1 490 2193
e. moira.hannon@thestar.ie
Advertising Manager: Paul Henderson
t. +353 1 499 3405
m. +353 86 257 6669
f. +353 1 490 7425
e. paul.henderson@thestar.ie

Irish Daily Star Sunday

Star House, 62a Terenure Road North,
Dublin 6W
General Enquiries
t. +353 1 490 1228
f. (News desk) +353 1 490 1358;
(Advertising) +353 1 490 7425
e. news.sunday@thestar.ie

■ *This is a Sunday national tabloid, sister
paper to the* **Irish Daily Star**

Editor: Gerard Colleran
Editor's Personal Assistant: Geraldine
D'Cruz
t. +353 1 499 3445
f. +353 1 490 2193
e. geraldine.d'cruz@thestar.ie
Deputy Editor: Des Gibson
t. +353 1 499 3445
f. +353 1 499 1358
e. des.gibson@thestar.ie
News Editor: Bernard Phelan
t. +353 1 499 3500
f. +353 1 490 1358
e. news.sunday@thestar.ie
Sports Editor: Gavan Beckton
t. +353 1 499 3495
f. +353 1 490 1358
e. gavan.beckton@thestar.ie
Chief Sub-Editor: Paul Mallon
t. +353 1 499 3474
f. +353 1 490 1358
e. paul.mallon@thestar.ie
Advertising Manager: Paul Henderson
t. +353 1 499 3405
m. +353 86 257 6669
f. +353 1 490 7425
e. paul.henderson@thestar.ie

Irish Examiner

Academy Street, Cork
General Enquiries
t. +353 21 427 2722
f. (News room) +353 21 427 5477
w. www.examiner.ie

■ *Daily mid-market broadsheet newspaper*
published in Cork. Founded in 1841 as the
Cork Examiner, *it has been in the control of*
the Crosbie family since 1872. In the mid-
1990s it dropped the 'Cork' from its title to
give it greater national appeal and make gains
against other mid-market titles. Its circulation
is around 64,000.

Editor: Tim Vaughan
t. +353 21 427 2722
f. +353 21 427 5477
e. editor@examiner.ie

Deputy Editor: Brian Carroll
t. +353 21 427 2722
f. +353 21 427 5477
e. brian.carroll@examiner.ie

Associate Editor: Jack Power
t. +353 21 427 2722
f. +353 21 427 5477
e. jack.power@examiner.ie

Chief Leader-Writer: Donal Musgrave
t. +353 21 427 2722
f. +353 21 427 5477
e. donal.musgrave@examiner.ie

Advertising Manager: Aidan Forde
t. +353 21 480 2218
f. +353 21 427 3846
e. aidan.forde@examiner.ie

Chief Business Correspondent: Brian
O'Mahony
t. +353 21 427 2722
f. +353 21 427 5477
e. brian.omahony@examiner.ie

Night Editor: Conor O'Donnell
t. +353 21 480 2102
f. +353 21 427 5477
e. news@examiner.ie

News Editor: John O'Mahony
t. +353 21 480 2102
f. +353 21 427 5477
e. news@examiner.ie

Sports Editor: Tony Leen
t. +353 21 480 2152
f. +353 21 427 5477
e. sport@examiner.ie;
tony.leen@examiner.ie

Editor of Feelgood Supplement: Irene
Feighan
t. +353 21 480 2722
f. +353 21 427 5477
e. irene.feighan@examiner.ie

Diary Editor: Ann Hurley
t. +353 21 480 2153
f. +353 21 427 5477
e. ann.hurley@examiner.ie

Business Editor: Kevin Mills
t. +353 21 480 2259
f. +353 21 427 5477
e. business@examiner.ie

Business Correspondent: Conor Keane
t. +353 21 480 2197
f. +353 21 427 5477
e. conor.keane@examiner.ie

Agri-business Correspondent: Ray Ryan
t. +353 21 480 2153
f. +353 21 427 5477
e. ray.ryan@examiner.ie

Farming Editor: Stephen Cadogan
t. +353 21 480 2365
f. +353 21 427 5477
e. stephen.cadogan@examiner.ie

Entertainment Editor: Ian Kilroy
t. +353 21 480 2374
f. +353 21 427 5477
e. ian.kilroy@examiner.ie

Image Editor: John O'Donovan
t. +353 21 480 2167
f. +353 21 427 5477
e. picturedesk@examiner.ie;
jod@examiner.ie
ISDN +353 21 480 6091
Modem +353 21 427 2749

Features Editor: Joe Dermody
t. +353 21 480 2213
f. +353 21 427 5477
e. joe.dermody@examiner.ie

Irish Examiner (Dublin Office)

80 Harcourt Street, Dublin 2
General Enquiries
t. +353 1 605 6350;
(Sales) +353 1 605 6305
f. (Editorial) +353 1 605 6355
w. www.examiner.ie
Political Reporter: Michael O'Farrell
t. +353 1 618 3643
m. +353 86 805 1152
f. +353 1 676 3122
e. michael.ofarrell@examiner.ie
Political Editor: Harry McGee
t. +353 1 618 4445
m. +353 87 263 1920
f. +353 1 676 3122
e. harry.mcgee@examiner.ie

Irish Farmer's Journal

Irish Farm Centre, Bluebell, Dublin 12
Editor and Chief Executive: Matt
Dempsey
t. +353 1 419 9500
f. +353 1 452 0876
e. mdempsey@farmersjournal.ie
w. www.farmersjournal.ie
■ *This weekly newspaper for the farming
community, first published in 1948, has a
circulation of more than 68,000. It provides
agricultural news, as well as technical and
country life features.*
Advertising Director: John Gill
e. jgill@farmersjournal.ie

Irish Independent

Independent News and Media, 27–32
Talbot Street, Dublin 1
Chief Executive, Ireland: Vincent
Crowley
t. +353 1 705 5333
f. +353 1 872 0304 / 873 1787
Group Managing Director: Gavin
O'Reilly
t. +353 1 705 5333/5710
f. +353 1 872 0304/873 1787
■ *Largest-selling Irish broadsheet and the
flagship Irish paper for its owners,*

Independent News and Media. The Irish
Daily Independent, *launched in 1891,
became the* Irish Independent *in 1905,
adopting a populist style featuring a large
use of photographs. It was traditionally aimed
at the Catholic middle class and the farming
community. Circulation currently stands at
160,000.*
Editor: Vincent Doyle
Deputy Editor: Michael Wolsey
e. mwolsey@unison.independent.ie
Group News Editor: Paul Dunne
e. pdunne@unison.independent.ie
Deputy Group News Editor: Dave
Halloran
e. dhalloran@unison.independent.ie
News Editor: Philip Molloy
t. (News desk) +353 1 705 5710
(10:00–17:00); +353 1 705 5720
(17:00–midnight)
e. news@unison.independent.ie;
pmolloy@unison.independent.ie
News Analysis Editor: Gerry
Mulligan
e. gmulligan@unison.independent.ie
Deputy News Editor: Annamaria
McEneaney
e. news@unison.independent.ie;
amcaneaney@unison.independent.ie
Assistant News Editor: Claire Grady
e. news@unison.independent.ie;
cgrady@unison.independent.ie
Assistant News Editor: Don Lavery
e. news@unison.independent.ie;
dlavery@unison.independent.ie
Group Financial Editor: Brendan
Keenan
t. +353 1 705 5630
f. +353 1 705 5707
e. finance@unison.independent.ie
Business Editor: Richard Curran
t. +353 1 705 5644
f. +353 1 705 5707
e. finance@unison.independent.ie
European Editor: Conor Sweeney
t. +322 218 0851

m. +32486 635 915
e. conorsweeney@hotmail.com
Group Sports Editor: Pat Courtney
e. pcourtney@unison.independent.ie
Sports Editor: P. J. Cunningham
e. pjcunningham@unison.
independent.ie
Political Editor: Gene McKenna
t. +353 1 618 3419
m. +353 86 854 0169
Political Reporter: Fionnán Sheehan
t. +353 1 618 3018
e. fsheehan@unison.independent.ie
Political Reporter: Senan Molony
t. +353 1 618 3162
e. smolony@oireachtas.irlgov.ie
Political Reporter: Brian Dowling
t. +353 1 618 3402
m. +353 87 222 6773
e. bdowling2@eircom.net
Political Reporter: Geraldine Collins
t. +353 1 618 3411
m. +353 86 264 8371
e. gcollins@unison.independent.ie
Political Staff: Sam Smyth
t. +353 1 618 3928
m. +353 87 222 6171
e. turk@indigo.ie
North-West Reporter: Anita Guidera
t. +353 74 515 43
m. +353 87 237 6733
South-East Reporter: Sarah Murphy
m. +353 86 804 8557
Belfast Reporter: Dominic Cunningham
t. +44 774 727 115
e. dominic.cunningham@
btinternet.com
Security Correspondent: Tom Brady
e. tbrady@unison.independent.ie
Features Editor: Peter Carvosso
e. pcarvosso@unison.independent.ie
Health Correspondent: Eilish O'Regan
e. eoregan@unison.independent.ie
Industrial Correspondent: Gerald Flynn
e. gflynn@unison.independent.ie

Motoring Correspondent: Eddie
Cunningham
e. ecunningham@unison.
independent.ie
Education Editor: John Walshe
e. jwalshe@unison.independent.ie
Supplements Editor: John Spain
e. jspain@unison.independent.ie
Consumer Affairs Correspondent:
Aideen Sheehan
e. asheehan@unison.independent.ie
Religious and Social Affairs
Correspondent: David Quinn
e. dquinn@unison.independent.ie
Arts Editor: Ian Baird
e. ibaird@unison.independent.ie
Books Editor: John Spain
e. jspain@unison.independent.ie
Consumer Affairs Correspondent:
Lorna Reid
m. +353 86 812 4715
e. lreid@unison.independent.ie
Group Photographic Manager: Liam
Mulcahy
t. +353 1 705 5749
m. +353 87 267 39 54
e. lmulcahy@unison.independent.ie
Photographic Editor: Padraig Beirne
e. pbeirne@unison.independent.ie
Deptuty Picture Editor: Ronan Lang
e. rlang@unison.independent.ie
Assistant Photographic Editor: Tom
Burke
e. tburke@unison.independent.ie
Property Editor: Cliodhna
O'Donoghue
t. +353 1 705 5723
f. +353 1 705 5778
e. property@unison.independent.ie;
codonoghue@unison.independent.ie
Southern Reporter: Ralph Riegel
t. +353 21 427 2494
f. +353 21 427 8231
Limerick Reporter: Eugene Hogan
m. +353 86 249 7290

Galway Reporter: Brian MacDonald
t. +353 91 525 587
m. +353 86 249 0122
f. +353 91 524 441
London Editor: Bernard Purcell
t. +44 207 828 4070; +44 370 756 257
f. +44 207 828 4303
e. bpurcell@unison.independent.ie

Irish Medical Times
Medical Publications Ireland Ltd,
24–26 Upper Ormond Quay,
Dublin 7
Editor
t. +353 1 817 6300
f. +353 1 817 6345
w. www.imt.ie
■ *This weekly newspaper covers news and developments in the Irish medical profession and has a circulation of more than 6,500.*

Irish Post, The
Cambridge House, Cambridge Grove,
London W6 0LE
w. www.irishpost.co.uk
■ *This is the weekly newspaper for the Irish in the UK.*
Editor: Frank Murphy
t. +44 208 735 9408
f. +44 208 741 3382
e. frankmurphy@irishpost.com
Editor: Sarah Finucane
t. +44 208 735 9418
f. +44 208 741 3382
e. sarahfinucane@irishpost.co.uk

Irish Sun, The
Fourth Floor, Bishop's House,
Redmond's Hill, Dublin 2
Bureau Chief and News Editor: Ronan O'Reilly
t. +353 1 479 2579
m. +353 86 817 2080
f. +353 1 479 2590
e. irishsun@the-sun.ie and ronan.o'reilly@the-sun.ie
w. www.thesun.co.uk

■ *The Irish edition of the highest-selling UK daily tabloid mixes domestic and UK content and currently has a circulation of about 115,000, making it the leading tabloid sold in Ireland. Its web site offers UK content only.*
Deputy News Editor: Myles McEntee
m. +353 86 823 3619
e. myles.mcentee@the-sun.ie

Irish Times
10–16 D'Olier Street, Dublin 2
General Enquiries
t. +353 1 675 8000
f. (News) +353 1 677 2130; (after 17:00) +353 1 679 3910
e. (Letters to Editor) lettersed@irish-times.ie; (Edition Information) itemail@irish-times.ie
w. www.ireland.com
■ *An elite daily newspaper, founded in 1859, published in Dublin with a circulation of about 120,000. The paper's traditional conservative and unionist position was transformed in the second half of the twentieth century into its current liberal, socially aware viewpoint. It is owned by the Irish Times Trust, which was set up in 1974 to ensure the paper's independence. The paper plans to move premises to a site in Tara Street.*
Managing Director: Maeve Donovan
Editor: Geraldine Kennedy
e. editorial@irish-times.ie
Deputy Editor: Paul O'Neill
e. poneill@irish-times.ie
Managing Editor: Eoin McVey
e. emcvey@irish-times.ie
Managing Editor (Features): Gerry Smyth
e. gsmyth@irish-times.ie
Managing Editor (Production): Joe Breen
e. jbreen@irish-times.ie
Investigations Editor: Peter Murtagh
e. pmurtagh@irish-times.ie
Foreign Editor: Paddy Smyth
e. psmyth@irish-times.ie
Opinion Editor: John Maher
e. jmaher@irish-times.ie

Duty Editor and Special Projects: Willy Clingan
  e. wclingan@irish-times.ie
Foreign Policy Editor and Duty Editor: Paul Gillespie
  e. pgillespie@irish-times.ie
Chief Sub-Editor: Liam Ryan
  e. lryan@irish-times.ie
Night Editors: Kevin O'Sullivan and Noel Costello
News Editor: Miriam Donohoe
  e. mdonohoe@irish-times.ie
Western and Marine Correspondent: Lorna Siggins
  e. lsiggins@irish-times.ie
Southern Correspondent: Barry Roche
  e. broche@irish-times.ie
North America Editor: Conor O'Clery
  t. +1 646 314 8731
  e. coclery@irish-times.ie
Chief Political Correspondent: Mark Brennock
  t. +353 1 618 3400
  m. + 353 87 233 5923
  e. mbrennock@irish-times.ie
Parliamentary Reporter: Marie O'Halloran
  t. +353 1 618 3018
  e. mohalloran@irish-times.ie
Political Correspondent: Mark Hennessy
  t. +353 1 618 3210
  m. +353 86 813 4191
  e. mark.hennessy@oireachtas.irlgov.ie
Parliamentary Reporter: Michael O'Regan
  t. +353 1 618 3294
  m. +353 86 338 9846
  e. moregan@oireachtas.irlgov.ie
Senior Business Correspondent: Arthur Beesley
  t. +353 1 675 8000
  m. +353 87 699 6080
  e. abeesley@irish-times.ie

Foreign Affairs Correspondent: Deaglán de Bréadún
  e. ddebreadun@irish-times.ie
Advertisement Sales Manager: Liam Holland
  e. lholland@irish-times.ie
Assistant Foreign Editor: Judith Crosbie
  e. jcrosbie@irish-times.ie
Features Editor: Sheila Wayman
  e. swayman@irish-times.ie
Business Editor: Barry O'Keefe
  e. finance@irish-times.ie;
  bokeefe@irish-times.ie
Deputy Business Editor: John McManus
  t. +353 1 679 8874
  e. jmcmanus@irish-times.ie
Sports Editor: Malachy Logan
  e. mlogan@irish-times.ie
Berlin Correspondent: Derek Scally
  t. +49 309 17 44388
  e. dscally@irish-times.ie
Religious Affairs Correspondent: Patsy McGarry
  e. pmcgarry@irish-times.ie
Chief Theatre Critic and Columnist: Fintan O'Toole
  e. fotoole@irish-times.ie
Fashion Editor: Deirdre McQuillan
  e. dmcquillan@irish-times.ie
Medical Correspondent: Muiris Houston
  e. mhouston@irish-times.ie
Legal Affairs Correspondent: Carol Coulter
  e. ccoulter@irish-times.ie
Literary Correspondent: Eileen Battersby
  e. ebattersby@irish-times.ie
Agriculture Correspondent: Sean MacConnell
  e. smcconnell@irish-times.ie
Literary Editor: Caroline Walsh
  e. cwalsh@irish-times.ie
Arts Editor: Deirdre Falvey
  e. dfalvey@irish-times.ie

Education Editor: Sean Flynn
 e. sflynn@irish-times.ie
Environment Editor: Frank McDonald
 e. fmcdonald@irish-times.ie
Irish Language Editor: Pól Ó Muirí
 e. pomuiri@irish-times.ie
Assistant Editor Special Projects and
Saturday Magazine Editor: Patsey
Murphy
 e. pmurphy@irish-times.ie
The Ticket Editor: Hugh Linehan
 e. theticket@irish-times.ie
Weekend Supplement Editor: Deirdre
Falvey
 e. dfalvey@irish-times.ie
Social Affairs Correspondent: Carl
O'Brien
 e. cobrien@irish-times.ie
Public Affairs Correspondent: Colm
Keena
 e. ckeena@irish-times.ie
Picture Editor: Peter Thursfield
 e. pthursfield@irish-times.ie
Motoring Correspondent: Michael
McAleer
 e. mmcaleer@irish-times.ie
Paris Correspondent: Lara Marlowe
 t. +331 4544 8656
 f. +331 4544 8656
 e. lmarlowe@irish-times.ie
Special Reports and Supplements
Editor: Orna Mulcahy
 e. omulcahy@irish-times.ie
Northern Editor: Gerry Moriarty
 t. +44 28 9032 3379 / 24
 f. +44 28 9023 1469
 e. gmoriarty@irish-times.ie

Irish Times (London Office)

76 Shoe Lane, London EC4A 3JB
London Editor: Frank Millar
 t. +44 20 7353 8981
 f. +44 20 7353 8070
 e. fmillar@irish-times.ie
 w. www.ireland.com

Kerryman, The

Clash Industrial Estate, Tralee, Co. Kerry
Editor: Declan Malone
Advertising Manager: Bernard O'Keeffe
 t. +353 66 714 5560
 f. +353 66 714 5572
 e. ads@kerryman.ie
 w. www.kerryman.ie
■ *Owned by Independent News and Media,
this is one of the largest Irish weekly regional
newspapers, with a circulation of 36,000 in Co.
Kerry. Published each Wednesday, it is the sister
paper to the* **Corkman.**

Kerry's Eye

22 Ashe Street, Tralee, Co. Kerry
Editor: Conor Lacey
 t. +353 66 712 3199
 f. +353 66 712 3163
 e. news@kerryseye.com
 w. www.kerryseye.com
■ *This weekly tabloid regional newspaper has
a circulation of 24,600 in Co. Kerry.*
Company Director and Advertising
Manager: Brendan Kennelly

Kildare Nationalist

Liffey House, Edward Street,
Newbridge, Co. Kildare
Editor: Vicki Weller
 t. +353 45 432 147
 f. +353 45 433 720
 e. editor@kildare-nationalist.ie and
 news@kildare-nationalist.ie
 w. www.kildare-nationalist.ie

Kildare Times

Unit 1, Eurospar Shopping Centre,
Fairgreen, Naas, Co. Kildare
Editors: Shay Fitzmaurice (Bray) and
Terry O'Mahoney
 t. +353 45 895 111
 f. +353 45 895 099
 e. kildaretimes@eircom.net
■ *Freesheet circulating in Co. Kildare.*

Kilkenny People

34 High Street, Kilkenny
Editor: Tom Molloy
t. +353 56 77 21015
f. +353 56 77 21414
e. info@kilkennypeople.ie
w. www.kilkennypeople.ie
■ *Weekly paper founded in 1892, with a circulation of 17,000 in Co. Kilkenny. Owned by Johnston Press.*
Advertising Manager: Peter Seaver

Killarney Advertiser

Woodlawn, Killarney, Co. Kerry
Editor: Cormac Casey
t. +353 64 32215
f. +353 64 32722
e. copy@killarneyadvertiser.ie
w. www.killarneyadvertiser.ie
■ *This freesheet circulates in the Killarney area of Co. Kerry.*

Kingdom, The

65 New Street, Killarney, Co. Kerry
Editor: John O'Mahony
t. +353 64 31932
f. +353 64 37099
e. news@the-kingdom.ie and john.omahony@the-kingdom.ie
w. www.the-kingdom.ie
■ *This is a weekly regional newspaper circulating in Co. Kerry.*
Advertising Manager: Catherine O'Sullivan
t. +353 64 37165
f. +353 64 34609
e. sales@the-kingdom.ie

Laois Nationalist

Coliseum Lane, Port Laoise, Co. Laois
Editor: Barbara Sheridan
t. +353 59 91 70113
e. barbara@laois-nationalist.ie
■ *Weekly regional paper circulating in Co. Laois*

Leinster Express

Dublin Road, Port Laoise, Co. Laois
Editor: John Whelan
t. +353 502 21666
f. +353 502 20491
e. lexpress@indigo.ie
w. www.unison.ie
■ *Founded in 1831, this weekly regional paper has a circulation of 18,000 in Cos. Laois, Offaly, Kildare, Carlow, Westmeath, Kilkenny and North Tipperary.*
Advertising Manager: Raymond McGowan

Leinster Leader

19 South Main Street, Naas, Co. Kildare
Editor: Michael Shearin
t. +353 45 897 302
f. +353 45 871 168
e. editor@leinsterleader.ie
w. www.unison.ie
■ *This is a weekly paper for Co. Kildare founded in 1881 and published each Wednesday. It is owned by a private company, The Leinster Leader Ltd, which now owns four other titles:* **Leinster Express, Dundalk Democrat, Offaly Express** *and* **Limerick Leader.**
Advertising Manager: Seamus Morahan
f. +353 45 897 647
e. advertising@leinsterleader.ie

Leitrim Observer

Hartley Business Park, Leitrim Road, Carrick-on-Shannon, Co. Leitrim
Editor: Claire Casserly
t. +353 71 96 20025
f. +353 71 96 20039
e. editor@leitrimobserver.ie
w. www.leitrimobserver.ie
■ *Weekly paper for Co. Leitrim with a circulation of 10,000. Owned by Johnston Press.*
Advertising Manager: Willie Donnellan
f. +353 71 96 20112
e. ads@leitrimobserver.ie

Letterkenny Listener

St Anne's Court, High Road,
Letterkenny, Co. Donegal
Editor-in-Chief: Michael Daly
t. +353 74 91 21014
f. +353 74 91 22881
e. editor@peoplespress.com
w. www.donegalnews.com
■ *This weekly regional newspaper aimed at readers in the Letterkenny area of Co. Donegal is part of the Derry Journal Group of Newspapers*

Liffey Champion

Mill Lane, Leixlip, Co. Kildare
Editor: Vincent Sutton
t. +353 1 624 5533
f. +353 1 624 3013
e. champnews@eircom.net
■ *Weekly local paper aimed at west Dublin and north Kildare with particular emphasis on the growing commuter towns of Lucan, Maynooth, Leixlip and Celbridge.*
Sales: Antoinette Tyrrell

Limerick Leader

54 O'Connell Street, Limerick
Editor: Brendan Halligan
t. +353 61 214 500
f. +353 61 401 424
e. editorial@limerickleader.ie
w. www.limerickleader.ie
■ *This paper was first published in 1889 and now has a circulation of about 27,000 in the Limerick and north Munster area. The paper is published four times a week, and there is also a weekend edition.*
Advertising Manager: Fergal Deegan
f. +353 61 314 804
e. advertising@limerickleader.ie

Limerick Post

Old Town Hall Centre, Rutland Street,
Limerick
Editor: Billy Ryan
t. +353 61 413 322
f. +353 61 417 684
e. news@limerickpost.ie
w. www.limerickpost.ie

■ *This is a weekly freesheet for Limerick, published each Thursday, which has a circulation of 40,000.*

Longford Leader

Leader House, Dublin Road, Longford
Managing Editor: Joe Flaherty
t. +353 43 45241
f. +353 43 41489
e. newsroom@longford-leader.ie
w. www.longford-leader.ie
■ *This weekly regional, published each Wednesday, has a circulation of 13,500 in Cos. Longford, Cavan, Westmeath, Roscommon and Leitrim. It is owned by Johnston Press.*
Advertising Manager: Margaret Faughnan
e. advertising@longford-leader.ie

Longford News

Earl Street, Longford
Editor: David Roe
t. +353 43 46342
f. +353 43 41549
e. info@longford-news.iol.ie
■ *This regional newspaper has a circulation of 9,500 in Co. Longford and surrounding areas. It is owned by the Alpha Newspaper Group.*
Advertising Manager: Nicky Bennett

Lucan Gazette

8 The Mall, Main Street, Lucan,
Co. Dublin
Editor: Ken Whelan
t. +353 1 601 0240
f. +353 1 601 0251
e. info@gazettegroup.com
■ *Local newspaper for the north west Dublin town launched in May 2004. It is owned by the Andersonstown News Group and is a sister paper of the* **Blanch Gazette.**

Mayo News

The Fairgreen, Westport, Co. Mayo
Editor: Seán Staunton
t. +353 98 25311
f. +353 98 26108
e. mayonews@anu.ie
w. www.mayonews.ie

■ *This is a weekly regional newspaper for Co. Mayo, founded in 1892, with a circulation of more than 9,000.*
Advertising Manager: Patrick Cawley

Meath Chronicle

Market Square, Navan, Co. Meath
Editor: Ken Davis
t. +353 46 90 79600
f. +353 46 90 23565
e. info@meath-chronicle.ie
w. www.meath-chronicle.ie
■ *This weekly regional paper has a circulation of 18,400 in Cos. Meath, Kildare, Westmeath and north Dublin.*

Medicine Weekly

Éireann Healthcare Publications,
25–26 Windsor Place, Dublin 2
Editor: Dara Gantly
t. +353 1 475 3300
f. +353 1 475 3311
e. editor@indigo.ie
■ *This weekly newspaper has news and feature articles on the Irish medical industry.*

Metro Éireann

213 North Circular Road, Dublin 7
Editor: Chinedu Onyejelem
t. +353 869 0670
m. +353 86 852 3397
f. +353 1 868 9142
e. news@metroeireann.com and editor@metroeireann.com
w. www.metroeireann.com
■ *This monthly newspaper was set up in 2002 and is now the primary source of information on the country's immigrant community and ethnic minorities.*

Midland Times

12–14 Dominick Street, Mullingar,
Co. Westmeath
Editor: Gerry Proctor
t. +353 44 35700
f. +353 44 35705
e. info@midlandtimes.ie
■ *A regional freesheet.*

Midland Tribune

Syngefield, Birr, Co. Offaly
Editor: John O'Callaghan
t. +353 509 20003
f. +353 509 20588
e. midtrib@iol.ie
■ *This weekly regional newspaper has a circulation of 16,000 in midland counties.*
Advertising Manager: Phyllis Byrne

Munster Express

37 The Quay, Waterford
Editor: Kieran Walsh
t. +353 51 872 141
f. +353 51 873 452
e. news@munster-express.ie
w. www.munster-express.ie
■ *This bi-weekly regional newspaper has a circualtion of 12,000 in Munster.*

Nationalist and Leinster Times

42 Tullow Street, Carlow
Editor: Eddie Coffey
t. +353 9391 70113
f. +353 9391 31442
e. eddie-coffey@carlow-nationalist.ie
w. www.carlow-leinstertims.ie
Advertising Manager: Christian Jago-Byrne
t. +353 9391 70103

Nationalist and Munster Advertiser

Queen Street, Clonmel, Co. Tipperary
Editor: Tom Corr
t. +353 52 22211
f. +353 52 72528
e. info@nationalist.ie and tcorr@nationalist.ie
w. www.nationalist.ie
■ *This weekly regional newspaper has a circulation of more than 15,000 in Co. Tipperary. Owned by Johnston Press.*
Advertising Manager: Phil Corby
e. ads@nationalist.ie

Nenagh Guardian

13 Summerhill, Nenagh, Co. Tipperary
Editor: Gary Cotter
t. +353 67 31214
f. +353 67 33401
e. gcotter@nenaghguardian.ie
w. www.nenaghguardian.ie

■ *This weekly provincial newspaper has a weekly circulation of more than 8,000 in north Tipperary.*
Advertising Managers: David Ryan and Gwyn Wallace

New Ross Standard

2 Mary Street, New Ross, Co. Wexford
Editor: Michael Ryan
t. +353 51 421 184
f. +353 51 422 462
e. michael.ryan@peoplenews.ie

■ *This regional weekly paper circulates in the New Ross area of Co. Wexford. It is part of the People Group of newspapers.*

News of the World

4th Floor, Bishop's Square, Redmond's Hill, Dublin 2
Assistant Editor (Ireland): Nick Bramhill
t. +353 1 479 2500
f. +353 1 479 2520
e. nick-bramhill@notw.ie
w. www.newsoftheworld.co.uk

■ *This is the Irish edition of the UK Sunday tabloid, mixing Irish news with content from the main UK version. Circulation: 166,500.*

North County Leader

Leader House, North Street, Swords, Co. Dublin
Editor: Christina Kelly
t. +353 1 840 0200
f. +353 1 840 0550
e. info@northcountyleader.com

Northern Standard

The Diamond, Monaghan
Editor: Martin Smyth
t. +353 47 82188
f. +353 47 84070
e. newsdesk@northernstandard.ie
w. www.northernstandard.ie

■ *This weekly regional newspaper has a circulation of 14,500 in Co. Monaghan and border areas.*
Advertising Manager: Bernie Smyth

Offaly Express

Bridge Street, Tullamore, Co. Offaly
Editor: John Whelan
t. +353 506 21744
f. +353 506 51930
e. lexpress@indigo.ie

■ *This weekly regional paper circulates in Co. Offaly. It shares its commercial staff with the Leinster Express.*

Offaly Independent

The Mall, Tullamore, Co. Offaly
Editor: Dave O'Connell
t. +353 506 51398
f. +353 506 25184
e. news@offalyindependent.ie

■ *This weekly regional newspaper circulates in Co. Offaly.*

People Newspapers

Channing House, Upper Rowe Street, Wexford

■ *Publishers of the magazine* **Ireland's Own** *and seven weekly newspapers:* **Bray People, Enniscorthy Guardian, Gorey Guardian, New Ross Standard, Wexford People, Wicklow People** *and* **Carlow People.**

People Newspapers (Dublin)

85–86 Omni Park Shopping Centre, Dublin 9
t. +353 1 862 1611
f. +353 1 862 1625
e. news@dublinpeople.com
w. www.dublinpeople.com

■ *This newspaper group was established in 1987. It began with the* **Northside People** *and now prints the east and west editions of the* **Northside People** *as well as the* **Southside People.** *It distributes more than 150,000 copies.*

Editors

Northside People: Neil Fetherston
 t. +353 1 862 1626
 e. neil@dublinpeople.com
North-West People: Aidan Kelly
 t. +353 1 816 2989
 e. aidan@dublinpeople.com
South-West People: Jack Gleeson
 t. +353 1 816 2923
 e. j.gleeson@dublinpeople.com

Provincial Farmer

Meath Chronicle, Market Square,
Navan, Co. Meath
Editor: Brian O'Loughlin
 t. +353 46 907 9612
 f. +353 46 902 3565
■ *This is a free monthly farming newspaper
circulated with the* Meath Chronicle.

Roscommon Champion

Abbey Street, Roscommon
Editor: Paul Healy
 t. +353 90 66 25051 / 2
 f. +353 90 66 25053
 e. roscommonchampion@eircom.net
 w. www.homepage.eircom.net/
 roscommonchampion
■ *Weekly regional newspaper circulating
mostly in Co. Roscommon. Founded in 1927,
its circulation stands at more than 9,000.*
Advertising Manager: Immacula Hoare

Roscommon Herald

Patrick Street, Boyle, Co. Roscommon
Editor: Christina McHugh
 t. +353 71 96 62004 / 62052
 f. +353 71 96 62926
 e. news@roscommonherald.ie
 w. www.roscommonherald.com
■ *Weekly regional newspaper, founded in 1859,
with a circulation of 11,000 in Co. Roscommon.*
Advertising Manager: Claire Morgan
 e. advertising@roscommonherald.ie

Scottish Radio Holdings

Clydebank Business Park, Clydebank,
Glasgow G81 2RX, Scotland

Chief Executive: David Goode
Company Secretary: Jane Tames
 t. +44 141 565 2200
 f. +44 141 565 2202
 e. radio@srh.co.uk
 w. www.srhplc.com
■ *This international media group owned
a large share of the Irish newspaper market
until June 2005. It grew from a consortium in
Glasgow in the early 1970s that won the third
commercial radio licence offered in the UK.
Now it has interests throughout Ireland, owning Morton Newspapers, one of Northern
Ireland's largest newspaper publishers, as well
as provincial papers in the Republic, including
the* Longford Leader, Kilkenny People,
Tipperary Star, Nationalist, *and* Leitrim
Observer. *The company also owns the Irish
radio stations Today FM and Dublin's FM104.
SRH now has two strong divisions throughout
the UK and the Republic. Its radio division
comprises 22 analogue services, one digital service and six digital licences, and SCORE Press,
while the newspaper division comprises 44
titles. In June 2005, Emap bought all its radio
businesses while Johnston Press took over
SCORE titles in Ireland.*

Sligo Champion

Wine Street, Sligo
Editor: Seamus Finn
 t. +353 7191 69222
 f. +353 7191 69040
 e. editor@sligochampion.ie
 w. www.unison.ie/sligo_champion
■ *Weekly regional paper for Co. Sligo,
founded in 1836, with a circulation of 14,000.*
Advertising Manager: Breda Potter

Sligo Weekender

Waterfront House, Bridge Street, Sligo
Editor: Brian McHugh
 t. +353 71 91 42140
 f. +353 71 91 74911
 e. brian.mchugh@sligoweekender.com
 w. www.sligoweekender.com
■ *Weekly regional newspaper circulating in
Sligo with a circulation of more than 9,000.*

Advertising Manager: Fergal
McDonagh
t. +353 71 91 74912
f. +353 71 91 42255

South City Express

PO Box 3430, Tallaght, Dublin 24
Editor: John Russell
t. +353 1 451 9000
f. +353 1 451 9805
e. sw@tallaghtonline.ie

Southern Star

Ilen Street, Skibbereen, Co. Cork
Editor: Liam O'Regan
t. +353 28 21200
f. +353 28 21212
e. editorial@southernstar.ie
w. www.southernstar.ie

■ *This weekly regional newspaper has a circulation of more than 15,000 in the south Co. Cork region.*

Advertising Manager: John Hamilton
e. advertising@southernstar.ie

Sunday Business Post

80 Harcourt Street, Dublin 2
t. +353 1 602 6000
f. +353 1 679 6496
e. info@spost.ie
w. www.thepost.ie

■ *This paper was launched in 1989 by four journalists as a financial weekly. Trinity Mirror bought the paper in 1997 and sold it to its present owners, Thomas Crosbie Holdings, for €10 million in April 2002. Its circulation stands at about 50,000.*

Managing Director: Fiachra O'Riordan
t. +353 1 602 6035
e. fiachra@sbpost.ie
Editor: Cliff Taylor
e. ctaylor@sbpost.ie
News Editor: Simon Carswell
e. scarswell@sbpost.ie
Deputy News Editor: Gavin Daly
e. gdaly@sbpost.ie
Assistant Editor: Kieron Wood
e. kwood@sbpost.ie

Assistant Editor and Crime
Correspondent: Barry O'Kelly
e. bokelly@sbpost.ie
Political Reporter: Pat Leahy
e. pat@sbpost.ie
Assistant Editor and Property Editor:
Gillian Nelis
e. gnelis@sbpost.ie
Assistant Editor and Design Editor:
Heather Warwicker
e. hwarwicker@sbpost.ie
Agenda Supplement Editor: Fiona
Ness
e. fness@sbpost.ie
Computers in Business Editor: Adrian
Weckler
e. aweckler@sbpost.ie
Media and Marketing Editor: Catherine
O'Mahony
e. comahony@sbpost.ie

Sunday Independent

Independent News and Media, 27–32
Talbot Street, Dublin 1
Reception
t. +353 1 705 5333
f. +353 1 705 5779
e. snews@unison.independent.ie
w. www.unison.independent.ie

■ *The sister paper to the* **Irish Independent** *is the highest-selling Sunday newspaper, with a circulation of more than 300,000. First published in 1906, it is the oldest Irish Sunday paper. It is owned by Independent News and Media.*

Editor: Aengus Fanning
f. +353 1 705 5575
e. afanning@unison.independent.ie
Deputy Editor and Features Editor:
Anne Harris
t. +353 1 705 5699
f. +353 1 705 5668
e. aharris@unison.independent.ie
Deputy Editor: Willie Kealy
t. +353 1 705 5690
e. wkealy@unison.independent.ie

Executive Editor (News): Jody Corcoran
t. +353 1 705 5693
m. +353 87 243 0636
e. jcorcoran@unison.independent.ie
News Editor: Ciarán Byrne
t. +353 1 705 5694
m. +353 86 173 9523
e. cbyrne@unison.independent.ie
Editor, Sunday Magazine: Brendan O'Connor
t. +353 1 705 5694
m. +353 87 222 6575
e. boconnor@unison.independent.ie
Political Correspondent: Joseph O'Malley
t. +353 1 618 3276
Business Editor: Shane Ross
f. +353 1 705 5719
e. sross@unison.independent.ie
Deputy Sports Editor: Seán Ryan
t. +353 1 705 5619
f. +353 1 705 5719
e. sryan@unison.independent.ie
Operations Editor: Campbell Spray
e. cspray@unison.independent.ie
Photographic Editor: Dave Conachy
t. +353 1 705 5674
e. dconachy@unison.independent.ie
Sports Editor: Adhamhnan O'Sullivan
t. +353 1 705 5680 / 1 / 2
e. aosullivan@unison.independent.ie

Sunday Mirror (Dublin Office)

4th Floor, Park House, 191–197 North Circular Road, Dublin 7
Editor: Christian McCashin
t. +353 1 868 8638 / 9
f. +353 1 868 8629
e. c.mccashin@mgn.co.uk
w. www.sundaymirror.co.uk
■ *Sister paper to the* **Irish Daily Mirror,** *this Sunday tabloid mixes Irish content and content from the main UK version. Reporters are based in Dublin, and production is carried out in its Belfast office. There is a separate*

version for northern readers. Circulation in the Republic is 51,303.

Sunday Times

Fourth Floor, Bishop's Square, Redmond's Hill, Dublin 2
Ireland Editor: Fiona McHugh
m. +353 86 600 9165
e. fiona.mchugh@Sunday-times.ie
News Editor: John Burns
t. +353 1 479 2424
f. +353 1 479 2421
e. john.burns@Sunday-times.ie
w. www.timesonline.co.uk
■ *The Irish edition of the UK quality broadsheet Sunday paper owned by News International features Irish news, sport, business, opinion and culture coupled with content from the main UK edition. It opened its Dublin office in 1996 and now has a circulation of more than 90,000.*
Political Correspondent: Richard Oakley
t. +353 1 618 3402
e. richard.oakley@Sunday-times.ie
Political Correspondent: Stephen O'Brien
t. +353 1 618 3402 [Leinster House]
m. +353 87 812 4716
e. stephen.obrien@Sunday-times.ie
Pictures Editor: Eileen Martin
e. eileen.martin@Sunday-times.ie
Managing Business Editor: Frank Fitzgibbon
e. frank.fitzgibbon@Sunday-times.ie
Business Editor: Tom McEnaney
e. tom.mcenaney@Sunday-times.ie
Sports Editor: Paul Rowan
e. paul.rowan@Sunday-times.ie
Property Editor: Brian Carey
e. brian.carey@Sunday-times.ie
Culture Ireland Magazine: Michael Ross
e. michael.ross@Sunday-times.ie
Money Editor: Margaret Ward
e. margaret.ward@Sunday-times.ie

Sunday Tribune

15 Lower Baggot Street, Dublin 2
General Enquiries
t. +353 1 661 5555
f. +353 1 661 5302
w. www.tribune.ie

■ *This quality broadsheet Sunday paper was launched in 1980 by the businessman Hugh McLoughlin but was dragged down when his tabloid* Daily News *collapsed. The title was bought, mainly by the journalist Vincent Browne and businessman Tony Ryan, and was re-launched in 1983. Now part-owned by Independent News and Media, it has a circulation in the 80,000s.*

Managing Director: Michael Roche
Editor: Noirin Hegarty
Advertising Manager: John Holland
e. jholland@tribune.ie
Political Editor: Stephen Collins
t. +353 1 618 3090 [Leinster House]
m. +353 87 235 5896
e. scollins@tribune.ie
Political Reporter: Shane Coleman
t. +353 1 618 3278 [Leinster House]
m. +353 87 236 1630
e. scoleman@tribune.ie
Pictures Editor: Máirín Gillespie
e. mgillespie@tribune.ie
Assistant News Editor and World
News Editor: Gerard Siggins
e. gsiggins@tribune.ie
Deputy News Editor: Olivia Doyle
e. newsdesk@tribune.ie and
odoyle@tribune.ie
Deputy Editor and News Editor:
Diarmuid Doyle
e. newsdesk@tribune.ie and
ddoyle@tribune.ie
Business Editor: Paul O'Kane
e. pkane@tribune.ie
Sports Editor: Philip Lannigan
e. sport@tribune.ie and
plannigan@tribune.ie
Property Editor: Helen Rogers
e. hrogers@tribune.ie

Sunday World

27–32 Talbot Street, Dublin 1
General Enquiries
t. +353 1 884 9000
f. +353 1 884 9001
e. news@sundayworld.com
w. www.sundayworld.com

■ *This Irish Sunday tabloid paper launched in 1973 has a circulation of more than 300,000. Its mixture of the style of a British tabloid and Irish content has thrived for three decades. Independent News and Media bought a controlling share of the paper in 1978.*

Managing Director: Michael Brophy
Managing Editor: John Shiels
Deputy Editor: Alan Murphy
Pictures Editor: Val Sheehan
Editor: Colm MacGinty
Deputy Editor: J. P. Thompson
Deputy Editor: Neil Leslie
Sports Editor: Brian Farrell
e. sport@sundayworld.com
News Editor: John Donlon
m. +353 87 267 7226
Advertising Manager: Gerry Lennon
f. +353 1 884 9002
Political Editor: Sean Boyne
m. +353 86 824 1075

Thomas Crosbie Holdings

97 South Mall, Cork
Chief Executive and Advertising
Manager: Angela Crowley
t. +353 21 230 4011
f. +353 21 230 4044
e. angela.crowley@tcm.ie
w. www.tch.ie

■ *This Cork media group has interests in radio and magazines but primarily in newspapers. Its main titles are the* Irish Examiner, Evening Echo *and* Sunday Business Post.

Editor: Jill O'Sullivan
t. +353 21 230 4000
f. +353 21 230 4044
e. jill.osullivan@tcm.ie

Tipperary Star

Friar Street, Thurles, Co. Tipperary
Editor: Michael Dundon
t. +353 504 21122
f. +353 504 21110
e. md@tipperarystar.ie
w. www.tipperarystar.ie
■ *This weekly regional newspaper has a circulation of 10,000 in Co. Tipperary. It is owned by Johnston Press.*
Advertising Manager: Paula St John

Tirconaill Tribune

Main Street, Milford, Co. Donegal
Editor: John McAteer
t. +353 74 91 53600
f. +353 74 91 53607
e. tirconailltribune@eircom.net
w. www.tirconaill-tribune.com

Topic Newspapers Ltd

6 Dominick Street, Mullingar, Co. Westmeath
Editor: Richard Hogan
t. +353 44 48 868
f. +353 44 43 777
e. topic@indigo.ie
■ *This company publishes and prints the regional newspapers Westmeath Topic, Offaly Topic and Meath Topic, which circulate in Cos. Westmeath, Offaly, Meath, Kildare and Longford. The titles share advertising.*
Advertising Manager: Tom Kiernan

Tralee Advertiser

Upper Rock Street, Tralee, Co. Kerry
Editor: Lionel Lynch
t. +353 66 712 2982
f. +353 66 712 9966
e. traleeadvertiser@eircom.net

Tuam Herald

Dublin Road, Tuam, Co. Galway
Editor: David Burke
t. +353 93 24183
f. +353 93 24478
e. editor@tuamherald.ie
w. www.unison.ie/tuam_herald

■ *A weekly regional paper circulating in the border area between Cos. Galway, Roscommon and Mayo. Founded in 1837, it has a circulation of 11,000.*
Advertising Manager: Miriam Farrell

Tullamore Tribune

Church Street, Tullamore, Co. Offaly
Editor: Gerard Scully
t. +353 506 21152
f. +353 506 21927
e. tulltrib@eircom.net
■ *This weekly regional paper has a circulation of 9,000 in Tullamore and surrounding areas.*
Advertising Manager: Phyllis Byrne

Vale Star/Mallow Star

19 Bridge Street, Mallow, Co. Cork
Editor: Steve Murphy
t. +353 22 22910
f. +353 22 22959
e. wob@vso.iol.ie

Waterford News and Star

25 Michael Street, Waterford
Editor: Peter Doyle
t. +353 51 309 543
f. +353 51 855 281
e. editor@waterford-news.com
■ *This weekly regional paper has a circulation of more than 15,000 in Co. Waterford. It is owned by Thomas Crosbie Media.*
Advertising Manager: Caroline Dower
t. +353 51 875 566
f. +353 51 856 317
e. sales@waterford-news.com

Waterford Today

36 Mayor's Walk, Waterford
Editor: Paddy Gallagher
t. +353 51 854 135
f. +353 51 854 140
e. info@waterford-today.ie
w. www.waterford-today.ie
■ *This freesheet circulates in Waterford.*
Advertising Manager: Niall Morrissey
m. +353 86 250 4169

Weekender Newspaper

6 Charter Buildings, Kennedy Road,
Navan, Co. Meath
Editor: Fergus Barry
  t. +353 46 90 22333
  f. +353 46 90 29864
  e. tebitto@indigo.ie
■ *This weekly regional newspaper circulates in Co. Meath.*

Weekly Observer

19 Bridge Street, Mallow, Co. Cork
Editor: Steve Murphy
  t. +353 22 22910
  f. +353 22 22959
  w. www.wob@vso.iol.ie

Western People

Kevin Barry Street, Ballina, Co. Mayo
Editor: James Laffey
  t. +353 96 60926
  f. +353 96 73458
  e. james.laffey@westernpeople.ie
  w. www.westernpeople.ie
■ *This is a weekly regional paper for Co. Mayo, founded in 1883, with a circulation of more than 21,000.*
Advertising Manager: David Dwane
  e. david.dwane@westernpeople.ie

Westmeath Examiner

19 Dominick Street, Mullingar, Co. Westmeath
Editor: Ronan O'Donoghue
  t. +353 44 42817
  f. +353 44 40640
  e. news@westmeathexaminer.ie
  w. www.westmeathexaminer.ie
■ *This weekly regional newspaper has a circualtion of 11,800 in Co. Westmeath.*
Advertising Manager: Dale Greenwood
  t. +353 44 48426
  e. advertise@westmeathexaminer.ie

Westmeath Independent

11 Seán Costello Street, Athlone,
Co. Westmeath
Editor: Dave O'Connell
  t. +353 90 64 72003
  f. +353 90 64 74474
  e. editor@westmeathindependent.ie
  w. www.westmeathindependent.ie
■ *This weekly regional newspaper circulates in Co. Westmeath.*

Wexford People

Channing House, Upper Rowe Street,
Wexford
Editor: Michael Ryan
  t. +353 53 40100
  f. +353 53 40195
  e. michael.ryan@peoplenews.ie
■ *This weekly regional, part of the People newspaper group, circulates in the Wexford area.*

Wicklow People

Main Street, Wicklow
Editor: Michael Ryan
  t. +353 404 67198
  f. +353 404 69937
  e. michael.ryan@peoplenews.ie
■ *This weekly regional paper is part of the People newspaper group and circulates in Co. Wexford. The total circulation for the group's titles in the county—the* Wicklow People, Bray People *and* Carlow People—*is 18,300.*

Wicklow Times

Bradán Media Sales, 1 Eglington Road,
Bray, Co. Wicklow
Editor: Shay Fitzmaurice
  t. +353 1 286 9111
  f. +353 1 286 9074
  e. wicklowed@localtimes.ie
■ *Freesheet for Co. Wicklow with a circulation of 37,500, with editions for the north, south and west of the county.*

Northern Ireland

Telephone numbers in Northern Ireland have the prefix 048 if dialled from the Republic and 004428 if dialled from elsewhere.

Alpha Newspapers Group

56 Scotch Street, Armagh BT61 7DQ
Group Company Secretary: Eddie McFeetors
t. +44 28 3752 2639
f. +44 28 7034 3606
w. www.ulsternet-ni.co.uk
■ *The proprietor of this leading Northern Ireland newspaper group is Lord Kilclooney, formerly John Taylor, ex-minister in the Stormont government and former Ulster Unionist MP. It increased its range of interests significantly when it bought the Northern Newspaper Group from the Troy family in 2003. Its weekly circulation now runs to 120,000, with titles in Dungannon, Omagh, Strabane, Armagh, Ballyclare, Larn, Carrickfergus and Rathfriland, Co. Down, as well as a freesheet in Co. Armagh. Among its titles are the* Antrim Guardian, Ballyclare Gazette, Ballymena Guardian, Ballymoney Chronicle, Carrickfergus Advertiser, Coleraine Chronicle, Coleraine Constitution, Larne Gazette, Limavady Chronicle, Limavady Constitution, Longford News, Magherafelt Constitution, Midland Tribune, Moyle Chronicle, Newtownabbey Guardian, Northern Constitution, Roscommon Champion, Ulster Gazette, Strabane Weekly News, Outlook, Tullamore Tribune, Tyrone Constitution *and* Tyrone Courier. *It also publishes the freesheets* Armagh Advertiser *and the* Leader *(Coleraine). The Alpha Group bought the* Athlone Voice *title in May 2005.*

Andersonstown News

Teach Basil, 2 Hannahstown Hill,
Belfast BT17 0LT
Managing Director: Máirtín Ó Muilleoir
t. (ROI): 048 9061 9000.
(elsewhere) +44 2890 619000

f. (ROI): 048 9060 5533.
(elsewhere) +44 2890 605533
e. mairtin@irelandclick.com
w. www.irelandclick.com
Editor: Robin Livingstone
Deputy Editor: Anthony Neeson
e. anthony@irelandclick.com
Classifieds: Linda Greenan
t. 048 9061 9000
e. linda@irelandclick.com
■ *A bi-weekly newspaper, published each Monday and Thursday, circulating in the greater Belfast area. The general-interest newspaper is part of the Andersonstown News Group, which also publishes the* North Belfast News, *the* South Belfast News *and the daily Irish-language newspaper* Lá. *The paper's web site offers paying subscribers an on-line version.*

Andersonstown News Group

Teach Basil, 2 Hannahstown Hill,
Belfast BT17 0LT
w. www.irelandclick.com
■ *This Northern Ireland newspaper group is made up of the bi-weekly* Andersonstown News, *the weekly* North Belfast News *and* South Belfast News *and the daily Irish-language paper* Lá. *In 2004 it moved into the Dublin market, launching the* Lucan Gazette *in south Dublin and its sister paper for north-west of the city, the* Blanch Gazette. *In 2005 it launched the newspaper* Daily Ireland.

Antrim Guardian

5 Railway Street, Antrim BT41 4AE
Editor: Liam Heffron
t. (ROI): 048 9446 2624.
(elsewhere) +44 28 9446 2624
f. (ROI): 048 9446 5551
e. antrimguardian@macunlimited.net
w. www.ulsternet-ni.co.uk

A weekly regional paper, published each Wednesday. Founded in 1970, its weekly circulation is 23,500. Along with its sister paper, the **Ballymena Guardian,** *it is owned by the* **Alpha Newspaper Group.** *Some content is available on its web site.*

Display Advertising Representative and Situations Vacant: Pat Dalton

Armagh-Down Observer

Ann Street, Dungannon, Co. Armagh
BT70 1ET
Editor: Desmond Mallon
  t. (ROI): 048 8772 2557.
  (elsewhere) +44 28 87722557
  f. (ROI): 048 8772 7334.
  (elsewhere) +44 28 87727334
  e. editor@observernewewspapersni.com
  w. none

Weekly paper, published every Thursday. It is part of the Observer newspaper group in Northern Ireland, which also publishes the **Ballymena Chronicle, Mid-Ulster Observer, Lurgan and Portadown Examiner, Armagh Observer, Dungannon Observer, Fermanagh News** *and* **Tyrone Democrat.**

Armagh Observer

Ann Street, Dungannon, Co. Armagh
BT70 1ET
Editor: Desmond Mallon
  t. (ROI): 048 8772 2557.
  (elsewhere) +44 28 87722557
  f. (ROI): 048 8772 7334.
  (elsewhere) +44 28 87727334
  e. editor@observernewewspapersni.com
  w. none

Weekly paper, published every Wednesday. It is part of the Observer newspaper group in Northern Ireland, which also publishes the **Ballymena Chronicle, Mid-Ulster Observer, Lurgan and Portadown Examiner, Armagh-Down Observer, Dungannon Observer, Fermanagh News** *and* **Tyrone Democrat.**

Ballymena Guardian

Alpha Newspapers Group, 20 Railway Road, Coleraine, Co. Derry BT52 1PD
Editor: Maurice O'Neill
  t. +44 28 703 43344
  f. +44 28 703 43606
  w. www.ulsternet-ni.co.uk

Weekly paper, published each Wednesday.
Advertising Manager: W. J. Lynn

Ballymena Times

22 Ballymoney Street, Ballymena, Co. Antrim BT43 6AL
Editor: Des Blackadder
  t. (ROI): 048 256 53300.
  (elsewhere): +44 28 25653300
  f. (ROI): 048 256 41517.
  (elsewhere) +44 28 256 41517
  e. edbt@mortonnewspapers.com
  w. www.ballymenatimes.com

This weekly paper, published each Wednesday, is a sister paper of the **Antrim Times.** *The combined circulation of the two titles is about 10,000. Both are owned by Morton Newspapers, which has a total of 27 titles in Ireland. The* **Ballymena Times** *has different editorial content from its sister, but they share advertising and have the same commercial staff. The web site shares content from both papers.*

Ballymoney and Moyle Times

6 Church Street, Ballymoney, Co. Antrim BT53 6HS
Editor: Lyle McMullen
Advertising Manager: Carmel Taylor
  t. (ROI): 048 27 666216.
  (elsewhere): +44 2827666216
  f. (ROI): 048 27 667066.
  (elsewhere): +44 2827667066
  e. edbm@mortonnewspapers.com

First published in 1989 as an offshoot of the **Ballymena Times,** *the general-interest paper now has sales of 4,500 in the north Antrim area. It is published on Tuesday evening, but the bulk of its sales are on Wednesday.*

Banbridge Chronicle

14 Bridge Street, Banbridge, Co. Down
BT32 3JS
Editor: Bryan Hooks
t. (ROI): 048 40662322.
(elsewhere): +44 28 40662322
f. (ROI): 048 40624397.
(elsewhere): +44 28 40624397
■ *Weekly paper published every Wednesday. It has a circulation of 7,600.*
Advertising Manager: Gina Fitzpatrick

Banbridge Leader

25 Bridge Street, Banbridge, Co. Down
BT32 3JL
Editor: Damien Wilson
t. (ROI) 048 40662745.
(elsewhere): +44 28 40662745
f. (ROI): 048 406 26378.
(elsewhere) +44 28 40626378
e. eddl@mortonnewspapers.com
w. www.mortonnewspapers.com

Belfast News

46–56 Boucher Crescent, Belfast
BT12 6QY
Editor: Julie McClay
t. (ROI): 048 9068 0000.
(elsewhere) +44 28 90 680000
f. (ROI): 048 9066 4412.
(elsewhere) +44 28 90 664 412
e. newsletter@mgn.co.uk
w. www.newsletter.co.uk
■ *This Belfast freesheet, published each Thursday, is a sister title of the* **News Letter.** *It is owned by the British venture capital company 3i, published by Century Newspapers, and managed through a holding company, Local Press Ltd.*

Belfast Telegraph

124–144 Royal Avenue, Belfast BT1
1EB
Reception and general enquiries
t. (ROI): 048 9026 4000.
(elsewhere): +44 28 90264000
f. (ROI): 048 90554518.
(elsewhere): +44 28 90554518
w. www.belfasttelegraph.co.uk
■ *The* **Belfast Telegraph** *is an evening paper and has the largest circulation in Northern Ireland, at around 111,000. It was founded in 1870 as the* **Belfast Evening Telegraph.** *Its traditional political outlook was mainstream unionist until 1953, when the editor, Jack Sayer, took a more liberal line to appeal to moderate nationalists. The paper was sold by Trinity Mirror to Anthony O'Reilly's Independent News and Media group.*
Managing Director: Derek Carvell
t. +44 28 9026 4160
f. +44 28 9033 1332
Editor: Edmund Curran
t. +44 28 90 264 400
f. +44 2890 554 518
e. editor@belfasttelegraph.co.uk
News Editor: Paul Connolly
t. +44 28 9026 4420
f. +44 28 90 554 540
e. newseditor@belfasttelegraph.co.uk;
pconnolly@belfasttelegraph.co.uk
Deputy News Editor: Ronan Henry
t. +44 28 9026 4420
f. +44 28 9055 4540
e. newseditor@belfasttelegraph.co.uk
Advertising Director: Simon Mann
t. +44 28 9026 4062
f. +44 28 9055 4581
Sport Assistant Editor: John Taylor
e. jtaylor@belfasttelegraph.co.uk
Sport Assistant Editor: Graham Hamilton
e. ghamilton@belfasttelegraph.co.uk
Agriculture Editor: Michael Drake
e. mdrake@belfasttelegraph.co.uk
Features Editor: Gail Walker
e. featureseditor@belfasttelegraph.co.uk;
Sports Editor: John Laverty
e. jlaverty@belfasttelegraph.co.uk
Business Editor: Nigel Tilson
e. ntilson@belfasttelegraph.co.uk
Letters to the Editor:
e. writeback@belfasttelegraph.co.uk
Picture Editor: Gerry Fitzgerald
e. gfitzgerald@belfasttelegraph.co.uk

Political Correspondent: Noel McAdam
  e. nmcadam@belfasttelegraph.co.uk
Political Correspondent: Chris Thornton
  e. cthornton@belfasttelegraph.co.uk
Property Correspondent: Mandi Millar
  e. mmillar@belfasttelegraph.co.uk
Religion Correspondent: Alf McCreary
  e. amccreary@belfasttelegraph.co.uk
Education Correspondent: Kathryn
Torney
  e. ktorney@belfasttelegraph.co.uk
Business Correspondent: Robin Morton
  e. rmorton@belfasttelegraph.co.uk
Golf News: Peter Hutcheon
  e. phutcheon@belfasttelegraph.co.uk
Health Correspondent: Nigel Gould
  e. ngould@belfasttelegraph.co.uk
North West Telegraph Editor: William
Allen
  t. +44 28 7134 8000
  e. wallen@belfasttelegraph.co.uk
London Editor: Brian Walker
  t. +44 7802 176 347
  e. bwalker@actona.demon.co.uk
Property Manager: Tommy Nolan
  t. +44 28 90 26 4005
  e. tommy.nolan@belfasttelegraph.co.uk
Newspaper Sales Controller: Julie
Stevenson
  t. +44 28 9026 4031
Advertising Sales Controller: Andrew
Harding
  t. +44 28 9026 4063
Advertising Sales Controller: Barbara
Campbell
  t. +44 28 9026 4117
Marketing Director: Richard McLean
  t. +44 28 9055 4769

Buy and Sell (Belfast Office)
Lyndon Court, Queen Street, Belfast
BT1 6BY
Business Advertising Advisor
  t. +44 28 9053 0066
  e. tradeads@buyandsell.ie
  w. www.buyandsell.ie

■ *Weekly newspaper providing free classified advertisements for private advertisers. Also provides business and international advertising and personal ads. The Northern Ireland paper edition is published on Fridays. A web edition is available.*

Carrickfergus Advertiser
31 High Street, Carrickfergus,
Co. Antrim BT38 7AN
Editor: Raymond Hughes
  t. (ROI): 048 93 363 651.
  (elsewhere) +44 28 93 363 651
  f. (ROI): 048 93 363 092.
  (elsewhere): +44 28 93 363 092.
■ *Weekly paper published each Wednesday, with a circulation of 7,500. Owned by the Alpha Newspaper Group.*

Carrick Times
19 North Street, Carrickfergus, Co.
Antrim BT38 7AQ
Editor: Hugh Vance
  t. (ROI): 048 93 351 992.
  (elsewhere): +44 28 93 351 992
  f. (ROI): 048 93 369 825.
  (elsewhere): +44 28 93 369 825
  e. edct@mortonnewspapers.com
  w. www.carricktimes.co.uk
■ *Weekly paper published each Thursday by the Morton Newspaper Group.*

Church of Ireland Gazette
3 Wallace Avenue, Lisburn, Co. Antrim
BT27 4AA
Editor: Rev. Canon I. M. Ellis
  t. (ROI): 048 92 67 5743.
  (elsewhere): +44 28 9267 5743.
  f. (ROI): 048 92 667 580.
  (elsewhere): +44 4892 667 580
  e. gazette@ireland.anglican.org
  w. gazette.ireland.anglican.org
■ *Weekly Church of Ireland newspaper. The week's Gazette can be e-mailed directly to subscribers.*

City News

22 Buncrana Road, Derry BT48 8AA
Editor-in-Chief: Pat McArt
  t. +44 28 71 27 2200
  f. +44 28 71 27 2260
  e. editorial@derryjournal.com
  w. www.derryjournal.com
■ *This paper, aimed at readers in Derry, is part of the Derry Journal Newspapers Group, owned by Local Press Ltd.*

Coleraine Chronicle

20 Railway Road, Coleraine, Co. Derry BT52 1EJ
Editor: John Fillis
  t. (ROI): 048 70343344.
  (elsewhere): +44 28 70343344
  f. (ROI): 048 70343606.
  (elsewhere): +44 28 70343606
  e. editor@colraine chronicle.com
  w. www.ulsternet-ni.co.uk
■ *The* Coleraine Chronicle *is part of the Alpha Newspaper Group. Its readership is based in the mid-Ulster region. As well as its Coleraine edition it has separate editions for Limavady, Ballycastle, Coleraine and Ballymoney.*

Coleraine Times

71 New Row, Market Court, Coleraine, Co. Derry BT52 1EJ
Editor: Lyle McMullen
  t. (ROI): 048 703 552 60.
  (elsewhere): +44 28 703 55 260
  f. (ROI): 048 703 56186.
  (elsewhere): +44 28 703 561 86
  e. edcr@mortonnewspapers.com
w. www.colerainetimes.com
■ *Weekly paper published each Wednesday by Morton Newspapers.*

Craigavon Echo

14 Church Street, Portadown, Co. Armagh BT62 3LQ
Editor: Victor Kelly
  t. (ROI): 048 38 336 111.
  (elsewhere): +44 38 336 111
  f. (ROI): 048 38 350 203.

  (elsewhere): +44 38 350 203
  e. edpt@mortonnewspapers.com
  w. www.mortonnewspapers.com
■ *Freesheet that is part of the Morton Newspaper Group.*

Daily Ireland

Teach Basil, 2 Hannahstown Hill, Belfast BT17 0LT
Editor: Maria McCourt
  t. 048 90 612345
  e. m.mccourt@dailyireland.com
  w. www.dailyireland.com
■ Daily Ireland *is a new compact Irish daily newspaper. Published in Belfast as part of the Andersonstown News Group, which is available in both Northern Ireland and the Republic, its main target area in the Republic is the border counties. The newspaper was launched in February 2005 and sees itself as a competitor to the* Irish News *in Northern Ireland. The newspaper has a more republican agenda than the* Irish News's *middle-class nationalist stance.*
Sales: Jacqueline O'Donnell
  t. +44 28 90 6066850
  e. j.odonnell@dailyireland.com

Derry Journal

22 Buncrana Road, Derry BT48 8AA
Editor-in-Chief: Patrick McArt
  t. +44 28 7127 2200.
  f. +44 28 7127 2260.
  e. editorial@derryjournal.com
  w. www.derryjournal.com
■ *The second-oldest title still in circulation, the* Derry Journal *was launched in 1772. Its readership is based in the north-west region. In 2004 it was sold by Trinity Mirror to the newly formed Local Press Ltd. Published twice-weekly, on Tuesday and Friday, its web site also offers full content.*
Advertising Manager: Marion Harkin
  f. +44 28 7127 2218

Derry Journal Newspapers Group

22 Buncrana Road, Derry BT48 8AA
Editor-in-Chief: Patrick McArt
  t. +44 28 7127 2200

f. +44 28 7127 2260
e. editorial@derryjournal.com
w. www.derryjournal.com

■ *This newspaper group is ultimately owned by the British venture capital company 3i, which manages it through a holding company, Local Press Ltd. The group publishes the City News, Derry Journal, Derry on Monday, Donegal Democrat, Donegal on Sunday, Donegal People's Press, Foyle News, Letterkenny Listener, and Sunday Journal.*
Editor-in-Chief Donegal Titles: Michael Daly

Derry News

26 Balliniska Road, Springtown Industrial Estate, Derry BT48 0LY
Editor: Joanne McCool
t. +44 28 71 296 600
f. +44 28 71 296 611
e. editor@derrynews.net

■ *Weekly paper published each Thursday.*

Derry on Monday

22 Buncrana Road, Derry BT48 8AA
Editor-in-Chief: Patrick McArt
t. +44 28 7127 2200
f. +44 28 7127 2260
e. editorial@derryjournal.com
w. www.derryjournal.com

■ *This Monday newspaper for readers in Derry is part of the Derry Journal Newspaper Group, owned by Local Press Ltd.*

Down Democrat

74 Market Street, Downpatrick, Co. Down BT30 6LZ
Chief Executive: Tom Brennan
t. +44 28 44 614 400
f. +44 28 44 61 2221
e. reception@downdemocrat.com
w. www.downdemocrat.com

■ *A weekly paper published every Tuesday. Its web site offers content to readers who register.*
Advertising Manager: Tina Maguire
t. +44 28 302 54 354
Editor: Terry McLaughlin
terry.mclaughlin@downdemocrat.com

Down Recorder

2–4 Church Street, Downpatrick, Co. Down BT30 6EJ
Editor: Paul Symington
t. (ROI): 048 44 613 711.
(elsewhere): +44 28 44 613 711
f. (ROI): 048 44 614 624.
(elsewhere): +44 28 614 624
w. www.thedownrecorder.com

■ *Weekly paper published every Wednesday, with a ciruculation of about 12,700.*
Advertising Manager: Carollyne Rogan

Dromore Leader

30a Market Square, Dromore, Co. Down BT25 1AW
Editor: Damien Wilson
t. +44 28 92 692 217
f. +44 28 40 626 378
e. eddl@mortonnewspapers.com
w. www.dromoreleader.com

■ *Weekly paper published each Wednesday. It is part of the Morton Newspaper Group.*

Dungannon News and Tyrone Courier

58 Scotch Street, Dungannon, Co. Tyrone BT70 1BD
Editor: Ian Greer
t. +44 28 877 26 171
e. tyrone.courier@ulsternet-ni.co.uk
w. www.ulsternet-ni.co.uk

■ *Weekly paper published each Wednesday, with a circulation of about 14,500.*

Dungannon Observer

Ann Street, Dungannon, Co. Tyrone BT70 1ET
Editor: Desmond Mallon
t. (ROI): 048 87 722 557.
(elsewhere): +44 28 8772 2557
f. (ROI): 048 87 727 334.
(elsewhere): +44 28 87 727 334
e. editor@observernewspapersni.com

■ *Weekly paper published each Friday.*

East Antrim Gazette

20 Main Street, Larne, Co. Antrim BT40 1SS

Editor: Raymond Hughes
t. (ROI): 048 28 277 450.
(elsewhere): +44 28 277 450
f. (ROI): 048 28 260 733.
(elsewhere): +44 28 260 733

East Antrim Times

Morton Newspaper Group, 8 Dunluce Street, Larne, Co. Antrim BT40 1SS
Editor: Hugh Vance
t. (ROI): 048 28 272 303.
(elsewhere): +44 28 272 303
f. (ROI): 048 28 260 255.
(elsewhere): +44 28 260 255
e. edlt@mortonnewspapers.com
w. www.mortonnewspapers.com
■ *This is part of the Morton Newspapers Group. It also publishes a monthly advertising newspaper, the* **East Antrim Advertiser,** *which is distributed free with the main paper.*

Farmers' Journal

8–10 East Bridge Street, Enniskillen, Co. Fermanagh BT74 7BU
Editor: Denzil McDaniel
t. +44 28 66 324 422
f. +44 28 66 325 047
e. info@impartialreporter.com
w. www.impartialreporter.com
■ *This weekly journal for the farming industry is included in the* **Impartial Reporter,** *which circulates in Co. Fermanagh and border counties.*

Farming Life

46–56 Boucher Crescent, Belfast BT12 6QY
Editor: David McCoy
t. (ROI): 048 90 680 000
(elsewhere): +44 28 90 680 000
f. (ROI): 048 90 664 412
(elsewhere): +44 28 90 664 412
e. david.mccoy@farminglife.com
w. www.farminglife.com
■ *A weekly paper, published each Saturday, aimed at Northern Ireland's farming community. This sister title to the* **News Letter** *is ultimately owned by the British*

venture capital company 3i, published by Century Newspapers and managed through a holding company, Local Press Ltd.
Classified Advertising Manager: Dorothy Allen
e. dorothy.allen@farminglife.com

Farm Week

14 Church Street, Portadown, Co. Armagh BT62 3LQ
Editor: Hal Crowe
t. +44 28 3833 9421
f. +44 28 3839 5409
e. edfw@mortonnewspapers.com
w. www.farmweek.net
■ *This weekly farming journal for Northern Ireland covers agricultural news and views. It is owned by Morton Newspapers.*

Fermanagh News

Observer Newspapers NI Ltd, Ann Street, Dungannon, Co. Tyrone BT70 1ET
Editor: Desmond Mallon
t. (ROI): 048 87 722 557.
(elsewhere): +44 28 8772 2557
f. (ROI): 048 87 727 334.
(elsewhere): +44 87 727 334
e. editor@observernewspapersni.com

Foyle News

Buncrana Road, Derry BT48 8AA
Editor-in-Chief: Patrick McArt
t. (ROI): 048 71 272 200.
(elsewhere): +44 28 71 272 200
f. (ROI): 048 71 272 260 (News).
(elsewhere): +44 28 71 272 260
e. editorial@derryjournal.com
w. www.derryjournal.com
■ *Twice-weekly paper, published each Tuesday and Friday, with a readership of around 25,000 each day in Derry and the surrounding region.*

Impartial Reporter

8–10 East Bridge Street, Enniskillen, Co. Fermanagh BT74 7BU
Editor: Denzil McDaniel
t. (ROI): 048 66 324 422.
(elsewhere): +44 28 66 324 422

f. (ROI): +048 66 325 047.
(elsewhere): +44 28 66 325 047
e. dmcdaniel@impartialreporter.com
w. www.impartialreporter.com
■ *Fermanagh's oldest newspaper, founded in 1825, the weekly* **Impartial Reporter** *is published each Thursday and circulates in Co. Fermanagh, Co. Tyrone and in the border counties of the south.*

Irish Daily Mirror (Belfast Office)

415 Holywood Road, Belfast BT42 2GU
Northern News Editor: Maurice Fitzmaurice
t. +44 28 90 568 006
f. +44 28 90 568 005
e. irish@mgn.co.uk (News desk);
fmaurice@mgn.co.uk
w. www.mirror.co.uk
■ *This is the Irish edition of the UK* **Daily Mirror,** *combining Irish and UK content for separate editions in the North and the Republic. News and sports staff are based in the Republic, while production is carried out in the paper's Belfast office. The web edition contains content from the UK edition only.*
Sports Editor: John Monaghan
e. news@irishmirror.ie
Circulation: 79,337

Irish News

113–117 Donegall Street, Belfast BT1 2GE
Managing Director: Dominic Fitzpatrick
t. +44 28 9032 2226
f. +44 28 9033 7505
e. newsdesk@irishnews.com
w. www.irishnews.com
■ *Northern Ireland daily newspaper published in Belfast and aimed primarily at the nationalist community. Independently owned by a prominent Belfast Catholic family, the Fitzpatricks, it has a circulation of about 50,000. The paper was established by clerical interests in 1891 and after partition became the voice of mainstream nationalism.*

Editor: Noel Doran
Assistant Editor: Stephen O'Reilly
News Editor: Stephen McCaffrey
t. +44 28 9033 7544
f. +44 28 9033 7505
Head of Content: Fiona McGarry
t. +44 28 9032 2226
f. +44 28 9033 7505
Deputy News Editor: Billy Foley
Southern Correspondent: Valerie Robinson
t. +353 522 2608
m. + 353 87 917 7494
f. +353 522 2608
e. valrobinson@eircom.net
Newry Office: Catherine Morrison
t. +44 28 30 25 7778
f. +44 28 30 25 1017
e. irnnewry@aol.com
Derry Correspondent: Seamus McKinney
t. +44 28 71 374 455
f. +44 28 71 374 455
Features: Joanna Barniff
Pictures Editor: Ann McManus
Political Correspondent: William Graham
Sports Editor: Thomas Hawkings
Business Editor: Gary McDonald
Farming Business: John Manley
Travel Editor: James Stinson
Marketing Manager: John Brolly
Deputy Advertising Manager: Seán Higgins
t. +44 28 9033 7509
f. +44 28 9033 7508
e. advertising@irishnews.com;
shiggins@irishnews.com
Advertising Manager: Paddy Meehan
t. +44 28 9033 7516
f. +44 28 9033 7508
e. advertising@irishnews.com;
pmeehan@irishnews.com

Lá

Teach Basil, 2 Hannahstown Hill,
Belfast BT17 0LT
General Enquiries
t. +44 28 9060 5050
f. +44 28 9060 5544
e. eolas@nuacht.com
w. www.nuacht.com
■ *Daily Irish language newspaper.*
Editor: Ciarán Ó Pronntaigh
Deputy Editor: Concubhar Ó Liatháin
e. concubhar@nuacht.com
Sub-Editor: Áine Nic Gearailt
Arts Editor: Philip Cummings
e. leabhar@nuacht.com
Education Editor: Dominic Ó Brolcháin
Advertising: Connla Lawlor

Lakeland Extra

8–10 East Bridge Street, Enniskillen,
Co. Fermanagh BT74 7BU
Editor: Denzil McDaniel
t. +44 28 66 32 4422
f. +44 28 66 325 047
e. dmcdaniel@impartialreporter.com
w. www.impartialreporter.com
■ *Freesheet published by the* **Impartial Reporter.**

Larne Times

8 Dunluce Street, Larne, Co. Antrim
Editor: Hugh Vance
t. +44 28 272 303
f. +44 28 260 255
w. www.larnetimes.com
■ *A weekly newspaper circulating in Co. Antrim, the* **Larne Times** *has been owned by Morton Newspapers Ltd since 1986. It is published each Thursday.*

The Leader

20 Railway Road, Coleraine, Co. Derry
Editor: Linda Faith Kelly
t. +44 28 7034 3344
f. +44 28 7034 3606
e. leader@colrainechronicle.com
w. www.ulsternet-ni.co.uk

Lisburn Echo

12A Bow Street, Lisburn, Co. Antrim
BT28 1BN
Editor: David Fletcher
t. +44 28 9267 9111
f. +44 28 9260 2904
w. www.mortonnewspapers.com
■ *Weekly freesheet published each Wednesday, owned by Morton Newspapers.*
Advertising Manager: David Fletcher

Londonderry Sentinel

Suite 3, Spencer House, Spencer Road,
Derry BT47 1AA
Editor: William McClelland
t. +44 71 348 889
f. +44 71 341 175
e. edls@mortonnewspapers.com
w. www.mortonnewspapers.com
■ *Weekly newpaper published each Wednesday, with a circulation of about 5,000 in the Derry area.*
Advertising Manager: Ann Jackson
e. adls@mortonnewspapers.com

Lurgan and Portadown Examiner

Observer Newspapers NI Ltd, Ann
Street, Dungannon, Co. Tyrone BT70
1ET
Editor: Desmond Mallon
t. +44 28 87 722 557
f. +44 28 87 727 334
e. editor@observernewspapersni.com

Lurgan Mail

4 High Street, Lurgan, Co. Armagh
BT66 8AW
Editor: Clint Aiken
t. + 44 28 38 327 777
f. +44 28 38 325 271
e. edlm@mortonnewspapers.com
w. www.lurganmail.com
■ *Weekly paper published each Friday with a circulation of almost 9,000 in the Lurgan area.*
Advertising Manager: Beryl Bickerstaff
e. adlm@mortonnewspapers.com

Mid-Ulster Echo

52 Oldtown Street, Cookstown,
Co. Tyrone BT80 8EF
Editor: Mark Baine
  t. +44 28 867 613 64
  f. +44 28 867 642 95
  e. admm@mortonnewspapers.com
■ *A weekly freesheet distributed to 12,000 homes in the mid-Ulster region each Wednesday and owned by the Morton Newspaper group.*

Mid-Ulster Mail

52 Oldtown Street, Cookstown,
Co. Tyrone BT80 8EF
Editor: Mark Baine
  t. +44 28 8676 2288
  f. +44 28 8676 4295
  e. admm@mortonnewspapers.com
  w. www.midulstermail.com
■ *The contact details for this weekly paper published each Thursday are the same for the paper's south Derry edition.*
Advertising Manager: Drewe McConell

Mid-Ulster Observer

Observer Newspapers NI Ltd, Ann Street, Dungannon, Co. Tyrone BT70 1ET
Editor: Desmond Mallon
  t. +44 28 87 722 557
  f. +44 28 87 727 334
  e. editor@observernewspapersni.com
■ *Weekly paper published each Wednesday.*

Morton Newspaper Group

2 Esky Drive, Portadown, Co. Armagh BT63 5YY
Chief Executive and Managing Director: Helene Hanna
  t. +44 28 3839 3939
  f. +44 28 3839 3940
  e. ads@mortonnewspapers.com
  w. www.production@mortonnews papers.com
■ *This is Northern Ireland's largest newspaper group, owning 22 titles throughout Ulster. The company is ultimately owned by the media*

conglomerate Scottish Radio Holdings, which bought the company in 1995. All editions are printed at the company's plant outside Portadown. The company now publishes a total of 25 weekly newspaper titles with a total weekly print order of more than 200,000 copies.
Company Secretary: Barry McConville

Mourne Observer and County Down News

Castlewellan Road, Newcastle, Co. Down BT33 0JX
Editor: Terence Bowman
  t. +44 28 4372 2666
  f. +44 28 4372 2666
  e. mobserver@btconnect.com
■ *An independent newspaper covering all of south Co. Down and some of the north of the county, with a circulation of about 12,000.*
Advertising Manager: Alice Bleue

Newry Democrat

45 Hill Street, Newry, Co. Down BT34 1AF
Editor: Caroline McEvoy
  t. +44 28 3025 4365
  f. +44 28 3025 1017
  e. caroline.mcevoy@newrydemocrat.com
  w. www.newrydemocrat.com
■ *A weekly paper circulating in the Newry area.*
Advertising Manager: Tina Maguire
  e. tina.maguire@newrydemocrat.com

Newry Reporter

4 Margaret Street, Newry, Co. Down BT34 1DF
Editor: Austin Smyth
  t. +44 28 3026 7633
  f. +44 28 3026 3157
  e. editor@newryreporter.com
Advertising Manager: Lowry Hodgett

News Letter

46–56 Boucher Crescent, Belfast BT12 6QY
General Enquiries
  t. +44 28 9068 0000

f. +44 28 9066 4412
w. www.newsletter.co.uk
■ *The oldest daily paper in Ireland and the first newspaper published in Ulster, this Belfast paper was founded in 1737. It has traditionally been a Protestant unionist paper, but it has adopted a more liberal stance in recent years. The* **News Letter** *was acquired from Trinity Mirror in late 2003 by the British venture capital company 3i. The paper is published by Century Newspapers and is managed through a holding company, Local Press Ltd. It currently has a circulation of 34,000.*
Editor: Austin Hunter
Assistant Editor: Helen Greenaway
News Editor: Jackie McKeown
 t. +44 28 90 660 030
 e. newsdesk@newsletter.co.uk
News Editor: Ric Clarke
 t. +44 28 9068 0005
 e. newsdesk@newsletter.co.uk
News Editor: Steven Moore
 t. +44 28 9068 0005
 e. newsdesk@newsletter.co.uk
Political Correspondent: Ciarán McKeown
Sales and Marketing Manager: William Berkley
Sports Editor: Brian Millar
Farming Life Editor: David McCoy
Travel and Tourism Editor: Geoff Hill
Pictures Editor: Martin Nangle
Advertising Manager: Shiona Rafferty
Women's Editor: Sandra Chapman
 t. +44 28 9068 0002
The Guide Editor (weekly entertainment listings): Geoff Magill
 t. +44 28 9068 0002

News of the World (Belfast Office)
72 High Street, Belfast BT1 2BE
Northern Ireland Reporter: Martin Breen
 t. + 44 28 9031 0031;
 +44 7770 350 629
w. www.newsoftheworld.co.uk

Newtownabbey Times
14 Portland Avenue, Glengormley,
Co. Antrim BT36 8EY
Editor: Hugh Vance
 t. +44 28 9084 3621
 f. +44 28 9083 7715
 e. ednt@mortonnewspapers.com
 w. www.mortonnewspapers.com
■ *Weekly newspaper, published on Thursdays.*
Advertising Director
 e. adnt@mortonnewspapers.com

Newtownards Chronicle and County Down Observer
25 Frances Street, Newtownards,
Co. Down BT23 3DT
Editor: John Savage
 t. +44 28 91 813 333
 f. +44 28 91 820 087
 e. news@ardschronicle.co.uk

Newtownards Spectator
Spectator Newspapers, 91 Main Street,
Bangor, Co. Down BT20 4AF
Editor: Paul Flowers
 t. +44 2891 270 270
 f. +44 2891 271 544
 e. editor@spectatornewspapers.co.uk

North Belfast News
253–255 Antrim Road, Belfast BT15 2GY
Editor: John Ferris
 t. +44 28 9058 4444
 f. +44 28 9058 4450
 e. johnferris@irelandclick.com
 w. www.irelandclick.com
Advertising Manager: Christina Sloam
 e. christina@irelandclick.com

North West Echo
Suite 3, Spencer House, Spencer Road,
Derry BT47 1AA
Editor: William McClelland
 t. +44 28 71 342 226
 f. +44 28 71 341 175
 e. edls@mortonnewspapers.com
 w. www.mortonnewspapers.com

■ *Freesheet circulating in Derry and surrounding areas. It is published each Wednesday and is owned by Morton Newspapers.*

Observer Newspaper Group
Ann Street, Dungannon, Co. Tyrone
BT70 1ET
Chief Executive and Editor-in-Chief:
Desmond Mallon
 t. +44 28 8772 2557
 f. +44 28 8772 7334
 e. editor@observernewspapers.com
■ *The Observer Group publishes the* **Armagh-Down Observer, Ballymena Chronicle and Antrim Observer, Dungannon Observer, Fermanagh News, Lurgan and Portadown Examiner,** *and* **Mid-Ulster Observer.**
Managing Director: Desmond Mallon

Outlook, The
Castle Street, Rathfriland, Co. Down
BT34 5QR
 t. +44 28 406 30781
 f. +44 28 406 31022
Editor: Ruth Rodgers
 e. ruth@outlooknews.co.uk

Portadown Times
14A Church Street, Portadown, Co.
Armagh BT62 3LQ
Editor: David Armstrong
 t. +44 28 38 336 111
 f. +44 28 38 350 203
 e. edpt@mortonnewspapers.com
 w. www.portadowntimes.com
■ *A weekly paper, published each Friday, with a circulation of about 12,000. It is owned by Morton Newspapers.*
Advertising Manager
 e. adpt@mortonnewspapers.com

Roe Valley Sentinel
32A Market Street, Limavady, Co.
Derry BT49 0AA
Editor: William McClelland
 t. +44 28 7776 4090
 f. +44 28 7772 2234

 e. edls@mortonnewspapers.com
 w. www.mortonnewspapers.com
■ *Weekly paper for Derry published each Wednesday and owned by Morton Newspapers.*

South Belfast News
2 Hannahstown Hill, Belfast BT17 0LY
Editor: Maria McCourt
 t. +44 28 90 619 000
 f. +44 28 90 620 602
 e. maria.mccourt@irelandclick.com
 w. www.irelandclick.com
■ *Weekly paper published each Friday, aimed at readers in the north of the city. It is owned by the Andersonstown News Group.*
Advertising Manager: Michelle Clarke
 e. michelle.clarke@irelandclick.com

Strabane Chronicle
Ulster Herald Series, 15 Upper Main
Street, Strabane, Co. Tyrone BT82 8AS
Editor: Michelle Canning
 t. +44 28 71 882 100
 f. +44 28 71 883 199
 w. www.strabanechronicle.com
■ *Weekly paper published each Thursday, with a circulation of about 5,000 in the Co. Tyrone area.*
Advertising Manager: Kathy Fitzpatrick

Strabane Weekly News
25–27 High Street, Omagh, Co.
Tyrone BT78 1BD
Editor: Wesley Acheson
 t. +44 28 82 242 721
 f. +44 28 82 243 549
 w. www.ulsternet-ni.co.uk
■ *Weekly paper published each Thursday in Strabane, with a circulation of about 2,000. It is owned by the Alpha Newspaper Group.*

Sunday Journal
Buncrana Road, Derry BT48 8AA
Editor-in-Chief: Patrick McArt
 t. +44 28 7127 2240
 f. +44 28 7127 2260
■ *Sunday newspaper from Local Press.*
Advertising and Sales: Caroline Morris

t. +44 28 7127 2234
e. caroline.morris@local-press.net
Editor: Eamonn Houston
e. eamonn.houston@local-press.net

Sunday Life
124–144 Royal Avenue, Belfast BT1
1EB
General Enquiries
t. +44 28 9026 4300
f. +44 28 9055 4507
w. www.sundaylife.co.uk

■ *This is the sister Sunday paper of the daily*
Belfast Telegraph *and is owned by*
Independent News and Media.
Editor: Martin Lindsay
t. +44 28 9026 4309
e. mlindsay@belfasttelegraph.co.uk
Pictures Editor: Darren Kidd
t. +44 28 9026 3178
Deputy Editor and News Editor:
Martin Hill
t. +44 28 9026 4305
e. mhill@belfasttelegraph.co.uk
Sports Editor: Jim Gracey
t. +44 28 9026 4308
e. jgracey@belfasttelegraph.co.uk

Sunday Mirror (Belfast Office)
415 Holywood Road, Belfast BT4 2GU
Editor: Derek Gallop
t. +44 28 9056 8000
f. +44 28 9056 8059
e. d.gallop@mgn.co.uk
w. www.sundaymirror.co.uk

■ *Sister paper of the* **Irish Daily Mirror,**
this Sunday tabloid mixes Irish content and
content from the main UK version. Reporters
are based in Dublin, and production is carried
out in its Belfast office. There is a separate ver-
sion for Northern readers.

Sunday World (Northern Ireland Edition)
3–5 Commercial Court, Belfast BT1
2NB
t. +44 28 9023 8118
w. www.sundayworld.com

■ *This Irish Sunday tabloid paper launched*
in 1973 has a circulation of more than
300,000. Its mixture of the style of a British
tabloid and Irish content has thrived for three
decades. Independent News and Media bought
a controlling share of the paper in 1978.

Tyrone Constitution
25–27 High Street, Omagh, Co.
Tyrone BT78 1BD
Editor: Wesley Acheson
t. +44 28 82 242 721
f. +44 28 82 243 549
w. www.ulsternet-ni.co.uk

Tyrone Herald
10 John Street, Omagh, Co. Tyrone
BT78 1DT
Editor: Darach MacDonald
e. editor@ulsterherald.com
t. +44 28 82 243 444
f. +44 28 82 242 206
w. www.ulsterherald.com

Tyrone Times
Unit B, Butter Market Centre, Thomas
Street, Dungannon, Co. Tyrone BT70
1HN
Editor: Peter Baines
t. +44 28 87 752 801
f. +44 28 87 752 819
e. edtt@mortonnewspapers.com
w. www.mortonnewspapers.com

■ *Weekly newspaper published each Friday*
and owned by Morton Newspapers.

Ulster Gazette and Armagh Standard
56 Scotch Street, Armagh BT61 7DF
Editor: Richard Stewart
t. +44 28 37 522 639
f. +44 28 37 527 029
e. ulstergazette@btconnect.com
w. www.ulsternet-ni.co.uk

■ *Weekly paper published each Wednesday,*
with a circulation of almost 11,000. It is owned
by the Alpha Newspaper Group.

Ulster Herald

10 John Street, Omagh, Co. Tyrone
BT78 1DT
Editor: Darach MacDonald
  t. +44 28 82 243 444
  f. +44 28 82 242 206
  e. editor@ulsterherald.com
  w. www.ulsterherald.com
■ *Weekly newspaper published every Thursday, with a circulation of 12,000 in the Co. Tyrone area. It is owned by the North West of Ireland Printing and Publicishing Company Ltd, which also publishes the* **Fermanagh Herald, Strabane Chronicle, Derry People** *and* **Donegal News.**
General Manager: Dominic McClements

Ulster Star

12A Bow Street, Lisburn, Co. Antrim
BT28 1BN
Editor: David Fletcher
  t. +44 28 92 67 9111
  f. +44 28 92 602 904
  e. edus@mortonnewspapers.com
  w. www.mortonnewspapers.com
■ *Weekly newspaper with a circulation of 12,600 in the Lisburn area. It is owned by Morton Newspapers.*
Advertisment Manager: Robert Abraham

3

TELEVISION:
IRELAND ON THE BOX

Helen Shaw

Irish television was born on New Year's Eve, 1961, with the launch of RTÉ television. For decades Irish audiences had only the RTÉ television channels, RTÉ 1 and 2, and the over-spill of the UK channels BBC and ITV. Today Irish audiences have a global choice of television from four Irish terrestrial channels, RTÉ 1 and 2, TG4 and TV3 as well as BBC Northern Ireland and UTV, along with dozens of UK, US and European channels. Ireland now has the second-highest penetration of digital television, after the UK, delivered through satellite and cable/MMDS. Despite a lack of digital terrestrial television, the vast majority of Irish television viewers have a minimum of 14–20 stations to watch. For many, the choice is far wider, ranging from the new UK digital channels such as BBC 3 and 4 to specialist genre channels such as History and Men and Motors. With over half a million digital subscribers in Ireland by March 2005, this meant that more than 59% of all pay television households were digital, or 38% of all television homes.[1]

The days when almost the entire nation watched one programme, like Gay Byrne's 'Late Late Show', may be gone, but domestic channels in Ireland still command high audiences, given the level of choice and competition. RTÉ's channels command approximately 35–44% of the market, with TV3 being the second most popular station, with 16% of the market. What has changed the character of the Irish television market in the past five years is the advent of BskyB, which supplies more than 25% of Irish homes with pay television via satellite.

1. ComReg, *Quarterly Market Commentary*, June 2005.

The television landscape

TV3, Ireland's first domestic private channel, was launched in 1998, some ten years after the legislation paving the way for independent television. With its advent, RTÉ, the public broadcaster, faced competition not just for viewers but for advertising, which at that stage represented two-thirds of its funding. TV3 is currently owned by CanWest, a Canadian global media corporation, and Granada Media Group; each has a 45% stake in the company. CanWest also has a stake in Ulster Television, UTV, which has its head office in Belfast and is part of the UK ITV network and itself a major player in the Irish radio market. RTÉ is now funded 50:50 by the television licence fee (currently €155 a year) and commercial revenue.[2]

For Irish viewers, the late 1990s brought choice with the advent of TG4, the Irish-language public broadcasting television channel, and TV3 but the most dramatic change came with the BSkyB introduction of satellite television, which quickly brought digital television offerings and the interactive 'red button' to hundreds of thousands of Irish viewers. This rapid roll-out of satellite digital television was in marked contrast to both the state's and RTÉ's failure to deliver digital terrestrial television (DTT). In 1998, Irish Government policy directed that RTÉ sell its 25% holding in Cablelink, the television cable company, which then had 330,000 subscribers. This generated millions for RTÉ, but an over-extended NTL was unable to invest in Ireland's cable network, and the vacuum was filled by BskyB, offering satellite dish solutions. The Irish DTT plan failed, as it was premised on RTÉ selling the transmission networks to fund it. However, as there were delays in selling the Irish network, the buoyancy that had witnessed the NTL deal was gone, and there were no serious cash buyers. Without a business plan, DTT was shelved and in the intervening years (from 2001 to 2004) BSkyB won the battle for the television digital market. NTL re-entered the market in late 2004, aggressively offering cable digital deals. By May 2005, 355,000 television homes were BskyB, with approximately 150,000 getting their packages from NTL. The other main provider in the Republic is Chorus, which uses cable and MMDS to deliver television. Chorus is owned by Liberty Media International and Princes Holdings (Independent News and Media). In May 2005 NTL was bought by United Global Com (UGC), a Liberty Media Company, bringing Chorus and NTL under the same corporate wing.

---

2. The RTÉ television licence is index-linked, subject to an external review. The last increase was €3 at the end of 2004.

Despite the collapse of the initial DTT plans in 2002, Irish Government policy remains committed to developing a terrestrial digital platform to safeguard the delivery of Irish content to Irish homes. In late March 2005 the Minister for Communications, Noel Dempsey, announced plans for a digital TV pilot in Dublin which would form the basis for a nationwide digital television scheme. The Dublin pilot will enable homes with a digital television set to receive up to twelve television and radio channels free, and has been influenced by the BBC's freeview scheme in the UK. The launch of the pilot scheme was confirmed on 29 June 2005 when the Government invited companies to bid for the scheme. According to the *Irish Times* (28 March 2005), the Government has already spent €2.6 million on digital television consultants in preparing its strategy, while RTÉ has spent more than €6 million on its digital plans, including the aborted sale of RTÉ networks in 2002. In mid-2004, consultants to the Government concluded that the only way forward for DTT in Ireland was for the state to fund the digital network and for RTÉ to lead it. A central cost in its introduction will be the conversion of the existing analogue net-work to digital, which is estimated at between €40 and €100 million, depending on the services and coverage envisaged. In May 2005 RTÉ announced that some of its €6.8 million surplus would go to fund digital broadcasting.

In 2004 the first regional television service was licensed in Waterford, and there are plans for an extension of both regional commercial television and community television. In January 2005 the BCI signed a contract with City Channel Ltd to provide a full Dublin television service on cable TV, and the new Dublin channel will be part of NTL's digital subscription package.

The television market

Television in the Republic gets 17% of advertising, which, as described in Chapter 9, hardly reflects its media weight. In 2003 RTÉ's channels had 62% of that revenue, with TV3 gaining nearly 35%.

By the end of 2004 RTÉ television was boasting of a prime-time national share in television of 44%, a significant achievement in the face of increased satellite and terrestrial competition. The prime-time hold was credited to increased spending on home-produced programming follow-ing the television licence increase at the end of 2002. Series such as the clothes show 'Off the Rails' and popular drama series such as 'The Clinic' and 'Love Is the Bug' were seen as winners, along with the news shoulders at 6 p.m. and 9 p.m. and the current affairs series 'Primetime'. RTÉ 2 was relaunched from Network 2 back to RTÉ 2, in order to increase the branding of all RTÉ services under the RTÉ umbrella, and a witty animation and marketing package supporting the relaunch was developed, with the aim of helping RTÉ 2 to increase its share in 2005. TV3 closed 2004 with a higher total national share than RTÉ 2 (13.5%, compared with 12.5%), while TG4 showed some growth over the year, hitting 3.1%, the same audience as Sky One in Ireland (Nielsen Media Research, Jan.–Dec. 2004).

Television stations and market share, 2004, Republic of Ireland and Northern Ireland

Broadcaster	Ownership	Stations	Market share (%)
RTÉ	Public body	RTÉ1, RTÉ 2	38.1
TG4	Public body	TG4	2.9
TV3	CanWest, Granada, private investors	TV3	13.4
BBC	Public body	BBC1, 2, 3 and 4	12.1
UK commercial	Various private investors	UTV, C4, E4, Sky 1/News, etc.	33.5

Source: European Institute for the Media, August 2004, D Kelvin Report, Ireland, p. 109.

Irish national television audience share, 2004

	RTÉ1	RTÉ2	TV3	TG4	BBC1	BBC2	UTV/ HTV	C4/ S4C	Sky One	Sky News	E4	Other	Total
Mon–Sun 03:00–26:59	25.8	12.5	13.5	3.1	6.6	3.8	6.7	4.2	3.1	1.6	1.4	17.7	100
Mon–Sun 18:00–23:29	32.3	11.5	13.8	2.7	6.1	3.2	7.8	3.9	3.1	0.9	1.1	13.6	100

Source: Nielsen Media Research, January–December 2004.

For TV3 the winners have been not home products but blockbuster reality shows like 'I'm a Celebrity, Get Me Out of Here' and UK soaps such as the long-running 'Coronation Street', which has extended runs with several episodes in one night in order to boost audiences. TV3's home-grown talent, David McWilliams, moved to the rival station RTÉ 1 to host an afternoon chat show, while TV3's political correspondent, Ursula Halligan, got her own television show focusing on politics.

While reality television and format shows are the name of the game in popular television, Irish television still thrives on home-grown talent, with RTÉ giving Ryan Tubridy his own Saturday night chat show and 'The Late Late Show with Pat Kenny' still pulling big audiences on Friday nights. RTÉ's summer experiment with Miriam O'Callaghan as a chat show host is the latest development. TV3 had a short-lived adventure in chat show land with Eamon Dunphy's show running against 'The Late Late Show'. This provided great entertainment for home audiences, who flicked between both shows, but ultimately failed for TV3.

Top 20 highest ranking Irish television programmes, 2004

Rank	Programme	Ch	Time	Date	TVR	'ooo	Share
1	The Late Late Toy Show	RTÉ1	21:37–23:37	Fri. 26 Nov.	25	940	63
2	You're a Star Live— The Result	RTÉ1	19:59–20:59	Sun. 07 Mar.	24.3	896	56
3	The Late Late Show	RTÉ1	21:37–23:38	Fri. 19 Mar.	22.2	818	63
4	Killinaskully—The Nativity	RTÉ1	21:37–22:00	Sat. 25 Dec.	21.7	814	51
5	Eurovision Song Contest	RTÉ1	20:00–23:14	Sat. 15 May	19.9	734	60
6	All-Ireland Football Final (Kerry v. Mayo)	RTÉ2	14:55–17:27	Sun. 26 Sep.	19.8	744	70
7	Coronation Street	TV3	20:29–20:56	Mon. 08 Mar.	19.7	726	52
8	All-Ireland Hurling Final (Cork v. Kilkenny)	RTÉ2	14:50–17:27	Sun. 12 Sep.	19.1	717	65
9	Prime Time Investigates — The Force of the Law	RTÉ1	21:37–22:26	Thu. 08 Jan.	19	701	50

Top 20 highest ranking Irish television programmes, 2004 *contd.*

Rank	Programme	Ch	Time	Date	TVR	'000	Share
10	Eastenders	RTÉ1	20:28–21:25	Sat. 25 Dec.	18.9	711	45
11	Rose of Tralee	RTÉ1	21:36–23:11	Tue 24 Aug.	18.8	694	52
12	Fair City	RTÉ1	20:04–20:31	Tue 06 Jan.	17.8	658	46
13	I'm a Celebrity—Get Me Out Of Here! Final	TV3	21:01–22:25	Mon 09 Feb.	17.4	642	41
14	Winning Streak	RTÉ1	20:20–21:12	Sat 18 Dec.	17.3	649	47
15	Agnes Browne	RTÉ1	21:29–23:09	Fri 09 Apr.	16.7	617	47
16	World Cup Qualifier (Ireland v. France)	RTÉ2	19:29–22:14	Sat 09 Oct.	16.4	617	46
17	Friends—The Final Episode	RTÉ2	21:33–22:28	Mon 24 May	16.3	601	42
=18	Winner Takes All	RTÉ1	20:34–21:01	Tue 28 Dec.	15.6	586	39
=18	Die Another Day	RTÉ1	22:04–24:06	Sat 25 Dec.	15.6	586	44
20	Daniel's Christmas Special	RTÉ1	21:30–22:27	Tue 28 Dec.	15.4	579	40

Source: RTÉ, 2005.

Note: Averaging option = any day, any time (best episode). News programmes are excluded. Minimum programme duration 20 minutes. Programmes are ranked on TVR (total viewer rating). Universe change September.

Future trends

Television sales in recent years have been boosted by the development of flat and plasma screens and by new DVD players and combined TV-DVD boxes. With the phasing out of video players, DVDs will continue to grow and the battle will be for the next phase of hard-drive DVD players and digital devices, which will allow consumers to programme DVD recordings without advertisements and to save television programmes to the hard drive of the home computer.

The future will see television morphing from the living-room box into mobile devices like the mobile phone and the laptop. Endemol, the world's largest production company, which produces the Big Brother franchise, has said that all its research focus and thinking is now on the mobile phone.

Television viewing has ironically decreased, despite the increase in the number of television stations, largely because of its lack of mobility and the significant pressure on the amount of time people can spend in front of a television set. Mobile television will allow television broadcasters to compete for commuter audiences stuck on trains and buses and in the back of cars.

Equally, more and more television-linked services, such as news, sports and entertainment, will be sold separately as mobile phone added-value services. For television companies the challenge is to increase television advertising revenue, despite reduced television hours and greater audience fragmentation. Expect more television mergers as the bigger media businesses seek to get more cross-media opportunities, so they can sell advertising across a range of platforms and reduce their costs of production. Since the Communications Act (2003) in the UK, foreign companies have been able to buy television channels there, so if Granada is bought by one of the top six, such as Viacom, TV3 ownership will change. Being part of a major US company would certainly enhance TV3's acquisition of key entertainment and films and raise the stakes in its competition with RTÉ. The battle to attract and hold our attention is likely to be even more intense with more television channels being launched in Ireland in the coming years, including Setanta Sport and Channel 6.

Republic of Ireland

National

Channel 6
PO Box 10192, Glenageary,
Co. Dublin
Directors: Michael Murphy, Pat
Donnelly
e. info@channel6.ie
■ *Launching late 2005. New commercial national TV station, catering for young adults, offering movies, comedy, series and music. Channel 6 will be delivered by satellite and is licensed in the UK.*

Radio Telefís Éireann (RTÉ) Television
Donnybrook, Dublin 4
t. +353 1 208 3111
f. +353 1 208 3080
e. info@rte.ie
w. www.rte.ie
■ *Irish national radio, television and online public service broadcasting company. RTÉ is funded by a television licence, with commercial advertisement on a roughly 50:50 basis. RTÉ has two terrestrial television channels, RTÉ 1 and RTÉ 2, and has a broadcasting production relationship with TG4, the Irish-language public broadcasting channel. RTÉ is broadcast on cable, satellite, and free to air. It does not have digital terrestrial television services yet but is exploring the possibility. RTÉ is managed by an Executive Board, headed by the Director General, Cathal Goan, and is governed by the RTÉ Authority, a government-appointed board, but may soon be regulated by an integrated broadcasting regulator, the Broadcasting Authority of Ireland.*
RTÉ Authority: Chairman Fintan Drury. Members: Maria Killian, Patricia King, Ian Malcolm, Patrick Marron, Úna Ní Chonaire, Stephen O'Byrnes and an RTÉ staff member to be elected by staff. Secretary to the Authority: Tom Quinn.

Email addresses of individuals follow the format firstname.lastname@rte.ie
RTÉ Director General: Cathal Goan
RTÉ Chief Financial Officer: Conor Hayes
RTÉ Director of Communications: Bride Rosney
Head of Group Human Resources: Peter Mulholland
RTÉ Managing Director of News and Current Affairs: Ed Mulhall
Managing Director of Television: Noel Curran
t. +353 1 208 2717
f. +353 1 208 3080
Director of Programmes: Clare Duignan
t. +353 1 208 3015
f. +353 1 208 3080
Commercial Director: Geraldine O'Leary
t. +353 1 208 2571
f. +353 1 208 3080
Director of Broadcast and Acquisitions: Dermot Horan
t. +353 1 208 2272
f. +353 1 208 3080
Business and Finance Executive: Michael Hyland
t. +353 1 208 3474
f. +353 1 208 3080
Head of Schedule Planning: Andrew Fitzpatrick
t. +353 1 208 2381
f. +353 1 208 3080
Manager, Transmission Traffic and Schedule Planning: Linda Graves
t. +353 1 208 2651
f. +353 1 208 3080
Communications Manager, Television: Cathriona Edwards
t. +353 1 208 3160
f. +353 1 208 3080

Assistant Director of Programmes: Mary Curtis
t. +353 1 208 2159
f. +353 1 208 3080
Commissioning Editor, Drama: Mary Callery
t. +353 1 208 3255
f. +353 1 208 3080
Commissioning Editor, Regional: Ray McCarthy
t. +353 1 208 2141
f. +353 1 208 3080
Commissioning Editor, Entertaining and Music: Kevin Linehan
t. +353 1 208 3385
Commissioning Editor, Children and Young People's Programming: Sheila DeCourcy
t. +353 1 208 2964
Commissioning Editor, Factual: Kevin Dawson
t. +353 1 208 3041
f. +353 1 208 3080
Commissioning Editor, Irish Language, Multi-Cultural and Educational Programmes: Mairéad Ní Nuadháin
t. +353 1 208 2951
f. +353 1 208 3080
Manager, Programme Support: Patricia Swan
t. +353 1 208 2740
f. +353 1 208 3080
Manager, Transmission Service: Isabel Charleton
t. +353 1 208 3943
f. +353 1 208 3080
Manager, Production and Facilities Integration Project: Anne Farrelly
t. +353 1 208 2075
f. +353 1 208 3080
Finance Director: Breda O'Keefe
t. +353 1 208 2189
f. +353 1 208 3080
Head of Technology: Pat Fenton
t. +353 1 208 2612

f. +353 1 208 3080
Director of Operations: John Hunt
t. +353 1 208 2839
f. +353 1 208 3080
Production Lawyer: Conor Sweeney
t. +353 1 208 4573
f. +353 1 208 3080
Head of Television Sport: Glenn Killane
t. +353 1 208 2217
f. +353 1 208 3032
News Editors: Ray Burke and Donal Byrne
t. +353 1 208 2177
Deputy News Editor: Orla de Barra
t. +353 1 208 2177
News Desk Assistant: Jennifer Smith
t. +353 1 208 2177
Television News Programme Editor: Barbara Fitzgerald
t. +353 1 208 4173
Television News Programme Editor: Morgan O'Kelly
t. +353 1 208 4068
Television News Programme Editor: Pat Brennan
t. +353 1 208 2177
Television News Programme Editor: Mary Butler
t. +353 1 208 3227
Television News Programme Deputy Editors: Donagh McGrath, Conor Fennell, Janet Martin and Conor Quinn
t. +353 1 208 3214
Television News Production Editor: Caroline Bleahen
t. +353 1 208 3207
Television News Production Editor: Joyce Jackson
t. +353 1 208 4815
Television News Production Editor: Sharon Kelly
t. +353 1 208 3945
Television News Foreign Editor: Margaret Ward
t. +353 1 208 2529

TG4

Baile na hAbhann, Co. na Gaillimhe
General Enquiries
t. +353 91 505 050
f. +353 91 505 021
e. eolas@tg4.ie
w. www.tg4.ie

■ *A national public service Irish-language television channel, broadcast by satellite, cable, webcast and free to air. TG4 sources original Irish programming from the independent production sector in Ireland. It was established and operates under the statutory umbrella of RTÉ, from which it receives an annual programme supply. TG4 also broadcasts a range of public service programmes in English. TG4 is funded directly by the state, with additional resources from commercial advertising revenue. It currently holds approximately 3% of the Irish television market share and from 2005 is available in Northern Ireland through a British-Irish all-island broadcasting initiative. TG4 is in the process of being established as an independent public broadcasting entity.*

Ceannasaí: Pól Ó Gallchóir
Ceannasaí's Office: Nóirín Uí Chonghaile
Leascheannasaí: Pádhraic Ó Ciardha
Programmes Department: Micheál Ó Meallaigh
Commercial Director: Pádraig Ó Dómhnaill
Director of Television: Alan Esslemont
Technical Manager: Neil Keaveney
Finance Manager: Mary Uí Chadhain
Commissioning Editors: Proinsias Ní Ghráinne, Máire Ní Chonláin
Commissioning (Sport): Rónán Ó Coisdealbha
Commissioning Administrator: Mary Ellen Ní Chualáin
Scheduler: Máire Aoibhinn Ní Ógáin
Programme Acquisitions: Deirbhile Ní Churraighín
Programme Publicity: Linda Ní Ghríofa
Marketing: Pádraic Ó Ráighne

Airtime Sales (Post-TV): Anna de Barra
Audience Research: Dave Moore
Broadcasting: Jill Uí Dhuinn Bhig
Legal: Andrea Martin
Dublin Office: Nóirín Ní Chonghaile
Nuacht TG4 Príomh-Eagarthóir (Chief News Editor): Michael Lally
t. +353 91 505 066
f. +353 91 505 005
Nuacht TG4 Eagarthóir Cúnta (Assistant News Editor): Joe Reddington
t. +353 91 505 067
Nuacht TG4 Eagarthóir Cúnta (Assistant News Editor): Tomás Ó Síocháin
Joe Reddington
Breandán Delap
t. +353 91 505 067
Nuacht Dublin Bureau
t. +353 1 208 3953
f. +353 1 208 2166
Eagraí Polaitíochta (Political Editor): Seósamh Mag Raollaigh
t. +353 1 618 3951
m. +353 87 270 7816
e. joegrealy@eircom.net

TG4 (Oifig Bhaile Átha Cliath)

80 Harcourt Street, Dublin 2
General Enquiries: Pádhraic Ó Ciardha
t. +353 1 476 3030
f. +353 1 476 3031
e. eolas@tg4.ie
w. www.tg4.ie

■ *The Dublin office of the national Irish-language television channel.*

Setanta Sport

Broadcasting House, 3A South Prince's Street, Dublin 2
General Enquiries
t. +353 1 474 8000
f. +353 1 474 8001
e. setanta.irl@setanta.com
w. www.setanta.com

■ *An independent private Irish company that provides dedicated sports television broadcasting and has a full sports channel, licensed in Ireland, available on digital platforms. The non-broadcasting wing of Setanta was subject to a management buy-out in late December 2004, which effectively separated production and broadcasting and created the independent production company Motive. Niall Cogley, CEO of Setanta Sport, was formerly Head of Sport at the rival RTÉ. Setanta Sport received a ten-year licence in 2004 for its new channel—the first new national Irish television station licensed under the 2001 Act.*

In March 2004, the BCI signed two pay-per-view, one-year broadcasting contracts with Setanta Sport under its trading company Setanta Sport PPV. These pay-per-view sports channels are on the BskyB digital platform in Ireland and the UK, Channel 435 and 436, and are available on cable platforms in the US. These sporting events include some world and European football events for which Setanta hold the rights, and for events such as the Scottish Football League matches, etc. These services are regulated under Section 36 (Satellite Content Contract) of the Broadcasting Act 2001.

Directors: Leonard Ryan, Michael O'Rourke
Chief Executive: Niall Cogley
Director of Marketing: Eleanor Collier
t. +353 1 474 4929
e. eleanor@setanta.com

Sky News (Ireland)

Alexandra House, Earlsfort Terrace, Dublin 2
General Enquiries
t. (News desk) +353 1 614 7666
f. +353 1 661 1402
e. news.ireland@bskyb.com
w. www.sky.com/skycom/home
■ *Provides a twice-nightly dedicated Irish television news service from Dublin, with bureaus in the west and north of Ireland.*
Managing Editor: Nick Purcell
t. +353 1 614 7920
News Editor: Joe Walsh

Account Director (Publicity): Neil O'Gorman
t. +353 1 678 9333
f. +353 1 661 1402
e. neil.ogorman@edelman.com
Planning Editor: Sally O'Herlihy
Account Manager (Publicity): Clodagh O'Hagan
t. +353 1 678 9333
f. +353 1 661 1402
e. clodagh.ohagan@edelman.com
Senior News Editor: Michael Wilson
t. +353 1 614 7620
f. +353 1 661 1402
e. m.c.wilson@bskyb.com
London News Desk
t. +44 207 705 3232
e. news.plan@bskyb.com
News Anchor: Gráinne Seoige
Correspondents: Ray Kennedy, Brian Daly

TV3

Westgate Business Park, Dublin 24
General Enquiries
t. +353 1 419 3333
f. +353 1 419 3300
e. info@tv3.ie
w. www.tv3.ie
■ *Ireland's independent commercial television channel, launched in 1998 and owned by CanWest and Granada Media Group, with minor interest still held by its founder, James Morris. TV3 holds approximately 13–14% of the Irish television market, with about 20% of the Irish television advertisement pie. TV3's key audience programmes include the UK soaps 'Emmerdale' and 'Coronation Street'.*
Chief Executive Officer and Managing Director: Rick Hetherington
Director of Government, Regulatory and Legal Affairs: David McMunn
Chief Financial Officer: Kathy Curran
Director of Programming: Matthew Salway

Director of News: Andrew Hanlon
t. +353 1 419 3344
f. +353 1 419 3322
e. andrew.hanlon@tv3.ie
Deputy Head of News: Bob Hughes
e. bob.hughes@tv3.ie
Director of Operations and
Technology: Peter Ennis
Director of Sales: Patrick Kiely
News Editor: Philippe Brodeur
t. +353 1 419 3347
f. +353 1 419 3300
e. news@tv3.ie
Assistant News Editor: Yvonne Doyle
t. +353 1 419 3344
f. +353 1 419 3300
e. yvonne.doyle@tv3.ie
Sports Editor: Stephen Cullinane
t. +353 1 419 3351
f. +353 1 419 3300
e. stephen.cullinane@tv3.ie
Commissioning Editor: Jane Gogan
t. +353 1 419 3353
f. +353 1 419 3439
e. jane.gogan@tv3.ie
Ireland AM
Presenters: Mark Cagney, Maura
Derrane, Alan Hughes
Producer: Debbie O'Donnell
t. +353 1 419 3400

Ulster Television (UTV) (Dublin Office)

64 Waterloo Road, Dublin 4
t. +353 1 664 3494
f. +353 1 664 3493
e. pdanaher@iol.ie
w. www.u.tv
■ *Dublin bureau for UTV.*
Dublin Correspondent: Patricia Danaher

Regional and Community Television

Cabletext Waterford

NTL, IDA Industrial Park, Cork Road,
Waterford

f. +353 5133 4433
e. edwat@ntl.com
w. www.ntl.com/ireland
■ *A 24-hour local channel covering Co.
Waterford. Provides 'Waterford at Eight', a
local television news and features programme
from Thursday to Sunday each week.
'Waterford at Eight' is produced by WLR FM.*
Waterford at Eight Producer: Gabrielle
Cummins

City Channel

Communications House, 2 Belmont
Court, Donnybrook, Dublin 4
t. +353 1 260 8074
e. dharvey@citychannel.ie
■ *A local niche television station, broadcasting 24 hours, 7 days a week, providing information and entertainment of specific interest to
the Dublin area.*
Director: David Harvey

Province 5 Television

Clogherboy House, Commons Road,
Navan, Co. Meath
t. +353 462 2665
f. +353 462 7880
e. info@province5.iol.ie
w. www.iol.ie/province5
■ *A community access television station,
broadcasting on Cable Management, Ireland's
cable television system, to more than 2,500
homes in the Navan area.*

SouthCoast TV (SCTV)

Enterprise House, Carrigaline, Cork
w. www.southcoasttv.net
Secretary: Eric Curtis
■ *Local television channel, covering Co. Cork
and west Waterford. SouthCoast TV offers
BBC 1, BBC2, HTV and Channel 4, plus
50 television and radio programme services.
Internet, video-on-demand and community
broadcasting will also be available.*

Northern Ireland

Telephone numbers in Northern Ireland have the prefix 048 if dialled from the Republic and 004428 if dialled from elsewhere.

BBC Northern Ireland (Television)

Broadcasting House, Ormeau Avenue,
Belfast BT2 8HQ
General Enquiries
  t. +44 28 9033 8000 / 8800
  f. +44 28 9033 8806
  w. www.bbc.co.uk/northernireland
■ *Part of the BBC network, BBC Northern Ireland is one of three BBC Nations services in Northern Ireland, Wales and Scotland. BBC Northern Ireland has radio, television, digital broadcasting and on-line services. Its television service provides programmes for the regional audience and for network BBC TV. The BBC is funded by a television licence, with no advertising. A Board of Governors regulates the BBC. BBC Northern Ireland as a tri-media production base has commissioning and editorial editors for both television and radio, so, unless specified as being solely television or radio, the manager listed has responsibilities for all production resources.*
  E-mail addresses of individuals follow the format
  firstname.lastname@bbc.co.uk

BBC Network:
BBC Director-General: Mark Thompson
BBC Deputy Director-General: Mark Byford
BBC Director of BBC Radio and Music: Jenny Abramsky
BBC Director of Television: Jana Bennett
BBC Director of Human Resources and Internal Communications: Stephen Dando
BBC Director of New Media and Technology: Ashley Highfield
BBC Acting Director, Marketing, Communications and Audiences: Jenny Lawrence
BBC Chief Operating Officer: John Smith
BBC Acting Director, Strategy and Distribution: Caroline Thomson

BBC Northern Ireland:
BBC National Governor for NI: Fabian Monds
Controller: Anna Carragher
Head of Broadcasting: Peter Johnston
Head of Programme Operations: Stephen Beckett
Head of Human Resources: Liz Torrans
Head of Programme Production: Mike Edgar
Head of Marketing Communications and Audiences: Kathy Bruce
Head of Creative Development: Bruce Batten
Head of News and Current Affairs: Andrew Colman
Managing Editor, Television: Peter McCann
Head of Drama: Patrick Spence
Commissioning Editor, Broadcast: Fergus Keeling
Editor, Television News: Angelina Fusco
Editor, Television Factual: Paul McGuigan
Editor, Television Current Affairs: Jeremy Adams
Editor, Political Programmes: Lena Ferguson
Editor (Foyle): Anna Leddy
Head of Learning and Interactive Services: Kieran Hegarty
Press Office
  t. +44 48 9033 8226 / 7
  f. +44 48 9033 8279
Press Office Manager: Una Carlin
Press Officer: Kevin McCauley

Press Officer: Caroline Cooper
Press Officer: Libby Kinney
Assistant Press Officer: Martin Flynn
Assistant Press Officer: Toni Cherry

Channel 9 TV (c9tv)

North West Television Services,
Television House, 1st Floor, 105–115
Spencer Road, Derry BT47 6GN
General Enquiries
  t. +44 28 7131 4400
  f. (news) +44 28 7134 6254;
  (accounts) +44 28 7132 9523
  e. info@c9tv.tv
  w. www.c9tv.tv
■ *Free-to-air terrestrial local television service
(Restricted Service Licensee) providing local
and in-house programming (news, sport,
current affairs, local interest programmes, interactive music and information) to the north-west
of Northern Ireland: Derry, Limavady,
Coleraine and Strabane.*
Station Manager: Gary Porter
News Editor: Jimmy Cadden
  jimmy@c9tv.tv

GMTV Belfast

ITN, Ascot House, 24–31 Shaftesbury
Square, Belfast BT2 7DB
General Enquiries
  t. (local) +44 28 9023 0923; (national)
  +44 28 9043 9138
  f. +44 28 9043 9395
  e. gmtv-itn.belfast@itn.co.uk
  w. www.gmtv.tv
■ *Provides the national breakfast-time service
as one of fifteen UK regional Channel 3 terrestrial television licences, with diverse programming, including news, regional production, and
provision for the deaf or hearing-impaired and
blind or partially sighted.*

GMTV (London Office)

London Television Centre, Upper
Ground, London SE1 9TT
General Enquiries
  t. +44 20 7827 7000
  f. +44 20 7827 7001
  w. www.gmtv.co.uk

■ *London office of GMTV. GMTV Belfast
provides the national breakfast-time service as
one of fifteen regional Channel 3 terrestrial
television licences, with diverse programming,
including news, regional production, and
provision for the deaf or hearing-impaired and
blind or partially sighted.*

Independent Television News (ITN)

Ascot House, 24–31 Shaftesbury
Square, Belfast BT2 7DB
General Enquiries
  t. +44 28 9023 0786
  f. +44 28 9043 9395
  w. www.itn.co.uk
■ *Provides a national and international news
service transmitted live and simultaneously
by the UK regional Channel 3 terrestrial television licensees (apart from GMTV). ITN also
provides news programmes for C4 and C5 and
has a 24-hour news service.*

Independent Television News (ITN) London Office

200 Gray's Inn Road, London WC1X
8XZ
General Enquiries
  t. +44 20 7833 3000
  f. +44 20 7430 4868
  e. editor@itn.co.uk
  w. www.itn.co.uk
■ *London office of ITN. ITN provides a
national and international news service transmitted live and simultaneously by the UK
regional Channel 3 terrestrial television
licensees (apart from GMTV). ITN also provides news programmes for the UK channels
C4 and C5 and has a 24-hour news service.*

NvTv

Northern Visions, 4 Lower Donegall
Street Place, Belfast BT1 2FN
  t. +44 28 9024 5495
  f. +44 28 9032 6608
  e. info@northernvisions.org
  w. www.northernvisions.org/nvtv
■ *Provides community television programmes
that are made with and by the various communities in Belfast.*

Community Media Development
Director: David Hyndman

Ulster Television (UTV)

Havelock House, Ormeau Road,
Belfast BT7 1EB
General Enquiries
 t. +44 28 9032 8122
 f. +44 28 9024 6695
 e. info@u.tv
 w. www.u.tv

■ *A Belfast-based media broadcaster, providing television programming to Northern Ireland and the Republic of Ireland largely via cable and satellite. CanWest, which owns 45% of TV3, also owns nearly 30% of UTV. UTV also owns a range of radio stations in the Republic, including Cork 96FM and FM102, formerly Lite FM, in Dublin.*

Chairman: John McGuckian
Chief Executive: John McCann
Press Office
 t. +44 28 9026 2187
 f. +44 28 9026 2219
Head of Press and Public Relations:
Orla McKibbin
 t. +44 28 9026 2188
 e. omckibbin@utvplc.com
Director of Television: Alan Bremner
 t. +44 28 9026 2083
 e. abremner@utvplc.com

News desk
 t. +44 28 9026 2000
 f. +44 28 9023 8381
 e. news@utvplc.com
Head of News and Current Affairs:
Rob Morrison
 t. +44 28 9026 2122
 f. +44 28 9024 6605
 e. rmorrison@utvplc.com
News Editor: Chris Hagan
 e. chagan@utvplc.com
Political Editor: Ken Reid
 t. +44 28 9026 2017
 e. kreid@utvplc.com
Sports Editor: Adrian Logan
 t. +44 28 9026 2111
 e. alogan@utvplc.com
Producer, 'Kelly': Patricia Moore
 t. +44 28 9026 2020
Producer, 'Insight': Trevor Birney
 t. +44 28 9026 2100

Sky News (Belfast Bureau)

Fanum House, Great Victoria Street,
Belfast BT2 7BE
 t. +44 28 9023 4099
 f. +44 28 9023 4016
Correspondent: Gary Honeyford

4

RADIO: THE AUDIO BOOM

Helen Shaw

Irish people love radio. Nearly 90% of the population tunes in to national, regional, local and community radio every day and listens for more than four hours a day—one of the highest radio audiences in the world.[1] Radio in Ireland has come a long way since the birth of 2RN in 1926, which later became Radio Éireann on the dial. From those roots came RTÉ Radio 1 and its sister services 2FM, Raidió na Gaeltachta and Lyric FM— the four 24-hour 7-day services from RTÉ, the public broadcaster in Ireland. But what really changed listening in Ireland was the birth of independent commercial radio from 1988–89. Today there are twenty-six local radio stations in the Republic, one regional and twenty community and special-interest radio stations, along with the independent national commercial station Today FM.[2] While the Irish radio landscape is now more colourful, it is also more competitive, and RTÉ, which operates solely in the national spectrum, has seen its share of the audience decline as new independent competitors are launched. In radio speak they talk of 'share' and 'reach', and this is how the competitive battle for ears is judged. A radio station's share reflects its slice of the audience and is the best indication of the strength of a station, while its reach reflects the extent of its audience, because it includes everyone tuning in to that station or programme, even if it's only for a very brief time. Reach is usually higher than share, so the reach of any local or regional station is 55%, while the share

1. According to the Joint National Listenership Research (JNLR) survey, 17 February 2005, 87% of Irish adults listen to radio, and the rate has been between 86 and 87% in the last few surveys.
2. There is also a licensed group of six hospital radio stations.

is 47%.[3] Sometimes reach is called 'listened yesterday', as that is what it reflects: the maximum number of people who listened for any period, or minutes, the day before the audience survey.

In Ireland radio audiences are measured by detailed surveys called the Joint National Listenership Research (JNLR), which are published every six months. The JNLR survey shows the strengths and weaknesses of individual stations in terms of their growth or decline, but its raw data is equally what creates economic value behind radio stations, in that it is how the advertising market assesses the value of stations and programmes and determines how much it will pay to sell advertisements to those radio audiences.

While RTÉ Radio's overall reach and share are in decline with the growth of more and more new stations, RTÉ Radio 1 and 2FM still broadcast the ten most listened-to programmes, from 'Morning Ireland', the RTÉ Radio 1 two-hour news breakfast show, which is the most popular radio programme on air, with 476,000 listeners a day.[4] Talk and speech radio rules in Ireland, not just for the national stations like RTÉ Radio 1, 2FM and Today FM but also for many of the local stations. Irish people like conversational radio, chat shows and phone-ins, to judge by the ratings that programmes like 'Gerry Ryan' and 'Liveline' get nationally and which are echoed in the programming strengths of national and local commercial radio as well.

Top ten weekday national radio programmes

	Programme	Station	Time block	Reach (%)	Number of adults (aged 15+)
1	Morning Ireland	RTÉ Radio 1	07:00–09:00	15	476,000
2	Gerry Ryan	RTÉ 2FM	09:00–12:00	12	382,000
3	Marian Finucane	RTÉ Radio 1	09:00–10:00	12	357,000
4	Liveline with Joe Duffy	RTÉ Radio 1	13:45–14:45	11	344,000
5	News at One	RTÉ Radio 1	13:00–13:45	10	324,000
6	Today with Pat Kenny	RTÉ Radio 1	10:00–12:00	9	301,000

3. JNLR, January–December 2004, released 17 February 2005.
4. JNLR, January–December 2004.

Top ten weekday national radio programmes *contd*

	Programme	Station	Time block	Reach (%)	Number of adults (aged 15+)
7	The Full Irish with Ryan Tubridy	RTÉ 2FM	06:00–09:00	8	243,000
8	Five Seven Live	RTÉ Radio 1	17:00–19:00	7	225,000
9	Gareth O'Callaghan	RTÉ 2FM	12:00–14:00	7	223,000
10	Michael Cahill	RTÉ 2FM	14:00–17:00	7	213,000

Based on Monday–Friday average programme listening reach for the national stations. These represent the most listened-to programmes on air in Ireland.

Source: Joint National Listnership Research (JNLR) and Market Research Bureau of Ireland (MRBI) Weekday Report, January–December 2004 (released 17 February 2005).

The radio landscape

In Ireland there are still far fewer radio choices than in most other European countries.[5] A recent policy review of both spectrum and licensing may lead to more stations and the completion of a regional network begun with the launch of Beat FM as a regional radio station in the southeast in 2003. RTÉ Radio 1's share has fallen to its present level of 24% from over 30% in a handful of years. The days of 'The Gay Byrne Show' in 1988 attracting nearly a million listeners reflected the public broadcasting monopoly, when anyone listening to talk radio was listening to the same station. Now and into the future, more and more diverse choices will fragment the radio market, providing wider offerings but equally ensuring that each station will hold smaller slices of both the audience and the advertising revenue pies. Today FM's target when it was launched in 1998 was a share of 15%, which it has never reached (its current share is 10%), and with more offerings on the way, smaller station shares will be the norm of the market. Lyric FM, RTÉ's classical music and arts channel, is now holding a national share of 2%, while the Irish-language station, Raidió na Gaeltachta, has less than 1%.

5. *Ox Review of Licensing of Radio Services in Ireland*, Department of Communications, Marine and Natural Resources, July 2004.

Radio share

	Share (%)	Change* (%)
Any regional or local	47	+1
RTÉ Radio 1	24	-1
RTÉ 2FM	17	=
Today FM	10	+1
RTÉ Lyric FM	2	+1
All RTÉ radio	**43**	**=**

*Compared with the previous survey.
Source: JNLR (January–December 2004).

The radio market

If Ireland has above-average radio listenership rates, it also enjoys above-average radio advertising revenue—partly because, unlike many other European countries, the public broadcasting stations also carry advertisements. In the UK, half the radio market is held by the BBC and is outside the reach of advertisers. While some argue that this leads to more money for the commercial sector, in reality it means that the radio sector is commercially under-developed. In the UK, less than 4.5% of total media spending in advertising goes into radio, compared with over 9% in Ireland.[6]

In recent years, the Irish radio market has, like many others, witnessed a move towards ownership consolidation. Several major media groups now own significant pieces of the radio landscape and are hitting the ceiling of the new BCI ownership limits at 17.9% (December 2004). These groups—Scottish Radio Holdings (SRH), a Glasgow media conglomerate; UTV, the Belfast media group; and Communicorp Group, the media and communications company of the Irish entrepreneur Denis O'Brien—have all been engaged in a series of consolidation and expansion moves in recent years. In June 2005, one of the major UK media groups, Emap, bought SRH for €587 million and took control of all SRH radio businesses in Ireland.

SRH wholly owned Ireland's only national independent radio station, Today FM (since 2001), and in 2004 it added Dublin's most successful independent, FM104, to its stable. SRH had recently bought one

6. *Ox Review*, p. 29.

of Ireland's most successful local stations, Radio Highland in Donegal, which has a 61% market share.

UTV, which is about to launch a new adult-oriented radio station in Belfast, owns Q102 (formerly Lite FM) in Dublin, 96 FM in Cork, a local station in Limerick (Limerick Live), and one in Drogheda (LMFM). Communicorp, through its radio subsidiary, wholly owns Spin FM and 98 FM in Dublin and controls Newstalk 106, the news and talk station in Dublin, which is lobbying to get a wider quasi-national licence in the future.

While the Dublin market is highly competitive, with a new station launching—Phantom FM, an alternative rock station, most regions have only one local station, and there is, to date, only one regional station, Beat FM, in the south-east, which was launched in 2003. The solo local stations often enjoy high audience ratings, like Highland, and have therefore been eyed with some interest by the consolidating media groups. Ironically, North-West Radio, which had a share of 55%, lost its licence in 2003 during the BCI's licence renewal process. In February 2005 the BCI, in a new policy statement, committed itself to issuing more radio licences in order to increase choice and diversity in the radio market. At the beginning of 2004 ComReg estimated that 25% of FM radio spectrum in Ireland remained unallocated, and there is no commercial use of medium wave.

Community radio in Ireland, unlike the UK, is a strong and growing sector, and there is now a community radio network which works together on training and development initiatives. Of the eighteen community stations, six are in the greater Dublin region and have played a significant part in building new urban community groups, while others, like Flirt FM in Limerick, are based in a university community.

Reach and market share, local stations (excluding Dublin and Cork)

Listenership (reach)	%	Market share	%
Highland Radio	69	Highland Radio	61
Mid-West Radio	66	Mid-West Radio	50
Shannonside/Northern Sound	60	WLR FM	48
Limerick's Live 95	56	Shannonside/Northern Sound	46
WLR FM	51	Radio Kerry	45

Source: JNLR; figures from survey period January–December 2004.

Future trends

In late 2004 the then Minister for Communications, Marine and Natural Resources, Dermot Ahern, promised changes in radio licensing. These changes were to support the audience's desire for choice, rather than the market's tendency to deliver the same content, based on the advertiser's wish to chase the 20 to 44-year-old audience. Beyond more analogue stations, the real challenge facing radio in Ireland is the transition to digital. A promised Government policy on digital audio broadcasting is expected. The European DAB-T (digital audio broadcasting, terrestrial) format has not proved widely successful in Europe, and its main success has been in the UK, where there is a new range of both public and commercial digital channels. By the end of 2004 there were more than 400 digital radio stations in the UK and more than a million DAB radio sets, with, ironically, some 8 million people tuning in to radio at home on their television sets. In Ireland, digital radio may bring new choices but it will also see radio become part of a multimedia bouquet of offerings in new hand-held devices and in integrated third-generation mobile phones.

The future of radio seems bright, as one of the key survival tactics it has is its mobility and flexibility. Radio was once transformed into an everyman tool by FM transistors, which moved radio from the middle-class home into the street and onto the Walkman personal stereo of the 1980s. In 2010 radio will still be personal and mobile but it will also be connected to the web, to telephones and to multimedia tools, which will mean the lines between sound and pictures will blur and interactivity will allow users to customise their 'radio' and create their own programmed schedule. When does radio stop being radio? the purists ask, probably echoing those who feared that 'real' listening and 'real' radio would end once it was squeezed into tiny transistors and ear-plugs. Technology is a stream; what remains constant is that radio, like the best forms of media, is still about communication.

Republic of Ireland

National

Radio Telefís Éireann (RTÉ)

RTÉ, Donnybrook, Dublin 4
General Enquiries
  t. +353 1 208 3111

■ *Ireland's national public broadcasting company, with full national television, radio and on-line services. Broadcasts four national radio channels, with 24-hour 7-day services, on a combination of FM, AM, long-wave, satellite, live streaming and audio files on line.*

  E-mail addresses of individuals are in the format firstname.lastname@rte.ie
RTÉ Director General: Cathal Goan
RTÉ Chief Financial Officer: Conor Hayes
RTÉ Managing Director of News and Current Affairs: Ed Mulhall
RTÉ Commercial Director: Geraldine O'Leary
RTÉ Director of Communications: Bride Rosney
Managing Director, Radio Business Unit: Adrian Moynes
PA to Managing Director: Lynn Davis
  t. +353 1 208 4521
  f. +353 1 208 4523
Finance Director, Radio: Kieran Barry
  t. +353 1 208 2026
Commercial Director, Radio: Antony Whittall
  t. +353 1 208 2487
  f. +353 1 208 2451
PA to Commercial Director: Celine Ennis
  t. +353 1 208 2482
Sales Manager: Ronan Murphy
  t. +353 1 208 3053
Television and Radio Sales (Belfast): Brian Kinder
  t. +44 48 9032 6441
Television and Radio Sales (London): John Ahern
  t. +44 207 615 1972

RTÉ Lyric FM

Cornmarket Square, Limerick
General Enquiries
  t. +353 61 20 7300
  f. +353 61 20 7390
  e. lyric@rte.ie
  w. www.rte.ie/lyricfm

■ *Ireland's classical music and arts radio channel, launched in 1999 and based in Limerick. Lyric FM was national station of the year in 2004.*

Head of Lyric FM: Aodán Ó Dubhghaill
  t. +353 61 20 7359

Presenters
Niall Carroll, Bernard Clarke, Carl Corcoran, Denis Costello, Gerry Godley, Aedín Gormley, Evelyn Grant, Donald Helme, Paul Herriott, Eamonn Lawlor, Eamonn Lenihan, Liz Nolan, Máire Nic Gearailt, Sean Rocks, Tim Thurston

Producers
Eoin Brady, Olga Buckley, Celia Donoghue, Evonne Ferguson, Gail Henry, John Hughes, Ethna Tinney, Sinéad Wylde

Programmes
Artszone
  e. arts.lyricfm@rte.ie
Blue of the Night
  e. blue.lyricfm@rte.ie
Breakfast
  e. breakfast.lyricfm@rte.ie
Concerts
  e. concerts.lyricfm@rte.ie
Drivetime Classics
  e. drivetime.lyricfm@rte.ie
Full Score
  e. thefullscore.lyricfm@rte.ie
Gloria
  e. gloria.lyricfm@rte.ie
Grace Notes/Reels to Ragas
  e. trad.lyricfm@rte.ie

Green Room Cinema
  e. cinema.lyricfm@rte.ie
Jazz Alley
  e. jazz.lyricfm@rte.ie
Lunchtime Choice
  e. requests.lyricfm@rte.ie
Lyric Notes
  e. notes.lyricfm@rte.ie
Third Wave
  e. wave.lyricfm@rte.ie

RTÉ Radio 1

RTÉ, Donnybrook, Dublin 4
General Enquiries
  t. +353 1 208 3111
  e. radio1@rte.ie
  w. www.rte.ie/radio1/
■ *Ireland's most popular radio station,*
with news, current affairs, talk, drama, arts
and music.
  RTÉ Radio 1's breakfast news show,
'Morning Ireland', is the most listened-to
show in Ireland, with some of the big names
in broadcasting on air, including Ryan
Tubridy, Pat Kenny and Joe Duffy during the
day.
  E-mail addresses of individuals are in
  the format firstname.lastname@rte.ie,
  unless otherwise indicated
Head of RTÉ Radio 1 and Deputy
Managing Director of RTÉ Radio:
Eithne Hand
  t. +353 1 208 2728
Managing Editor, Radio News:
Michael Good
  t. +353 1 208 2149
Features, Arts and Drama Editor:
Lorelei Harris
  t. +353 1 208 2604
Current Affairs Editor: John McMahon
  t. +353 1 208 2443
Development Editor: Ann Marie
O'Callaghan
  t. +353 1 208 2094
  f. +353 1 208 2739
  e. annmarie.ocallaghan@rte.ie

Regional Editor: Tom McGuire
  t. +353 90 647 4543
Senior Press Officer: Jennifer Taaffe
  t. +353 1 208 2312
Sports, Music and Irish-Language
Editor: Paddy Glackin
  t. +353 1 208 2426
Programmes
Risin' Time
Presenter: Maxi
  t. +353 1 208 3392
  text +353 87 627 2222
  e. maxi@rte.ie
Morning Ireland
Presenters: David Hanly, Aine Lawlor
and Cathal Mac Coille
  e. morningireland@rte.ie
Editors: Shane McElhatton, Lisa
Pereira, Niall Martin, Hilary McGouran
The Tubridy Show
Presenter and Producer: Ryan Tubridy
Producers: Paul Russell and Yvonne
Judge
  t. + 353 1 208 2290
  f. + 353 1 208 2559
  e. tts@rte.ie
Today with Pat Kenny
Presenter: Pat Kenny
  t. +353 1 208 3280
Producer: Marian Richardson
  t. +353 1 208 2776
  on air 1850 715 900
  NI/UK 0845 785 7777
  f. +353 1 208 2634
  text +353 87 627 2222
  e. todaypk@rte.ie
John Creedon
Presenter: John Creedon
Producers: John Creedon, Donna
O'Sullivan
  on air 1850 715 808
  text +353 87 627 2222
  e. creedon@rte.ie
News at One
Presenter: Seán O'Rourke
Editor: Bernadette O'Sullivan

t. +353 1 208 3223
f. +353 1 208 2011
e. newsatone@rte.ie
World Report and This Week
Presenters: Gerald Barry, Roisín Duffy,
Paul Maguire
Editor: Gerald Barry
t. +353 1 208 2705
f. +353 1 208 3086
Liveline
Presenter: Joe Duffy
Producer: Ann Marie Power
Series Producer: Margaret Curley
liveline@rte.ie
free RoI 1850 715 815
free NI 0800 614 616
t. +353 1 208 3263/2984
f. +353 1 208 2424
text +353 87 627 2222
e. joe@rte.ie
Rattlebag
Presenter: Myles Dungan
Producer: Nuala O'Neill
t. +353 1 208 2986
24-hour phone +353 1 208 3445
e. rattle@rte.ie
Ronan Collins
Presenter: Ronan Collins
free RoI 1850 715 900
free NI/UK 0345 857 777
Five Seven Live
Presenter: Rachael English
Producer: Conor P. Kavanagh
t. +353 1 208 3270
f. +353 1 208 3027
e. 57live@rte.ie
Tonight with Vincent Browne
Presenter: Vincent Browne
t. +353 1 208 3267
Series Producer: Eamon Keane
t. +353 1 208 3267
free RoI, on air 1850 715 150
free NI/UK 0845 785 3333
text (22:00 to 23:30 only) +353 87
627 2222
e. tonightvb@rte.ie

Bowman Saturday 8:30
Presenter and Producer: John Bowman
t. +353 1 668 3147
Saturday View
Presenter: Rodney Rice
Producer: Noelle O'Reilly
e. saturdayview@rte.ie
weekdays +353 1 208 3268/2660
free RoI, on air 1850 715 900
free NI/UK 0845 761 4616
e. ricer@rte.ie
The Sunday Show
Presenter: Tom McGurk
Producer: Síle Yeats
e. sundayshow@rte.ie
Sunday Miscellany
Producer: Cliodhna Ní Anluain
Farm Week
Producer and Presenter: Frances Shanahan
t. +353 1 208 2337
f. +353 1 208 3983
m. +353 87 688 7958
e. farmweek@rte.ie

RTÉ Radio 2FM

RTÉ, Donnybrook, Dublin 4
General Enquiries
t. RoI 1850 715 922
t. NI 0345 585 285
text +353 87 772 0000
e. info@2fm.ie
w. www.rte.ie/2fm

■ *2FM is RTÉ's popular music and chat
channel aimed at 15 to 35-year-olds, with the
iconic Gerry Ryan on air from 09:00 to 12:00
every day.*
Head of 2FM: John Clarke
t. +353 1 208 2061
f. +353 1 208 3092
Presenters
Aidan Leonard:
aidanleonard@2fm.ie
Conor G: conorg@2fm.ie
Cormac Battle: cormac@2fm.ie
Damian Farrelly:
damianfarrelly@2fm.ie

Damien McCaul:
damienmccaul@2fm.ie
Dave Fanning: dave@2fm.ie
Dan Hegarty: dan@2fm.ie
Gerry Ryan: gerryryan@2fm.ie
Jenny Huston: jenny@2fm.ie
John Clarke: jc@2fm.ie
John Kenny: johnkenny@2fm.ie
John Power: johnpower@2fm.ie
Larry Gogan: larry@2fm.ie
Mark McCabe: markmccabe@2fm.ie
Michael Cahill: michaelcahill@2fm.ie
Mr Spring: mrspring@2fm.ie
Rick O'Shea: rick@2fm.ie
Wes Darcy: wesdarcy@2fm.ie
Will Leahy: saturday@2fm.ie
Ruth Scott: breakfast@2fm.ie

Programmes

Breakfast with Rick and Ruth
Presenters: Rick O'Shea and Ruth Scott
e. breakfast@2fm.ie

The Gerry Ryan Show
Presenter: Gerry Ryan
t. +353 1 208 2063
e. gerryryan@2fm.ie
Producer: Siobhan Hough
t. +353 1 208 2066
f. +353 1 208 3245

Gareth O'Callaghan
Presenter: Gareth O'Callaghan
e. gareth@2fm.ie

The Big Afternoon with Michael Cahill
Presenter: Michael Cahill
e. michaelcahill@2fm.ie

Larry Gogans's Golden Hour
Presenter: Larry Gogan
e. larry@2fm.ie

Dave Fanning
Presenter: Dave Fanning
e. dave@2fm.ie

Newsbeat
Presenter: Avril Hoare
Producer: Eamonn Falvey
Reporter: Pat McGrath
e. newsbeat@2fm.ie

RTÉ Raidió na Gaeltachta (Conamara)
Casla, Co. na Gaillimhe
General Enquiries
t. +353 91 50 6677
f. +353 91 50 6666; (news)
+353 91 50 6688
e. rnag@rte.ie
w. www.rte.ie/rnag

■ *RTÉ's full radio service in Irish, with head office in Casla and a network of regional offices around the country.*
Head of Raidió na Gaeltachta: Tomás Mac Con Iomaire
t. +353 91 50 6677
f. +353 91 50 6666
e. tomas.macconiomaire@rte.ie

Programmes

Adhmhaidin
Nuacht agus cúrsaí reatha (news and current affairs)
Presenter: Norita Ní Chartúir

An Saol ó Dheas
Clár irise, á chur i láthair ó Bhaile na nGall (magazine programme from Baile na nGall)
Presenter: Mícheál Ó Sé

An Chaint sa Chathair
Clár irise á chur i láthair ó Bhaile Átha Cliath (magazine programme from Dublin)
Presenter: Dónall Ó Braonáin

RTÉ Raidió na Gaeltachta (Regional Office)
C/o RTÉ, Donnybrook, Dublin 4
General Enquiries
t. +353 1 208 2033
f. +353 1 208 3350
e. rnag@rte.ie
w. www.rte.ie/rnag

RTÉ Raidió na Gaeltachta (Regional Office)
Doirí Beaga, Co. Dhún na nGall
General Enquiries
t. +353 74 953 1244
f. +353 74 953 1645

e. rnag@rte.ie
w. www.rte.ie/rnag

RTÉ Raidió na Gaeltachta (Regional Office)

Baile na nGall, Co. Chiarraí
General Enquiries
t. +353 66 915 5114
f. +353 66 915 5291
e. rnag@rte.ie
w. www.rte.ie/rnag

Today FM

Today FM House, 124 Upper Abbey Street, Dublin 1
General Enquiries
t. +353 1 804 9000
f. +353 1 804 9099
e. live@todayfm.com
w. www.todayfm.com

■ *Ireland's national commercial independent radio station, offering music and talk to an 18+ audience. Today FM, launched in 1998 and broadcasts on FM and on line. Broadcasters include Ian Dempsey at breakfast, Ray D'Arcy in the morning and Matt Cooper at evening drive time. Today FM is 100% owned by Emap.*

Chief Executive Officer: Willie O'Reilly
News Editor: Cathy Farrell
Programme Manager: Tom Hardy

Programmes

The Ian Dempsey Breakfast Show
Presenter: Ian Dempsey
e. dempsey@todayfm.com
The Ray D'Arcy Show
Presenter: Ray D'Arcy
t. +353 1 804 9011
e. ray@todayfm.com
Co-presenter: Jenny Kelly
t. 353 1 804 9035
e. jkelly@todayfm.com
Tony Fenton's Show
Presenter: Tony Fenton
e. tfenton@todayfm.com
The Phil Cawley Show
Presenters: Phil Cawley and Ruth O'Neill

e. philip@todayfm.com
e. roneill@todayfm.com
The Last Word
Presenter: Matt Cooper
e. lastword@todayfm.com
Producer: Barbara Loftus
t. 353 1 804 9020

Local and regional

98FM

The Malt House, Grand Canal Quay, Dublin 2
General Enquiries
t. +353 1 670 8970
f. +353 1 670 8969
e. online@98fm.ie
w. www.98fm.ie

■ *Local Dublin city and county commercial independent radio station playing contemporary music from the 1980s onwards for 25 to 44-year-olds on FM and on line. 98FM is owned by Communicorp Group, Denis O'Brien's radio and media holdings.*

General Manager: Ciarán Davis
Financial Controller: Edel Quinn
Head of Sales: Michael Brady
Head of Marketing: Aisling Walsh
Head of News: Teena Gates
Associate Programme Director: John Taylor
Production Manager: Dara O'Beirne
Sports Editor: Johnny Lyons

Programmes

The Morning Crew
Presenters: Dermot Whelan and Dave Moore
t. 1850 715 981
text +353 86 600 0981
e. theallnewmorningcrew@98fm.ie
Home Run with Brian McColl
Presenter: Brian McColl
t. 1850 715 981
text +353 86 600 0981
e. homerun@98fm.ie

Beat 102–103 FM

Broadcasting Centre, Ardkeen,
Dunmore Road, Waterford
General Enquiries
t. +353 5 184 9102
f. +353 5 184 9103
e. info@beat102103.com
w. www.beat102103.com
■ *Regional radio station, broadcasting to Cos. Carlow, Kilkenny, Waterford, Wexford and south Tipperary on FM and on line. Target audience 15 to 34-year-olds. Contemporary music and talk relevant for the target audience. Beat FM was launched in 2003. It is the first regional station in Ireland and is seen as a 'pilot' for regional station formats by the licensing regulator, the Broadcasting Commission of Ireland (BCI).*
Chief Executive: Kieran McGeary
Sales Manager: Karen Cheevers
Financial Controller: Gerry Sheridan
Programme Controller: Kieran McGeary
Head of Music: Leigh Doyle
Head of Production: Andy McCloskey
Technical Engineer: Pat Maher
Head of News and Head of Sport: Gabrielle Cummins

Clare FM

Abbeyfield Centre, Francis Street,
Ennis, Co. Clare
General Enquiries
t. +353 65 682 8888
f. +353 65 682 9392
e. info@clarefm.ie
w. www.clarefm.ie
■ *Local Co. Clare commercial independent radio station, broadcasting music and talk, news and current affairs to a 20+ audience on FM and on line.*
Chairperson: Michael Evans
Chief Executive Officer: Liam O'Shea
Station Administration: John O'Flaherty
Head of News: John Drummy
Head of Sports: Mike McCartney

Head of Sales and Marketing: Susan Murphy
e. sales@clarefm.ie
Programmes
Morning Focus (10:00 to 12 noon, Monday to Friday)
t. Studio RoI 1850 400 964
Presenter: Cian Ó Síocháin
Producer: Mark Dunphy
e. focus@clarefm.ie

Cork 96FM/103FM County Sound

Broadcasting House, Patrick's Place,
Cork
General Enquiries
t. +353 21 455 1596
f. +353 21 455 1500
e. info@96fm.ie
w. www.96fm.ie
■ *Local Cork city and county commercial independent radio station, broadcasting news, current affairs and music for a local 20+ audience on FM and on line. Cork 96FM/103FM is owned by UTV, the Belfast media company. Neil Prendeville is the region's version of Pat Kenny and Gerry Ryan, and the station is one of the more popular local franchises in the country.*
Managing Director: Ronan McManamy
Head of Sales: Joy Hennebry
Head of News and Sport: Barry O'Mahony
e. news@96fm.ie
Head of Administration: Alma Malone
Commercial Director: Sean Barry
Station Manager: Michael Brett
Programme Director: Neil Prendeville
Promotions Manager: Elaine Fitzgerald
e. sales@96fm.ie
Programmes:
Opinion Line (09:00 to 12 noon, Monday to Friday)
t. Studio RoI 1850 715 996
Presenter: Neil Prendeville
e. neil@96fm.ie
Researchers: Frank O'Brien, Trish Drinan

Cork 96FM/103 FM County Sound (Bandon)

Weir Street, Bandon, Co. Cork
General Enquiries
t. +353 23 4 3103
f. +353 23 4 4294
e. info@96fm.ie
w. www.96fm.ie

Cork 96FM/103 FM County Sound (Mallow)

Gouldshill, Mallow, Co. Cork
General Enquiries
t. +353 22 4 2430
f. +353 22 4 2488
e. info@96fm.ie
w. www.96fm.ie

Dublin's Country 106.8 FM

Radio Centre, Killarney Road, Bray,
Co. Wicklow
General Enquiries
t. +353 1 272 4770
f. +353 1 272 4753
e. mail@dublins1068.com
w. www.dublins1068.com
■ *Local Dublin commercial independent radio station, broadcasting country and Irish music and news to a 25+ audience on FM and on line.*
E-mail addresses for individuals are in the format firstname.lastname@dublins1068.com
Chief Executive: Sean Ashmore
Programme Director: Robert Walshe
Sales Manager: Brian McGrath
Head of Production: Kevin Blessing

East Coast FM

Radio Centre, Killarney Road, Bray,
Co. Wicklow
General Enquiries
t. +353 1 272 4700
f. +353 1 272 4701
e. mail@eastcoast.fm
w. www.eastcoast.fm

■ *Local Co. Wicklow commercial independent radio station, broadcasting music, news, sport, current affairs and local issues to 15 to 55-year-olds on FM.*
General Manager: Ciara O'Connor
Head of News: Gareth Farrell
Newsroom +353 1 272 4721
e. newsdesk@eastcoast.fm
Sales and Marketing Manager: Paul Bailey
Financial Controller: Sue Fletcher
Programme Director: Joe Harrington
Production Manager: Robert Diggins
Programmes
The Morning Show (09:00 to 12 noon, Monday to Friday)
Presenters: Tracey Clifford, Declan Meehan
Producers: Claire Darmody and Owen Dawson

FM104

Hume House, Pembroke Road,
Dublin 4
General Enquiries
t. +353 1 500 6600
f. +353 1 668 9545
e. sales@fm104.ie
w. www.fm104.ie
■ *Local Dublin city and county commercial independent radio station, broadcasting contemporary music hits to 15 to 34-year-olds on FM and on line. FM104 is owned by Emap.*
Managing Director and Financial Controller: Tim Fenn
e. timf@fm104.ie
Sales Director: Margaret Nelson
Head of News: Aisling Bastable
e. news@fm104.ie
Head of Sport: Hazel Nolan
Programme Director: David Kelly
e. davek@fm104.ie
Head of Marketing: Helena Kelly
Production Manager: Andy Matthews

Galway Bay FM

Sandy Road, Galway
General Enquiries
t. +353 91 77 0000
f. +353 91 75 2689
e. info@galwaybayfm.ie
w. www.galwaybayfm.ie

■ *Local Galway city and county commercial independent radio station, broadcasting music, news, sport, current affairs and local issues to 15 to 55-year-olds on FM and on line.*

Chief Executive Officer: Keith Finnegan
Managing Director: Gerry Rabbitt
Head of Sales and Marketing: Paddy Madden
e. sales@galwaybayfm.ie
Head of News: Bernadette Prendergast
e. bprendergast@galwaybayfm.ie
Financial Controller: Gerry Rabbitt
e. gerry@galwaybayfm.ie
Programme Controller: Keith Finnegan
e. keith@galwaybayfm.ie

Programmes
Keith Finnegan (10:00 to 12 noon, Monday to Friday)
Presenter: Keith Finnegan
e. keith@galwaybayfm.ie
Researcher: Fionnuala Rabbitt
e. comments@ galwaybayfm.ie

Highland Radio

Pine Hill, Letterkenny, Co. Donegal
General Enquiries
t. +353 74 912 5000
f. +353 74 912 5344
e. enquiries@highlandradio.com
w. www.highlandradio.com

■ *Local Co. Donegal commercial independent radio station, broadcasting music (country and pop), news, current affairs and sport to a 20+ audience on FM and on line. Highland Radio is the most popular local radio station in the Republic, with a market share of over 60%, but it also has a significant number of listeners on the other side of the border, in Co. Derry. Bought by Scottish Radio Holdings in March 2005 for €6 million, now owned by Emap.*

Managing Director: Charlie Collins
Traffic and Programming Co-ordinator: Linda McGroarty
Promotions Manager: Shaun Doherty
Senior Producer: Lisa Burkitt
Sales Co-ordinator: Kevin Collins
Head of Production: Canice Wilson
Accounts and Staffing Co-ordinator: Mary Duffy
Financial Controller: Hazel Russell
Head of News: Donal Kavanagh
e. news@highlandradio.com
Head of Sports: Charlie Collins

Programmes
The Shaun Doherty Show (10:00 to 13:00, Monday to Friday)
Presenter: Shaun Doherty
e. shaundoherty@highlandradio.com
Producer/Researcher: Caroline Orr

KCLR 96FM

Broadcast Centre, Carlow Road, Kilkenny
General Enquiries
t. +353 56 779 6296
f. +353 56 779 6299
e. info@kclr96fm.com
w. www.kclr96fm.com

■ *Local commercial independent radio station for Cos. Carlow and Kilkenny, broadcasting music, news, current affairs and sport with a local emphasis to an adult 15+ age group on FM. KCLR 96FM replaced Radio Kilkenny in the licensing round of 2003, when Radio Kilkenny lost its licence. KCLR went on air in 2004 and is headed by John Purcell, with Sue Nunn, formerly of Radio Kilkenny, working as News Editor.*

Chief Executive Officer: John Purcell
News Editor: Sue Nunn
e. news@kclr96fm.com
Programme Controller: John Purcell
Programme Co-ordinator: Mags Murphy
Advertising Sales: Debra O'Neill

Kfm

Kfm Broadcast Centre, M7 Business
Park, Newhall, Naas, Co. Kildare
General Enquiries
  t. +353 45 89 8999/84 9109
  f. +353 45 89 8993
  e. info@kfmradio.com
  w. www.kfmradio.com
■ *Local Co. Kildare commercial independent
radio station, broadcasting contemporary music
and focusing on local news, current affairs and
sport on FM.*
General Manager and Director: Clem
Ryan
Production Engineer: Emily Owens
Commercial Director: Padraig O'Dwyer
  e. sales@kfmradio.com
News Editor: Ciara Plunkett
  e. ciara@kfmradio.com
Deputy News Editor: Susan Molloy
  e. susan@kfmradio.com
Sports Editor: Killian Whelan
  e. sport@kfmradio.com
Advertising Traffic: Gavin McDaid
Programme Director: Noel Shannon
  t. +353 45 849 102
  m. +353 87 239 8215
  e. noel@kfmradio.com
Programmes
*Today (09:00 to 12 noon, Monday to
Friday)*
Presenter: Noel Shannon
Producer: Marie O'Riordan
  t. Studio (RoI) 1850 200 536
  e. marie@kfm.ie

Limerick's Live 95 FM

Radio House, Dock Road, (PO Box
295), Limerick
General Enquiries
  t. +353 61 46 1900
  f. +353 61 41 9595
  e. mail@live95fm.ie
  w. www.live95fm.ie
■ *Local Limerick city and county commercial
independent radio station, broadcasting
contemporary music with news features and
sport to a 20+ audience on FM and on line.*
Chief Executive: David Tighe
Head of Sales: Gerry Long
  e. sales@live95fm.ie
Programme Director: David Tighe
Head of News: Joe Nash
  e. news@live95fm.ie
Financial Controller: Tracey Wilmott
Programmes
*Limerick Today (09:00 to 12 noon,
Monday to Friday)*
  t. Studio +353 61 461 995
  e. limericktoday@live95fm.ie
Presenter: Ed Myers
Researcher: Anne-Marie Geraghty

LM FM

Broadcasting House, Rathmullen Road,
Drogheda, Co. Louth
General Enquiries
  t. +353 41 983 2000
  f. +353 41 983 2957
  e. info@lmfm.ie
  w. www.lmfm.ie
■ *Local Cos. Louth and Meath commercial
independent radio station, broadcasting music
and talk and focusing on local issues to adults
over 25 (daytime) and 15 to 30-year-olds
(nighttime) on FM. UTV bought LM FM at
the close of 2004, adding the station to its now
significant radio stable in the Republic.*
Chief Executive Officer: Michael
Crawley
Head of News: Michael Carolan
  e. mcarolan@lmfm.ie
Deputy News Editor: Ruth O'Connell
Sales Manager: Eileen Duggan
Chief Engineer: Eddie Caffrey
Sports Editor: Brendan Cummins
Programme Controller: Eamonn Doyle
Programmes
The Eamonn Doyle Show
Presenter: Eamonn Doyle
  e. edoyle@lmfm.ie

Midlands 103

The Mall, William Street, Tullamore,
Co. Offaly
General Enquiries
t. +353 50 65 1333
f. +353 50 65 2546
e. goodcompany@midlandsradio.fm
w. www.midlandsradio.fm
■ *Local Cos. Laois, Offaly and Westmeath
commercial independent radio station, broad-
casting music hits and talk to adults aged 25+
on FM.*
Chief Executive Officer: Albert
Fitzgerald
Programme Director: Fran Curry
Administration Manager: Rebecca
Donnelly
Head of Sales: Eleanor Lahart
Head of News: Will Faulkner
e. newsroom@midlandsradio.fm
Head of Sport: Damien Moran
Accounts Director: Joan Blackweir
Programmes
*Midlands Today (10:00 to 12 noon,
Monday to Friday)*
e. midlandstoday@midlandsradio.fm
t. Comment RoI 0818 300 103
Presenter: Fran Curry
Researcher: Rebecca Rush

Mid West Radio

Clare Street, Ballyhaunis, Co. Mayo
General Enquiries
t. +353 818 3000 55
f. +353 94 963 0285
e. info.mo@mnwr.ie
w. www.mnwr.ie
■ *Local Co. Mayo commercial independent
radio station, broadcasting chart music with an
emphasis on the local and Irish to adults aged
18+ on FM and online. In mid 2005, Mid
West Radio launched a new internet radio
service aimed at the Irish abroad, called
Mid West Irish Radio, which is on
www.midwestirishradio.com.*
Chief Executive Officer: Paul Claffey
Station Manager: Chris Carroll

Financial Controller: Enda Carberry
Programme Director: Paul Claffey
Head of News: Teresa O'Malley
Head of Sales and Marketing: Tina
Mitchell
Programmes
*The Tommy Marren Show (09:00 to
11:00, Monday to Friday)*
Studio +353 94 963 0169
Text, on air +353 87 900 4141
Presenter: Tommy Marren
e. tommy@mnwr.ie
*The Mid Morning Show (11:00 to
13:00, Monday to Friday)*
Presenter: Paul Claffey
e. paul@mnwr.ie
Studio +353 94 963 0169
Text, on air +353 87 900 4141
Producer: Gerry Glennon
e. gerry@mnwr.ie

Newstalk 106 FM

Warrington House, Mount Street,
Dublin 2
General Enquiries
t. +353 1 644 5100
f. +353 1 661 1602
e. info@newstalk106.ie
w. www.newstalk106.ie
■ *Local Dublin city and county commercial
independent radio station, broadcasting talk-
based programming with news, sport and traffic
to a 25+ audience on FM and on line.
Newstalk 106 FM is controlled by Denis
O'Brien's company Communicorp Group.
Eamon Dunphy, previously a national broad-
caster with Today FM's 'The Last Word', now
hosts the Newstalk breakfast programme, while
George Hook presents evening drive time.*
Chief Executive: Dan Healy
Head of Sales: Cera Ward
Head of News: John Keogh
Station Editor: Vacant
Financial Controller: Patrick Hand
Foreign Affairs Editor: Karen Coleman
e. karen@newstalk106.ie
Sports Editor: Ger Gilroy

Programmes

The Breakfast Show with Eamon Dunphy

Presenter: Eamon Dunphy
t. +353 1 644 5133
e. dunphy@newstalk106.ie
Producer-Researchers: Daire Whelan, Hugh Ormond
t. +353 1 644 5122

The Orla Barry Show

Presenter: Orla Barry
t. +353 1 644 5108
e. orlabarryshow@newstalk106.ie

City Edition

Presenter: Declan Carty
t. +353 1 644 5111
e. cityedition@newstalk106.ie

Lunchtime with Damien Kiberd

Presenter: Damien Kiberd
t. +353 1 644 5113
e. damien@newstalk106.ie
Producer-Researcher: Patricia Monaghan

Sean Moncrieff Presents Moncrieff

Presenter: Sean Moncrieff
t. +353 1 644 5109
e. afternoon@newstalk106.ie
Producer-Researcher: Jonathon Doyle

The Right Hook with George Hook

Presenter: George Hook
t. +353 1 644 5103
e. therighthook@newstalk106.ie
Producer-Researcher: Brian Reynolds

Northern Sound Radio (Cavan)

26A Bridge Street, Cavan
General Enquiries
t. +353 49 436 1666
f. +353 49 436 1668
e. info@northernsound.ie
w. www.northernsound.ie
■ *Local Cos. Cavan and Monaghan commercial independent radio station, broadcasting local news, information and current affairs and contemporary music to 18 to 55-year-olds on FM.*
Chief Executive: Richard A. Devlin

Northern Sound Radio (Monaghan)

Dawson Street, Monaghan
General Enquiries
t. +353 47 72 666
f. +353 47 84 447
e. info@northernsound.ie
w. www.northernsound.ie
■ *Local Cos. Cavan and Monaghan commercial independent radio station, broadcasting local news, information and current affairs and contemporary music to 18 to 55-year-olds on FM.*
Chief Executive: Richard A. Devlin
t. +353 43 47 777
e. richard@northernsound.ie
Agency Co-ordinator: Mel O'Brien
Chief Engineer: Jimmy Naughton
Production Manager: Deirdre Kelly
Station Manager and Head of News: Fintan Duffy
e. fintan@northernsound.ie
Head of Programmes: Joe Finnegan
Advertising Traffic: Mel O'Brien
Sales Manager: Cathy Casey

Ocean FM (Donegal)

Gruagorm House, Main Street, Donegal
t. +353 74 972 5024
f. +353 74 972 5025
w. www.oceanfm.ie

Ocean FM (Leitrim)

Unit 2, Library Corner, Old Church Street, Manorhamilton, Leitrim
t. +353 71 985 5761
f. +353 71 985 5762
w. www.oceanfm.ie

Ocean FM (Sligo)

North-West Business Park, Collooney, Sligo
t. +353 71 911 8100
free RoI 1850 20 0060
text +353 86 805 1025
f. +353 71 911 8101
e. info@oceanfm.ie
w. www.oceanfm.ie

■ *Local Cos. Sligo, Leitrim and Donegal commercial independent radio station, broadcasting local news, information and current affairs and contemporary music to 18 to 55-year-olds on FM. Ocean FM won the north-west licence in a controversial decision by the board of the Broadcasting Commission of Ireland (BCI) in 2003, taking North West Radio, one of the most popular local stations, off the air. The BCI decision was later upheld by the courts following challenges from North West.*

Chief Executive Officer: Tim Collins
General Manager and Programme Director: Robert Walshe
  e. robert.walshe@oceanfm.ie
Head of Sales and Marketing: Padraig O'Dwyer
  e. sales@oceanfm.ie
Head of News and Sport: Niall Delaney
  e. news@oceanfm.ie

Programmes
North West Today
Presenter: Robert Walshe
  e. robert.walshe@oceanfm.ie
Producer: Margaret Carr Flynn

Phantom FM

Phantom FM, 12 Camden Row, Dublin 8
General Enquiries
  t. +353 1 478 0363
  m. (text) +353 87 619 5171
  f. +353 1 476 2138
  e. worldwide@phantomfm.com;
  (studio) studio@phantomfm.com
  w. www.phantomfm.com
■ *Local Dublin city and county independent radio station, broadcasting alternative rock music to a young audience on FM and on line. Licensed in mid-2004. Phantom FM was a long-time pirate radio station in Dublin before succeeding in the last licensing round. N.B. Launch delayed to late 2005 due to legal challenge over its license award.*
News Department: Steve Conway, Sinead Geraghty

Q102 FM

Glenageary Office Park, Glenageary, Co. Dublin
General Enquiries
  t. +353 1 662 1022
  f. +353 1 662 9974
  e. admin@q102.ie
  w. www.q102.ie
■ *Local Dublin city and county commercial independent radio station, broadcasting news, traffic, weather, current affairs and music favourites to adults aged 30+ on FM and on line. Q102 is owned by UTV, the Belfast media company. It was formerly known as Lite FM but was relaunched in 2004.*

Chief Executive Officer: Scott Williams
Direct Sales Manager: Chris Meagher
Programme Director: Ian Walker
Financial Controller: Nicola Carroll
Head of News: Eileen Brophy
  t. +353 1 618 3616
  m. +353 87 252 1044
  e. eileen.brophy@q102.ie
News Desk
  t. +353 1 201 3811
  f. +353 1 201 3815
  e. news@q102.ie

Radio Kerry

Maine Street, Tralee, Co. Kerry
General Enquiries
  t. +353 66 712 3666
  f. +353 66 712 7491
  e. elma@radiokerry.ie
  w. www.radiokerry.ie
■ *Local Co. Kerry commercial independent radio station, broadcasting news, current affairs, sport, talk, music and special-interest programmes to 25-year-olds+ (and specific programmes to 15 to 24-year-olds) on FM and on line. Radio Kerry has both a strong radio legacy, as one of the first local stations to go on air, and a significant local market share.*
Chief Executive Officer: Paul Byrne
Head of Sales and Marketing: Melanie O'Sullivan
Finance Manager: Marie Sweeney

Programme Coordinator: John Herlihy
Head of News, Sport and Current
Affairs: Sinead Spain
  e. news@radiokerry.ie
Programmes
Kerry Today
  e. kerrytoday@radiokerry.ie
Presenter: Rory O'Sullivan
  t. +353 66 719 1201
Producer-Researcher: Theresa Murphy
  t. +353 66 719 1220

Red FM 104–106
Unit 1, University Technological
Centre, Curraheen Road, Bishopstown,
Cork
General Enquiries
  t. +353 21 486 5500
  f. +353 21 486 5501
  e. info@redfm.ie
  w. www.redfm.ie
■ *Local Cork city and county commercial
independent radio station, broadcasting contemporary music, news, talk and traffic information
to a youth audience (15 to 34-year-olds) on
FM and on line. Thomas Crosbie Holdings are
shareholders in Red FM.*
Chief Executive: Henry Condon
Programme Director: Carol O'Beirne
Head of News: Lana O'Connor
  e. news@redfm.ie
National Sales Director: Niall Whelan
  t. +353 21 486 5531
  e. sales@redfm.ie
Financial Controller: Paul Cotter
Sports Editor: Kieran McSweeney
  e. sports@redfm.ie

Shannonside 104FM
Unit 8, Master Tech Business Park,
Athlone Road, Longford
General Enquiries
  t. +353 43 47 777 (Longford);
  +353 90 662 5525 (Roscommon)
  f. +353 43 4 9384 (Longford);
  +353 90 662 5529 (Roscommon)
  e. info@shannonside.ie
  w. www.shannonside.ie

■ *Local Cos. Longford, Roscommon and
South Leitrim commercial independent
radio station, broadcasting news, information,
current affairs and contemporary music with
a local and Irish emphasis to 18 to 55-year-olds
on FM.*
Chief Executive: Richard A. Devlin
  e. richard@shannonside.ie
Head of Sales: Kathy Casey
Financial Controller: Richard Devlin
Chief Engineer: Jimmy Naughton
  e. jimmy@shannonside.ie
Production Manager: Deirdre Kelly
Advertising Traffic: Mel O'Brien
Programme Controller: Joe Finnegan
  e. joe@shannonside.ie
Head of News: Seamus Duke
  e. news@shannonside.ie
Programmes
*Joe Finnegan (09:20 to 12 noon,
Monday to Friday)*
  t. during programme 1850 796 796
  text +353 87 120 0900
Presenter: Joe Finnegan
  e. joe@shannonside.ie
Producer: Eugene Murphy

South East Radio
Custom House Quay, Wexford
General Enquiries
  t. +353 53 4 5200
  f. +353 53 4 5295
  e. info@southeastradio.ie
  w. www.southeastradio.ie
■ *Local Co. Wexford commercial independent
radio station, broadcasting contemporary music,
news, specialist and information programmes
with a local emphasis to 25 to 55-year-olds on
FM and on line.*
Managing Director: Eamonn Buttle
General Manager: Liam Dwyer
  e. ldwyer@southeastradio.ie
Head of Sales: Marion Barry
  t. +353 53 4 2333
  e. sales@southeastradio.ie
Head of Programmes: Clive Roylance
  e. clive@southeastradio.ie

Head of News: Ellen Lynch
e. news@southeastradio.ie

Spin 1038 FM

73 North Wall Quay, Dublin 1
General Enquiries
t. +353 1 877 2100
f. +353 1 855 0711
e. info@spin1038.com
w. www.spin1038.com

■ *Local Dublin city and county commercial
independent radio station, broadcasting contemporary music to 15 to 34-year-olds on FM and
on line. Spin 1038 is aimed at a youth music
audience and is headed by the former head of
RTÉ 2FM, Liam Thompson. Spin FM is now
100% owned by Communicorp Group.*

E-mail addresses for individuals follow
the format lastname.firstname@
spin1038.com
Chief Executive Officer and Financial
Controller: Tom Wright
Head of Sales: Peter Barry
Programme Director: Liam Thompson
Programming Manager: Chris Doyle
Head of Marketing: Robyn Macken
Head of News: Trish Laverty
Financial Controller: Tom Wright
News and Current Affairs
Producer: Damien O'Meara
t. (free RoI) 1850 774 636
e. talk@spin1038.ie

Tipp FM

Davis Road, Clonmel, Co. Tipperary
General Enquiries
t. +353 52 2 5299/6222
f. +353 52 2 5447
r. reception@tippfm.com
w. www.tippfm.com

■ *Local Co. Tipperary commercial independent radio station, broadcasting contemporary
music with 30% news and current affairs to 24
to 50-year-olds on FM and on line.*

Chief Executive Officer: Ethel Power
Financial Controller: Mark O'Sullivan
Promotions and Sponsorship Manager:

Aidan O'Doherty
e. sales@tippfm.com
General Sales Manager: Raymond
Mulligan
e. sales@tippfm.com
News Editor: Seamus Martin
t. +353 52 25 456
m. +353 87 247 9163
e. news@tippfm.com

Programmes

*Tipp Today (10:00 to 12 noon, Monday
to Friday)*
Presenter: Seamus Martin
e. seamusmartin@tippfm.com
Producer: Geraldine Heffernan
e. geraldine@tippfm.com

West Limerick 102

Shannon Development Enterprise
Centre, Sheehan's Road, Newcastle,
Co. Limerick.
t. +353 69 66 200
Chairperson: Michael J. Noonan
Vice-Chairperson: Mary Kelly
Station Manager: Diarmuid McIntyre
Franchise area: West Limerick
Frequency: 102 MHz

■ *Audience details: The entire population of
all ages, both rural and urban, in the west
Limerick area.*
*Programme policy: Programming will be based
on community access and will reflect the various community interests and needs of the audience. The schedule will offer a diversity of programme content to cover all communities and
communities of interest in west Limerick.*

Broadcasting hours: 7 a.m. to 1 a.m.,
seven days a week.

WLR FM (Dungarvan)

Castle Street, Harbour Bay, Dungarvan,
Co. Waterford
General Enquiries
t. +353 58 43951
f. +353 58 45822
e. reception@wlr.com
w. www.wlrfm.com

■ *Local Waterford city and county commercial independent radio station, broadcasting news, sport, current affairs, local issues and music to 15 to 55-year-olds on FM and on line.*
Managing Director: Des Whelan
  e. des@wlrfm.com

WLR FM (Waterford)

Broadcast Centre, Ardkeen, Dunmore Road, Waterford
General Enquiries
  t. +353 51 87 7592
  f. +353 51 87 7420
  e. reception@wlr.com
  w. www.wlrfm.com
■ *Local Waterford city and county commercial independent radio station, broadcasting news, sport, current affairs, local issues and music to 15 to 55-year-olds on FM and on line.*
Managing Director: Des Whelan
  e. des@wlrfm.com
Director of Programmes: Billy McCarthy
Financial Controller: Gerry Sheridan
Advertising Manager: Tim Hassett
Production Manager: Lisa Dignam
Head of Music: Michael Byrne
Head of Sport: Catherine Power
  e. sport@wlrfm.com
Head of News: Liz Reddy
  m. +353 86 679 4796
  e. news@wlrfm.com
Head of Sales and Marketing: Tim Hassett
  e. sales@wlrfm.com

Community

Cashel and District Community Radio

Halla na Féile, Cashel, Co. Tipperary
General Enquiries
  t. +353 62 6 3500
  f. +353 62 6 3513
■ *Cashel town and district community radio station, broadcasting to the urban and rural community 09:00–11:00 and 19:00–22:00*

Monday to Friday, 09:00–11:00 and 19:00–21:00 Saturday and 09:00–12:00 and 19:00–21:00 Sunday on FM.
Chairperson: P. J. Irwin
Vice-Chairperson: Martin Browne
Secretary: Kevin Muldoon
Public Relations Officer: Anne Devitt

Community Radio Castlebar

Market Square, Castlebar, Co. Mayo
General Enquiries
  t. +353 94 902 5555
  f. +353 94 902 5989
  e. crcfm@eircom.net
  w. www.castlebar.ie/crcfm
■ *Castlebar town and community radio station, broadcasting entertainment, education and information programmes to the town and district of Castlebar, 09:00–22:00 Monday to Sunday, on FM and on line.*
Chairperson: Martin Waters
Station Manager: Peter Killeen
Secretary: Pat Stanton
News and Current Affairs: Peter Killeen
Sponsorship, Sales and Advertising: Paddy Cummins

Community Radio Youghal

League of the Cross Hall, Catherine Street, Youghal, Co. Cork
General Enquiries
  t. +353 24 9 1199/2288
  f. +353 24 9 1199
  e. info@youghalradio.com
  w. www.youghalradio.com
■ *Youghal town and district community radio station, broadcasting information and entertainment to the wider community, 09:00–18:00 Monday to Friday and 09:00–20:00 Saturday and Sunday, on FM.*
Chairperson: Seamus Murphy
Technical Director: Noel Cronin

Connemara Community Radio

Letterfrack, Co. Galway
General Enquiries
  t. +353 95 4 1616
  f. +353 95 4 1628

e. info@connemarafm.com
w. www.connemarafm.com

■ *North-west Connemara community radio station, broadcasting talk and music with a local community emphasis, 11:00–09:00 Monday to Sunday, on FM.*

Chairperson: Peter Veldon
Station Manager: Pat Walshe
News and Current Affairs: Grainne O'Malley

Cork Campus Radio

Level 3, Áras na Mac Léinn, National University of Ireland, Cork
General Enquiries
t. +353 21 490 2170/2008/3974
f. +353 21 490 3108
e. radio@ucc.ie
w. www.corkcampusradio.ucc.ie

■ *Cork city and university community radio station, broadcasting talk and music to students and the wider community and enabling community participation in programming, 08:00–17:30 Monday to Friday, on FM and on line.*

Chairperson: Donnchadh Ó hAodha
Station Manager: Catriona Chambers
Station Producer: Kieran Hurley

Dublin South FM

The Old School, Loreto Avenue, Dublin 14
General Enquiries
t. +353 1 493 0377
f. +353 1 493 0520
e. info@dublinsouthfm.ie
w. www.dublinsouthfm.ie

■ *South Dublin community radio station, broadcasting community-focused programming to parts of Dundrum, Churchtown, Rathfarnham, Ballinteer, Kilmacud, Goatstown, Stillorgan, Windy Arbour, Milltown, Mount Merrion and Sandyford, 16:00–21:00 Monday to Sunday, on FM.*

Chairperson: John O'Brennan
Station Manager: Mary Napier
Head of News: Martin Walsh
Head of Programmes: Brendan Hickey
Producer: Mike Purcell

Dundalk 100 FM

Dundalk Media Centre, Partnership Court, Park Street, Dundalk, Co. Louth
General Enquiries
t. +353 42 935 7496
f. +353 42 935 7478
e. info@dundalkfm.com
w. www.dundalkfm.com

■ *Dundalk town and district community radio station, broadcasting community programming and encouraging the participation of the community, 08:30–13:00 Monday to Friday, and 08:00–23:30 Saturday and Sunday on FM.*

Chairperson: Niall Byrne
Secretary and Station Manager: Alan Byrne

Flirt FM

Áras na Mac Léinn, National University of Ireland, Galway
General Enquiries
t. +353 91 75 0445
f. +353 91 52 5700
e. flirtfm@nuigalway.ie
w. www.flirtfm.nuigalway.ie

■ *Galway city and university community radio station, broadcasting to the student and wider population of Galway, 08:00–12:00 and 17:00–22:00 Monday to Thursday and 08:00–12:00 Friday, on FM and on line.*

Chairperson: Seán Mac Íomhair
Station Manager: Áine Lyne
News Editor: Sinead Connolly
Current Affairs: Jennifer Allen
Sports: John Nolan

Near FM

Northside Civic Centre, Bunratty Road, Dublin 17
General Enquiries
t. +353 1 867 1016
f. +353 1 848 6111
e. nearfm@iol.ie
w. www.nearfm.ie

■ *North-east Dublin community radio station, broadcasting community development and access programming to the community and enabling community participation, 08:00–00:00 Monday to Sunday, on FM. Near FM has been in the forefront of community radio programming and has developed several radio initiatives, including multi-cultural programming.*

Chairperson: Jack Byrne

Station Manager: Sally Galiana
  e. sally@nearfm.ie

Head of Sports: Fergus Carroll
  e. sport@nearfm.ie

Phoenix FM

Unit 333, Services Centre,
Blanchardstown Centre, Dublin 15
General Enquiries
  t. +353 1 822 7222
  f. +353 1 822 7209
  e. phoenixfm@iol.ie
  w. www.iolfree.ie/~phoenixfm
■ *Dublin 15 community radio station, broadcasting talk, music, local news and community affairs to Blanchardstown, Castleknock, Carpenterstown, Clonsilla, Mulhuddart and Corduff, 19:00–23:00 Monday to Friday and 15:00–22:00 Saturday and Sunday on FM.*

Chairperson: David Hughes

Programme Controller: Trevor Webster

Personnel Manager: Chris Hitchcock

Technical Manager: Gerry Garvey

Radio Corca Baiscinn (South West Clare Community Radio)

Community Centre, Circular Road,
Kilkee, Co. Clare
General Enquiries
  t. +353 65 908 3022
  f. +353 65 905 6602
  e. swccr@eircom.net
  w. www.iol.ie/~ycradio/CRFSWC-CR.html
■ *Loop Head and Doonbeg community radio station, broadcasting talk, information and entertainment to the community and enabling local participation, 10:00–13:00 Monday to Friday and 14:00–17:00 Saturday and Sunday, on FM.*

Chairperson: Morgan Roughan

Secretary: Mary Farren

Treasurer: Jim McAnespie

Station Manager: Catriona Chambers

Raidió na Life

7 Merrion Square, Dublin 2
General Enquiries
  t. +353 1 661 6333
  f. +353 1 676 3966
  e. rnl106@iol.com
  w. www.rnl106.com
■ *Greater Dublin community radio station, broadcasting music and talk to Irish-speakers of all ages, 16:30–08:00 Monday to Friday and 12:00–08:00 Saturday and Sunday, on FM and on line.*

Cathaoirleach (Chairperson): Marion Gunn

Station Manager, Advertising Manager and Director of Programmes: Fionnuala Mac Aodha

Station Producer: Seán Ó Cearúil

Head of News: Maebh Ní Fhallúin

Raidió Pobail Inis Eoghain (ICRFM)

Carndonagh, Co. Donegal
General Enquiries
  t. +353 77 2 9105
  f. +353 77 2 9107
  e. studio@icrfm.ie
  w. www.icrfm.ie
■ *North Inishowen community radio station, broadcasting talk and local content and enabling community participation 11:00–07:00 Monday to Friday, on FM.*

Cathaoirleach (Chairperson) and Station Manager: Jim Doherty

Station Producer: P. J. Mc Laughlin

Head of News and Sport: Charlie Shields

Tallaght FM

Level 3, The Square, Tallaght,
Dublin 24
General Enquiries
  t. +353 1 462 3333
  f. +353 1 462 3444

e. info@tallaghtfm.com
w. www.tallaghtfm.com

■ *South-west Dublin community radio station, broadcasting talk and music to the community of Tallaght and district, 12:00–22:00 Monday to Saturday, on FM.*

Chairperson: Mark O'Toole
Station Manager: Roderic Smyth
Station Producer: Christine O'Beirne

Tipperary Mid West Community Radio

St Michael's Street, Tipperary
General Enquiries
t. +353 62 5 2555
f. +353 62 5 2671
e. tippmidwest@radio.fm
w. www.tipperarymidwestradio.com

■ *South-west Tipperary community radio station, broadcasting information, education and entertainment to Tipperary and the mid-west of the county, 07:00–24:00 Monday to Friday, on FM.*

Chairperson: Michael Maguire
Vice-Chairperson: Jim Fitzgerald
Sales: Colette O'Hallaran
Assistant Hon. Secretary: Breda Ryan
Hon. Treasurer: Denis Hartnett
Public Relations Officer: Martin Quinn
Head of News: Maurice Crotty
Sports Editor: Shane Heffernan
Production Manager: P. J. Cummins

West Dublin Access Radio

Ballyfermot Community Civic Centre, Ballyfermot Road, Dublin 10
General Enquiries
t. +353 1 620 7193
f. +353 1 620 7193
e. bcasey@eircom.net

■ *West Dublin community radio station, broadcasting information, entertainment and education to the wider community, 13:30–17:40 Monday to Friday, on FM.*

Chairperson: Gerard Royal
Secretary: Robert Healy
Station Manager: Rosaleen Lynch

Wired FM (Limerick)

Mary Immaculate College, South Circular Road, Limerick
General Enquiries
t. +353 61 31 5773
f. +353 61 31 5776
e. wiredfm@mic.ul.ie
w. www.wiredfm.mic.ul.ie

Wired FM (Moylish)

Institute of Technology, Moylish, Limerick
General Enquiries
t. +353 61 30 8215
f. +353 61 31 5776
e. wiredfm@lit.ie
w. www.wiredfm.mic.ul.ie

■ *Student community radio station, broadcasting music (especially Irish music), news and features on youth, third-level and community-oriented issues, 08:30–10:00, 12:00–14:00, 16:30–22:00 Monday to Thursday, 17:00–19:30 Fridays, with repeat broadcasts 11:00–13:30 Sundays, on FM.*

Chairperson: Michael Breen
Station Manager: Nessa McGann

Special interest

Dublin City Anna Livia FM

Unit 6, Docklands Innovation Park, East Wall Road, Dublin 3
General Enquiries
t. +353 1 865 8020
f. +353 1 836 6063
e. dcalfm@annalivia.com
w. www.annaliviafm.com

■ *Dublin city and county special interest radio station, broadcasting talk-based programmes and specialist music to 25 to 65-year-olds, 07:00–14:00 Monday to Friday and 08:00–14:00 Saturday and Sunday, on FM.*

Chairperson: Margaret Roche
Secretary: Blaise Barron
Head of News: Shona Murray
Head of General Programming: Aidan Lonergan
Station Manager: B. J. A. Jones

Hospitals and institutions

Beaumont Hospital Radio

Beaumont Hospital, Beaumont Road,
Dublin 9
General Enquiries
  t. +353 1 809 2486
  f. +353 1 837 6982
  e. bhrrequests@eircom.net
■ *Beaumont Hospital radio, broadcasting music, news and information to patients and staff 24 hours a day on FM.*
Chairperson and Station Manager:
David Dennehy

CUH FM Hospital Radio

Cork University Hospital, Wilton, Cork
General Enquiries
  t. +353 21 434 2117
  f. +353 21 434 3307
■ *Cork University Hospital radio station, broadcasting news and music programming to the patients and staff on FM.*
Chairperson: Martin Corbett
Station Manager: Noel Welch

Limerick Regional Hospital Radio

Limerick Regional Hospital,
Dooradoyle, Limerick
General Enquiries
  t. +353 61 30 1072/48 2423
  e. radio107.2fm@mwhb.ie
■ *Limerick Regional Hospital radio station, broadcasting music and programming to the patients and staff on FM.*
Station Manager: Tom O'Sullivan
Radio Assistant: Ray Fennelly

Mater Hospital Radio, Dublin

Eccles Street, Dublin 7
General Enquiries
  t. +353 1 803 2300/2301
  f. +353 1 803 2300
  e. pledden@indigo.ie

■ *Mater Public and Private Hospital radio station, broadcasting music and programming to patients and staff of both hospitals on FM.*
Chairperson and Station Manager: Peter
Ledden

St Ita's Hospital Radio

St Ita's Hospital, Portrane, Co. Dublin
General Enquiries
  t. +353 1 843 6633
  f. +353 1 843 6633
  e. 97.4@oceanfree.net
■ *St Ita's Hospital radio, broadcasting music and programming to the patients and staff on FM.*
Chairperson: Seamus Murphy
Station Manager: Tom Noctor

South Tipperary General Hospital Radio

Western Road, Clonmel, Co.
Tipperary
General Enquiries
  t. +353 52 7 7104
  f. +353 52 7 7105
  e. info@stghradio.org;
  requests@stghradio.org
  w. www.stghradio.org
■ *South Tipperary General Hospital radio station, broadcasting music and programming to patients and staff, 16:00–22:00 weekdays and 10:00–18:00 Saturdays and Sundays, on FM.*
Station Manager: John Savage
Assistant Manager: Ann Kavanagh

Northern Ireland

Telephone numbers in Northern Ireland have the prefix 048 if dialled from the Republic and 004428 if dialled from elsewhere.

3C (Continuous Cool Country)
General Enquiries
e. info@3cdigital.com
w. www.3cdigital.co.uk
■ *Terrestrial 24-hour digital radio station, broadcasting country music. Available on digital radio (DAB), freeview digital terrestrial television, and on line. Not available on FM.*
Presenters
Pat Geary
e. pat.geary@3cdigital.com
Dave Johanssen
e. dave@3cdigital.com
Derek Shirlaw
e. derek.shirlaw@3cdigital.com
John MacCalman
e. john.maccalman@3cdigital.com

BBC Radio Foyle
8 Northland Road, Derry BT48 7JD
General Enquiries
t. +44 28 7137 8600
w. www.bbc.co.uk/northernireland/
e. radiofoyle/index.shtml
■ *Part of the BBC network, a regional BBC radio station broadcasting information, education, music and entertainment on FM, medium wave, digital radio (DAB), freeview and on line, in conjunction with BBC Radio Ulster and BBC Northern Ireland.*
E-mail addresses follow the format
firstname.lastname@bbc.co.uk
Head of BBC Radio Foyle: Anna Leddy
Programmes
The Morning Programme
Presenter: Paul McFadden
text +44 778 620 0931
The Mark Patterson Show
Presenter: Mark Patterson
t. +44 28 7126 6522
text +44 778 620 0931

BBC Radio Ulster
Broadcasting House, Ormeau Avenue, Belfast BT2 8HQ
General Enquiries
t. +44 28 9033 8000
w. www.bbc.co.uk/northernireland/
radioulster/index.shtml
■ *Part of the BBC network, a BBC 'national' radio station broadcasting information, education, music and entertainment on FM, medium wave, digital radio (DAB), freeview and on line as part of BBC Northern Ireland. A Board of Governors regulates the BBC.*
E-mail addresses follow the format
firstname.lastname@bbc.co.uk
BBC Director of BBC Radio and Music: Jenny Abramsky
BBC NI Controller: Anna Carragher
BBC NI Head of Radio Ulster: Susan Lovell
Programmes
Good Morning Ulster
Presenters: Wendy Austin, Seamus McKee and Conor Bradford
Evening Extra
Presenters: Mark Carruthers and Audrey Carville

Citybeat 96.7 FM
46 Stranmillis Embankment, Belfast BT9 5FN
General Enquiries
t. +44 28 9020 5967; (requests) +44 28 9020 0967
f. +44 28 9020 0023
e. info@citybeat.co.uk
w. www.citybeat.co.uk
■ *Radio station broadcasting music, news and information programming to a 25 to 49-year-old adult audience within a 20-mile radius of Belfast on FM, digital radio (DAB) and on line.*

Chairperson: Robin Burgess
Station Director: John Rosborough
Programme Controller: Owen Larkin
  e. owen.larkin@citybeat.co.uk
Sales Director: Dorothy McDade
  e. dorothy.mcdade@citybeat.co.uk
Promotions Manager: David Johnson
  e. david.johnson@citybeat.co.uk
News Editor: Marc Mallett
  e. marc.mallett@citybeat.co.uk
Commercial Producer: Eddie
McDermott
  e. eddie.mcdermott@citybeat.co.uk
Head of Music: Stuart Robinson
  e. stuart.robinson@citybeat.co.uk

Cool FM

Kiltonga Industrial Estate, Belfast Road,
Newtownards, Co. Down BT23 4ES
PO Box 974, Belfast BT1 1RT
General Enquiries
  t. +44 28 9181 7181
  f. +44 28 9181 4974
  e. music@coolfm.co.uk
  w. www.coolfm.co.uk
■ *Radio station broadcasting music and talk
to the greater Belfast area on FM, digital radio
(DAB) and on line. Now owned by Emap.*
Managing Director and Programme
Controller: David Sloan
Head of Music: John Paul Ballantine
Publicity and Promotions Manager:
Alastair McDowell

Downtown Radio

Kiltonga Industrial Estate, Belfast Road,
Newtownards, Co. Down BT23 4TJ
General Enquiries
  t. +44 28 9181 5555
  f. +44 28 9181 5252
  e. programmes@downtown.co.uk
  w. www.downtown.co.uk
■ *Radio station broadcasting music and talk
to greater Belfast, Derry, Limavady,
Enniskillen, Omagh, South Down, Ballymena,
Newcastle and Larne on FM, AM digital radio
(DAB) and on line. Now owned by Emap.*

Managing Director and Programme
Controller: David Sloan
Head of News, Sport and Features:
Harry Castles
Sales Manager: Rodney Bell
Publicity and Promotions Manager:
Alastair McDowell

Kiss 100

Scriptor Court, Farringdon Road,
London EC1R 3AD, England
General Enquiries
  t. +44 20 7837 1100
  e. info@kiss100.com
  w. www.kiss100.com
■ *Radio station broadcasting dance music and
talk on digital radio (DAB) and on line. Not
available on FM.*

Magic 105

PO Box 105, Lurgan, Co. Armagh
BT66 7WA
General Enquiries
  t. +44 28 3834 5555; (studio) +44 28
  3834 2555
  e. sales@magic105.net
  w. www.magic105.net
■ *Local radio station broadcasting music from
the 1970s and 80s to an adult audience.*

Mid 106

2C Park Avenue, Cookstown,
Co. Tyrone BT80 8AH
General Enquiries
  t. +44 28 8675 8696
■ *Local radio station broadcasting music (par-
ticularly Irish and country) and talk to
Cookstown, Magherafelt, Dungannon and dis-
tricts, on FM and on line.*

Q97.2 (Causeway Coast Radio)

24 Colyfin Road, Coleraine, Co. Derry
BT52 2NU
General Enquiries
  t. +44 28 7035 9100; (requests) +44
  28 7034 4972
  e. info@q972.fm
  w. www.q972.fm

■ *Local radio station broadcasting music-based entertainment to the Causeway Coast, on FM and on line. Part of the Q Radio network.*

Q101.2FM West (Enniskillen)

1 Belmore Mews, 2 New Street,
Enniskillen, Co. Fermanagh BT74 6AH
General Enquiries
   t. +44 28 6632 0777
   e. requests@q101west.fm
   w. www.q101west.fm

Q101.2FM West (Omagh)

42A Market Street, Omagh,
Co. Tyrone BT78 1EH,
General Enquiries
   t. +44 28 8224 5777
   e. requests@q101west.fm
   w. www.q101west.fm

Q102.9

Riverview Suite, 87 Rossdowney
Road, Waterside, Co. Derry
BT47 5SU
General Enquiries
   t. +44 28 7134 4449
   f. +44 28 7131 1177
   e. manager@q102.fm
   w. www.q102.fm

■ *Local radio station broadcasting music and talk to Northern Ireland on FM, digital radio (DAB) and on line. Flagship station of the Q Radio network, which includes Q97.2 FM and Q101 West (Omagh and Enniskillen).*
Q Network Managing Director: Frank McLaughlin

Special interest

BFBS Radio 1

Headquarters Northern Ireland,
BFPO 825
General Enquiries
   t. (studio) +44 28 9226 6666; (office)
   +44 28 9226 6688
   f. +44 28 9226 6677

   e. bfbsni@bfbs.com
   w. www.ssvc.com/bfbs/radio/nire-land/index.htm

■ *Radio station broadcasting information, music and community issues to current and former members of the British armed forces, AM and on line.*

Féile FM

473 Falls Road, Belfast BT12 6DD
General Enquiries
   t. +44 28 9031 3440
   f. +44 28 9031 9150
   e. info@feilebelfast.com
   w. www.feilebelfast.com

■ *Féile FM is a festival community radio station, which broadcasts for two four-week periods each year, prior to and during Draíocht and St Patrick's Day in March and the August Féile.*

Board of Directors: Gerry Adams, Siobhan O'Hanlon, Geraldine McAteer, Ciarán Quinn

Irish Christian Broadcasters (ICB)

16 Battlehill Road, Portadown,
Co. Armagh BT62 4ER
General Enquiries
   t. +44 28 3835 4503
   w. www.gracefellowship.ie/icbweb-page.htm

■ *Christian radio station broadcasting on AM.*

Shine FM

c/o Youth with a Mission, 45
Cloghskelt Road, Castlewellan, Co.
Down BT31 9QF
General Enquiries
   t. +44 28 4067 1919
   e. admin@shine.org.uk
   w. www.shinefm.fsnet.co.uk

■ *Local community access radio station, broadcasting a Christian message to Banbridge and district.*

Hospital

Antrim Hospital Radio

Antrim Area Hospital, 45 Bush Road,
Antrim BT41 2RL
Secretary
t. +44 28 9442 4161 (voicemail)
e. antrimhospitalradio@hotmail.com
w. www.nihr.org.uk/antrim
/index.html
■ *Hospital radio station broadcasting music and talk to the patients and staff of the Antrim Area Hospital.*

Mater Hospital Radio, Belfast

Mater Hospital, Crumlin Road, Belfast
BT14 6AB
General Enquiries: Davy Downes
t. +44 28 9074 1211
w. www.nihr.org.uk/mater/
index.html
■ *Hospital radio station broadcasting music and talk to the patients and staff of the Mater Hospital.*

Radio Craigavon

Basement Area, Craigavon Area
Hospital, Lisniskey, Lurgan Road,
Portadown, Co. Armagh BT63 5QQ
Manager: Jim Kerr
t. +44 28 3861 2507 (studio voice-mail)
e. jimkerr.home@btinternet.com
■ *Hospital radio station broadcasting music and talk to the patients and staff of the Craigavon Area Hospital.*

Radio Mid-Ulster

Mid-Ulster Hospital, Hospital Road,
Magherafelt, Co. Derry BT45 5EX
Chairman: Tom McKeown
t. +44 28 7963 1031
e. studio@radiomid.co.uk
w. www.radiomid.co.uk/index.html
■ *Hospital radio station broadcasting music and talk to patients and staff.*

Radio Moyle

Flat 3, Moyle Hospital, Gloucester
Avenue, Larne, Co. Antrim BT40
1RW
Secretary: George Cunningham
t. +44 28 2827 5431 (ex. 6296)
e. radiomoyle@hotmail.com
w. www.nihr.org.uk/moyle/
index.html
■ *Hospital radio station, broadcasting music and talk to the patients and staff of the Moyle Hospital, 17:30–22:00 Sunday to Friday.*

Radio Valley

Lagan Valley Hospital, Hillsborough
Road, Lisburn, Co. Antrim BT28 1JP
General Enquiries: Richard Hogg
t. +44 28 9267 1151
■ *Hospital radio station broadcasting music and talk to the patients and staff of the Lagan Valley Hospital.*

Ulster Hospital Radio

Ulster Hospital, Upper Newtownards
Road, Belfast BT16 0RH
Chairman: Andrew Kane
t. +44 28 9048 4511 (ex. 2124)
e. info@ulsterradio.co.uk
w. www.nihr.org.uk/ulster/
index.html
■ *Hospital radio station broadcasting music and talk to patients and staff.*

Internet

Liquid Sound Radio

22 Ardcarn Drive, Dundonald, Belfast
BT5 7RS
Chairman: Scott Longworth
t. +44 78 8052 6035
e. chairman@liquidsoundradio.tk
w. www.liquidsoundradio.tk

5

NEW MEDIA: RIDING THE TECHNOLOGY WAVE

Dr Aphra Kerr

New media are rapidly becoming old media as they diffuse through Irish society. Mobile phones have been in the vanguard in terms of penetration, but the domestic take-up of the internet and video game consoles are following rapidly. These new media provide a range of content, including voice, music, videos and games. Irish new media companies are small to medium-sized companies and serve both the domestic and global markets.

In the Republic, new media content and services have been very lightly regulated, and government policy has concentrated on enabling business innovation. However, initial patterns of diffusion and use have been unequal, an issue known as the digital divide. Further, the need to educate people about how to use new media, media literacy, and the need to protect children from certain forms of content and certain users are emerging policy issues.

New media penetration and use in Ireland

ComReg, the Irish telecommunications regulator, reported that mobile phone penetration was 96% in Ireland in March 2005.[1] This percentage equals the penetration rate of landline phones, and access is evenly spread through different demographic groups. Basic text and image-based messaging services, for example downloading ring tones and accessing sports results, are very popular with Irish users. Next-generation mobile technologies will see the provision of more media-rich applications and 'adult'

1. See ComReg, Quarter 1 2005 Survey, published June 2005.

content both to mobile phones and other mobile devices. Indeed Ireland now boasts the second highest European SMS, text messaging, rate with ninety-two texts per person per month by mid 2005.

A survey of Ireland's main internet service providers conducted by Nua and the Digital Media Centre in October 1995 found that there were 4,800 companies and 1,800 private users of the internet in Ireland. Within a relatively short time this situation has changed dramatically. An Amárach survey conducted in 2004 found that 46% of Irish households had access to the internet and that the dominant place of access was the home. However, in this survey, significant differences in access emerged, with younger people from ABC1 households more than twice as likely to have access to the internet. With regard to use it appears that sending e-mail, booking holidays and buying books or concert tickets were the most popular applications with Irish users.[2]

An interesting experiment in relation to the internet in Ireland was the Eircom Information Age Town competition. In 1996, towns with a population of more than 30,000 inhabitants competed to win an integrated telecommunications infrastructure worth €19 million. From 1997 to 2002 the winning town, Ennis, had the highest rate of home access to the internet of any Irish town.[3] The money was spent on upgrading the local network, subsidising home computer use, training and community applications.

Finally, figures for the household penetration of video game consoles (PlayStation 2, GameCube or X-box) are rather more difficult to find. Sony claims that household penetration of their video game platforms in Ireland is second only to Japan. The Central Statistics Office household budget survey, 1999–2000, found that spending on computer games is increasing but is still significantly behind spending on other media.[4] A survey conducted by Amárach in 2001 found that only 6% of the total information and communications spending by Irish households was on game consoles and software.[5]

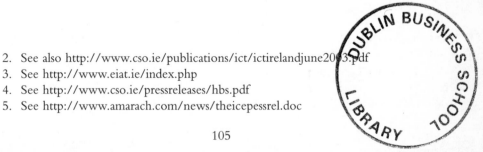

2. See also http://www.cso.ie/publications/ict/ictirelandjune2003.pdf
3. See http://www.eiat.ie/index.php
4. See http://www.cso.ie/pressreleases/hbs.pdf
5. See http://www.amarach.com/news/theicepessrel.doc

New media companies

In Ireland, many of the companies that pioneered new media production in the 1990s came from more traditional media sectors.[6] 'New media' includes a broad range of devices, and new media companies rarely produce for a single media device: multi-platform content strategies are much more common.

By 2002 a Forfás report estimated that there were 282 active 'digital content' companies in Ireland, employing between 4,000 and 4,500 people.[7] These companies produced both technologies and content for new media, ranging from companies that concentrated on entertainment (games, digital film, digital television), digital libraries and e-learning to companies that produced consumer and business information services. Almost 150 of these companies concentrated on entertainment services and applications for the Irish and global markets. Forfás noted that the industry was at a relatively early stage of development and largely comprised very small enterprises that concentrated on content creation and design. The greatest number of companies could be found in web design, followed by digital television, digital film and e-learning.

The Forfás report identified a total of 78 companies offering web design services to commercial customers. Of these, only five were in non-Irish ownership. Many of these companies are members of the Irish Internet Association, which acts to promote the industry, assists companies in networking and lobbies the government. Recent international arrivals in this sector are Google, eBay and Overture.

According to ComReg figures, the Irish mobile phone market is one of the most profitable markets in Europe for network operators. It is therefore surprising that, despite deregulation, the network market is dominated by two companies: Vodafone, which holds 54% of the market, and O_2, which holds a further 40%. Independent mobile content providers must negotiate with these two companies in order to offer services to Irish mobile users. As mobile phones increase in sophistication, games are becoming another important application. Eirplay Games, Selatra, Upstart and TKO Software are companies that develop and localise games for

6. Kerr, A. (1999). The Development of Multimedia in Ireland. In: *Europe Appropriates Multimedia. A Study of the National Uptake of Multimedia in Eight European Countries and Japan.* R. Williams and R. Slack. Trondheim, Norwegian University of Science and Technology: pp. 215–278

7. Forfás (2002) *A Strategy for the Digital Content Industry in Ireland*, Dublin. Available on line at http://www.forfas.ie/pubs_index.htm

mobile phones both at home and abroad.

Despite the growing market for video and computer games, there are very few companies actually producing these types of games in Ireland. Both Microsoft and Vivendi have substantial localised operations in Ireland, but indigenous companies are largely start-ups and face considerable barriers to entry. Nevertheless, Torc Interactive and Kapooki Games are developing video and computer games aimed at the UK and US markets.[8] In 2004, Irish game companies formed a chapter of the International Game Developers' Association both to promote the Irish games industry and to help companies to develop.

Each year Irish new media companies can participate in the Irish Internet Association's Net Visionary Awards, the Irish Digital Media Awards and the Darklight Digital festival. Companies can also participate in the European-wide EUROPRIX Multimedia Top Talent award.[9] Irish students and companies have been particularly successful at the European level, both in nominations and prizes.

New media policy

From the late 1990s, numerous consultancy reports identified new media as an economic sector with much potential for growth. Government policies to promote new media production and consumption are dispersed through a range of policy areas, from information society, education, telecommunications and industrial development to innovation policies. Recent initiatives include the development of the Internet Advisory Board and the extension of the film censor's role to include digital games.[10]

Probably the most significant government initiative to promote the new media industry has been the development of the Digital Hub. This project has involved the redevelopment of nine acres of land in the Liberties area of central Dublin and the provision of enterprise space for new media companies. The project began in 2001, and an early tenant was Media Lab Europe, a branch of the Massachusetts Institute of Technology in Boston. Forty companies are now established in the area, employing approximately 400 people. The project also organises new media training,

8. Kerr, A. (2003). Live Life to the Power of PS2: locating the digital games industry in the new media environment. *Irish Communications Review*, Vol. 9. See http://www.icr.dit.ie/volume9/articles/Kerr.pdf

9. See http://www.toptalent.europrix.org; http://www.darklight-filmfestival.com; and http://www.digitalmedia.ie

10. See http://www.iab.ie

seminars, exhibitions and competitions, like Dare to be Digital, which tries to encourage students to enter the games industry. The Diageo Learning Liberties Initiative has supported a range of enterprise and community learning projects in the area.[11] The closure of MIT Media Lab Europe at the beginning of 2005 has been seen in the media as a body blow to the research and innovation aspect of the Digital Hub project. However, a second research phase, this time involving Irish research institutions and universities, is due to replace it. While Media Lab closed following the Government's decision not to continue subsidising the project, the digital media cluster at the Digital Depot site has been quietly flourishing, with several of the digital games, animation and mobile phone applications companies expanding rapidly. The US internet retail engine Amazon has now based one of its units in the Digital Hub.

Future trends

One of the most important issues in this industry is access to broadband, both for companies and users. Despite growing rates of internet access and use, access to the internet in Ireland is largely by dial-up modems (73% of users at the end of 2004), and this has meant that the growth of both e-commerce and on-line entertainment applications has been slow. The introduction of flat-rate internet pricing schemes and the government policy of developing high-speed metropolitan area networks in towns around the country may go some way towards alleviating the problem. This issue is particularly important in border areas, given the high levels of broadband penetration in Northern Ireland. A related issue is that, while access to the internet has increased, use is still structured by age and class.

Finally, many of the 'risks' associated with the use of the internet will also emerge with other new media in the future, as their networking and graphical capabilities increase. While the government has established the Internet Advisory Board, the development of new media content classification systems and the promotion of media literacy have yet to become part of the government's policy agenda, despite its emergence in policy arenas elsewhere in Europe. The trend throughout Europe has been towards integrated regulation of content and policy of both broadcast and new media, and this is likely to be an emerging debate in Ireland.

11. See http://www.thedigitalhub.com/home/default.asp

Faster and smaller: Moore's Law and the gadget

Neil Leyden

In 1965, Gordon Moore, joint founder of Intel Technologies (now one of the largest technology employers in Ireland) made a famous observation. This observation, commonly known as Moore's Law, noted the exponential growth in the number of transistors per integrated circuit and predicted that this trend would continue year after year. In lay person's terms, this meant that since 1965 the processing power of microchips has doubled every eighteen months. As a result of this, personal computers have got faster and faster and we now have complex integrated circuits appearing in everything from dishwashers to key rings.

But do we need them? Do we really want to watch television on our mobile phones? Do we really want our fridges to tell us that the milk is out of date, or to wear smart tags so advertising signs can recognise us and offer personalised discounts? Maybe not, but, as Nicholas Negroponte, the founder of the Media Lab in MIT and Europe, warns, 'the history of technological development shows that we consistently overestimate short term assimilation and underestimate the long term consequences.'

Simply put, although we don't think we want them, the chances are that once we do have them we will be hooked. A perfect example of this is the way that the Irish have embraced the mobile phone. It seems a distant memory when the first brick-like analogue mobile phones came on the market. However, once they went digital and became smaller and cheaper the mobile became the essential life-style tool. Now 15 to 24-year-olds say the mobile is their number 1 technology tool, above even the television.

It could be argued that the mobile phone isn't really a phone any more. Voice services are now just a part of the overall function and services associated with the mobile. Phones are invariably becoming personal organisers, MP3 players, web browsers, cameras, and hand-held game consoles. For example, data revenue for O2 Ireland was 21.8% of total revenue in 2004, and this is continuing to rise. With the advent of 3G, data services such as e-mail, internet browsing, picture and video messaging will generate more revenues for the operators in the form of data traffic.

However, the march of technological innovation offers no guarantees for the life expectancy of any given business model. Technological innovations that inadvertently upset business models are called 'disruptive technologies', and there are two potentially formidable disruptive technologies on the horizon for the mobile operators.

The first is called wi-fi, which is the technology that wireless local area networks (LANs) are based on. Although this technology has been around for a while, it is only recently that wi-fi cards have become standard in most laptops. Wi-fi cards allow users to access broadband networks through the wireless radio frequency where available. Wi-fi hotspots are now being widely provided by both fixed-line and mobile operators to hotels, airport lounges, cafés and pubs—often allowing customers to surf free of charge, with the trade-off for the provider being that the customer will then purchase more goods and services if they stay in the vicinity. Mobile operators can also charge the customer for using their hotspot access if the provider doesn't wish to cover the full costs. As a result, wi-fi cards are now being built in to the next-generation mobile phones and PDAs, meaning that mobile users will be able to use the internet in an increasing range of venues. No particular threat, you might think, to the mobile operators—that is, until you add two other potentially disruptive technologies: voice over IP (VoIP) and WiMAX.

VoIP quite simply uses the internet to make phone calls. The voice call—made from a landline or a computer—is digitised and switched over to the internet, which completes the call, nationally or internationally. This means that the customer can make an international phone call for the price of a local one, because the internet becomes the middleman between the two exchanges. Now when this technology is added to a mobile phone and used on a wi-fi hotspot, strictly speaking customers will be able to make international mobile calls for next to nothing, or potentially free.

WiMAX, on the other hand, is a standards-based wireless technology, being pushed heavily by Intel, which provides high-throughput broadband connections over long distances. WiMAX can provide metropolitan area network connectivity at speeds of up to 75 Mb/sec and be used to transmit signal as far as 30 miles. Potentially, this could mean the provision of cost-effective wireless connectivity for everyone in cities and towns, allowing for the maximum usage of applications like VoIP.

But business models are flexible and the smart move with the times. Another famous disruptive technology was 'peer-to-peer' software, most memorably epitomised by the Napster free software (another competitor, Kazaa, developed their technology into the leading VoIP service, Skype). Napster was heralded as the potential ruin of the music industry, as flagrant piracy would take hold and artists and studios would go broke. It would be the day the music died. Then Apple came up with the iPod and turned everything on its head. With a mixture of minimalist design, technological innovation and end-to-end service provision, Apple has created the consumer device of the decade—so far! By October 2004 Apple had sold 2 million iPod devices, and many analysts have forecast easily double that number for the holiday-sales-fuelled first quarter of 2005.

Where they differed from what went before is that they manage the whole process from end to end—keeping both customers and copyright holders in the loop. Apple provides the proprietary iTunes software—a 'peer to peer' technology that manages the sharing of content between your computer and your device—and also allows you to purchase songs over the internet, through their iTunes stores, having done a deal with all the major labels. The latest versions of the iPod have a 40 Gb storage capacity, allowing the storage of up to 15,000 songs. In November 2004, U2 became involved in an unprecedented endorsement deal with Apple, allowing Apple to sell a customised U2 iPod, which would be preloaded with all of U2's back catalogue. In the wings, Sony are desperately trying to relaunch their ground-breaking Walkman brand for the digital generation, but they have a lot of ground to cover.

At the core is still Moore's Law, which guarantees faster and faster processing power and more and more capacity for memory. Alongside that, the entrepreneurial mind and consumer demand means that we are rapidly heading toward a society where we will be surrounded by silent, ubiquitous computing power, with all our mobile gadgets and gizmos accessing the numerous networks that will facilitate our entertainment and social desires as well as our business needs. When we consider that nanotechnology will bring this computing power down to the subatomic level, the potential for the future is mind-boggling.

Neil Leyden, Calico Media, The Digital Hub, Dublin.

Amárach Consulting

37 Northumberland Road, Dublin 4
Chief Executive: Gerard O'Neill
t. +353 1 660 5506
f. +353 1 660 5508
e. gerard.oneill@amarach.com
w. www.amarach.com
■ *This is a specialist in predictive market research, consumer trend analysis and business forecasting. Amárach provides media and technology market research and analysis for media institutions such as ComReg.*
Director: John Trainor
john.trainor@amarach.com
Director: Michael McLoughlin
michael.mcloughlin@amarach.com

AMAS

38 Lower Leeson Street, Dublin 2
Managing Director: Aileen O'Toole
t. +353 1 661 0499
f. +353 1 6611 360
e. info@amas.ie
w. www.amas.ie
■ *This is an e-government and e-business firm, focused on strategy, content and marketing, assisting public and private organisations to develop and redevelop their on-line channels around best practice principles.*

Amazon

The Digital Depot, The Digital Hub, Thomas Street, Dublin 8
w. www.amazon.com
■ *New Irish research and development centre for the on-line retail centre, based in the Digital Depot since April 2005.*

Athena Media

Digital Depot, The Digital Hub, Thomas Street, Dublin 8
Managing Director: Helen Shaw
t. +353 1 488 5850/1
m. +353 87 675 4375
e. helenshaw@athenamedia.ie
w. www.athenamedia.ie
■ *This content production and media consultancy company specialises in digital media and makes content for multimedia: radio, television, on-line and books. It is a source of consultancy expertise in media policy and digital media.*

Beyond International

The Digital Depot, The Digital Hub, Thomas Street, Dublin 8
w. www.beyond.com.au
■ *Irish centre for the Australian cross-media production and distribution company.*

Big Top Multimedia

First Floor, 26 Eustace Street, Dublin 2
Director: Richard Fitzpatrick
t. +353 1 6708311
w. www.bigtopmultimedia.com
■ *This multimedia company offers clients web design, web hosting, e-commerce, e-newsletters and consultancy services, among others.*

Blinck Mobile Ltd

The Digital Depot, The Digital Hub, Thomas Street, Dublin 8
e. info@blinck.com
w. www.blinck.com
■ *Irish centre for the Dutch digital media company.*

Boulder Media

The Digital Hub, Thomas Street, Dublin 8
Managing Director: Mark Downey
t. +353 1 6794645
w. www.bouldermedia.com
■ *Boulder Media produces animation for television and the internet and is providing work for the US Cartoon Network.*

Cable and Wireless Ireland Ltd

1 Airton Road, Tallaght, Dublin 24
Managing Director: Noreen O'Hare
t. +353 1 404 0333
f. +353 1 404 0339
e. enquiries.ireland@cw.com
w. www.cw.com/ie
■ *This international company provides communications and ICT infrastructure to Irish firms.*

Caboom

10 St Stephen's Green, Dublin 2
Contact: Al Byrne
t. +353 1 672 7077
f. +353 1 672 7043
e. info@caboom.ie
w. www.caboom.ie
■ *This media production company specialises in advertisements, television production and digital media content.*

Calico Media

The Digital Depot, The Digital Hub,
Thomas Street, Dublin 8
Contact: Neil Leyden
t. +353 1 489 3672
e. neil@calico.ie
w. www.calico.ie

Cambridge Animation Systems (Digital Animation Media)

The Digital Hub, Thomas Street,
Dublin 8
Contact: Cormac Slevin
■ *This company has been pioneering the development of cutting-edge 2D cartoon animation software since its foundation in 1990.*

Capiche Design

Unit 5, 10–13 Thomas Street, The
Digital Hub, Dublin 8
Contact: Gabriel Walsh, Adrian
McLoughlin
t. +353 1 453 5805
f. +353 1 453 5804
e. info@capichedesign.com
w. www.capichedesign.com
■ *This graphic design company offers its clients creative work on corporate identity, packaging and point of sale, as well as brochures and web design.*

Certification Europe

The Digital Hub, Thomas Street,
Dublin 8
Chief Executive Officer
Michael Brophy
t. +353 1 679 6666
f. +353 1 679 3235
e. info@certificationeurope.com
w. www.certificationeurope.com
■ *This ICT company provides assessment and certification services to the Irish and international markets.*

Chorus

Limerick Enterprise and Development
Park, Roxboro Road, Limerick
Chief Executive: Phil Freedman
t. +353 61 272 120
f. +353 61 272 777
e. info@chorus.ie
w. www.chorus.ie
■ *This is a provider of multichannel television, broadband and telephone services to 725,000 Irish homes. It employs 550 workers in its Limerick operation.*
Public Relations Manager: Edwina Gore
e. egore@chorus.ie

Cibenix

Digital Depot, The Digital Hub,
Thomas Street, Dublin 8
Chief Executive Officer: Garry
McCollum
t. +353 1 488 5840
f. +353 1 488 5844
e. info@cibenix.com
w. www.cibenix.com
■ *This company helps mobile operators to get more revenue from existing data services, such as news, sports, music and games. It makes these data services more visible and more accessible by the subscriber.*

Creative Inputs

121–123 Ranelagh, Dublin 6
Contact: Martin MacDonnell
t. +353 1 4972711
f. +353 1 4972779
e. mmacdonnell@creativeinputs.ie
w. www.creativeinputs.ie
■ *This graphic design studio develops projects ranging from corporate identity and annual reports to promotional material.*

Cyesta

Digital Depot, The Digital Hub,
Dublin 8
Contact: James Wolsey
t. +353 1 489 3630
f. +353 1 633 5515
e. info@cyesta.com
w. www.cyesta.com
■ *This company provides anti-piracy services and systems to owners of intellectual property rights. Its core customers are in both the entertainment industries and other industries marketing branded goods that are affected by piracy and counterfeiting.*

Daft.ie

The Digital Hub, Thomas Street,
Dublin 8
Contact: Eamonn Fallon
t. 1580 880 880
f. +353 1 658 1073
e. info@daft.ie
w. www.daft.ie
■ *Daft.ie provides low-cost on-line advertising to Irish estate agencies, landlords, home-owners and tenants. It covers property for sale, property to let, accommodation sharing, office spaces, retail spaces, short-term apartments, holiday homes, parking spaces and new homes.*

Dara Creative Communications

19 Magennis Place, Dublin 2
Contact: Denise Kinsella
+353 1 672 5222
f. +353 672 5226
e. info@daracreative.ie
w. www.daracreative.ie
■ *This is a graphic design and communications consultancy.*

DHR Communications

157 Thomas Street, The Digital Hub,
Dublin 8
Contact: Dermot Ryan
t. +353 1 707 1929
e. info@dhr.com
w. www.dhr.com

Digital Hub Development Agency

10–13 Thomas Street, Dublin 8
Chief Executive Officer: Philip Quinn
t. +353 1 480 6200
f. +353 1 480 6201
e. info@thedigitalhub.com
w. www.thdigitalhub.com
■ *This is a government-funded project to create an international digital enterprise area in Dublin, containing developing media enterprise companies.*

Digital Media Forum

The Digital Depot, Thomas Street,
Dublin 8
Chairman: Neil Leyden
t. +353 1 489 3605
e. info@digitalmediaforum.net
w. www.digitalmediaforum.net
■ *This group comprises twenty-two companies around the Digital Hub representing the digital media industry. It creates enterprise resources for member-companies.*

DVM TV

The Digital Depot, The Digital Hub,
Dublin 8
Brian Darcy
t. +353 1 488 5812
e. sales@dvm.tv
w. www.dvm.tv
■ *This company provides a premium digital media service whereby customers can purchase local information and entertainment from the best media brands in the country in each media category, such as news, sport, entertainment, cars, travel and more.*

Eircom

St Stephen's Green West, Dublin 2
Chief Executive: Philip Nolan
t. +353 1 671 4444
e. pressoffice@eircom.net
w. www.eircom.net
■ *This is Ireland's leading communications company and was originally established as a government department. It was bought by Valentia Telecommunications Ltd in 2001 and became Eircom Ltd. Its mobile subsidiary,*

Eircell, was sold to Vodafone. The company's chairman is Anthony O'Reilly.

Chief Financial Officer: Peter Lynch

Eirplay Games

The Digital Depot, Thomas Street, Dublin 8

Contact: Peter Lynch

t. +353 1 4885816

f. +353 1 488 5801

e. info@eirplaygames.com

w. www.eirplaygames.com

■ *This is a developer and distributor of mobile entertainment software. It has published more than ten mobile games and won the Irish Digital Media Award for Game Developer of the Year in 2004.*

Empower.ie

e. webmaster@empower.ie

w. www.empower.ie

■ *This portal site was set up by thirty-five county and city enterprise boards to simply and cost-effectively create their web sites.*

Equinox eBusiness Solutions

The Windmill Offices, The Digital Depot, The Digital Hub, Thomas Street, Dublin 8

t. +353 1 677 6800

f. +353 1 677 6804

e. sales@equinox.ie

w. www.equinox.ie

■ *e-Commerce digital media company.*

European Biometrics Forum

The Digital Depot, Thomas Street, Dublin 8

Contact: Cathy McKeon

t. +353 1 488 5810

w. www.eubiometricsforum.com

■ *This forum contains some of Europe's leading privacy, technology and visibility experts, specialising in the future of the biometrics industry, which deals in automated methods of recognising a person based on a physiological or behavioural characteristic, including fingerprinting, retinal and iris scanning, hand and finger geometry, voice patterns, facial recognition, and other techniques.*

Fluid Rock

The Digital Hub, 157 Thomas Street, Dublin 8

Contact: Ruth MacPartlin

t. +353 1 6330005

e. ruth.mcpartlin@fluid-rock.com

w. www.fluid-rock.com

■ *This company specialises in the development of digital solutions, from web sites and CD-ROMs to enterprise-level content management systems. Its core businesses include strategic and technical consultancy, project management, digital design and development*

Google Ireland

1st and 2nd Floors, Gordon House, Barrow Street, Dublin 4

Division Controller: Angus Kelsall

f. +353 1 436 1001

e. Ireland@google.com

w. www.google.ie

■ *Google was founded by Larry Page and Sergey Brin and is the world's largest on-line search engine. Is can also be accessed from wireless platforms, including WAP and i-mode phones. Google's European Operations offices are in Dublin.*

Havok

The Digital Depot, Thomas Street, Dublin 8

Contact: David O'Meara

t. +353 1 472 4300

f. +353 1 671 0022

e. w.

www.havok.com

■ *This company develops gaming technology that is used in game development for the PlayStation2, Xbox, GameCube and the PC.*

Hewlett-Packard Ireland

Liffey Park Technology Campus, Barnhall Road, Leixlip, Co. Kildare

Managing Director: Martin Murphy

t. +353 1 615 0000

f. +353 1 615 8296

e. martin.murphy@hp.com

w. www.hp.com/ie

■ *This global IT company employs more than 4,200 at its Leixlip plant, providing ICT infrastructure to companies of all sizes. It also provides personal computers to customers.*

IBM Ireland (Sales and Marketing Office)

Oldbrook House, 24–32 Pembroke Road, Dublin 4
Managing Director: Michael Daly
  t. +353 1 815 4462
  f. +353 1 815 4040
  e. ibmenquire@ibm.com/ie
  w. www.ibm.com/ie
■ *The multinational IT company, established in Ireland in 1956, has 3,700 full-time employees, developing computer systems, software, network systems and microsystems.*

Intel

Collinstown Industrial Park, Leixlip, Co. Kildare
General Manager: Jim O'Hara
  t. +353 1 606 7000
  f. +353 1 606 7070
  w. www.intel.ie
■ *This multinational ICT company employs about 4,700 people at its Leixlip plant, its European manufacturing centre, where it produces microprocessrs and communication silicon chips.*

Irish Internet Association

The Digital Hub, Thomas Street, Dublin 8
Contact: Irene Gahan
  t. +353 1 453 5707
  e. irene@iia.ie
  w. www.iia.com
■ *Professional body for internet businesses.*

Journeyman Productions

The Digital Hub, Thomas Street, Dublin 8
Managing Director: Cóilín Ó Scolaí
  t. +353 1 4537644
  f. +353 1 4734586
  e. info@journeyman.ie
  w. www.journeymanproductions.com

■ *This is a full-service digital media production company, providing products and services for the audio-visual, publishing and interactive digital media market.*

Kapooki Games

5 Talbot Street, Dublin 1
Chief Executive Officer: Michael Griffin
  t. +353 1 874 5833
  f. +353 1 878 7919
  e. info@kapooki.com
  w. www.kapooki.com
■ *This is an Irish gaming company and a registered Xbox developer.*

Kavaleer Productions

The Digital Depot, Thomas Street, Dublin 8
Creative Directors: Andrew Kavanagh, Gary Timpson, Damien Byrne
  +353 1 488 5873
  f. +353 1 488 5801
  e. info@kaveleer.com
  w. www.kaveleer.com
■ *This is an animation and live-action production company.*

Kratos

The Digital Hub, Thomas Street, Dublin 8
Managing Director: Brian Whelan
  +353 1 6807100
  f. +353 1 6334658
  e. info@kratos.ie
  w. www.kratos.ie
■ *This company provides digital media products, training and support.*

Lightbox Multimedia

Digital Depot, The Digital Hub, Thomas Street, Dublin 8
Managing Director: Tom Hayes
  +353 1 489 3615
  f. +353 1 6335593
  e. info@lightbox.ie
  w. www.lightbox.ie
■ *This is a web site design and development company.*

Lincor Solutions

The Digital Hub, Thomas Street,
Dublin 8
Contact: Richard Cooke
  t. 353 1 477 5800
  e. info@lincor.ie
  w. www.lincor.com
■ *Digital media services for health care.*

Meteor

4030 Kingswood Avenue, Citywest
Business Park, Naas Road, Dublin 24
Chief Executive: Robert Haulbrook
  t. +353 1 4307000
  e. info@meteor.ie
  w. www.meteor.ie
■ *This is Ireland's third mobile phone operator.*

Microsoft Ireland

Carmanhall Road, Sandyford, Dublin 18
Directors: Matt Rossmessl, Paul Rellis,
Dermot Igoe, Joseph Macri, Kevin Fay
  t. +353 1 295 3826 and 1850 940940
  e. information@microsoft.ie
  w. www.microsoft.com/ireland
■ *This multinational software and internet technologies company employs 1,200 workers in Ireland.*

Mobile Tornado

The Digital Depot, Thomas Street,
Dublin 8
Contact: Stuart Kelly
  +353 1 489 3610
  f. +353 1 489 3620
  e. info@mobiletornado.com
  w. www.mobiletornado.com
■ *This company develops integrated voice and data solutions that are accelerating the employment of data services over current wireless networks and devices.*

Moving Media

The Digital Depot, Thomas Street,
Dublin 8,
Managing Director: Simon Factor
  +353 1 488 1487
  f. +353 1 488 1488

  e. email@movingmedia.ie
  w. www.movingmedia.tv
■ *Moving Media provide expert services to support the modernisation and preservation of sound and image collections by transferring them to digital file formats.*

Novell Ireland Software

Treasury Building, Lower Grand Canal
Street, Dublin 2
Directors: Lorcan Murtagh and Richard
Commins
  t. +353 605 8000
  f. +353 1 605 8200
  e. info_ireland@novell.com
  w. www.novell.com
■ *This multinational net systems company employs 108 people.*

NTL

Building P2, East Point Business Park,
Dublin 3
Managing Director: Graham Sutherland
  t. +353 1 245 8000
  f. +353 1 245 8001
  e. graham.sutherland@ntl.com
  w. www.ntl.ie
■ *This is a provider of cable television and telecommunications services, bought by the US company UGC in May 2005.*
Public Relations Manager: Anna-Maria
Barry
  e. annamaria.barry@ntl.ie

O2 Ireland

76 Lower Baggot Street, Dublin 2
Chief Executive: Danuta Grey
  t. +353 1 609 5000
  f. +353 1 609 5010
  e. w. www.o2.ie
■ *This mobile phone operator has almost 1.4 million customers and employs 1,450 people in Ireland.*
Head of Corporate Affairs: Johanna
Cassells
  e. johanna.cassells@o2.com

Phoenix Safety

The Digital Hub, 10–13 Thomas
Street, Dublin 8
Contact: Sean Fennell
  +353 1 4730550
  f. +353 1 4730566
  e. info@phoenixsafety.ie
  w. www.phoenixsafety.ie
■ *This company offers professional and consultancy services for implementing health and safety workplace programmes in a broad range of industries.*

PixAlert International

The Digital Hub, 10–13 Thomas
Street, Dublin 8
Contact: John Nolan
  +353 1 707 8860
  e. info@pixalert.com
  w. www.pixalert.com
■ *Digital media security company offering digital media management tools.*

Pixel Soup

The Digital Depot, Thomas Street,
Dublin 8
Contact: Philip Lynch
  +353 1 4736300
  f. +353 1 4736166
  e. info@pixelsoup.ie
  w. www.pixelsoup.ie
■ *This digital design company can deliver projects in a range of media, including DVD production, CD-Rom and web design.*

Recruit Ireland

97 South Mall, Cork
Managing Director: Tom Crosbie
  t. +353 21 491 0000
  f. +353 21 491 0099
  e. tom.crosbie@recruitireland.com
  w. www.recruitireland.com
■ *This is a jobs web site for employers and those seeking work, owned by Thomas Crosbie Holdings, owners of the* **Examiner** *and* **Sunday Business Post.**

Reverse Perspective

The Digital Depot, The Digital Hub,
Thomas Street, Dublin 8
Contact: Helen Maguire
  +353 1 639 1529
  e. info@reversespace.com
  w. www.reversespace.com
■ *This is a media company producing 3D full-colour holograms.*

Rí Productions

The Digital Hub, Thomas Street,
Dublin 8
Creative Director: Gordon Murphy
  e. info@ri-productions.com
  w. www.ri-productions.com
■ *Rí Productions is a digital communications company specialising in design and direction, with a particular emphasis on digital video.*

Screentime ShinAwiL

The Digital Depot, The Digital Hub,
Thomas Street, Dublin 8
Managing Director: Larry Bass
  +353 1 488 5855
  f. +353 1 488 5871
  e. info@shinawil.ie
  w. www.screentime.tv
■ *This is a specialist television production company operating in Australia, New Zealand, Ireland and the UK, producing drama, reality, infotainment, entertainment, game shows, documentaries and children's television.*

Selatra

National Software Centre,
Loughmahon, Blackrock, Co. Cork
Chief Executive: Sean Cronin
  t. +353 21 230 7180
  f. +353 21 230 7179
  e. info@selatra.com
  w. www.selatra.com
■ *Selatra publishes Java games for mobile phones and can also provide the associated technology for the delivery of these games to mobile phones globally.*

ShopAD

The Digital Hub, Thomas Street,
Dublin 8
Contact: Stephen Galvin
t. +353 1 679 3001
f. +353 1 679 3219
e. info@shopadz.com
w. www.shopadz.com
■ *This digital media company provides digital signage and in-store digital advertising for businesses.*

Siemens

Fitzwilliam Court, Leeson Close,
Dublin 2
t. +353 1 216 2000
f. +353 1 216 2399
e. infoireland@fujitsu-siemens.com
w. www.siemens.ie
■ *This electronics company provides services throughout the market, including the communications sector.*

Sky Ireland

Alexandra House, Earlsfort Terrace,
Dublin 2
Director: Mark Deering
t. +353 1 614 7666
f. +353 1 661 1402
e. news.ireland@bskyb.com
w. www.sky.com
■ *This is the Irish office of Sky News. BSkyB also sells satellite television to Irish audiences.*

Sonas Innovation (Sonasi)

The Digital Hub, Thomas Street,
Dublin 8
Contact: Fergal Marrinan
t. +353 1 679 3900
e. info@sonasi.com
w. www.sonasi.com
■ *This company provides consultancy on and develops e-government strategies and systems for public and private-sector clients.*

Space Synapse

The Digital Depot, The Digital Hub,
Thomas Street, Dublin 8
Managing Director: Anna Hill
t. +353 1 488 5853
e. anna@spacesynapse.com
w. www.spacesynapse.com
■ *This company makes artistic work that is influenced by the meeting of art, science and innovation.*

Sportsbrand Media

The Digital Depot, Thomas Street,
Dublin 8
Contact: Conor Gallagher
+353 1 489 3616
f. +353 1 488 5801
e. team@sportsbrandmedia.com
w. www.sportsbrandmedia.com
■ *This company aims to create more innovative brand strategy and design within the sports industry.*

TKO Software

The Digital Hub, Thomas Street,
Dublin 8
General Manager: Will Golby
e. pr@tko-software.com
w. www.tko-software.com
■ *This video game production company develops games on consoles, personal computers and wireless phone handsets.*

Torc Interactive

Drumhaggart, Muff, Co. Donegal
Producer: Tony Kelly
t. +353 74 936 8603
e. info@torcinteractive.com
w. www.torcinteractive.com
■ *This is an Irish gaming company established in Co. Donegal.*

Twelve Horses

The Digital Hub, Thomas Street,
Dublin 8
Contact: David Malone
t. +353 1 2402500
f. +353 1 240 2555
e. info@twelvehorses.net
w. www.twelvehorses.com
■ *Twelve Horses is a leading provider of e-mail and web-based marketing and business automation solutions.*

Upstart Games

1–2 Exchange Street, Dublin 2
Chief Executive Officer: Barry O'Neill
t. +353 1 674 6323
f. +353 1 629 5199
e. info@upstartgames.com
w. www.upstartgames.com
■ *This company develops and publishes games played on mobile phones and has offices in Ireland, Japan and the United States.*

Vodafone Ireland

Mountain View, Leopardstown, Dublin 18
Chief Executive: Teresa Elder
t. +353 1 203 7777
e. pressoffice@vodaphone.com
w. www.vodafone.ie
■ *This international mobile phone operator has 1.8 million customers in Ireland and employs 1,500 people.*
Press Officer: Tara Delaney

Xwerx

Digital Depot, Digital Hub, Dublin 8
Contact: Sean Murphy
t. +353 1 489 3646
e. info@xwerx.com
w. www.xwerx.com
■ *This is a multimedia company.*

Zamano

Digital Depot, Digital Hub, Thomas Street, Dublin 8
Contact: Eoin Ó Ceallacháin
t. +353 1 488 5820
f. +353 1 488 5821
e. info@zamano.com
w. www.zamano.com
■ *This company provides mobile applications to mobile network operators, B2C brands, retail chains, media companies and enterprise customers.*

Zenark

Digital Hub, Thomas Street, Dublin 8
Contact: Gary Noone
t. +353 1 415 0933
e. info@zenark.com
w. www.zenark.com
■ *This company designs and supplies tailored software services for clients in multiple industries, including media, financial, print management, entertainment and software development.*

Zink Films

Digital Hub, Thomas Street, Dublin 8
Contact: Gary O'Neill
t. +353 1 488 5845
e. gary@zincfilms.com
w. www.zincfilms.com

6

BOOKS: READING THE FUTURE

Dr Mark O'Brien

The books landscape

Until the 1970s the Irish books world was small. The publishing landscape was marked by few bookshops and even fewer publishers. Small print runs were the norm and fewer than 200 titles were published in any given year. But things changed gradually from the mid-1960s. The closed intellectual climate of de Valera's Ireland began to dissipate as Ireland embraced free trade under Seán Lemass. As foreign investment flooded into the country, Ireland changed culturally. Urbanisation, greater participation of women in the work force, free second-level education, the emergence of Irish television and the relaxation of censorship provisions in 1967 challenged the old certainties. It was, as one writer observed, 'a time for questioning: how, why, when?'

In this environment, the publishing industry made editions of formerly banned works available to an increasingly educated and literate public. This, coupled with the emergence of new writers, new publishing houses and greater print runs, saw the publishing industry grow from strength to strength. Its share of the home market—traditionally dominated by British publishers—rose steadily as the range, diversity and quality of books increased year by year. By the turn of the century, the boom years of the Celtic Tiger, Irish publishers were producing nearly a thousand new titles a year. There are now more than eight thousand different titles in print.

Among the most prominent publishing houses in Ireland are Blackstaff Press, Four Courts Press and Gill & Macmillan. Other prominent publishing houses include Brandon Books, Lilliput Press, O'Brien Press, Poolbeg

Press and Townhouse. New publishing houses continue to emerge, such as the Liffey Press and Liberties Press. Within the university publishing sector, Cork University Press and UCD Press are significant. In recent years several international publishers have set up Irish offices, dramatically changing the face of publishing and giving Irish writers new access to the UK market. Among the better-known arrivals are Penguin Ireland and Hodder Headline. Prospective authors should check the web sites of individual publishing houses for information on the types of books published and book proposal protocols, but the best advice is to get a good agent.

Book publishers in Ireland are collectively represented by CLÉ (the Irish Book Publishers' Association), which is a cross-border body founded in 1970. With fifty-four members, the membership of CLÉ has increased in recent years. It now includes most of the major publishing houses in Ireland, with a mixture of trade, general, legal and academic publishers. As a trade association it has an interest in legislative and other influences on the industry's working environment. It provides publishers with a platform from which to discuss issues of common concern and also promotes the publications of its members at various book fairs around the world. CLÉ in turn is a member of the International Publishers' Association and the Federation of European Publishers.

The growth in overseas sales of Irish works (usually fiction or memoirs) is helped in no small way by the Ireland Literature Exchange, which is funded by the Arts Council, the Arts Council of Northern Ireland, Bord na Leabhar Gaeilge and the government's Cultural Relations Committee. Founded in 1994, it has helped fund the translation of more than five hundred titles into forty languages. The criteria for translation funding are simple: the book must be clearly identifiable as a work of Irish literature, although the subject itself need not be concerned with Ireland. In recent years the South American and Asian markets have become the focus of translation activity, in order to expand these markets.

The books market

Relative to its size, Ireland has a healthy book publishing industry. Although there are dominant participants in the market, the greater availability of publishing technology has ensured the growth of many independent publishing houses with niche markets. While the home market is undoubtedly the most important market for all publishers, overseas trade has also become an increasingly important source of revenue. The late

1980s and early 1990s witnessed a huge growth in international interest in Irish books, helped in no small way by the advent of the internet and book clubs aimed at the Irish diaspora. Between 1994 and 2000, total exports grew from €3.55 million to €6.35 million. After the terror attacks in New York in 2001, and with the euro rising against the dollar, the export market fell back towards the 1994 level.

Home and export markets (€m)

	2003	2000	1997	1994
Home	72.73 (93.8%)	56.88 (90%)	44.19 (88.5%)	38.6 (91.6%)
European Union	2.85 (3.7%)	4.7 (7.4%)	4.19 (8.4%)	2.41 (5.7%)
Non-EU	1.96 (2.5%)	1.65 (2.6%)	1.52 (3.1%)	1.14 (2.7%)
Total	77.54	63.23	49.90	42.16

Source: CLÉ (Irish Book Publishers' Association). Value of Irish-published works only.

The book market in Ireland is broadly segmented into two distinct sectors, the educational market (primary, secondary and third-level books) and the general market (fiction, non-fiction and children's publications). Over the last ten years, sales in both sectors have grown each year. The total (home and exports) sales for both sectors increased from €42.16 million in 1994 to €77.54 million in 2003. In the educational market, sales jumped from €29.08 million in 1994 to €54.03 million in 2003. While sales in the all three segments of the educational market increased, the most pronounced increase was in the primary school book segment, as a result of the introduction of several new curriculums.

Educational market (€m)

	2003	2000	1997	1994
Primary	21.99 (40.7%)	14.22 (34.5%)	9.52 (29.4%)	8.89 (30.6%)
Secondary	29.44 (54.5%)	24.38 (59.1%)	21.20 (65.5%)	18.54 (63.8%)
Third-level	2.60 (4.8%)	2.67 (6.5%)	1.65 (5.1%)	1.65 (5.7%)
Total	54.03	41.27	32.38	29.08

Source: CLÉ (Irish Book Publishers' Association). Value of Irish-published works only.

Likewise, all three segments of the general market (fiction, non-fiction and children's publications) experienced sales growth between 1994 and 1997. The largest increase was experienced in the sale of works of non-fiction, which increased from €10.41 million in 1994 to €18.27 million in 2003. The fiction segment also experienced an increase in sales, growing from €1.52 million to €3.44 million over the same period.

General (non-educational) market (€m)

	2003	2000	1997	1994
Non-fiction	18.27 (77.7%)	16.38 (75.9%)	13.97 (79.7%)	10.41 (79.6%)
Fiction	3.44 (14.6%)	3.43 (15.9%)	2.29 (13%)	1.52 (11.7%)
Children's	1.80 (7.6%)	1.78 (8.2%)	1.27 (7.2%)	1.14 (8.7%)
Total	23.51	21.59	17.52	13.08

Source: CLÉ (Irish Book Publishers' Association). Value of Irish-published works only.

The general market continues to depend heavily on affluent professional consumers for the bulk of its sales. 'Heavy book buyers'—those who buy ten or more books a year—represent an important part of the market. The book-buying habit is spread through all age ranges, but there is a slightly higher propensity to buy books among those aged between 25 and 54 than among other groups. Autobiographies are among the most popular choices, for those buying non-fiction, while romance novels and the 'chick-lit' genre of 'Brigid Jones' remain popular among fiction buyers. Ireland's romance writers, from Maeve Binchy, Deirdre Purcell and Patricia Scanlon to today's mix of Sheila O'Flanagan, Cathy Kelly and Cecelia Ahern, have proved to be excellent exports, while in other fiction, Colm Tóibín and Joe O'Connor are both international sellers.

Future trends

There are several concerns facing Irish publishers. How to strengthen growth in the home and overseas markets is of primary concern. Likewise, the pressure from booksellers to increase the discount (profit margin) from publishers is omnipresent. As with the newspaper industry, the issue of libel is of crucial concern to non-fiction book publishers. One libel action is enough to put a severe, even fatal, strain on most publishing houses. This creates a 'chilling effect' that makes publishers avoid areas of legitimate public interest. Very often publishers cannot afford to fight cases, as the chances of recovering their legal costs from unsuccessful plaintiffs are very slim. Nonetheless, with the emergence of a new generation of successful Irish writers, the future of the Irish publishing industry looks stable. The real challenge for the book publishing industry will be its relationship with the new media world. As more and more homes go broadband, people will seek more information in multimedia formats that can be used in interactive ways, similar to the way DVDs have enhanced the film and television market by offering consumers more. The publishing companies that embrace the online challenge and see their content appearing in both traditional book and multimedia forms are more likely to swim in the sea of digital convergence.

Top ten fiction books sold in the Republic of Ireland, 2004

	Author	Publisher	Number sold	Price
The Da Vinci Code	Brown, Dan	Corgi	131,359	€9.54
Angels and Demons	Brown, Dan	Corgi	54,816	€10.04
PS, I Love You	Ahern, Cecelia	HarperCollins	43,148	€13.71
Where Rainbows End	Ahern, Cecelia	HarperCollins	42,210	€13.15
The Curious Incident of the Dog in the Night-Time	Haddon, Mark	Vintage	40,829	€9.45
The Star of the Sea	O'Connor, Joseph	Vintage	37,287	€9.98
PS, I Love You	Ahern, Cecelia	HarperCollins	34,467	€9.64
Digital Fortress	Brown, Dan	Corgi	34,443	€9.42
Deception Point	Brown, Dan	Corgi	25,813	€10.11
Two for Joy	Scanlan, Patricia	Bantam Books	22,464	€9.54

Source: Neilsen BookScan.

Top ten non-fiction books sold in the Republic of Ireland, 2004

	Author	Publisher	Number sold	Price
You Are What You Eat: The Plan That Will Change Your Life	McKeith, Gillian	Michael Joseph	37,247	€17.21
A Short History of Nearly Everything	Bryson, Bill	Black Swan	31,208	€12.32
From Dún Síon to Croke Park: The Autobiography	Ó Muircheartaigh, Mícheál	Penguin Ireland	26,525	€20.29
The Bookseller of Kabul	Seierstad, Asne	Virago	23,066	€10.13
The Official Driver Theory Test		Prometric Ireland	22,021	€16.64
Eats, Shoots and Leaves: The Zero Tolerance Approach to Punctuation	Truss, Lynne	Profile Books	21,238	€14.49
Rules of the Road		Department of the Environment	20,705	€2.50
Guinness World Records, 2005		Guinness	20,470	€17.40
My Life	Clinton, Bill	Hutchinson	14,348	€30.07
Dublin City and District Street Guide	Ordnance Survey	Ordnance Survey of Ireland	13,876	€11.43

Source: Neilsen BookScan.

Republic of Ireland

A & A Farmar
Beech House, 78 Ranelagh, Dublin 6
t. +353 1 496 3625
f. +353 1 497 0107
e. afarmar@iol.ie
w. www.farmarbooks.com
■ *Publisher of non-fiction books on food and wine, Irish interest, Irish literature and social history.*
Directors: Anna Farmar and Tony Farmar

Advance Publications (APL Group)
Acorn House, 38 St Peter's Road, Dublin 7
General Enquiries
t. +353 1 868 6640
f. +353 1 868 6651
e. info@aplgroup.net
w. www.aplgroup.net
■ *Publisher of in-house publications for businesses and associations, including association yearbooks, catalogues, annual reports, monthly magazines and organisation handbooks.*

An Gúm
27 North Frederick Street, Dublin 1
t. +353 1 889 2800
f. +353 1 873 1140
e. angum@forasnagaeilge.ie
w. www.gaeilge.ie
■ *Publisher of Irish-language books, with academic, children's, educational, fiction, textbook, music, dictionary (general and terminology) titles.*
Executive Officer: Barra Mac Aodha Bhuí

Anvil Books
45 Palmerston Road, Dublin 6
t. +353 1 497 3628
e. dardisanvil@eircom.net
■ *Publisher of books for children and historical non-fiction (especially the period 1916 to 1924).*
Managing Director: Rena Dardis

Arlen House
PO Box 222, Galway
t. +353 86 820 7617
f. +353 86 820 7617
e. arlenhouse@ireland.com
■ *Publisher of books in feminist and academic areas.*
Publisher: Alan Hayes

Ashville Media Group
Apollo House, Tara Street, Dublin 2
t. +353 1 432 2200
f. +353 1 672 7100
e. info@ashville.com
w. www.ashville.com
■ *Publisher of magazines, yearbooks and diaries, periodicals and books for businesses.*
Editor: Meg Walker

Association of Freelance Editors, Proofreaders and Indexers (AFEPI)
w. www.afepi.ie
■ *Trade organisation, providing information on freelances working in publishing and protecting the interests of members.*
Joint Chairs:
Brenda O'Hanlon
t. +353 1 295 2194
e. brenda@ohanlonmediaservices.com
Priscilla O'Connor
t. +353 1 6012846
e. priscillaoconnor@eircom.net

Attic Press
Youngline Industrial Estate, Pouladuff Road, Togher, Cork
t. +353 21 490 2980
f. +353 21 431 5329
e. corkuniversitypress@ucc.ie
w. www.corkuniversitypress.com
■ *A subsidiary of Cork University Press and publisher of books on Irish and women's studies, history, fiction, health and life-style, and practical reference books.*

Editor: Tom Dunne
  e. tdunne@ucc.ie
General Enquiries: as Cork University
Press
  t. www.corkuniversitypress.com

Ballylough Books

Chestnut Lodge, Callaghane,
Co. Waterford
  t. +353 51 38 2538
  f. +353 51 38 2538
  e. ballyloughbooks@eircom.net
  w. homepage.eircom.net/~ballylough-books
■ *Publisher of books about Waterford, along with autobiographies and anthologies.*
Publisher: Tom Fewer

Blackhall Publishing

33 Carysfort Avenue, Blackrock,
Co. Dublin
  t. +353 1 278 5090
  f. +353 1 278 4446
  e. blackhall@eircom.net
  w. www.blackhallpublishing.com
■ *Publisher of business, management and law books.*
General Enquiries: Ruth Garvey

Blackwater Press

Hibernian Industrial Estate, Greenhills
Road, Tallaght, Dublin 24
  t. +353 1 413 7200
  f. +353 1 413 7280
  e. audrey.keating@folens.ie
  w. www.folens.ie
■ *Publisher of books including biography, political commentary, sport, children's and general fiction, reference and humour. An imprint of Folens Publishers.*
Publisher: John O'Connor

Bradshaw Books

Tigh Filí, Thompson House,
MacCurtain Street, Cork
  t. +353 21 450 9274
  f. +353 21 455 1617
  e. admin@cwpc.ie
  w. www.tighfili.com
■ *Publisher of poetry books.*
General Enquiries: Máire Bradshaw

Brandon Books

Brandon/Mount Eagle, PO Box 32,
Cooleen, Co. Kerry
  t. +353 66 915 1463
  f. +353 66 915 1234
  w. www.brandonbooks.com
■ *Publisher of fiction and non-fiction books in the areas of biography, memoirs, popular history, current affairs and modern politics.*
Editorial Director: Steve MacDonogh

Breacadh

Casla, Co. na Gaillimhe
  t. +353 91 50 6952
  f. +353 91 50 6951
  e. breacadh@eircom.net
  w. www.breacadh.ie
■ *Publisher of Irish-language books.*
Manager: Nóirín Ní Ghrádaigh

Celtic Publications

16 Grove Lawn, Malahide,
Co. Dublin
  t. +353 1 845 6860
  f. +353 1 816 8680
  e. info@celticpublications.com
  w. www.celticpublications.com
■ *Publisher of books and other educational materials to promote Ireland as a destination for learning English as a foreign language, and Irish history, music, art and culture.*
Publisher: Marianne Quinn

Childnames.net

27 Villarea Park, Glenageary, Co.
Dublin
  t. +353 87 936 9888
  e. info@childnames.net
  w. www.childnames.net
■ *Publisher of books for children and books of children's names.*
General Enquiries: John Gallagher

Children's Press

45 Palmerston Road, Dublin 6
t. +353 1 497 3628
f. +353 1 496 8263
e. dardisanvil@eircom.net
■ *Publishes children's and young adults' books. An imprint of Anvil Books.*
Publisher: Rena Dardis

Church of Ireland Publishing

Church of Ireland House, Church Avenue, Dublin 6
t. +353 1 492 3979
f. +353 1 492 4770
e. susan.hood@rcbdub.org
w. www.ireland.anglican.org
■ *Publisher of books and leaflets on Church of Ireland regulations, church history and genealogy in Ireland.*
Publications Officer: Susan Hood

Cló Iar-Chonnachta

Indreabhán, Co. na Gaillimhe
t. +353 91 59 3307
f. +353 91 59 3362
e. cic@iol.ie
w. www.cic.ie
■ *Publisher of Irish-language books and music. Books include anthologies of poetry, short stories and songs, novels, teenage fiction, children's books, theses and history books. Some books are published in English or in English and Irish. Many titles are available in audio format. Publishes music, including traditional, sean-nós from all over Ireland, Cajun, country and Cape Breton.*
General Manager: Deirdre O'Toole

Coiscéim

Tig Bhríde, 91 Howth Road, Dublin 13
t. +353 1 832 0131
■ *Irish-language publisher. Recent titles have been poetry, novels and short stories, children's books, quiz books, memoirs and reference works.*
Publisher: Pádraig Ó Snodaigh

Cois Life

62 Rose Park, Dún Laoghaire, Co. Dublin
t. +353 1 280 7951
f. +353 1 280 7951
e. eolas@coislife.ie
w. www.coislife.ie
■ *Publisher of literary and academic works in Irish. Recent titles have included books for learners of Irish and books in the areas of young people, plays, fiction and poetry. Academic monographs are also published, in the series Lúb ar Phár.*
Directors: Caoilfhionn Nic Pháidín and Seán Ó Cearnaigh

Collins Press

West Link Park, Doughcloyne, Wilton, Cork
t. +353 21 434 7717
f. +353 21 434 7720
e. enquiries@collinspress.ie
w. www.collinspress.ie
■ *Publisher of a wide range of mostly non-fiction books. Recent titles have been in the areas of history, archaeology, photography, biography, walking guides, fiction and general Irish interest.*
Publisher: Con Collins

ColourBooks

105 Baldoyle Industrial Estate, Dublin 13
t. +353 1 832 5812
f. +353 1 832 5825
e. sales@colourbooks.ie
w. www.colourbooks.ie
■ *Book printer supplying publishers in Ireland and Europe.*
Sales Executive: Gerry Kelly

Columba Press

55A Spruce Avenue, Stillorgan Industrial Park, Blackrock, Co. Dublin
t. +353 1 294 2556
f. +353 1 294 2564
e. sean@columba.ie
w. www.columba.ie

■ *Publisher of books on spirituality, religion, history, counselling and the arts. European distributor for several American and Canadian publishers. Irish distributor for British and Irish imprints.*
Publisher: Seán O Boyle
t. +353 1 294 2556 (ext 207)

Cork University Press

Youngline Industrial Estate, Pouladuff Road, Togher, Cork
t. +353 21 490 2980
f. +353 21 431 5329
e. corkuniversitypress@ucc.ie
w. www.corkuniversitypress.com or www.corkuniversity.org
■ *Publisher of academic books. Recent titles have been in the areas of Irish studies, Irish cultural history, archaeology, landscape studies, music, art history, literary criticism and poetry.*
Publications Director: Mike Collins
e. mike.collins@ucc.ie
Editorial Manager: Tom Dunne
e. t.dunne@ucc.ie

Cumann Leabharfhoilsitheoirí Éireann (CLÉ)

25 Denzille Lane, Dublin 2
t. +353 56 775 6333
e. info@publishingireland.com
w. www.publishingireland.com
■ *Irish Book Publishers' Association, including trade, general, legal and academic publishers.*
Administrator: Jolly Ronan

Currach Press

55A Spruce Avenue, Stillorgan Industrial Park, Blackrock, Co. Dublin
t. +353 1 294 2556
f. +353 1 294 2564
e. info@currach.ie
w. www.currach.ie
■ *Publisher and imprint of the Columba Bookservice. Recent titles have been in the areas of Irish history, biography, politics, current affairs, sport, music and the arts.*
Publisher: Brian Lynch
m. +353 86 821 4842

Dedalus Press

13 Moyclare Road, Dublin 13
t: +353 1 8392034
f: +44 870 127 2089
e. info@dedaluspress.com
w. www.dedaluspress.com
■ *Publisher of new Irish poetry and poetry in translation in various European languages.*
General Enquiries: Pat Boran

Drumlin Publications

Nure, Manorhamilton, Co. Leitrim
t. +353 71 985 5237
f. +353 71 985 6063
e. drumlin@eircom.net
w. www.drumlinpublications.com
■ *Publisher of Irish-language and English-language books. Recent titles have been in the areas of Irish culture, history, religion, poetry, dancing and music.*
Publisher: Proinnsíos Ó Duigneáin

Dublin Institute of Advanced Studies (School of Celtic Studies)

10 Burlington Road, Dublin 4
t. +353 1 668 0748
f. +353 1 668 0561
e. mriordan@celt.dias.ie
w. www.dias.ie
■ *Irish-language and Celtic-language publisher. Publishes bibliographies, manuscripts, periodicals, collections and information bulletins on the Irish language, Irish literature, Irish history and genealogy, Welsh, Breton and Hiberno-Latin.*
Publications Officer: Michelle O'Riordan

Educational Company of Ireland

Ballymount Road, Dublin 12
t. +353 1 450 0611
f. +353 1 450 0993
e. info@edco.ie
w. www.edco.ie
■ *Publisher of primary and post-primary educational books. Titles are in the areas of English, Irish, mathematics, SESE/SPHE, history, geography, science, music, business, French, home economics, CSPE, technology,*

accountancy, biology and graphics. Exam paper books are also published.

Senior Editor: Clíona Ní Bhréartúin

European Foundation

Wyattville Road, Loughlinstown,
Co. Dublin
t. +353 1 204 3240
f. +353 1 282 6456
w. www.eurofound.eu.int
■ *Publisher of studies and position papers on European social policy in English and other languages of the European Union.*

Editor in Chief: Mary McCaughey
e. mcu@eurofound.eu.int
Editor: Hilary O'Donoghue
e. hod@eurofound.eu.int
Editor: Linda Longmore
e. llo@eurofound.eu.int
Editorial Assistant: Clare Deasley
e. cde@eurofound.eu.int

Flax Mill Publications

34 Ballypark, Flax Mill Lane,
Drogheda, Co. Louth
t. +353 41 982 6221/984 2071
■ *Publisher of books in the areas of feminism, spirituality, geography and landscape features.*

Flyleaf Press

4 Spencer Villas, Glenageary, Co.
Dublin
t. +353 1 284 5906
e. flyleaf@indigo.ie
w. www.flyleaf.ie
■ *Publisher of books on Irish genealogy and family history.*

Managing Editor: Jim Ryan

Four Courts Press

7 Malpas Street, Dublin 8
t. +353 1 453 4668
f. +353 1 453 4672
e. info@four-courts-press.ie
w. www.four-courts-press.ie
■ *Publisher of academic books in the areas of Celtic and medieval studies, ecclesiastical history, modern history, art, literature and law. Also publishes under the Open Air imprint.*

Managing Director and Publisher:
Michael Adams
Marketing, Promotion and Foreign
Rights: Ronan Gallagher
Editorial Production: Martin Fanning

Gallery Press

Loughcrew, Oldcastle, Co. Meath
t. +353 49 854 1779 (+fax)
e. gallery@indigo.ie
w. www.gallerypress.com
■ *Publisher of books of poetry, plays and prose by contemporary Irish authors.*

General Enquiries: Peter Fallon

Geography Publications

24 Kennington Road, Dublin 6W
t. +353 1 456 6085
f. +353 1 456 6085
e. info@geographypublications.com
w. www.geographypublications.com
■ *Publisher of books on Irish history, geography and biography.*

Gill & Macmillan

Hume Avenue, Park West, Dublin 12
t. +353 1 500 9500
f. +353 1 500 9599
w. www.gillmacmillan.ie
■ *Publisher of fiction and non-fiction books and educational textbooks. Imprints: Tivoli, Newleaf and Gateway. Provides distribution services to other Irish publishers.*

General Enquiries
e. info@gillmacmillan.ie
General Non-Fiction Publishing: Fergal
Tobin
e. ftobin@gillmacmillan.ie
University and College Publishing and
Further Education and PLC Publishing:
Marion O'Brien
e. mobrien@gillmacmillan.ie
School Publishing: Hubert Mahony
e. hmahony@gillmacmillan.ie
School Publishing: Anthony Murray
e. amurray@gillmacmillan.ie

Government Publications

51 St Stephen's Green, Dublin 2
t. +353 1 453 1588
f. +353 1 478 0645
e. fintan.butler@opw.ie
w. www.irlgov.ie
■ *Publisher of government reports and books
on all aspects of Irish government.*
Assistant Director: Fintan Butler

Hodder Headline Ireland

Unit 8 Castlecourt Shopping Centre,
Castleknock, Dublin 15
t. +353 1 824 6288
f. +353 1 824 6289
e. info@hhireland.ie
w. www.hhireland.ie
■ *Publisher of Irish non-fiction and fiction,
popular and literary books; the Irish division of
the Hodder Headline Group.*
Managing Director: Breda Purdue
  e. breda.purdue@hhireland.ie
Publisher: Ciara Considine
  e. ciara.considine@hhireland.ie
Senior Editor: Claire Rourke
  e. claire.rourke@hhireland.ie
Sales Manager: Ruth Shern
  e. ruth.shern@hhireland.ie

Institute of Public Administration

Vergemount Hall, Clonskeagh,
Dublin 6
t. +353 1 240 3600
f. +353 1 269 8644
w. www.ipa.ie
■ *Publisher of books and periodicals on
public service administration and management.
Titles cover the following themes: economics,
education, government and politics, health
care management, international affairs, law,
local government, personnel, public affairs
and social administration. Publishes the*
Administration Yearbook and Diary.
General Enquiries: Eileen Kelly
  e. ekelly@ipa.ie

Irish Academic Press

44 Northumberland Road, Dublin 4
t. +353 1 668 8244
f. +353 1 660 1610
e. info@iap.ie
w. www.iap.ie
■ *Publisher of academic books.*
General Enquiries: Rachel Milotte

Irish Times Books

4th Floor, Ballast House, Aston Quay,
Dublin 2
t. +353 1 472 7125
f. +353 1 472 7110
e. noconnor@irish-times.com
w. www.ireland.com
■ *Publisher of books, including reprints from
the* **Irish Times,** *humour, satire and genealogy.*
General Enquiries: Niall O'Connor

Kerryman

Clash Industrial Estate, Tralee, Co. Kerry
t. +353 66 712 1666
f. +353 66 714 5570
w. www.kerryman.ie
■ *Publisher of non-fiction books in the areas
of Irish history and poetry.*
Editor: Declan Malone
  e. ads@kerryman.ie

Liberties Press

51 Stephens Road, Dublin 8
t. +353 1 838 6383
w. www.libertiespress.com
■ *Publisher of non-fiction books in areas
including sport, health, food, music, history and
politics.*
General Enquiries
  info@libertiespress.com
Editorial Director: Seán O'Keeffe
  sean@libertiespress.com

The Liffey Press

Ashbrook House, 10 Main Street,
Raheny, Dublin 5
t. +353 1 851 1458
f. +353 1 851 1459
e. info@theliffeypress.com
w. www.theliffeypress.com

■ *Publisher of Irish-focused non-fiction books in the areas of culture, social policy, arts and literature, current events, politics, education, economics and related fields.*
Managing Director: David Givens

Lilliput Press

62–63 Sitric Road, Dublin 7
t. +353 1 671 1647
f. +353 1 671 1233
e. info@lilliputpress.ie
w. www.lilliputpress.ie
■ *Publisher of books with a broad Irish theme on art and architecture, autobiography and memoirs, biography and history, ecology and environmentalism, essays and literary criticism, philosophy, current affairs and popular culture, fiction, drama and poetry.*
Publisher: Antony Farrell

Martello Press

6 Brookfield Avenue, Blackrock,
Co. Dublin
t. +353 1 288 7317
f. +353 1 288 7353
e. info@martellopress.ie
w. www.martellopress.ie
■ *Provides lithographic and digital printing, graphic design and typesetting.*
Managing Director: Joe Behan

Maverick House

Main Street, Dunshaughlin,
Co. Meath
t. +353 1 824 0077
f. +353 1 824 1746
e. info@maverickhouse.com
w. www.maverickhouse.com
■ *Publisher of non-fiction and current affairs books.*
Managing Director: Jean Harrington

Media Publications

21 Main Street, Blackrock, Co. Dublin
t. +353 1 283 2401
f. +353 1 283 3899
e. mediapub@eircom.net
■ *Publisher of the* **Irish Media Guide,** *a free annual guide to the Irish media, distrib-uted to listed companies.*
Publisher: Mark O'Donoghue

Mentor Publications Ltd

43 Furze Road, Sandyford Industrial Estate, Dublin 18
t. +353 1 295 2112
f. +353 1 295 2114
e. all@mentorbooks.ie
w. www.mentorbooks.ie
■ *Publisher of fiction and non-fiction adult and children's books and educational materials.*
Managing Director: Danny McCarthy

Mercier Press

Douglas Village, Cork
t. +353 21 489 9858
f. +353 21 489 9887
e. books@mercierpress.ie
w. www.mercierpress.ie
■ *Publisher of non-fiction books on history, folklore and politics.*
CEO: Clodagh Feehan

Merlin Publishing

16 Upper Pembroke Street, Dublin 2
t. +353 1 676 4373
f. +353 1 676 4368
w. www.merlin-publishing.com
■ *Publisher of non-fiction books in areas including politics, history, crime and humour. Also publishes under the Wolfhound Press imprint.*
Sales and Marketing Manager: Chenile Keogh
e. ChenileK@merlin.ie

National Gallery of Ireland

Merrion Square, Dublin 2
t. +353 1 663 3518
f. +353 1 661 9898
e. bookshop@ngi.ie
w. www.nationalgallery.ie
■ *Publisher of art, art education and art col-lection catalogues.*
Retail and Publications Manager:
Lydia Furlong

National Library of Ireland Publications

Kildare Street, Dublin 2
t. +353 1 603 0200
f. +353 1 676 6690
e. coflaherty@nli.ie
w. www.nli.ie
■ *Publisher of books, booklets and packs of facsimile documents that are especially suitable for school use, as well as collections of literary and cultural interest.*
General Enquiries: Colette O'Flaherty

New Island Books

2 Brookside, Dundrum Road, Dublin 14
t. +353 1 298 9937
f. +353 1 298 7912
w. www.newisland.ie
■ *Publisher of fiction and non-fiction books in the literary and political areas.*
Editor: Deirdre Nolan
e. editor@newisland.ie
Publicity and Production: Fidelma Slattery
e. fidelma.slattery@newisland.ie
Publicity and Marketing Manager: Joseph Hoban
e. joseph.hoban@newisland.ie

Oak Tree Press

19 Rutland Street, Cork
t. +353 21 431 3855
f. +353 21 431 3496
e. info@oaktreepress.com
w. www.oaktreepress.com
■ *Publisher of business books and other publications.*
General Enquiries: Brian O'Kane

O'Brien Press

20 Victoria Road, Dublin 6
t. +353 1 492 3333
f. +353 1 492 2777
e. books@obrien.ie
w. www.obrien.ie
■ *Publisher of adult and children's fiction and non-fiction books.*
Managing Director: Michael O'Brien

Ordnance Survey Ireland

Phoenix Park, Dublin 8
t. +353 1 802 5300
w. www.osi.ie
■ *Producer of urban, rural, tourist and leisure mapping and publisher of information on geodetic services, papers on the new co-ordinate system and more general publications. All publications are available as PDF files.*
Chief Executive: Richard Kirwan
e. richard.kirwan@osi.ie

Penguin Ireland

25 St Stephen's Green, Dublin 2
t. +353 1 661 7695
f. +353 1 661 7696
e. info@penguin.ie
w. www.penguin.ie
■ *Publisher of Irish-interest literary and commercial fiction and non-fiction books.*
Editor: Brendan Barrington
t. +353 1 661 7693
e. brendan.barrington@penguin.ie
Managing Director: Michael McLoughlin
t. +353 1 661 7690
e. michael.mcloughlin@penguin.ie
Senior Editor: Patricia Deevy
t. +353 1 661 7699
e. patricia.deevy@penguin.ie

Philomel Productions

1 Queen's Gate Place Mews, London SW7 5BG, England
t. +44 207 581 2303
f. +44 207 589 2264
e. philomelbooks@hotmail.com
■ *Publisher based in the UK and Ireland. Recent titles have been in the areas of cognition and cognitive psychology; fairy tales, folk tales, fables, magical tales and traditional stories; Indo-European languages; general literary studies; literary history and criticism; modern fiction; works by individual poets (from the nineteenth century); early learning and early learning concepts.*
Director (Ireland): Dónall Ó Riagáin
e. oriagain@gofree.indigo.ie

Poolbeg

123 Grange Hill, Baldoyle Industrial
Estate, Dublin 13
t. +353 1 832 1477
f. +353 1 832 1430
e. poolbeg@.poolbeg.com
w. www.poolbeg.com
■ *Publisher of fiction and non-fiction books and provider of online bookshop.*
Publisher: Paula Campbell

Prim-Ed Publishing

Bosheen, New Ross, Co. Wexford
t. +353 51 440 075
f. +353 51 422 982
e. sales@prim-ed.com
w. www.prim-ed.com
■ *Publisher of photocopiable teaching resources for primary school and special-needs lower secondary pupils, written by practising classroom teachers.*

Rathbane Publishing (Cló an Rátha Bháin)

Atlantic View House, Lisdoonvarna,
Co. Clare
t. +353 65 707 4486
e. rathbane@iol.ie
w. www.iol.ie/~rathbane
■ *Publisher of books and other material connected with North Clare and the Burren.*
Editors: John Doorty and Kit Uí Chéirín

Relay Books

Tyone, Nenagh, Co. Tipperary
t. +353 67 31 734
f. +353 67 31 734
e. relaybooks@eircom.net
■ *Publisher of books relating to the local history of North Tipperary.*
Publisher: Donal A. Murphy

Royal Irish Academy

19 Dawson Street, Dublin 2
t. +353 1 676 2570
f. +353 1 676 2346
e. info@ria.ie
w. www.ria.ie
■ *Publisher of books, scholarly journals, series and monographs. Titles are in the areas of language, history, archaeology and sciences.*
General Enquiries: Hugh Sheils
e. h.shiels@ria.ie

Salmon Publishing

Knockeven, Doolin, Co. Clare
t. +353 65 708 1941
f. +353 65 708 1941
e. info@salmonpoetry.com
w. www.salmonpoetry.com
■ *Publisher of books of Irish poetry.*

Sitric Books

62–63 Sitric Road, Dublin 7
t. +353 1 671 1682
f. +353 1 671 1233
w. www.sitric.com
■ *Subsidiary of Lilliput Press and publisher of fiction and non-fiction books for a young and modern readership. Recent titles have been in areas including journalism, first-person narratives, crime fiction and popular mass-market women's fiction.*
General Enquiries: Antony Farrell

Tír Eolas

Newtownlynch, Doorus, Kinvara,
Co. Galway
t. +353 91 637 452
f. +353 91 637 452
e. info@tireolas.com
w. www.tireolas.com
■ *Publisher of books, guides and maps that provide information on Irish history, archaeology, landscape, culture and tradition.*
General Enquiries: Anne Korff

Townhouse

Trinity House, Charleston Road,
Dublin 6
t. +353 1 497 2399
f. +353 1 497 0927
e. books@townhouse.ie
w. www.townhouse.ie
■ *Publisher of Irish-interest books in areas such as the environment, gardening, mythology, folklore and music, sport, history, genealogy,*

literature and criticism, spirituality and commercial fiction.
Publishing Assistant: Joanna Brogan
Publisher and Managing Director:
Treasa Coady
Sales and Production Manager: Helen
Gleed O'Connor
Editor (Non-Fiction): Marie Heaney

University College Dublin Press

Newman House, 86 St Stephen's
Green, Dublin 2
t. +353 1 716 7397
f. +353 1 716 7211
e. ucdpress@ucd.ie
w. www.ucdpress.ie
■ *Publisher of academic books in the areas of history and politics, social sciences, science and the environment, languages, literature and music. Study guides are also published.*
Publisher: Barbara Mennell

Veritas

7–8 Lower Abbey Street, Dublin 1
t. +353 1 878 8177
f. +353 1 878 6507
e. publications@veritas.ie
w. www.veritas.ie
■ *Publisher of general religious books and liturgical and catechetical texts.*
Director, Product Development: Maura
Hyland

Whytes

38 Molesworth Street, Dublin 2
t. +353 1 676 2888
f. +353 1 676 2880
e. info@whytes.ie
w. www.whytes.ie
■ *Publisher of books and catalogues of Irish art and collectibles.*
General Enquiries: Ian White

Woodtown Music Publications

Dame House, Dame Street, Dublin 2
t. +353 1 677 8943
f. +353 1 679 3664
e. wholesale@crl.ie or
   claddaghrecords@crl.ie
■ *Publisher of music scores.*
Company Secretary: Jane Bolton

Wynkin deWorde

PO Box 257, Galway
t. +353 91 581 441
f. +353 91 581 441
e. info@deworde.com
w. www.deworde.com
■ *Publisher of adult and children's books. Also promotes the work of authors from Europe and the Middle East.*
Editorial: Valerie Shortland
Managing Director: Roger Derham

Northern Ireland

Telephone numbers in Northern Ireland have the prefix 048 if dialled from the Republic and 004428 if dialled from elsewhere.

Abbey Press

12 The Pines, Jordanstown, Co. Antrim BT37 0SE
t. +44 28 3026 3142
f. +44 28 3026 2514
e. mgrogan@abbeycbs.co.uk
w. www.abbeycbs.co.uk
■ *Publisher of literary biography, memoirs, fiction, history, politics and academic books, with a strong poetry list.*
Administrator: Mel McMahon
Editor: Adrian Rice

Adleader Publications

15 Chartwell Park, Belfast BT8 6NG
t. +44 28 9079 7902
f. +44 28 9079 1454
e. mail@adleader.co.uk
w. www.adleader.co.uk
■ *Publisher of the* **Energy Institute Yearbook and Directory for Northern Ireland**, **Filmscan** *(a film, television and video directory for Ireland),* **Crewfinder Cymru** *(a film and television directory for Wales), and the* **Northern Ireland Bar Library Directory.**
Publisher: Stan Mairs, Hilary Ingram
Production Manager: Gavin Doherty

Appletree Press

Old Potato Station, 14 Howard Street South, Belfast BT7 1AP
t. +44 28 9024 3074
f. +44 28 9024 6756
e. reception@appletree.ie
w. www.brandedbooks.ie
■ *Publisher of Irish-interest gift books, guidebooks, books on history, music, humour, criticism and stationery, in eight languages.*
Managing Director: John Murphy

Blackstaff Press

4c Heron Wharf, Sydenham Business Park, Belfast BT3 9LE
t. +44 28 9045 5006
f. +44 28 9046 6237
e. info@blackstaffpress.com
w. www.blackstaffpress.com
■ *Publisher of books, mainly (but not exclusively) of Irish interest, including history, politics, fiction, poetry and humour.*
General Enquiries: Patsy Horton

Colourpoint Books

Colourpoint House, Jubilee Business Park, 21 Jubilee Road, Newtownards, Co. Down BT23 4YH
t. +44 28 9182 0505
f. +44 28 9182 1900
e. info@colourpoint.co.uk
w. www.colourpoint.co.uk
■ *Publisher of Irish-interest, transport, educational, military and religious books.*

Cranagh Press

University of Ulster, Cromore Road, Coleraine, Co. Derry BT52 1SA
t. +44 28 7032 4187
f. +44 28 7032 4925
e. cranagh@ulst.ac.uk
w. www.ulst.ac.uk/cranagh
■ *Design and publishing house, covering typesetting, image-sourcing, cover design, final proofing and printing of books, booklets and pamphlets.*

Guildhall Press

Unit 4, Community Services Units, Bligh's Lane, Creggan, Derry BT48 0LZ
t. +44 28 7136 4413
f. +44 28 7137 2949
e. info@ghpress.com
w. www.ghpress.com

■ *Publisher of local history and wider-interest books on the history of the past thirty years in the north of Ireland. A community organisation providing web publishing and design for local business and community groups.*
Manager: Paul Hippsley

Lagan Press
Unit 4, 1a Bryson Street, Belfast
BT5 4ES
t. +44 28 9045 5571
m. +44 79 0171 4670
f. +44 28 9045 5571
e. lagan-press@e-books.org.uk
w. www.lagan-press.org.uk
■ *Publisher of poetry, drama and literary fiction in Irish and English, with an emphasis on the north of Ireland.*
General Enquiries: Pól Ó Muirí

Lapwing Publications
1 Ballysillan Drive, Belfast BT14 8HQ
t. +44 28 9029 5800
e. lapwing-poetry.co.uk
■ *Publisher of poetry books.*
Publisher: Dennis Greig

SLS Legal Publications (NI)
School of Law, Queen's University,
Belfast BT7 1NN
t. +44 28 9097 5224
f. +44 28 9032 6308
w. www.sls.qub.ac.uk
■ *Publisher of legal practitioners' textbooks,* the **Bulletin of Northern Ireland Law** *and legal journals.*

General Enquiries: Miriam Dudley
  e. m.dudley@qub.ac.uk
Publications Editor: Sara Gamble
  e. s.gamble @qub.ac.uk

The Stationery Office (TSO Ireland)
16 Arthur Street, Belfast BT1 4GD
t. +44 28 9023 8451
f. +44 28 9023 5401
e. enquiries@tsoireland.com
w. www.tsoireland.com
■ *Provides information management services in design, print production and buying, and publishing.*
General Enquiries: Dan Lavery
  e. dan.lavery@tso.co.uk

Ulster Historical Foundation
Balmoral Buildings, 12 College Square
East, Belfast BT1 6DD
t. +44 28 9033 2288
f. +44 28 9023 9885
e. enquiry@uhf.org.uk
w. www.ancestryireland.com
■ *Publishes historical, educational and genealogical source books and guides to genealogy, gravestone inscriptions and local history.*
Administrative Officer (Publications):
Marie Heading
Executive Director: Fintan Mullan
Project Manager and Publications:
Andrew Vaughan

7

MAGAZINES AND PERIODICALS: OFF THE SHELF

Dr Mark O'Brien

The magazine landscape

The magazine stands are full of choice these days, but in Ireland the magazine industry has been going through a period of rapid change, with intense competition from UK and international titles and a battle for advertising. As well as enjoying something of a boom during the Celtic Tiger years, in 1998 the VAT rate on magazines was cut from 21% to 12.5%, bringing Ireland's rate into line with most other European states. There are currently more than 360 magazines—consumer and trade—produced at various frequencies in the Republic. There is an equally thriving periodical industry north of the border. The industry can be broken down into broad categories or genres, such as women's life-style, men's life-style, television guides, specialist interest (sport, music, business, food, car, home decor), general interest (current affairs and mixed content), trade (construction, catering, banking, etc.) and listings (entertainment, recruitment, classified advertisements).

Like the newspaper industry, Irish magazines and periodicals have to compete with a multitude of expensively produced British titles. In addition, Irish newspapers have become keen to lure female readers by including magazines with content similar to that formerly the preserve of the magazine industry. Some encouraging developments occurred in the sector in 2004. The high-profile magazines produced by Smurfit Communications were subject to a management buyout by its Chief Executive, Norah Casey, and is now Harmonia. Vincent Browne, the founder of investigative publications such as *Nusight* and *Magill*, launched the *Village*, a new 80-page weekly current affairs magazine, in mid-2004. In a similar vein, *Magill* was relaunched under new owners as a high-end 80-page glossy magazine at the end of 2004. Whether the market can support both remains to be seen.

The Periodical Publishers' Association of Ireland (PPAI) represents the great majority of magazine and periodical publishers in Ireland, north and south. Its forty members produce more than 150 consumer, consumer specialist, business and professional publications. Formed in 1999, the association promotes the interests of magazine and periodical publishers and is a member of the European Federation of Magazine Publishers.

The magazine and periodical market

The Irish magazine industry became embroiled in something of a controversy in mid-2002 when Smurfit Communications conceded that it had been inflating its self-reported circulation figures of three of its flagship titles: *Woman's Way*, *Irish Tatler* and *U Magazine*. For decades, advertisers had had to be content with publishers' own statement of circulation figures. The PPAI responded by introducing mandatory auditing under its code of verification. All PPAI magazines and periodicals with a circulation over 50,000 a year that seek commercial advertising are now audited by the Audit Bureau of Circulation. As with newspapers, magazines and periodicals rely on circulation and readership figures to attract advertising. With so many publications produced, it is possible only to give a breakdown of the most prominent titles from each genre.

Circulation of top selling Republic of Ireland magazines, 2003

	Frequency	Circulation ('000)
Women's life-style		
U Magazine	Monthly	52
VIP	Monthly	32
Woman's Way	Weekly	31
Social & Personal	Monthly	25
Modern Woman	Monthly	24

Circulation of top selling Republic of Ireland magazines, 2003 *contd.*

	Frequency	Circulation ('000)
Irish Tatler	Monthly	22
Image	Monthly	22
Sport		
Irish Golf World	6 per year	50
Golf Ireland	8 per year	37
Breaking Ball	11 per year	20
Gaelic World	Monthly	15
Irish Rugby Review	11 per year	12
Irish Golf Review	Quarterly	12
Business		
Initiative	Monthly	162
Banking Ireland	Quarterly	21
Smart Company	Bi-monthly	21
Business & Finance	Fortnightly	10
Business Plus	Monthly	9
Decision	6 per year	7
General		
The Phoenix	Fortnightly	19
Hot Press	Fortnightly	19
In Dublin	Fortnightly	30
The Dubliner	Monthly	10
The Village	Weekly	N/A
Television guides		
RTÉ Guide	Weekly	118
TV Now	Weekly	35

Source: PPAI web site (Cawley Nea survey of Irish magazine industry, 2003).

There is also a thriving magazine industry north of the border, with more than seventy titles of varying frequencies published locally. The most popular is the weekly *TV Times*, with a circulation of 38,000 per issue. Among the most popular monthly magazines are *Ulster Tatler* (circulation 12,786), *Northern Woman* (circulation 13,000), *Motoring & Home Life (25,000)* and *Ulster Business* (circulation 5,635). There are no audited circulation or readership figures for Irish sales of British magazines or periodicals. However, self-reported publishers' statements for 2003 show very healthy sales. There are more than fifty prominent life-style titles available (with varying frequencies of publication), ranging from those aimed at men, women and teenagers to those specialising in sport, films, home décor, gardening, music and current affairs. Among the best-selling titles are *Hello!* (45,000), *Woman* (32,103), *Woman's Own* (27,343), *Sugar* (21,515), *Heat* (25,000), *FHM* (20,000), *Glamour* (20,000) and *National Enquirer* (18,648).

However, despite such high circulation figures, advertisers are more disposed to advertise in Irish magazines—it is cheaper, the circulation and readership figures are audited, and in the eyes of advertisers there is little sense in buying expensive space in a British magazine if the target audience for the advertisement is an Irish one. Between 2001 and 2003, advertising revenue for Irish magazines increased from €17 million to €34 million. The magazine industry now accounts for 2.9% of annual media advertising expenditure, and advertising accounts for approximately 31% of average magazine revenue.

Readership of selected titles, 2002/2003 (%)

Title	All adult	Men	Women	ABC1	C2DE	15–34 years	35+ years
RTÉ Guide	13.4	10.4	16.4	12.2	13.5	12.9	13.8
Woman's Way	6.4	1.1	11.5	5.6	7.0	5.5	7.0
Irish Tatler	1.2	0.4	2.1	1.7	0.9	1.7	0.9
U	2.5	0.3	4.6	3.2	2.1	4.1	1.3
Hot Press	0.9	1.2	0.5	1.3	0.6	1.5	0.4

Source: JNRS/Lansdowne. In 2004 the magazine *PPA Ireland* gave the consumer magazine award to *U* magazine from Harmonia, with publisher of the year going to Niall Stokes of *Hot Press*.

Future trends

With the long-running VAT issue resolved since 1998, the cost of paper and increased competition from well-produced British titles remain the most pressing issues for the magazine and periodical industry. Irish publications know that they must stay competitive if they are to survive. One obvious way of being competitive is to keep the cover price down. In 2003 some Irish magazines cut their cover price to try to increase their circulation. *U Magazine* cut its price to €1 per issue and as a result its sales rose by 47%—17,000 copies—by the end of the year. In a similar vein, *Irish Tatler* halved its price to €2 and increased its circulation by 29%, selling an extra 5,000 copies per issue. In contrast, *Image*, its main competitor, stuck by its cover price of €3.70 and saw its sales drop by 7.6%. It is not clear how many new regular readers will be retained through such methods, but it demonstrates at least that the magazine industry is fighting for its survival.

For some publishing groups involved in magazines and periodicals the role of e-magazines and the impact of the internet as a publishing medium will depend on the adoption of broadband in Ireland and Northern Ireland. In the United States, for example, where home broadband is now commonplace, most major magazines operate full subscriber e-magazines, such as *Businessweek*. One major positive factor for Irish publishing houses is that growing spending power means more Irish people have disposable income for high-end genre magazines such as food, home, lifestyle and technology publications. Some publishers still see gaps in the market for publications aimed at children, teenagers and parents, reflecting the national statistics which show the Irish birth rate, and population, continuing to rise.

Republic of Ireland

AA Motoring
Goldstar Media Ltd, 7 Cranford
Centre, Montrose, Dublin 4
Editor: Neil Briscoe
  t. +353 1 260 0899
  f. +353 1 260 0911
  e. info@drivemagazine.com
■ *This is a quarterly magazine for members
of the Automobile Association (AA).*

Ability
National Resource Centre, Old
Nangor Road, Clondalkin, Dublin 22
Editor: Shani Williamson
  t. +353 1 457 2329
  f. +353 1 457 2328
  e. swilliamson@iasbah.ie
  w. www.iasbah.ie
■ *This is a quarterly magazine of the Irish
Spina Bifida and Hydrodcephalus Association*

Abroad
Woodfield Publishing, 2nd Floor,
35 Harcourt Street, Dublin 2
Editor and Publisher: Michael Collins
  t. +353 1 475 7248
  f. +353 1 475 7301
  e. michael@abroadmagazine.com
  w. www.abroadmagazine.com
■ *Published bi-monthly, this magazine covers
travel, tourism, hotels and overseas property.*

Accountancy Ireland
83 Pembroke Road, Dublin 4
Editor: Daisy Downes
  t. +353 1 637 7240
  f. +353 1 668 5685
  e. ddownes@accountancyireland.ie
  w. www.accountancyireland.ie
■ *This journal for chartered accountants in
Ireland is published six times a year and is
aimed at accountants and business executives.*

Accountancy Plus
9 Ely Place, Dublin 2
Editor: Coleen Quinn
  t. +353 1 676 7353
  f. +353 1 661 2367
  e. cpa@cpaireland.ie
  w. www.cpaireland.ie
■ *Quarterly journal of the Institute of
Certified Public Accountants in Ireland.*

Afloat
Irish Marine Press Publications Ltd, 2
Lower Glenageary Road, Dún
Laoghaire, Co. Dublin
Editor: David O'Brien
  t. +353 1 284 6161
  f. +353 1 284 6192
  e. info@afloat.ie
  w. www.afloat.ie
■ *This is a boating magazine, published ten
times a year.*

Ageing Matters in Ireland
Age Action Ireland Ltd, 30–31 Lower
Camden Street, Dublin 2
Editor: Paul Murray
  t. +353 1 475 6989
  f. +353 1 475 6011
  e. library@ageaction.ie
  w. www.ageaction.ie
■ *This is a monthly bulletin for elderly
people.*

Aisling Quarterly, The
Inis Mór, Aran Islands, Co. Galway
Co-Editors: Tess Harper and Dara
Molloy
  t. +353 99 61245
  f. +353 99 61968
  e. aismag@iol.ie
  w. www.aislingmagazine.com
■ *This is a quarterly alternative life-style
magazine covering Celtic spirituality, social
and environmental issues.*

All-Ireland Kitchen Guide

Ashgrove House, Kill Avenue, Dún
Laoghaire, Co. Dublin
Publisher: Mike Keenan
  t. +353 1 272 2616
  f. +353 1 272 2617
  e. homesinteriors@ireland.com
■ *This is a glossy homes, décor and interiors*
magazine.

Amnesty International

48 Fleet Street, Dublin 2
Acting Editor: Roxane Macara
  t. +353 1 677 6361
  f. +353 1 677 6392
  e. magazine@amnesty.ie
  w. www.amnesty.ie
■ *Published three times a year, this is the*
newsletter of the human rights organisation's
Irish section.

An Taisce

Tailors' Hall, Back Lane, Dublin 8
Editors: Judy Osborne and Cóilín Mac
Lochlainn
  t. +353 1 454 1786
  f. +353 1 453 3255
  e. admin@antaisce.org
  w. www.antaisce.org

Aquaculture Ireland

BIM, Crofton Road, Dún Laoghaire,
Co. Dublin
Editor: Fiach Ó Brolcháin
  t. +353 1 285 9111
  m. +353 87 261 1597
  f. +353 1 285 7823
  e. silchester@eircom.net
■ *Published bi-monthly, this is the journal of*
the Irish Aquaculture Industry Association.

Archaeology Ireland

PO Box 69, Bray, Co. Wicklow
Editor: Tom Condit
  t. +353 1 276 5221
  f. +353 1 276 5207
  e. info@wordwellbooks.com
  w. www.wordwellbooks.com

■ *This quarterly magazine is aimed at profes-*
sional archaeologists and those with an interest
in the area.

Architecture Ireland

Nova Publishing, 9 Sandyford Office
Park, Dublin 18
Editor: Sandra O'Connell
  t. +353 1 295 8115
  f. +353 1 295 9350
  e. mail@architectureireland.ie
  w. www.architectureireland.ie
■ *This is the official journal for the Royal*
Institute of Architects of Ireland and is pub-
lished ten times a year.

Arts Ireland

Irish Emigrant Publications, Cathedral
Building, Middle Street, Galway
Editor: Oonagh Montague
  t. +353 91 569 158
  f. +353 91 569 178
  e. oonagh@emigrant.ie
  w. www.emigrant.ie
■ *This is a monthly bulletin covering Irish*
arts and theatre. It has a circulation of 12,500,
published via e-mail and internet.

Astronomy and Space

Astronomy Ireland, PO Box 2888,
Dublin 5
Editor: David Moore
  t. +353 1 847 0777
  f. +353 1 847 0771
  e. info@astronomy.ie
  w. www.astronomy.ie
■ *Monthly magazine of Astronomy Ireland*
with articles on astronomy and space news as
well as listings of events visible in the skies
above Ireland.

Auto Ireland

Harmonia, 2 Clanwilliam Court, Lower
Mount Street, Dublin 2
Editor: Brian Foley
  t. +353 1 240 5300
  f. +353 1 661 9757
  e. automags@harmonia.ie
  w. www.harmonia.ie

■ *This is a bi-monthly magazine for car enthusiasts.*

Auto Trade Journal

Automotive Publications, Glencree House, Lanesborough Road, Roscommon
Managing Editor: Padraic J. Deane
t. +353 9066 25676
f. +353 9066 25636
e. pdeane@autopub.ie
w. www.autopub.ie
■ *This trade magazine for the motor trade is published bi-monthly.*

Autowoman

Harmonia, 2 Clanwilliam Court, Lower Mount Street, Dublin 2
Editor: Serena Davies
t. +353 1 240 5300
f. +353 1 661 9757
e. automags@harmonia.ie
w. www.harmonia.ie
■ *Quarterly car magazine for women.*

Baby & Child

Goldstar Media Ltd, 7 Cranford Centre, Montrose, Dublin 4
Editor: Gemma Tipton
t. +353 1 260 0899
f. +353 1 260 0911
e. gtipton@eircom.net
■ *Annual parenting magazine for parents of babies and young children.*

Backpacker Ireland

2nd Floor, 35 Harcourt Street, Dublin 2
Publisher: Michael Collins
t. +353 1 475 7262
m. +353 86 858 3585
f. +353 1 475 7301
e. editor@backpacker.ie
w. www.backpacker.ie
■ *This is a monthly magazine for backpackers and tourists, covering tourism, listings, reviews and a guide to going out.*

Backspin

The Golf Business, 'Birkdale', 4 Rathmichael Manor, Loughlinstown, Co. Dublin
Editor: Declan O'Donoghue
t. +353 1 282 7269
f. +353 1 282 7483
e. golfbiz@eircom.net
■ *This is a quarterly magazine for golf fans.*

Books Ireland

11 Newgrove Avenue, Dublin 4
Publisher: Jeremy Addis
t. +353 1 269 2185
f. +353 1 260 4927
e. booksi@eircom.net
■ *Printed nine times a year, this magazines features publishing and bookselling news, along with reviews of Irish-interest books and listings of recent and future publications.*

Bookview Ireland

Irish Emigrant Publications, Cathedral Buildings, Middle Street, Galway
Editor: Pauline Ferrie
t. +353 91 569 158
f. +353 91 569 178
e. ferrie@emigrant.ie
w. www.emigrant.ie
■ *This is a monthly newsletter aimed at Irish emigrants providing news and reviews of the latest Irish-interest books.*

Build Your Own House and Home

Dyflin Publications Ltd, 99 South Circular Road, Dublin 8
Editor: Roisín Carabine
t. +353 1 416 7900
f. +353 1 416 7901
e. roisincarabine@dyflin.ie
w. www.buildyourownhome.ie
■ *Published in conjunction with the Royal Institute of Architects in Ireland, this annual magazine contains articles about building a home.*

Business & Finance

1–4 Swift's Alley, Dublin 2
Editor: Gabi Thesing
t. +353 1 416 7800
f. +353 1 416 7898
e. gabi@bandf.net
w. www.bandf.ie
■ *This is a fortnightly business news magazine, with news and feature articles on finance topics.*

Business Plus

Nalac Ltd, 30 Morehampton Road,
Dublin 4
Editor: Nick Mulcahy
t. +353 1 660 8400
f. +353 1 660 4540
e. info@businessplus.ie
w. www.bizplus.ie
■ *This is a monthly business magazine with news and features on finance topics.*

Business World

6 Merrion Row, Dublin 2
Alan Soughley
t. +353 1 661 8625
f. +353 1 676 7667
e. newsdesk@businessworld.ie
w. www.businessworld.ie
■ *This is an on-line business information source for the Irish market, with extra subscription-based updates on specific sectors.*

Business2Arts

44 East Essex Street, Dublin 2
Editor: Siobhán Broughan
t. +353 1 672 5336
f. +353 1 672 5373
e. info@business2arts.ie
w. www.business2arts.ie
■ *This quarterly newsletter covers business sponsorship of the arts.*

A Buyer's Guide to Irish Art

Ashville Media Group, Apollo House,
Tara Street, Dublin 2
Editors: Meg Walker and Jane Humphries
t. +353 1 432 2200
f. +353 1 672 7100
e. info@ashville.com
w. www.ashville.com
■ *This is a twice-yearly guide to the Irish art scene.*

Cancerwise

Eireann Healthcare Publications, 25–26
Windsor Place, Dublin 2
Managing Editor: Cora Mannion
t. +353 1 475 3300
f. +353 1 475 3311
e. cmannion@eireannpublications.ie

Cara

Harmonia, 2 Clanwilliam Court, Lower
Mount Street, Dublin 2
Editor: Tony Clayton-Lea
t. +353 1 240 5300
f. +353 1 661 9757
e. tonycl@harmonia.ie
w. www.harmonia.ie
■ *This is the free in-flight magazine for Aer Lingus, providing travel features, reviews and interviews. It is published ten times a year.*

Checkout

Checkout Publications Ltd, Adelaide
House, 3 Adelaide Street, Dún
Laoghaire, Co. Dublin
Editor: Terence Cosgrave
t. +353 1 230 0322
f. +353 1 230 0629
e. info@checkout.ie
w. www.checkout.ie
■ *This monthly food and drink trade magazine is issued to manufacturers, suppliers and distributors throughout Ireland.*

Children's Wear in Ireland

Future Communications, 5 Main
Street, Blackrock, Co. Dublin
Editor: Paul Golden
t. +353 1 283 6782
f. +353 1 283 6784
e. futura@indigo.ie
■ *This twice-yearly publication covers the children's clothing industry.*

Circa Art Magazine

43–44 Temple Bar, Dublin 2
Editor: Peter FitzGerald
t. +353 1 679 7388
f. +353 1 679 7388
e. editor@recira.com
w. www.recirca.com
■ *This journal of contemporary visual arts is published four times a year.*

Clár na nÓg

National Youth Council of Ireland,
3 Montague Street, Dublin 2
Editor: Vacant
t. +353 1 478 4122
f. +353 1 478 3974
e. press@nyci.ie
w. www.youth.ie
■ *This monthly electronic magazine is produced by the National Youth Council of Ireland and distributed to youth leaders and organisations.*

Classmate

Dublin City Council, 16–19
Wellington Quay, Dublin 2
Editor: Emma Donnelly
t. +353 1 672 3896
f. +353 1 672 3921
e. comms@dublincity.ie
w. www.dublincity.ie
■ *This quarterly newsletter produced by Dublin City Council is aimed at primary schoolchildren.*

Commercial Interiors of Ireland

Unit F5, Bymac Centre, North West
Business Park, Dublin 15
Editor: Muriel Bolger
t. +353 1 822 4477
f. +353 1 822 4485
e. admin@pembrokepublishing.com
■ *This is an annual trade magazine for institutions and professional organisations with an interest in commercial interior design.*

Commercial Law Practitioner

Round Hall Ltd, 43 Fitzwilliam Place,
Dublin 2
Editor: Brian Hutchinson
t. +353 1 662 5301
f. +353 1 622 5302
e. info@roundhall.ie
w. www.roundhall.ie
■ *Published eleven times a year, this journal deals with commercial law issues, with articles from Ireland and elsewhere.*

Computerscope

Scope Communications, Prospect
House, 3 Prospect Road, Dublin 9
Editor: David D'Arcy
t. +353 1 882 4444
f. +353 1 830 0888
e. david.darcy@scope.ie
w. www.techcentral.ie
■ *This is a monthly computer and information technology magazine, which has a controlled free circulation.*

Confetti

Dyflin Publications Ltd, 99 South
Circular Road, Dublin 8
Editor: Ciara Elliott
t. +353 1 416 7900
f. +353 1 416 7901
e. ciara@dyflin.ie
w. www.confetti.ie
■ *This is a quarterly bridal, fashion and beauty magazine circulating throughout Ireland.*

Construction

Dyflin Publications Ltd, 99 South
Circular Road, Dublin 8
Editor: Kathy Laverty
t. +353 1 416 7900
f. +353 1 416 7901
e. construction@dyflin@ie
■ *This monthly magazine is the official journal of the Construction Industry Federation.*

Construction and Property News

Jemma Publications Ltd, Marino
House, 52 Glasthule Road, Sandycove,
Co. Dublin
Editor: Maev Martin
t. +353 1 280 0000
f. +353 1 280 1818
e. m.martin@jemma.ie

■ *This monthly trade magazine is aimed at the building and construction industry.*

Construction Information Service (CIS) Report

Newmarket Information Ltd,
66 Ranelagh, Dublin 6
Managing Director: Tom Moloney
  t. +353 1 491 0043
  f. +353 1 491 0092
  e. info@cisireland.com
  w. www.cisireland.com
■ *This weekly information bulletin gives information on all types of building projects.*

Construct Ireland

Fáilte House, Hannover Street East,
Dublin 2
Editor: Jeff Colley
  t. +353 1 210 3618
  f. +353 1 210 8437
  e. info@constructireland.ie
  w. www.constructireland.ie
■ *This twice-monthly trade magazine deals with on sustainable development and construction.*

Consumer Choice

43–44 Chelmsford Road, Dublin 6
Editor: Kieran Doherty
  t. +353 1 497 8600
  f. +353 1 497 8601
  e. cai@consumerassociation.ie
  w. www.consumerassociation.ie
■ *This subscription-only independent monthly magazine gives consumers information on products and services and current consumer affairs. It is produced by the Consumers' Association of Ireland.*

Conveyancing and Property Law Journal

Round Hall Ltd, 43 Fitzwilliam Place,
Dublin 2
Editor: Deborah H. Wheeler
  t. +353 1 662 5301
  f. +353 1 662 5302
  e. info@roundhall.ie
  w. www.roundhall.ie

■ *This property law journal is published four times a year.*

Cork Now

Cork Now Productions Ltd, 4 South
Terrace, Cork
Editor: Eileen Bennett
  t. +353 21 484 7393
  f. +353 1 21 484 7394
  e. www.corknow.ie
■ *This Cork-focused magazine is published six times a year and covers life-style, health, home and beauty issues.*

Cosantór, An

Public Relations Section, Defence
Forces HQ, Infirmary Road, Dublin 8
Editor: Corporal Paul Hevey
  t. +353 1 804 2000
  f. +353 1 677 9018
  e. ancosantoir@defenceforces.iol.ie
■ *This magazine for Defence Forces personnel is published ten times a year.*

Credit Union Review

17 Castle Street, Dalkey, Co. Dublin
Editor: Joe Joyce
  t. +353 1 285 9111
  e. silchester@eircom.net
■ *This official journal of the Irish League of Credit Unions is published twice a month.*

Cumhacht

PwDI, Jervis House, Jervis Street,
Dublin 1
Editor: Tim Ryan
  t. +353 1 662 4649
  f. +353 1 676 1940
  e. tim@foleyryancommunications.com
  w. www.pwdi.ie
■ *This is a quarterly newsletter for People with Disabilities in Ireland.*

Decision

Dillon Publications, PO Box 7130,
Dublin 18
Editor: Frank Dillon
  t. +353 1 278 0841
  f. +353 1 295 4368

e. info@decisionireland.com

w. www.decisionireland.com

■ *Published six times a year, this management magazine focuses on current Irish business trends and circulates to the top management of leading Irish companies*

Diabetes Ireland

MedMedia Ltd, 25 Adelaide Street, Dún Laoghaire, Co. Dublin

Editor: Dave Southern

t. +353 1 280 3967

f. +353 1 280 7076

e. dave.southern@diabetes.ie

w. www.diabetes.ie

■ *This is the quarterly journal for the Diabetes Federation of Ireland.*

Diabetes Wise

Eireann Healthcare Publications, 25–26 Windsor Place, Dublin 2

In-house Editor: Tim Ilsley

t. +353 1 475 3300

f. +353 1 475 3311

e. ilsley@eireannpublications.ie

w. www.eireannpublications.ie

■ *This is a quarterly publication for diabetes patients and their carers and family.*

Digital Media Services Directory

Digital Media House, 9 Baggot Court, Dublin 2

Publisher and Editor: Damien Ryan

t. +353 1 669 1750

f. +353 1 669 1769

e. dryan@digitalmedia.ie

w. www.digitalmedia.ie

■ *This is the annual guide to developments and trends in the digital media sector.*

Doctor's Deskbook

Maxwell Designs, 49 Wainsfort Park, Dublin 6

Editor: Dr Bill Maxwell

t. +353 1 492 4034

f. +353 1 492 4035

e. maxwell@doctorsdeskbook.ie

■ *This is the annual reference book for general practitioners in Ireland.*

Doctrine and Life

Dominican Publications, 42 Parnell Square, Dublin 1

Editor: Bernard Tracey OP

t. +353 1 873 1355

f. +353 1 873 1760

e. sales@dominicanpublications.com

w. www.dominicanpublications.com

■ *Published ten times a year, this religious magazine covers developments in the Church in Ireland and globally.*

Drinks Industry Ireland

Louisville Publishing Ltd, Louisville, Enniskerry, Co. Wicklow

Editor: Pat Nolan

t. +353 1 204 6230

f. +353 1 204 6231

e. drinksinireland.indigo.ie

■ *This trade magazine for publicans, hoteliers, night-club owners and all sectors of the drinks industry is published ten times a year.*

Drive

Goldstar Publications Ltd, 7 Cranford Centre, Montrose, Dublin 4

Editor: Neil Briscoe

t. +353 1 260 0899

f. +353 1 260 0911

e. info@drivemagazine.ie

w.www.drivemagazine.ie

■ *This motoring magazine is published twice a month.*

Drystock Farmer

IFP Media, 31 Dean's Grange Road, Blackrock, Co. Dublin

Editor: Paul O'Grady

t. +353 1 289 3305

f. +353 1 289 6406

e. paul@ifpmedia.com

w. www.ifpmedia.com

■ *This is the quarterly journal of the Irish Cattle and Sheep Farmers' Association.*

Dubliner, The

Dubliner Media Ltd, 23 Wicklow Street, Dublin 2

Editor: Trevor White

RTÉ

IRELAND'S
PUBLIC SERVICE
BROADCASTER

Dublin City University
Ollscoil Chathair Bhaile Átha Cliath

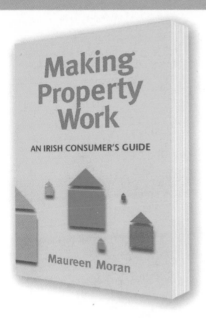

Creating a centre of excellence
for digital media
in the heart of Dublin City

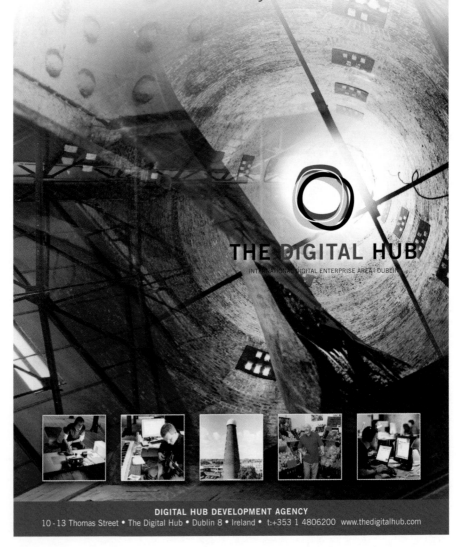

THE DIGITAL HUB
INTERNATIONAL DIGITAL ENTERPRISE AREA | DUBLIN

It's been a

V

INTAGE
YEAR

THE SUNDAY BUSINESS POST

52,115*

Sales are bubbling over

Up by 1% (502 copies)

* ABC Jan - June 2004

For advertising information contact 01-6026000

THE SUNDAY BUSINESS POST
IRELAND'S FINANCIAL, POLITICAL AND ECONOMIC NEWSPAPER

The Broadcasting Commission of Ireland

Promoting choice, diversity and consistent quality in the Irish broadcasting sector.

Broadcasting Commission of Ireland
Coimisiún Craolacháin na hÉireann

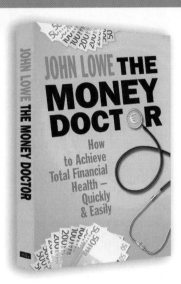

The Institute of Art, Design & Technology, which incorporates the **National Film School**, offers an exciting range of courses at undergraduate and postgraduate levels.

iadt
DUN LAOGHAIRE
National Film School

The Institute provides a creative interdisciplinary environment that is unique in Ireland where art, design and media disciplines are complemented by a high level of expertise in professional practice, digital media technologies and new business models.

Dun Laoghaire
Institute of Art, Design &
Technology
O2 National Digital Media Awards
Higher Education Award
2003 and 2004

– Radio Broadcasting
– Makeup for Film, TV and Theatre
– Modelmaking and Design for Film and Media
– Photography
– Animation
– Film and Video Studies
– Production Design
– Interactive Media
– Film and Television Production

Dun Laoghaire
Institute of Art, Design &
Technology
Kill Avenue, Dun Laoghaire,
Co. Dublin, Ireland
t: + 353 (0) 1 214 4600
f: + 353 (0) 1 214 4700
www.iadt.ie

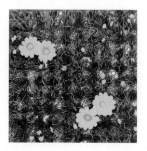

t. +353 1 635 9822
f. +353 1 675 2158
e. editor@thedubliner.ie
w. www.thedubliner.ie
■ *This is a Dublin-focused monthly magazine covering art, films, food, music and style.*

Dublin Evening Classes Guidebook

Oisín Publications, 4 Iona Drive, Dublin 9
Editor: Liam Ó hOisín
t. +353 1 830 5236
f. +353 1 830 7860
e. oisinpr@iol.ie
w.www.eveningclasses.ie
■ *This is an annual guide to available evening classes in Dublin.*

Dublin Historical Record

Old Dublin Society, City Assembly House, 58 South William Street, Dublin 2
Honorary Editor: Theo Mortimer
t. +353 846 1443
e. theomortimer@eircom.net
■ *Published half-yearly, this magazine features the history and antiquities of Dublin.*

Dublin Review, The

PO Box 7948, Dublin 1
Editor and Publisher: Brendan Barrington
t. +353 1 678 8627
f. +353 1 678 8627
e. brendan_barrington@yahoo.com
w. www.thedublinreview.com
■ *This is a quarterly magazine of essays, fiction and reportage, published in book format.*

Dublin University Law Journal

Round Hall Ltd, 43 Fitzwilliam Place, Dublin 2
Editor: Neville Cox
t. +353 1 662 5301
f. +353 1 662 5302
e. info@roundhall.ie
w. www.roundhall.ie
■ *This annual journal features articles on contemporary Irish law.*

Easy Food

Zahra Publishing, 1st Floor, 19 Railway Road, Dalkey, Co. Dublin
Editor: Lucy Taylor
t. +353 1 235 1394
f. +353 235 4434
e. editoreasyfood@zahrapublishing.com
w. www.easyfood.ie
■ *This food magazine is published twice a month and is aimed at consumers looking for easy-to-cook nutritious food.*

Economic and Social Review, The

4 Burlington Road, Dublin 2
Editor: Gillian Davidson
t. +353 1 667 1525
f. +353 1 668 6231
e. press@esri.ie
w. www.esri.ie
■ *This is a quarterly journal for the social sciences and for economic and social studies.*

Education

Keelin Ltd, 9 Maypark, Malahide Road, Dublin 5
Editor: Niall Gormley
t. +353 1 832 9243
f. +353 1 832 9246
e. education@clubi.ie
w. www.educationmagazine.ie
■ *This publication, printed five times a year, deals with Irish education and circulates in secondary schools and third-level institutions.*

Education Matters

47 Watson Avenue, Killiney, Co. Dublin
Editor: Phyllis Mitchell
t. +353 1 285 1696
f. +353 1 285 2275
e. info@educationmatters.ie
w. www.educationmatters.ie
■ *This fortnightly electronic journal covers education issues.*

Éigse: A Journal of Irish Studies

National University of Ireland, 49
Merrion Square, Dublin 2
Editor: Prof. Pádraig A. Breatnach
e. padraig.breatnach@ucd.ie
w. www.nui.ie/eigse
■ *This journal, published by the National University of Ireland, features a wide range of research in Irish language and literature and academic book reviews. It usually appears once a year.*

Eircom Live

Eircom, St Stephen's Green West,
Dublin 2
Editor: Seán Creedon
t. +353 1 671 4444
f. +353 1 478 1211
e. screedon@eircom.ie
■ *This is the Eircom staff newspaper, published ten times annually.*

Émail

European Union House, Dawson
Street, Dublin 2
Editors: Tim Ryan and Kate Healy
t. +353 1 634 1121
e. kate.healy@cec.eu.int
w. www.euireland.ie
■ *This is the free weekly newsletter of the European Union's Dublin Office.*

Employment Law Report

Round Hall Ltd, 43 Fitzwilliam Place,
Dublin 2
Editor: Cliona Kimber
t. +353 662 5301
f. +353 1 662 5302
e. info@roundhall.ie
w. www.roundhall.ie
■ *Six issues of this report, covering all aspects of company law, are published each year.*

Energy and Environment Management

Premier Publishing Ltd, 52–53
Morrison Chambers, 32 Nassau Street,
Dublin 2

Editor: Ronan McGlade
t. +353 679 6700
f. +353 1 679 6701
e. ronan@prempub.com
w. www.prempbl.com
■ *This subscription magazine is published twice a month.*

Engineers Journal

IFP Media, 31 Dean's Grange Road,
Blackrock, Co. Dublin
Editor: Mary Sweetman
t. +353 1 289 3305
f. +353 1 289 6406
■ *This is the monthly journal of the Institution of Engineers of Ireland.*

Environmental Management Ireland

Nestron Ltd, 68 Middle Abbey Street,
Dublin 1
Editor: Annette O'Riordan
t. +353 1 872 0734
f. +353 1 872 0856
e. envmi@indigo.ie
w. www.environmentalmanagement.ie
■ *A bi-monthly business publication aimed at managers, featuring environmental controls on all sections of industry and commerce in Ireland.*

Equality News

Equality Authority, 2 Clonmel Street,
Dublin 2
Editor: t. +353 1 417 3333
■ *This quarterly journal from the Equality Authority covers current development in equal opportunities employment and related issues.*

Euro Food & Drink

Dame Publishing Ltd, Block 4, Usher's
Court, Usher's Quay, Dublin 8
Editor: Geoff Percival
t. +353 1 671 9766
f. +353 1 679 9646
e. editorial@eurofoodanddrink.com

Event Guide, The

D and K Media Ltd, Regus House,
Harcourt Road, Dublin 2

Editor: Kieran Owens
t. +353 1 477 3933
e. info@eventguide.ie
w. www.eventguide.ie
■ *This fortnightly guide to films, music, art, drama and other cultural events is distributed free.*

Fáilte/Wecome

Mac Communications, Taney Hall, Eglinton Terrace, Dundrum, Dublin 14
Editor: Sarah McQuaid
t. +353 1 296 0000
f. +353 1 296 0383
e. info@maccommunications.ie
■ *The annual on-board magazine of Irish Ferries.*

Farm & Plant Buyers Guide

Unit 6, Leopardstown Office Park, Dublin 18
Editor and Publisher: Ray M. J. Egan
t. +353 1 240 5555
f. +353 1 294 3303
e. info@cpg.ie
w. www.farmandplant.ie
■ *This is a monthly bulletin for buyers of farm and plant machinery.*

Feasta

43 Na Cluainte, Trá Lí, Co. Chiarraí
Editor: Pádraig Mac Fhearghusa
t. +353 66 712 4169
e. feasta@eircom.net
w. www.feasta.ie
■ *This is a monthly Irish-language arts and political journal.*

Film Ireland

Film Base, 6 Eustace Street, Dublin 2
Editor: Lir Mac Cárthaigh
t. +353 1 679 6716
f. +353 1 679 6717
e. info@filmbase.ie
w. www.filmbase.ie
■ *This magazine, which covers the Irish and international film industry, is published twice a month.*

Finance

Fintel House, 6 The Mall, Beacon Court, Sandyford, Dublin 18
Editor: Ken O'Brien
t. +353 1 293 0566
f. +353 1 0560
e. info@finance-magazine.com
w. www.financedublin.com
■ *This monthly business and finance magazine covers the companies in the Irish Financial Services Centre, Dublin.*

Fins

1 Clonard, Blackrock Road, Cork
Chief Editor: Tony Lynch
t. +353 21 491 7251
e. editor@finsmag.com and feedback@finsmag.com
w. www.finsmag.com
■ *This water sports magazine is published four times a year.*

Fitzwilliam Post

39 Upper Fitzwilliam Street, Dublin 2
Editor: Michael Dunne
t. +353 1 882 8611
f. +353 1 676 3564
e. fitzwilliampost@eircom.net
■ *This paper is published fifteen times a year and is given free to businesses in central Dublin.*

Fleet Car

D'Alton Street, Claremorris, Co. Mayo
Editor: Jarlath Sweeney
t. +353 94 937 2819
f. +353 94 936 2814
e. enquiries@fleet.ie
w. www.fleet.ie
■ *This is a quarterly trade magazine for the car transport industry, published as a supplement to* **Fleet Management**.

Flying In Ireland

PO Box 10004, Churchtown, Dublin 14
Editor: Laurence Dwyer
w. www.flyinginireland.com
e. editor@flyinginireland.com

Focus

National Council for the Blind in
Ireland, Whitworth Road, Dublin 9
Editor: Joe Bollard
t. +353 1 830 7033
f. +353 1 830 7787
e. joebollard2@eircom.net
w. www.ncbi.ie
■ *This is a fortnightly magazine on visual
impairment issues produced by the National
Council for the Blind in Ireland.*

Focus on Ireland and the Wider World

Comhlámh, 10 Upper Camden Street,
Dublin 2
Editorial contact
Conall Ó Caoimh
t. +353 1 478 34490
f. +353 1 478 3738
e. conall@comhlamh.org
w. www.comhlamh.org
■ *This magazine is produced by members of
the development organisation Comhlámh, giving news and analysis of development issues.*

Food and Drink Business

Premier Publishing Ltd, 52–53
Morrison Chambers, 32 Nassau Street,
Dublin 2
Editor: Mike Rohan
t. +353 679 6700
f. +353 679 6701
e. prempbl@iol.ie
w. www.prempbl.com
■ *This is a monthly subscription-based trade
magazine for the food and drink industry.*

Food and Drink Manufacturing Solutions

Advance Publications Ltd, Acorn
House, 38 St Peter's Road, Dublin 7
Editor: Willo Litzouw
t. +353 1 868 6640
f. +353 1 868 6651
e. willo@aplgroup.net
w. www.aplgroup.net

■ *This is a quarterly trade magazine available
on subscription and geared towards food and
drink manufacturers and suppliers.*

Food and Wine Magazine

Harmonia, 2 Clanwilliam Court,
Dublin 2
Editor: Ernie Whalley
t. +353 1 240 5300
f. +353 1 661 9757
e. foodandwine@harmonia.ie
w. www.harmonia.ie
■ *This is a monthly magazine for consumers,
featuring articles on food, wine, entertaining
and restaurant reviews.*

Food Ireland

Tara Publishing Ltd, Poolbeg House,
1–2 Poolbeg Street, Dublin 2
Editor: John Walshe
t. +353 1 241 3000
f. +353 1 2413040
e. johnwalshe@tarapublishingco.com
■ *This is an annual directory and guide for
the food, drink and processing industry.*

Food Service Ireland

Premier Publishing Ltd, 52–53
Morrison Chambers, 32 Nassau Street,
Dublin 2
Editor: Mike Rohan
t. +353 1 679 6700
f. +353 1 679 6701
e. prempbl@iol.ie
w. www.prempbl.com
■ *This is a subscription trade magazine, published twice a month, for the food service sector.*

Footwear in Ireland

Futura Communications, 5 Main
Street, Blackrock, Co. Dublin
Editor: Paul Golden
t. +353 1 283 6782
f. +353 1 283 6784
e. futura@indigo.ie
■ *This is a trade magazine published twice a
year.*

Forum
MedMedia Ltd, 25 Adelaide Street,
Dún Laoghaire, Co. Dublin
Editor: Niall Hunter
t. +353 1 280 3967
f. +353 1 280 7076
e. mail@medmedia.ie
■ *This is the monthly journal of the Irish College of General Practitioners, circulated to all Irish GPs.*

Furrow, The
The Furrow Trust, St Patrick's College,
Maynooth, Co. Kildare
Editor: Ronan Drury
t. +353 1 708 3741
f. +353 1 708 3908
e. furrow.office@may.ie
w. www.thefurrow.ie
■ *This is a monthly journal for the contemporary Catholic Church, featuring contributions from leading clerics, lay writers and public figures.*

Futura
Futura Communications, 5 Main
Street, Blackrock, Co. Dublin
Editor: Paul Golden
t. +353 1 283 6782
f. +353 1 283 6784
e. futura@indigo.ie
■ *This a monthly fashion and footwear magazine.*

Gaelic World
13a Abbey Lane, Abbey Farm,
Celbridge, Co. Kildare
Editor: Owen McCann
t. +353 1 627 9666
f. +353 1 627 9667
e. gaelicworld@eircom.net
■ *This is the official Gaelic Athletic Association monthly magazine.*

Galway Magazine
32 Kilkerrin Business Park, Liosbán
Industrial Park, Tuam Road, Galway
Editor: Michael Lally

t. +353 91 758 811
e. info@irelandguides.ie
w. www.irelandguides.ie
■ *This is an annual magazine concentrating on the Galway region.*

Galway Now Magazine
Golden Egg Productions Ltd, 1A
Clarinbridge Business Park,
Clarinbridge, Co. Galway
Editor: Eileen Bennett
t. +353 91 777 077
f. +353 91 777 080
e. galwaynow@iol.ie
w. www.galwaynow.com
■ *This glossy life-style magazine, centred on Galway, publishes ten issues a year.*

Garda News
6th Floor, Phibsboro Tower, Dublin 7
t. +353 1 830 3166
f. +353 1 830 6396
e. gardanews@agsi.ie
■ *This is the publication of the Association of Garda Sergeants and Inspectors.*

Garda Review
Dyflin Publications, 44 South Circular
Road, Dublin 8
Editor: Neil Ward
t. +353 1 416 7900
f. +353 1 416 7901
e. gardareview@gra.cc
■ *This is the monthly magazine of Garda-related news, with features, comment and analysis on policy, law and industrial relations.*

Garda Times
Ashville Media Group, Apollo House,
Tara Street, Dublin 2
Editor: Ruairi Kavanagh
t. +353 1 432 2200
f. +353 1 672 7100
e. ruairi@ashville.com
w. www.ashville.com
■ *This quarterly journal is the official publication of the Association of Garda Superintendents.*

Gay Community News

Unit 2, Scarlet Row, Essex Street West,
Dublin 8
Editor: Brian Finnegan
t. +353 1 671 9076
f. +353 1 671 3549
e. editor@gcn.ie
w. www.gcn.ie
■ *This monthly magazine for gay and lesbian readers features news, features, opinion and event listings. It has a circulation of about 12,000 and is published by the National Lesbian and Gay Federation.*

Gazeta

55 Lower O'Connell Street, Dublin 1
Editor: Sergei Tarugin
t. +353 1 874 0004
f. +353 1 874 0404
w. www.russianireland.com
e. sales@russianireland.com

Genuine Irish Old Moore's Almanac, The

MAC Communications Ltd, Taney
Hall, Eglinton Terrace, Dublin 14
Editor: Sarah McQuaid
t. +353 1 296 0000
f. +353 1 296 0383
e. info@maccommunications.ie
w. www.maccommunications.ie
■ *This annual guide is aimed primarily at the farming community and features information on marts and fairs, with a monthly weather guide.*

Golf Ireland

PO Box 8111, Swords, Co. Dublin
Editor: Dermot Gilleece
t. +353 18078122
f. +353 1 807 8203
e. sales@121golf.com
w. www.121golf.com
■ *This magazine for golfers is published ten times a year.*

Gradireland

77 Pembroke Street, Dublin 4
Director: Adrian Wood
t. +353 1 667 6291
f. +353 1 660 6623
w. www.gradireland.com
■ *This is an annual directory of graduate jobs and postgraduate study options, distributed to Irish universities, north and south.*

Guideline

Institute of Guidance Counsellors,
17 Herbert Street, Dublin 2
Editor: Fred Tuite
t. +353 502 33333
f. +353 502 33314
e. careersheywood@eircom.net
■ *This bi-monthly magazine contains news for guidance counsellors in schools and colleges.*

Hallel

Region of the Isles of the Cistercian
Order of the Strict Observance, Mount
St Joseph Abbey, Roscrea, Co. Tipperary
Editor: Ciarán Ó Sabhaois OCSO
t. +353 505 21711
f. +353 505 22198
e. hallel@msjroscrea.ie
■ *This review of monastic liturgy is published twice a year.*

Health, Living and Wellbeing

Mercury Media, 11 Lower Fitzwilliam
Street, Dublin 2
Editor: Maire Loftus
t. +353 1 611 0941
e. marie@healthandliving.ie
w. www.hlaw.ie
■ *This is a monthly health magazine.*

HeartWise

Eireann Healthcare Publications, 25–26
Windsor Place, Dublin 2
Editor: Tim Ilsley
t. +353 1 475 3300
f. +353 1 475 3311
e. tilsley@eireannpublications.ie

Heritage Outlook

Rothe House, Parliament Street, Kilkenny
Editor: Isabel Smyth
t. +353 56 777 0777
f. +353 56 777 0788
e. mail@heritagecouncil.com
w. www.heritagecouncil.ie

Highball

Ashville Media Group, Apollo House, Tara Street, Dublin 2
Editor: Damian Dowds
t. +353 1 432 2200
f. +353 1 672 7100
e. damian.dowd@ashville.com
w. www.ashville.com
■ *This is the official monthly GAA magazine for fans and players.*

History Ireland

PO Box 69, Bray, Co. Wicklow
Editor: Tommy Graham
t. +353 1 276 5221
f. +353 1 276 5207
e. info@worldwellbooks.com
■ *This magazine, published four times a year, is aimed both at professional historians and those with an interest in the field.*

Hogan Stand

Lynn Publications Ltd, Kells Business Park, Kells, Co. Meath
Editor: John Lynch
t. +353 46 92 41 923
f. +353 46 92 41926
e. lynnpublications@eircom.net
w. www.hoganstand.com
■ *This is a monthly GAA magazine.*

Hospitality Ireland

Madison Publications, 3 Adelaide Street, Dún Laoghaire, Co. Dublin
Editor: Áine Flynn
t. +353 1 236 5880
f. +353 1 230 0325
e. info@hospitality-ireland.com
w. www.hospitality-ireland.com

■ *This is a bi-monthly trade magazine for the food and hospitality sector.*

Hotel and Catering Review

Jemma Publications Ltd, Marino House, 52 Glasthule Road, Sandycove, Co. Dublin
Editor: Frank Corr
t. +353 1 280000
f. +353 1 280 1818
e. f.corr@jemma.ie
■ *This monthly trade magazine reviews developments in the hotel and catering industry.*

Hotel and Restaurant Times

Monwick Publications, HR House, Carton Court, Maynooth, Co. Kildare
Publishing Editor: Cyril McAree
t. + 353 1 628 5447
f. + 353 1 628 5447
e. editorial@hotelandrestauranttimes.ie
w. www.hotelandrestauranttimes.ie

Hot Press

13 Trinity Street, Dublin 2
Editor and Publisher: Niall Stokes
t. +353 1 241 1500
f. +353 1 241 1538
e. info@hotpress.com
w. www.hotpress.com
■ *This fortnightly music, culture and current affairs magazine has a circulation of more than 19,000.*

House & Home

Dyflin Publications Ltd, 99 South Circular Road, Dublin 8
Editor: Roisín Carabine
t. +353 416 7900
f. +353 1 416 7901
e. roisin@houseandhome.ie
w. www.houseandhome.ie
■ *This interiors and housing magazine is published bi-monthly.*

Housing Times

267 Upper Kilmacud Road, Dublin 14
Editor: Donal Buckley
t. +353 1 295 1367
e. bucko@indigo.ie

House Hunter

ABC Publications, 78 Lower Leeson
Street, Dublin 2
Editor: Simon Christian
t. +353 639 8887
f. +353 1 639 8889
e. abcpublications@eircom.net
■ *This domestic property magazine is published twice a month.*

HRD Ireland

Irish Institute of Training and
Development, Leinster Mills,
Osberstown, Naas, Co. Kildare
Editor: Mary-Rose O'Sullivan
t. +353 45 881 166
f. +353 45 881 192
■ *Published four times a year, this trade magazine deals with training and human resource development issues.*

IE Sports Review

Irish Emigrant Publications, Cathedral
Building, Middle Street, Galway
Editor: Liam Ferrie
t. +353 1 91 569 158
f. +353 91 569 178
e. info@emigrant.ie
w. www.irishemigrant.com
■ *This bi-weekly bulletin gives Irish and British sports results and reports to an audience of mostly Irish emigrants, reaching a circulation of 10,500.*

Image

Image Publications Ltd, 22 Crofton
Road, Dún Laoghaire, Co. Dublin
Editor: Sarah McDonnell
t. +353 1 280 8415
f. +353 1 280 8309
w. www.image.ie
■ *A women's magazine containing interviews and features on style, beauty, health and women's issues.*

IMPACT News

Nerney's Court, Dublin 1
Editor: Bernard Harbour
t. +353 1 817 1500
e. bharbour@impact.ie
w. www.impact.ie
■ *This bulletin, published ten times a year, is sent directly to members of the Irish Municipal, Public and Civil Trade Union and has a circulation of 33,500.*

InBusiness

17 Merrion Square, Dublin 2
Editor: Ciara O Mahony
t. +353 1 661 2888
f. +353 1 661 2811
e. ciara.omahony@chambers.ie
w. www.chambers.ie

In Dublin

Page 7 Media, Unit 6, Leopardstown
Office Park, Dublin 18
Editor: Aisling Donnelly
t. +353 1 240 5554
f. +353 1 294 3303
e. info@indublin.ie
w. www.indublin.ie
■ *This weekly freesheet contains entertainment listings and reviews as well as guides to eating out. It has a circulation of 30,000.*

Industrial Relations News

121–3 Ranelagh, Dublin 6
Editor: Brian Sheehan
t. +353 1 497 2711
f. +353 1 497 2779
e. bsheehan@irn.ie
w. www.irn.ie
■ *This weekly subscription magazine covers industrial relations news. It is also published on line.*

In Production

Caherdaniel, Co. Kerry
Editor: David Hare
t. +353 66 947 5986
f. +353 66 947 5488
e. inpro@iol.ie

Inside Government Magazine

Derryshalagh Publications Ltd, 19
Irishtown Road, Dublin 4
Managing Director: Joe Murphy
t. +353 1 231 3593

f. +353 1 677 7752

e. ingov@eircom.net

■ *This monthly magazine on current government issues is mailed to all elected representatives, workers in government and civil service, as well as local authorities and universities.*

Inside Ireland

PO Box 1886, Dublin 16

Editor: Brenda Weir

t. +353 1 493 1906

f. +353 1 493 4538

e. insideireland@eircom.net

w. www.insideireland.com

■ *This quarterly direct-mail bulletin provides information on Ireland, mainly to foreign subscribers, with supplements on genealogy.*

Insight Magazine

Harmony Publications Ltd, Roslyn Park, Sandymount, Dublin 4

Editor: Gary Culliton

t. +353 1 205 7242

f. +353 1 205 7202

e. insight@rehab.ie

■ *This monthly magazine covers health and social affairs.*

Intercom

Veritas House, 7–8 Lower Abbey Street, Dublin 1

Editor: Sister Mary O'Brien

t. +353 1 878 8177

f. +353 1 878 6507

e. intercom2004@eircom.net

■ *This is a monthly magazine for clergy and Church workers.*

Intouch

Irish National Teachers' Organisation (INTO), 35 Parnell Square, Dublin 1

Editor: Tom O'Sullivan

t. +353 1 804 7700

f. +353 1 872 2462

e. editor@into.ie

w. www.into.ie

■ *This is the newsletter of the INTO, circulated to 30,000 readers ten times a year.*

Investor, The

Digital Media House, 9 Baggot Court, Dublin 2

Editor: Barry McCall

t. +353 1 669 1750

f. +353 1 669 1769

e. barry@digitalmedia.ie

w. www.digitalmedia.ie

■ *Published six times a year, this gives financial information for private investors and entrepreneurs.*

IPA Journal

Concept Publications, Unit B2, Riverview Business Park, Dublin 12

Managing Editor: Karina Colgan

t. +353 1 456 8453

f. +353 1 456 8454

e. ipajournal@iol.ie

w. www.conceptpublications.ie

IPU Review

IPU, Butterfield House, Butterfield Avenue, Dublin 14

Editor: Dr Majella Lane

t. +353 1 493 6401

e. ipu@iol.ie

■ *This is the monthly journal of the Irish Pharmaceutical Union, with a circulation of 2,500.*

Ireland at Your Leisure

Ashville Media Group, Apollo House, Tara Street, Dublin 2

Editor: Meg Walker

t. +353 1 432 2200

f. +353 1 672 7100

e. info@ashville.com

w. www.ashville.com

■ *This is the official publication of Avis, Budget Rent-a-car, Dan Dooley Rent-a-Car, Irish Car Rentals and Murray's Europcar.*

Ireland of the Welcomes

Fáilte Ireland, Baggot Street Bridge, Dublin 2

Editor: Letitia Pollard

t. +353 1 602 4000

f. +353 1 607 4335

e. letitia.pollard@failteireland.ie

w. www.irelandofthewelcomes.com

■ *Published six times a year, this magazine deals with Irish life and culture. Much of its 100,000 circulation is in the US.*

Ireland's Antiques and Period Properties

20–21 South William Street, Dublin 2

Editor: Rosemary Whelan

t. +353 1 677 4847

e. iapp@indigo.ie

■ *This guide to antiques and period properties is published three times a year.*

Ireland's Auto Trader

Paramount Court, Corrig Road, Sandyford Industrial Estate, Dublin 18

t. +353 1 449 0600

f. +353 1 449 0606/0607

e. enquiries@autotrader.ie

w. www.autotrader.ie

■ *Motoring magazine and on-line car sales available throughout Ireland.*

Ireland's Eye

6 Dominick Street, Mullingar, Co. Westmeath

Editor and Publisher: Tom Kiernan

t. +353 44 48868

f. +353 44 43777

e. topic@indigo.ie

w. www.irelandseye.com

■ *This is a monthly general-interest magazine with a strong Irish character. It is on sale in Ireland and the UK, as well as having subscription sales to the US.*

Ireland's Greyhound Weekly

Mohober, Mullinahone, Co. Tipperary

Editor: Michael Fortune

t. +353 52 53885

f. +353 52 53886

e. irishgw@eircom.net

■ *This magazine gives a weekly review of the Irish greyhound scene.*

Ireland's Horse Review

Review Publishing Group, Garden Street, Ballina, Co. Mayo

Managing Editor: Liam Geddes

t. +353 96 73500

f. +353 96 72077

e. info@irelands-horsereview.ie

w. www.irelands-horsereview.com

■ *This is a monthly Irish equestrian magazine.*

Ireland's Issues

Byzantium Publishing Ltd, 30 Gardiner Place, Dublin 1

Editor: Seán Kavanagh

t. +353 1 873 5137

f. +353 1 873 5143

e. issuesmag@iolfree.ie

■ *This fortnightly current affairs and interviews magazine is sold by the homeless and unemployed.*

Ireland's Own

The People Newspapers Ltd, Channing House, Upper Rowe Street, Wexford

Editors: Phil Murphy and Seán Nolan

t. +353 53 401 40

f. +353 53 40191

w. www.finnvalley.ie/irelandsown/

■ *This is a weekly journal of fiction and literature with a strong traditional Irish flavour.*

Irish 4x4 & Off-Road

Whelan Byrne Associates, 2 Sunbury, Kilcullen, Co. Kildare

Editor: Brian Byrne

t. +353 45 481090

e. admin@whelanbyrneassociates.ie

w. www.irishcarnews.ie

Irish America Magazine

Suite 2100, 875 Avenue of the Americas, New York, NY 10001, USA

Editor: Patricia Harty

t. +1 212 725 2993

f. +1 212 244 3344

e. irishamag@aol.com

w. www.irishamerica.com

Irish Angler's Digest

Shannon Oughter, Sligo
Editor: E. Parkes
t. +353 71 91 47841
f. +353 71 91 47841
e. parkes@indigo.ie
w. www.irishanglersdigest.com
■ *This is a monthly magazine for angling enthusiasts.*

Irish Arts Review

Irish Arts Review Ltd, State
Apartments, Dublin Castle, Dublin 2
Editor: John Mulcahy
t. +353 1 679 3525
f. +353 1 632 8647
e. editorial@irishartsreview.com
w. www.irishartsreview.com
■ *This quarterly magazine gives a review of the Irish art and design industry.*

Irish Banking Review

Irish Bankers' Federation, Nassau
House, Nassau Street, Dublin 2
Editor: Felix O'Regan
t. +353 1 671 5299
f. +353 1 679 6680
e. felix.oregan@ibf.ie
w. www.ibf.ie
■ *This quarterly magazine covers policy and industry trends in the banking sector.*

Irish Birds

BirdWatch Ireland, Rockingham
House, Newcastle, Co. Wicklow
Editor: Stephen Newton
t. +353 1 281 9878
f. +353 1 281 9763
e. snewton@birdwatchireland.org
w. www.birdwatchireland.ie
■ *This is the annual journal of BirdWatch Ireland and covers birdwatching and conservation.*

Irish Brides and Homes Magazine

Crannagh House, 198 Rathfarnham
Road, Dublin 14
Editor: Jane Phillips
t. +353 1 490 0550
f. +353 1 490 6763
e. info@irishbridesandhomes.ie
w. www.irishbridesandhomes.ie
■ *This is a quarterly magazine for women who are getting married.*

Irish Broker

Holyrood Publications, 134–6 Baldoyle
Industrial Estate, Dublin 13
Managing Editor: Paul Gibson
t. +353 1 839 5060
f. +353 1 839 5062
e. holyrood@clubi.ie

Irish Building Magazine

35A Patrick Street, Dún Laoghaire, Co.
Dublin
Managing Director: Colin Walsh
t. +353 1 280 6030
f. +353 1 284 6328
e. irishbuilding@eircom.net
■ *This is a business management magazine for construction industry executives.*

Irish Car

Whelan Byrne Associates, 2 Sunbury,
Kilcullen, Co. Kildare
Editor: Brian Byrne
t. +353 45 481 090
e. admin@whelbyrneassociates.ie
w. www.irishcarnews.ie
■ *This is a monthly magazine for motoring enthusiasts.*

Irish Computer

CPG House, Glenageary Office Park,
Dún Laoghaire, Co. Dublin
Editor: Eamon McGrane
t. +353 1 284 7777
f. +353 1 284 7584
e. emcgrane@cpg.ie
w. www.irishcomputer.ie
■ *This monthly computer magazine, with a circulation of 42,000, covers news for the computer industry.*

Irish Computer Directory and Diary

Computer Publications Group, CPG House, Glenageary Office Park, Dún Laoghaire, Co. Dublin
Sales Manager: Stephen Pearson
t. +353 1 284 7777
f. +353 1 284 7584
e. spearson@cpg.ie
■ *This yearbook gives a directory of computer goods on the Irish market.*

Irish Construction Industry Magazine

Commercial Publications Ltd, 24 Idrone Lane, Blackrock, Co. Dublin
Editor: Michael Hayes
t. +353 1 283 3233
f. +353 1 2833254
e. mhayes@irishconstruction.com
w. www.irishconstruction.com

Irish Crime

101 Grange Way, Baldoyle Industrial Estate, Dublin 13
Editor: Michael Sheridan
t. +353 1 839 8008
f. +353 1 839 8007
e. crime@newcenturypublishing.com
w. www.newcenturypublishing.com
■ *This magazine covers all aspects of crime and is published twice a month.*

Irish Criminal Law Journal

Thomson Round Hall Ltd, 43 Fitzwilliam Place, Dublin 2
House Editor: Paul Anthony McDermott
t. +353 1 662 5301
f. +353 1 662 5302
e. info@roundhall.ie
■ *This quarterly journal features scholarly articles on criminal law and criminology.*

Irish Current Law Monthly Digest

Thomson Round Hall Ltd, 43 Fitzwilliam Place, Dublin 2
Editor: Martin McCann
t. +353 1 662 5301
f. +353 1 662 5302

e. info@roundhall.ie
■ *This monthly journal gives a round-up of higher court judgments and developments in all forms of legislation.*

Irish Cycling Review

PO Box 7992, Dún Laoghaire, Co. Dublin
Editor: Frank Quinn
t. +353 1 284 0137
f. +353 1 284 0137
e. quinnf@oceanfree.net
■ *Published three times a year, this magazine is aimed at Irish cycling enthusiasts.*

Irish Economic and Social History

Economic and Social History Society of Ireland, c/o Department of Modern History, Trinity College, Dublin 2
Editors: Prof. S. J. Connolly, School of History, Queen's University, Belfast, and Dr Neal Garnham, Academy for Irish Cultural Heritages, University of Ulster, Derry
■ *This is an annual scholarly journal dealing with economic and social history.*

Irish Educational Studies

Educational Studies Association of Ireland, Drumcondra Education Centre, Drumcondra Road, Dublin 9
Editor: Ciarán Sugrue
t. +353 1 857 6400
f. +353 1 857 6499
e. info@ecdrumcondra.ie
■ *This scholarly journal of education research is published three times a year.*

Irish Electrical Review Retail

Sky Publishing Ltd, 5 Main Street, Blackrock, Co. Dublin
Publisher: Patrick J. Codyre
t. +353 1 283 6755
f. +353 1 283 6784
e. ier@indigo.ie
■ *This monthly trade bulletin outlines news and developments for independent retailers, multiples and buyer groups.*

Irish Electrical Review Trade

Sky Publishing Ltd, 5 Main Street,
Blackrock, Co. Dublin
Publisher: Patrick J. Codyre
t. +353 1 283 6755
f. +353 1 283 6784
e. ier@indigo.ie
■ *This monthly trade bulletin outlines
news and developments for wholesalers and
contractors.*

Irish Emigrant, The

Irish Emigrant Publications, Cathedral
Building, Middle Street, Galway
Publisher: Liam Ferrie
t. +353 91 569 158
f. +353 91 569 178
e. iepro@emigrant.ie
w. www.irishemigrant.com
■ *This weekly newsletter gives Irish news for
the Irish community around the world. Its
print edition is published in Boston and New
York, while it is also published on the web and
as an electronic newsletter.*

Irish Employment Law Journal

Round Hall Ltd, 43 Fitzwilliam Place,
Dublin 2
Editor: Cliona Kimber
t. +353 1 289 3305
f. +353 1 289 6406
e. info@roundhall.ie
w. www.roundhall
■ *This journal covering trends in employment
law is published five times a year.*

Irish Engineers' Journal

IFP Media, 31 Dean's Grange Road,
Blackrock, Co. Dublin
Editor: Bernard Potter
t. +353 1 289 3305
f. +353 1 289 6406
e. bernard@ifpmedia.com
w. www.ifpmedia.com

Irish Entrepreneur

Morrissey Media Ltd, Clondaw House,
Clondaw Lower, Ferns, Co. Wexford

Editor: Maree Morrissey
t. +353 53 36884
f. +353 53 36881
e. info@irishentrepreneur.com
w. www.irishentrepreneur.com
■ *A magazine for Irish entrepreneurs.*

Irish Farmer's Journal

Irish Farm Centre, Bluebell, Dublin 12
Editor: Matt Dempsey
t. +353 1 419 9500
f. +353 1 452 0876
e. mdempsey@farmersjournal.ie
w. www.farmersjournal.ie

Irish Farmers' Monthly

IFP Media, 31 Dean's Grange Road,
Blackrock, Co. Dublin
Editor: Paul O'Grady
t. +353 1 289 3305
f. +353 1 289 6406
e. paul@ifpmedia.com
w. www.ifpmedia.com
■ *This is a monthly magazine dealing with
farmers' issues with a circulation of 24,000.*

Irish Field, The

Irish Farm Centre, Bluebell, Dublin 12
Managing Editor: Leo Powell
t. +353 1 405 1100
f. +353 1 455 4008
e. info@irishfield.ie
w. www.irishfield.ie
■ *This weekly newspaper dealing with all
aspects of the Irish horseracing industry has a
circulation of more than 14,000.*

Irish Food

31 Dean's Grange Road, Blackrock,
Co. Dublin
Editor: Miriam Atkins
t. +353 1 289 3305
f. +353 1 289 6406
e. miriamp@ifpmedia.com
w. www.ifpmedia.com
■ *This trade magazine has a controlled circulation among foreign food and drink buyers in
Europe.*

Irish Forestry

Society of Irish Foresters, Enterprise
Centre, Ballintogher, Co. Sligo
Editor: Eugene Hendrick
t. +353 71 916 4434
f. +353 71 913 4904
e. sif@eircom.net
w. www.societyofirishforesters.ie
■ *This is the twice-yearly journal of the*
Society of Irish Foresters.

Irish Garden, The

PO Box 69, Bray, Co. Wicklow
Editor: Gerry Daly
t. +353 1 286 2649
f. +353 1 286 4215
e. edit@tig.iol.ie
w. www.theirishgarden.com
■ *This magazine for gardening enthusiasts is*
published ten times a year.

Irish Hairdresser

PO Box 28, An Post Mail Centre,
Coosan, Athlone, Co. Westmeath
Editor: Maeve O'Healy-Harte
t. +353 87 988 9771
e. mohh@eircom.net
■ *This hairdressing trade magazine is pub-*
lished twice a month.

Irish Hardware

Jemma Publications, Marino House, 52
Glasthule Road, Sandycove, Co. Dublin
Editor: Martin Foran
t. +353 1 280 0000
f. +353 1 280 1818
e. m.foran@jemma.ie
■ *This is a monthly hardware trade magazine*
for hardware and DIY shops.

Irish Homes Magazine

Cyndale Enterprises Ltd, 48 North
Great George's Street, Dublin 1
Editor: Berenice Brindley
t. +353 1 878 0444
f. +353 1 878 7740
e. info@irishhomes.ie
w. www.irishhomes.ie

■ *This is a bi-monthly magazine dealing*
with interiors and home décor.

Irish Interiors

Unit F5, Bymac Centre, Northwest
Business Park, Dublin 15
Editor: Muriel Bolger
t. +353 1 822 4477
f. +353 1 822 4485
e. admin@pembrokepublishing.com
■ *This magazine, covering interior design and*
décor, is published twice a year.

Irish Journal of Education

Educational Research Centre, St
Patrick's College, Drumcondra Road,
Dublin 9
Editor: Thomas Kellaghan
t. +353 1 837 3789
f. +353 1 837 8997
w. www.erc.ie
■ *This annual publication, available on sub-*
scription, features scholarly articles on all
aspects of education.

Irish Journal of Family Law

Thomson Round Hall Ltd,
43 Fitzwilliam Place, Dublin 2
Editor: Geoffrey Shannon
t. +353 1 662 5301
f. +353 1 662 5302
e. info@roundhall.ie
w. www.roundhall.ie
■ *This quarterly legal magazine features*
articles on all aspects of family law.

Irish Journal of Management

Blackhall Publishing, 27 Carysfort
Avenue, Blackrock, Co. Dublin
Editors: Teresa Brannick, NUID; Norma
Heaton, UU; and Patrick Flood, UL
t. +353 1 278 5090
f. +353 1 278 4446
e. info@blackhallpublishing.com
■ *This journal of the Irish Academy of*
Management, published twice a year, prints
articles on research in Irish business.

Irish Journal of Medical Science
2nd Floor, International House, 20–33
Lower Hatch Street, Dublin 2
Editor: Thomas N. Walsh
t. +353 1 662 3706
f. +353 1 661 1684
e. journal@rami.ie
w. www.rami.ie
■ *This is the quarterly journal of the Royal Academy of Medicine in Ireland.*

Irish Journal of Psychological Medicine
25 Adelaide Street, Dún Laoghaire, Co. Dublin
Editor: Prof. Brian Lawlor
t. +353 1 280 3967
f. +353 1 280 7076
e. mail@medmedia.ie
■ *This is a research journal distributed to psychiatrists in Ireland and overseas.*

Irish Jurist
Thomson Round Hall Ltd,
43 Fitzwilliam Place, Dublin 2
Editor: Prof. Finbar McAuley
t. +353 1 662 5301
f. +353 1 662 5302
■ *This annual legal periodical, founded in 1848, features academic articles on legal issues.*

Irish Law Reports Monthly
Thomson Round Hall Ltd, 43
Fitzwilliam Place, Dublin 2
House Editor: Hilary Delany
t. +353 1 662 5301
f. +353 1 662 5302
e. info@roundhall.ie
■ *Published fourteen times a year, this gives reports of judgments in the higher courts.*

Irish Law Times
Thomson Round Hall Ltd,
43 Fitzwilliam Place, Dublin 2
Editor: David P. Boyle
t. +353 1 662 5301
f. +353 1 662 5302
e. info@roundhall.ie

■ *This journal, published twenty times a year, provides up-to-date information on cases, personal injury awards and new legislation.*

Irish Marketing and Advertising Journal
45 Upper Mount Street, Dublin 2
Editor: Seamus Bagnall
t. +353 1 661 1660
f. +353 1 661 1632
e. editor@irishmarketingjournal.ie
w. www.adworld.ie
■ *This marketing and advertising journal for professionals working in the sector is published monthly.*

Irish Marketing News
IRN Publications, 121–3 Ranelagh, Dublin 6
Managing Editor: Julie Colby
t. +353 1 497 2711
f. +353 1 497 2779
e. jcolby@irn.ie
■ *This is the official magazine of the Marketing Institute of Ireland and is published twice a month.*

Irish Media Contacts Directory
Media Information Services, PO Box 8250, Dún Laoghaire, Co. Dublin
Managing Editor: Mike Burns
t. +353 1 284 5892
f. +353 1 284 5059
e. medinfserv@eircom.net
■ *This is a twice-yearly guide to the print and broadcast media in Ireland sold by subscription and direct order.*

Irish Medical Directory
Medical Information Systems, PO Box 5049, Dublin 6
Editor: Dr Maurice Guéret
t. +353 1 492 6040
f. +353 1 492 6040
e. info@imd.ie
w. www.imd.ie
■ *This is an annual directory of health services and health care professionals throughout the country.*

Irish Medical Journal

IMO House, 10 Fitzwilliam Place,
Dublin 2
Editor: Dr John Murphy
t. +353 1 676 7273
f. +353 1 661 2758
e. imj@imj.ie
w. www.imj.ie
■ *This is the official journal of the Irish Medical Organisation (IMO) and covers news and trends in the medical profession.*

Irish Medical News

MAC Communications, Taney Hall,
Eglinton Terrace, Dublin 14
Editor: Gary Finnegan
t. +353 1 296 000
f. +353 1 296 0383
e. gfinnegan@maccommunications.ie
w. www.imj.ie
■ *This is a weekly newspaper covering medical and political news in the industry. It has a circulation of 6,802.*

Irish Medical Times

Medical Publications Ireland Ltd,
24–26 Upper Ormond Quay, Dublin 7
Editor: Colin Kerr
t. +353 1 817 6300
f. +353 1 817 6335
e. colin.kerr@imt.ie
w. www.imt.ie

Irish Motor Industry

IFP Ltd, 31 Dean's Grange Road,
Blackrock, Co. Dublin
Editor: Daniel Attwood
t. +353 1 289 3305
f. +353 1 289 6406
e. daniel@ifpmedia.com
w. www.ifp.ie
■ *This is the official journal of the Society of the Irish Motor Industry (SIMI), which is distributed monthly to its members, giving news and information on national and international events.*

Irish Pharmacist

Eireann Healthcare Publications, 25
Windsor Place, Dublin 2
Editor: Stephen Meyler
t. +353 1 475 3300
f. +353 1 475 3311
e. drlove@eireannpublications.ie
■ *This is a monthly trade magazine for pharmacists.*

Irish Pharmacy Journal

18 Shrewsbury Road, Dublin 4
t. +353 1 283 7294
f. +353 1 283 7678
e. journal@pharmaceuticalsociety.ie
■ *This is the official journal of the Pharmaceutical Society of Ireland and is published ten times a year.*
Editor: Val Harte

Irish Planning and Environmental Law Journal

Thomson Round Hall Ltd,
43 Fitzwilliam Place, Dublin 2
Editor: Emma Galligan
t. +353 1 662 5301
f. +353 662 5302
e. info@roundhall.ie
w.www.roundhall.ie
■ *This quarterly trade magazine gives news updates on planning and environmental law.*

Irish Practice Nurse

Eireann Healthcare Publications, 25–26
Windsor Place, Dublin 2
Editor: Anne-Marie Hardiman
t. +353 1 475 3300
f. +353 1 475 3311
e. ahardiman@eireannpublications.ie
■ *This trade magazine for nurses is published twice a month.*

Irish Printer

Jemma Publications Ltd, Marino
House, 52 Glasthule Road, Sandycove,
Co. Dublin
Editor: Nigel Tynan
t. +353 1 280 0000

f. +353 1 280 1818

e. n.tynan@jemma.ie

■ *This monthly trade magazine for the printing industry is distributed to printers and publishers.*

Irish Property Buyer

Clarendon Communications,
33 Clarendon Street, Dublin 2
Editor: Angela Long

t. +353 1 635 1699

f. +353 1 635 1696

e. editoripb@eircom.net

■ *This property magazine is published bi-monthly.*

Irish Psychiatrist, The

Eireann Healthcare Publications,
25 Windsor Place, Dublin 2
Editor: Maura Henderson

t. +353 1 475 3300

f. +353 1 475 3311

e. mhenderson@eireannpublications.ie

■ *This trade magazine for psychiatrists is published twice a month.*

Irish Psychologist, The

CX House, 2A Corn Exchange Place,
Dublin 2

t. +353 1 474 9160

f. +353 1 474 9161

e. info@psihq.ie

w. www.psihq.ie

■ *This is the monthly newsletter of the Psychological Society of Ireland, and review articles can be submitted at any time.*

Irish Racing Calendar

Horse Racing Ireland, Thoroughbred
County House, Kill, Co. Kildare
Editor: Martin Murphy

t. +353 45 842 800

f. +353 45 842 801

e. info@hri.ie

w. www.horseracingireland.ie

■ *This industry newsletter is distributed to owners, jockeys and all horseracing professionals.*

Irish Red Cross Review

Irish Red Cross Society, 16 Merrion
Square, Dublin 2
Editor: Aoife MacEoin

t. +353 1 676 5135

f. +353 1 661 4461

e. info@redcross.ie

w. www.redcross.ie

■ *This is the quarterly journal distributed to policy-makers and journalists, as well as Red Cross members.*

Irish Review, The

Cork University Press, Youngline
Industrial Estate, Pouladuff Road,
Togher, Cork
Editors: Colin Graham, Michael
Cronin and Claire O'Halloran

t. +353 21 490 2980

f. +353 21 431 5329

e. corkunip@ucc.ie

w. www.corkuniversitypress.com

■ *This critical review of literature, arts, history and science is published twice a year.*

Irish Rugby Review

PO Box 7992, Dún Laoghaire,
Co. Dublin
Editor: Frank Quinn

t. +353 1 284 0137

f. +353 1 284 0137

e. quinnf@oceanfree.net

■ *This magazine reviews the Irish rugby scene and is published eleven times a year.*

Irish Runner

PO Box 1227, Dublin 8
Editor: Frank Greally

t. +353 1 620 0089

e. editor@irishrunner.ie

w.www.irishrunner.ie

■ *This is a magazine for running enthusiasts, published twice a month.*

Irish Scientist Yearbook, The

Oldbury Publishing Ltd, 55 Kimmage
Road West, Dublin 12
Editor: Geraldine Van Esbeck

t. +353 1 465 2310
f. +353 1 465 2311
e. irishscientist@oldbury.ie
w. www.irishscientist.ie
■ *This annual book gives a review of scientific and technological activities throughout Ireland.*

Irish Skipper, The

MAC Communications Ltd, Taney Hall, Eglinton Terrace, Dublin 14
Editor: Cormac Burke
t. +353 74 956 2843
f. +353 1 74 954 8940
e. skippereditor@iol.ie
■ *This is the monthly journal of the Irish fishing and aquaculture industry.*

Irish Soccer Magazine

PO Box 7992, Dún Laoghaire, Co. Dublin
Editor: Frank Quinn
t. +353 1 284 0137
f. +353 1 284 0137
e. quinnf@oceanfree.net
■ *This magazine for soccer fans is published nine times a year.*

Irish Social Worker

Irish Association of Social Workers, 114–16 Pearse Street, Dublin 2
Editor: Lorna Kavanagh
t. +353 1 677 4838
f. +353 1 671 5734
e. iasw@eircom.net
w. www.iasw.ie
■ *This is the official journal of the Irish Association of Social Workers.*

Irish Stock Market Annual, The

Coliemore House, Coliemore Road, Dalkey, Co. Dublin
Publisher: Mark O'Neill
t. +353 1 284 8911
f. +353 1 204 8177
e. info@privateresearch.ie
■ *This annual review of the Irish stock market is distributed to those dealing in the stock market, as well as being sold in some bookshops.*

Irish Tatler

Clanwilliam House, 2 Clanwilliam Place, Dublin 2
Editor: Elizabeth McCormack
t. +353 1 240 5300
e. emccormack@harmonia.ie
w. www.harmonia.ie
■ *This monthly women's magazine features articles on fashion, beauty, food, careers and relationship issues. Its readership is aged between 30 and 45.*

Irish Theological Quarterly

St Patrick's College, Maynooth, Co. Kildare
Editor: Vincent Twomey SVD
t. +353 1 708 3496
f. +353 1 628 9063
e. itqeditor@may.ie
■ *This quarterly magazine features articles by leading national and international theologians. It is produced by members of the Faculty of Theology at St Patrick's College, Maynooth.*

Irish Travel Trade News

A12 Calmont Park, Ballymount Road, Dublin 12
Editor: Michael Flood
t. +353 1 450 2422
f. +353 1 450 2954
e. editor@irishtraveltradenews.com
■ *This is a monthly trade magazine for the travel industry.*

Irish Trucker

Lynn Publications Ltd, Kells Business Park, Kells, Co. Meath
Editor: John Lynch
t. +353 46 92 41923
f. +353 46 9241 926
e. lynnpublications@eircom.net
w. www.irishtrucker.com
■ *This is a monthly trade magazine for the trucking industry.*

Irish Veterinary Journal

31 Dean's Grange Road, Blackrock, Co. Dublin
Editor: Catriona Boyle

t. +353 1 289 3305
f. +353 1 289 6406
e. catriona@ifpmedia.com
w. www.ifpmedia.com
■ *This is the monthly trade journal of Veterinary Ireland, covering all aspects of the industry.*

Irish Youthwork Scene

Irish Youthwork Centre, NYF,
20 Lower Dominick Street, Dublin 1
Editor: Fran Bissett
t. +353 1 872 9933
f. +353 1 872 4183
e. fbissett@nyf.ie
w. www.iywc.com
■ *This newsletter is published four times a year and features articles on youth-related issues.*

Iris Oifigiúil

Government Supplies Agency, 51 St Stephen's Green, Dublin 2
Editor: Mick Dunne
t. +353 1 647 6838
f. +353 1 647 6842
e. irisoifigiuil@opw.ie
w. www.irisoifigiuil.ie
■ *This is the official state gazette, published twice a week.*

It's All about Living

Ashville Media Group, Apollo House,
Tara Street, Dublin 2
Editor: Claire O'Mahony
t. +353 1 432 2200
f. +353 1 672 7100
e. info@ashville.com
w. www.ashville.com
■ *This quarterly newsletter is the official publication of the health insurers VHI and is distributed to all members.*

Journal, The

James Wims, Brandsma, Killucan,
Co. Westmeath
Ireland Editor: James Wims
t. +353 44 76744
m. +353 86 838 8006

■ *This is the twice-monthly magazine of the Chartered Institute of Journalists and the Institute of Journalists.*

Journal of Music in Ireland

Edenvale, Esplanade, Bray, Co. Wicklow
Editor: Toner Quinn
t. +353 1 286 7292
f. +353 1 286 7292
e. editor@thejmi.com
w. www.thejmi.com
■ *This magazine contains reviews and articles on traditional, contemporary, classical and jazz music. It is published every two months.*

Journal of the Irish Dental Association

Irish Dental Association, 10 Richview Office Park, Clonskeagh Road,
Dublin 14
Editor: Dr Aisling O'Mahony
t. +353 1 283 0499
f. +353 1 283 0515
e. info@irishdentalassoc.ie
w. www.dentist.ie
■ *This is the quarterly professional journal of the Irish Dental Association.*

Kiss

Vymura Ltd, 3 Ely Place, Dublin 2
Editor: Susan Vasquez
t. +353 1 676 9832
f. +353 1 480 4799
e. info@kiss.ie
w. www.kiss.ie

KT Parenting

HRM Printers, 51 Allen Park Road,
Stillorgan, Co. Dublin
Editor: Suzanne Gunn
t. +353 1 205 6895
f. +353 1 210 0884
e. kindergartentimes@ireland.com
■ *This is a quarterly parenting magazine.*

Law Society Gazette

Law Society of Ireland, Blackhall Place,
Dublin 7

Editor: Conal O'Boyle
t. +353 1 672 4828
f. +353 1 672 4877
e. c.oboyle@lawsociety.ie
w. www.lawsociety.ie
■ *This magazine, featuring professional news and information for solicitors, is published ten times a year.*

Licensed Vintners' Association Directory and Diary

Tara Publishing Company Ltd, Poolbeg House, 1–2 Poolbeg Street, Dublin 2
Managing Director: Fergus Farrell
t. +353 1 241 3095
f. +353 1 241 3010
■ *This is the official annual publication of the Irish Vintners' Association, circulated free to members in the licensed trade.*

Licensing World

Jemma Publications Ltd, Marino House, 52 Glasthule Road, Sandycove, Co. Dublin
Editor: Nigel Tynan
t. +353 1 280 0000
f. +353 1 280 1818
e. n.tynan@jemma.ie
■ *This is a montly trade magazine for the licensed trade.*

Lifeboats Ireland

15 Windsor Terrace, Dún Laoghaire, Co. Dublin
Editor: Claire Brennan
t. +353 1 284 50 50
f. +353 1 284 5052
e. lifeboatsireland@rnli.org.uk
■ *This is the annual journal of the Royal National Lifeboat Institution in Ireland, with a circulation of 7,500.*

Lifetimes

26A Phibsborough Place, Dublin 7
Editor: Tricia Coogan
t. +353 1 830 6667
f. +353 1 830 6833
e. lifetimes@dna.ie

Local Authority Times

Institute of Public Administration, 57–61 Lansdowne Road, Dublin 4
Editor: Mark Callanan
t. +353 1 240 3632
f. +353 1 668 9135
e. mcallanan@ipa.ie
w. www.ipa.ie
■ *This local government news magazine, published four times a year, is distributed among all local authority representatives and staff.*

Local News

Local News Publications, Bank House Centre, 331 South Circular Road, Dublin 8
Editor: Jason O'Toole
t. +353 1 453 4011
f. +353 1 454 9024
e. thelocalnews@iol.ie

Macra na Feirme Yearbook and Diary

Ashville Media Group, Apollo House, Tara Street, Dublin 2
Editor: Meg Walker
t. +353 1 432 2200
f. +353 1 672 7100
e. info@ashville.com
w. www.ashville.com
■ *This is the yearbook of the Irish young farmers' organisation.*

Magill

Magoo Ltd, 1–4 Swift's Alley, Dublin 8
Editor: Eamonn Delaney
t. +353 1 416 7800
f. +353 1 416 7899
e. magilleditorial@bandf.net
■ *This is a recently relaunched politics and current affairs magazine that has a tradition of investigative journalism.*

Manufacturing Ireland

Advance Publications Ltd, Acorn House, 38 St Peter's Road, Dublin 7
Editor: Willo Litzouw
t. +353 1 868 6640
f. +353 1 868 6651

e. willo@aplgroup.net

w. www.aplgroup.net

■ *This trade magazine for the manufacturing sector is published ten times a year.*

MAPS (Media, Advertising, Promotions and Sponsorship)

MAC Communications Ltd, Taney Hall, Eglinton Terrace, Dundrum, Dublin 14

Editor: Sarah McQuaid

t. +353 1 296 0000

f. +353 1 296 0383

e. info@maccommunications.ie

■ *Published annually, this is the official media directory of the Association of Advertisers in Ireland.*

Marine Times

Anvil Court, New Row, Killybegs, Co. Donegal

Editor: Mark McCarthy

t. +353 74 973 1239

f. +353 74 973 1822

e. marinetimes@eircom.net

w. www.marinetimes.ie

■ *This is a monthly fishing and marine life magazine.*

Marketing

1 Albert Park, Sandycove, Co. Dublin

Editor: Michael Cullen

t. +353 1 284 4456

f. +353 1 280 7735

e. cullen@marketing.ie

w. www.marketing.ie

■ *This monthly subscription magazine is sent to advertising, PR and other media executives.*

Maternity

Ashville Media Group, Apollo House, Tara Street, Dublin 2

Editor: Meg Walker

t. +353 432 2200

f. +353 1 672 7100

e. info@ashville.com

w. www.ashville.com

■ *This is the annual publication for maternity hospitals.*

Mayo Magazine

32 Kilkerrin Business Park, Liosbán Industrial Estate, Tuam Road, Galway

Managing Editor: Michael Lally

t. +353 91 758 811

e. info@irelandguides.ie

w. www.irelandguides.ie

■ *This annual magazine offers a guide on aspects of Co. Mayo.*

Medical Missionaries of Mary Magazine

MMM Communications, Rosemount Terrace, Booterstown, Co. Dublin

Editor: Sister Isabelle Smyth

t. +353 1 288 7180

f. +353 1 283 4626

e. mmm@iol.ie

w. www.mmmworldwide.org

■ *This is the annual magazine of an organisation comprising nuns and lay people dedicated to helping the poor around the world.*

Medico-Legal Journal of Ireland

Thomson Round Hall Ltd, 43 Fitzwilliam Place, Dublin 2

In-House Editor: Susan Rossney

t. +353 1 662 5301

f. +353 1 662 5302

e. susan.rossney@thomson.com

w. www.ucd.ie/~legalmed

■ *This twice-yearly journal covers medical law issues.*

Menswear in Ireland

Futura Communications Ltd, 5 Main Street, Blackrock, Co. Dublin

Publishing Director: Patrick J. Codyre

t. +353 1 283 6782

f. +353 1 283 6784

e. futura@indigo.ie

■ *This is a trade magazine for the men's retail sector, with a circulation of 4,000.*

Midlands Magazine

PO Box 28, An Post Mail Centre, Coosan, Athlone, Co. Westmeath

Editor: Maeve O'Healy-Harte
t. +353 87 988 9771
e. info@midlandsmagazine.ie
■ *This is a quarterly life-style magazine, concentrating on the midlands area.*

Milltown Studies
Milltown Institute of Theology and
Philosophy, Miltown Park, Dublin 6
Editor: Dr Kieran O'Mahony OSA
t. +353 1 269 8388
f. +353 1 269 2528
e. komahony@milltown-institute.ie
w. www.miltown-institute.ie
■ *This twice-yearly scholarly journal
publishes articles and reviews on philosophy
and theology.*

Modern Medicine
Eireann Publications, 25 Windsor
Place, Dublin 2
Editor: Maura Henderson
t. +353 46 90 21442
f. +353 46 90 23565
e. mhenderson@eireannpublications.ie
■ *This bi-monthly publication covers trends
and issues in clinical medicine.*

Modern Woman
The Meath Chronicle, Market Square,
Navan, Co. Meath
Editor: Margot Davis
t. +353 1 46 907 9600
f. +353 46 902 3565
e. harriet@meath-chronicle.ie
■ *This is a national monthly paper for
women and is published by the* **Meath
Chronicle,** *which distributes a Co. Meath
edition with the* **Meath Chronicle.**

Moments
Ashville Media Group, Apollo House,
Tara Street, Dublin 2
Editor: Meg Walker
t. +353 1 432 2200
f. +353 1 672 7100
e. info@ashville.com
■ *This is the official annual magazine of the
Jury Doyle Hotel Group.*

Mongrel
69 Middle Abbey Street, Dublin 1
Editor: Sam Bungey
t. +353 874 7548
f. +353 1 633 5968
e. info@mongrel.ie
w. www.mongrel.ie
■ *This free monthly magazine is aimed at
readers aged between 18 and 25. It contains
interviews, reviews and photojournalism.*

Motoring Life
Cyndale Enterprises Ltd, 48 North
Great George's Street, Dublin 1
Editor: Geraldine Herbert
t. +353 1 878 0444
f. +353 1 878 7740
e. info@motoringlife.ie
■ *Founded in 1946, this bi-monthly motoring
magazine features car reviews and an annual
buyer's guide.*

Motor Market
The Publishing Company, Unit 5,
Woodpark, Sallynoggin, Co. Dublin
Editor: Brendan Barrett
t. +353 1 284 0266
f. +353 1 284 0860
e. publishingco@indigo.ie
w. www.motormarket.ie
■ *This is a weekly magazine with new and
second-hand cars for sale.*

Motorshow
Automotive Publications, Glencree
House, Lanesborough Road,
Roscommon
Editor: Padraic J. Deane
t. +353 90 662 5676
f. +353 90 663 7410
e. pdeane@autopub.ie
w. www.motorshow.ie
■ *This is an annual magazine for car enthusiasts, featuring a car buyer's guide.*

Moving In
Argyll Communications, 29
Charlemont Lane, Dublin 3
Editor: Clodagh Edwards

t. +353 1 833 0560

f. +353 1 833 0826

e. clodagh.edwards@argyllcommuni-
cations.ie

■ *This is a bi-monthly interiors and house-
buying guide for those moving into a new
home.*

NCBI News

NCBI, Whitworth Road, Dublin 9

Editor: Frank Callery

t. +353 1 830 7033

f. +353 1 830 7787

e. info@ncbi.ie

w. www.ncbi.ie

■ *Published six times a year in print, in
braille, in audio and on the web, this is the
newsletter for the National Council for the
Blind in Ireland.*

Northwest Visitor's Guide

32 Kilkerrin Business Park, Liosbán
Industrial Estate, Tuam Road, Galway

Managing Editor: Michael Lally

t. +353 91 758 811

e. info@irelandguides.ie

w. www.irelandguides.ie

■ *This is an annual guide to the north-west
for tourists and visitors.*

Nursing in the Community

MedMedia Publications, 25 Adelaide
Street, Dún Laoghaire, Co. Dublin

Editor: Tara Horan

t. +353 1 280 3967

f. +353 1 280 7076

e. nursing@medmedia.ie

■ *This monthly trade magazine is circulated
to nurses in the Republic.*

Obair

51 St Stephen's Green, Dublin 2

Editor: George Moir

t. +353 1 647 6128

f. +353 1 647 6491

e. george.moir@opw.ie

w. www.opw.ie

■ *This is the bi-annual magazine for staff
and customers of the Office of Public Works.*

Organic Matters

Irish Organic Farmers' and Growers'
Association, Harbour Road, Kilbeggan,
Co. Westmeath

Editors: David Storey and Cáit Curran

t. +353 93 55707

e. d.storey@indigo.ie and
ccurran@ireland.com

w. www.organicmattersmag.com

■ *This magazine, published six times a year,
deals with organic farming and gardening and
is circulated to members of the Irish Organic
Farmers' Association.*

Outlook

Kimmage Manor, Whitehall Road,
Dublin 12

Editor: Mary Rieke Murphy

t. +353 1 492 8519

f. +353 1 492 8586

e. editoroutlook@eircom.net

■ *This bi-monthly missionary magazine is
published by the Holy Ghost Mission.*

Outsider

The Outsider Media Ltd, 32 Lower
Leeson Street, Dublin 2

Publisher and Editor-in-Chief:
Damian Hackett

t. +353 1 283 8523

f. +353 1 283 8525

e. info@outsider.ie

w. www.outsider.ie

■ *This monthly outdoor pursuits magazine
features articles on sports such as climbing,
kayaking and mountain biking.*

PC Live!

Media Team Ltd, Trintech Building,
South County Buisiness Park,
Leopardstown, Dublin 18

Editor: Stephen Cawley

t. +353 1 207 4288

f. +353 1 207 4299

e. stephen.cawley@mediateam.ie

w. www.pclive.ie

■ *This is a monthly computer and internet
magazine, with a circulation of 10,000.*

Peatland News

Irish Peatland Conservation Council,
Bog of Allen Conservation Centre,
Rathangan, Co. Kildare
Editor: Catherine O'Connell
t. +353 45 860133
f. +353 45 860481
e. bogs@ipcc.ie
w. www.ipcc.ie
■ *This bogland information and conservation newsletter is published twice a year.*

Phoenix

Penfield Enterprises Ltd, 44 Lower
Baggot Street, Dublin 2
Editor: Paddy Prendiville
t. +353 1 661 1062
f. +353 1 662 4532
e. goldhawk@indigo.ie
w. www.phoenix-magazine.com
■ *This is a fortnightly current affairs and satirical magazine.*

Pioneer

Pioneer Total Abstinence Association,
27 Upper Sherrard Street, Dublin 1
Chairperson: Micheál Mac Gréil
t. +353 1 874 9464
f. +353 1 874 8485
e. pioneer@jesuit.ie
w. www.pioneertotal.ie
■ *This is the monthly journal of the Pioneer Association, a Catholic organisation whose members vow not to drink alcohol or take drugs.*

Plan: The Business of Building

Plan Magazines Ltd, 5–7 Main Street,
Blackrock, Co. Dublin
News Editor: Denise McGuire
t. +353 1 278 8161
f. +353 1 278 8133
e. info@planmagazine.ie
w. www.planmagazine.ie
■ *This is a monthly trade magazine for the building industry.*

Plantman

1 The Green, Kingswood Heights,
Dublin 24
Managing Editor: Patrick Murphy
t. +353 1 452 0898
f. +353 1 452 0898
e. info@plantmanmagazine.com
w. www.plantmanmagazine.com
■ *This is a monthly trade magazine for the quarrying industry.*

Poetry Ireland Review

120 St Stephen's Green, Dublin 2
Editor: Peter Sirr
t. +353 1 478 9974
f. +353 1 478 0205
e. poetry@iol.ie
w. www.poetryireland.ie
■ *This is a quarterly poetry magazine, publishing poems, reviews and articles from new and established poets.*

Portfolio

Unit 8, Docklands Innovation Park,
Dublin 3
Publisher: Gerry Proctor
t. +353 1 672 5831
f. +353 1 677 4823
e. info@portfolio.ie
■ *This monthly freesheet covers the Irish Financial Services Centre and the Docklands as well as other businesses in the city.*

Practical Employment Law

Thomson Round Hall Ltd,
43 Fitzwilliam Place, Dublin 2
In-house contact: Susan Rossney
t. +353 1 662 5301
f. +353 1 662 5302
e. susan.rossney@thomson.com
■ *This is a twice-yearly manual giving a guide to employment law.*

Private Research

Coliemore House, Coliemore Road,
Dalkey, Co. Dublin
Publisher: Mark O'Neill
t. +353 1 284 8911

f. +353 1 204 8177
■ *This monthly trade magazine gives an analysis of private companies.*

Professional Insurance Broker, The
Foley Ryan Communications,
69 Fitzwilliam Square, Dublin 2
Editor: John Millet
t. +353 1 662 4649
f. +353 1 676 1940
e. info@foleyryancommunications.com
w. www.piba.ie
■ *This is the official journal of the Professional Insurance Brokers' Association, published quarterly.*

Professional Ireland
Irish Emigrant Publications, Cathedral
Building, Middle Street, Galway
Publisher: Liam Ferrie
t. +353 91 569 158
e. info@emigrant.ie
w. www.emigrant.ie
■ *This weekly newsletter gives professional job listings in Ireland and abroad. It prints editions in the US and is available by e-mail bulletin.*

Property Professional, The
Foley Ryan Communications,
69 Fitzwilliam Square, Dublin 2
Editor: Tim Ryan
t. +353 1 662 4649
f. +353 1 676 1940
e. info@foleyryancommunications.com
■ *This is the official journal of the Institute of Professional Auctioneers and Valuers, published quarterly.*

Property Valuer, The
IAVI, 38 Merrion Square, Dublin 2
Editor: Valerie Bourke
t. +353 1 661 1794
f. +353 1 661 1797
e. info@iavi.ie
w. www.realestate.ie
■ *This is the quarterly journal of the Irish Auctioneers' and Valuers' Institute, which represents estate agents and auctioneers.*

Prudence
Dyflin Publications Ltd, 99 South
Circular Road, Dublin 8
Editor: Alanna Gallagher
t. +353 1 416 7990
f. +353 1 416 7901
e. alanna@prudence.ie
w. www.prudence.ie

Public Affairs Ireland
53 Glasthule Road, Glasthule,
Co. Dublin
Directors: Don Bergin and Garrett
Fennell
t. +353 1 284 5300
f. +353 1 284 5178
e. info@publicaffairsireland.com
w. www.publicaffairsireland.com
■ *This is a monthly guide to political and legislative affairs. It also publishes electronically a weekly commentary on forthcoming parliamentary business.*

Public Affairs News
Pan Publications Ltd, 10 Merrion
Square, Dublin 2
Editor: Veronica McDermott
t. +353 1 662 3436
f. +353 1 662 3437
e. info@panltd.com
w. www.panltd.com
■ *This is a monthly political and economic digest.*

Public Sector Times
Bradán Publishing, 5 Eglinton Road,
Bray, Co. Wicklow
Managing Editor: Shay Fitzmaurice
t. +353 1 286 9111
f. +353 1 286 9074
e. psted@localtimes.ie
■ *This monthly newspaper features news on the civil and public service and is distributed to senior public sector executives.*

Public Service Review
Public Service Executive Union,
30 Merrion Square, Dublin 2

Editor: Tom Geraghty
t. +353 1 676 7271
f. +353 1 661 5777
e. info@pseu.ie
w. www.pseu.ie
■ *This is the official journal of the Public Service Executive Union, the union for senior civil servants, published every two months.*

Reach: Journal of Special Needs Education in Ireland
Irish Association of Teachers in Special Education, Drumcondra Education Centre, Drumcondra Road, Dublin 9
Editor: Patricia Lynch
t. +353 1 884 2035
e. pat.lynch@spd.dcu.ie
w. www.iatseireland.com
■ *This is the journal of special needs education, published twice a year; it aims to be a resource for teachers in the sector.*

Reality Magazine
75 Orwell Road, Dublin 6
Editor: Gerard R. Moloney CSsR
t. +353 1 492 2488
f. +353 1 492 2654
e. info@redemptoristpublications.com
w. www.redemptoristpublications.com
■ *A monthly Catholic magazine, published by the Irish Redemptorists.*

Religious Life Review
42 Parnell Square, Dublin 1
Editor: Thomas McCarthy OP
t. +353 1 873 1355
f. +353 1 873 1760
e. thomas.mccarthy@dominicanpublications.com
■ *This religious magazine is published six times a year.*

Renovate Your House and Home
Dyflin Publications Ltd, 99 South Circular Road, Dublin 8
Editor: Róisín Carabine
t. +353 1 416 7900
f. +353 1 416 7901
e. roisin@houseandhome.ie

w. www.dyflin.ie
■ *This is an annual glossy interiors magazine.*

Retail News
Tara Publishing Company Ltd, Poolbeg House, 1–2 Poolbeg Street, Dublin 2
Editor: John Walshe
t. +353 1 241 3095
f. +353 1 241 3010
e. kathleenbelton@tarapublishingco.com
w. www.retailnews.ie
■ *This grocery trade magazine is published ten times a year. It is the official magazine of the grocers' organisation, RGDATA.*

Room
Goldstar Media Ltd, 7 Cranford Centre, Stillorgan Road, Dublin 4
Editor: Eleanor Flegg
t. +353 1 260 0899
f. +353 1 260 0911
e. jamesgspl@eircom.net
■ *This is an interiors magazine, published bi-annually.*

RTÉ Guide
RTÉ Publishing, RTÉ, Donnybrook, Dublin 4
Editor: Aoife Byrne
t. +353 1 208 2920
f. +353 1 208 3085
e. rteguide@rte.ie
w. www.rte.ie
■ *This is the weekly official television and listings magazine for RTÉ, featuring interviews, features and reviews.*

Running Your Business
Firsthand Publishing, 24 Terenure Road East, Dublin 6
Managing Director: Donal McAuliffe
t. +353 1 490 2244
f. +353 1 492 0578
e. info@ryb.ie
■ *This is the official magazine of the Small Firms Association.*

Runway Airports

Aer Rianta, Collinstown House,
Dublin Airport, Co. Dublin
Editor: Mark McDermott
t. +353 1 814 4273
f. +353 1 814 4663
e. runway@indigo.ie
■ *This bi-monthly magazine is the house
magazine of Aer Rianta, the Irish airport
authority.*

Sacred Heart Messenger, The

Messenger Publications, 37 Lower
Leeson Street, Dublin 2
Editor: Rev. Patrick Carberry SJ
t. +353 1 676 7491
f. +353 1 661 1606
e. sales@messenger.ie
w. www.messenger.ie
■ *This is a monthly religious magazine.*

Salesian Bulletin

SDB Media, Salesian House, Maynooth
Road, Celbridge, Co. Kildare
Editor: Fr Pat Egan SDB
t. +353 1 455 5605
f. +353 1 455 8781
e. frpegan@iol.ie
w. www.homepage.eircom.net/
~sdbmedi
■ *This is a quarterly religious magazine.*

Saoirse

223 Parnell Street, Dublin 1
Editor: Ruairí Óg Ó Brádaigh
t. +353 1 872 9747
f. +353 1 872 9757
e. saoirse@iol.ie
w. www.rsf.ie
■ *This is the monthly newsletter of
Republican Sinn Féin.*

Saol na nOileán

Comhdháil Oileáin na hÉireann, Inis
Oírr, Co. Galway
Editorial and Advertising contact: Bríd
Seoige
t. +353 99 75096
f. +353 99 75103

e. comhdhail.oilean@indigo.ie
w. www.oileain.ie
■ *This free quarterly English and Irish
newsletter is distributed to houses on off-shore
islands.*

Saothar

Irish Labour History Society, Beggar's
Bush, Haddington Road, Dublin 4
Editors: Dónal Ó Drisceoil and Dr
Fintan Lane
t. +353 1 668 1071
e. d.odriscoll@ucc.ie and
fintanlane@ireland.com
w. www.ilhsonline.org/saothar.htm
■ *This is the annual scholarly journal of the
Irish Labour History Society.*

Science

Faculty of Science and Health, Dublin
City University, Collins Avenue
Extension, Dublin 9
Managing Editor: Gillian Murphy
t. +353 1 700 5840
e. gillian.murphy@dcu.ie
w. www.ista.ie
■ *Published four times a year, this is the official journal of the Irish Science Teachers'
Association and contains articles on scientific
topics, forthcoming events and reviews.*

Science Spin

1A Longwood Avenue, Dublin 8
Editors: Seán Duke and Tom Kennedy
t. +353 1 454 5230
e. tom@sciencespin.com
w. www.sciencespin.com
■ *This quarterly magazine contains news and
features about science in Ireland.*

Scripture in Church

Dominican Publications, 42 Parnell
Square, Dublin 1
Editor-in-Chief: Martin McNamara MSC
t. +353 1 872 1611
f. +353 1 873 1760
e. subscriptions@dominicanpublica-
tions.com

■ *This is a quarterly newsletter that aims to aid the celebration of Mass.*

Search

RE Resource Centre, Holy Trinity Church, Rathmines, Dublin 6
Editor: Rev. Canon K.V. Kennerley
t. +353 1 497 2821
f. +353 1 497 2821
■ *This Church of Ireland journal is published three times a year.*

Senior Times

S&L Promotions Ltd, 4 Fitzwilliam Square East, Dublin 2
Editor: John Low
t. +353 1 676 1811
f. +353 1 676 1944
e. slpromotions@iol.ie
w. www.seniortimes.ie
■ *This life-style magazine for the over-fifties is published eight times a year.*

Shannon Region Visitor's Guide

32 Kilkerrin Business Park, Liosbán Industrial Estate, Tuam Road, Galway
Managing Editor: Michael Lally
t. +353 91 758 811
e. info@irelandguides.ie
w. www.irelandguides.ie
■ *This is an annual guide for tourists and visitors to the Shannon region.*

Shelflife

CPG House, Glenageary Office Park, Dún Laoghaire, Co. Dublin
Managing Editor: Colette O'Conor
t. +353 1 201 3720
f. +353 1 284 7584
w. www.shelflife.ie
■ *This trade magazine for the retail sector is published monthly, with a circulation of 8,500.*

Signal

Ashville Media Group, Apollo House, Tara Street, Dublin 2
Editor: Ruairí Kavanagh
t. +353 1 432 2200
f. +353 1 672 7100

e. info@ashville.com
w. www.ashville.com
■ *Published bi-annually, this is the official journal of the Representative Association of Commissioned Officers.*

Síocháin

Concept Publications, Unit B2, Riverview Business Park, New Nangor Road, Dublin 12
Managing Editor: Karina Colgan
t. +353 1 456 8453
f. +353 1 456 8454
e. siochainmagazine@eircom.net
■ *This is the official magazine for the Garda Síochána Retired Members' Association.*

Sláinte

GP Communications, 108 Lower Baggot Street, Dublin 2
Editor: Kay Marham
t. +353 1 662 9452
f. +353 1 678 9855
e. slainte@gpcomm.com or info@inst-er.com
■ *This health magazine is published quarterly.*

Smart Company

Mediateam Ltd, Trintech Building, South County Business Park, Leopardstown, Dublin 18
Editor: Stephen Cawley
t. +353 1 207 4271
f. +353 1 207 4299
e. stephen.cawley@mediateam.ie
w. www.techcentral.ie
■ *This is a quarterly magazine for small to medium-sized businesses.*

Social & Personal

21st Century Media Ltd, 19 Nassau Street, Dublin 2
Editor and Publisher: P. J. Gibbons
t. +353 1 633 3993
f. +353 1 633 4353
e. info@socialandpersonal.ie
w. www.socialandpersonal.ie
■ *This is a monthly style and fashion magazine.*

Socialist Voice

7 Bloom Lane, Dublin 1
Editorial Collective
t. +353 1 874 7981
e. cpoi@eircom.net
■ *This is a monthly newspaper covering politics, culture and economics from a socialist viewpoint.*

Spirituality

Dominican Publications, 42 Parnell
Square, Dublin 1
Editor: Tom Jordan OP
t. +353 1 873 1355
f. +353 1 873 1760
e. editor.spirituality@dominicanpublications.com
w. www.dominicanpublications.com
■ *This Catholic religious magazine is published six times a year.*

Sporting Press

Davis Road, Clonmel, Co. Tipperary
Editor: J. L. Desmond
t. +353 52 21422
f. +353 52 25018
e. news@sportingpress.ie
w. www.sportingpress.ie
■ *This is a weekly greyhound and coursing newspaper.*

Studia Hibernica

St Patrick's College, Drumcondra
Road, Dublin 9
Editorial Company Secretary:
Dr Uáitéar Mac Gearailt
t. +353 1 884 2000
f. +353 1 837 6197
w. www.spd.dcu.ie/main/news/
StudiaHibernica.shtml
■ *This annual scholarly journal features articles on Irish language, history, archaeology and folklore.*

Studies

35 Lower Leeson Street, Dublin 2
Editor: Fergus O'Donoghue SJ
t. +353 1 676 6785
f. +353 1 676 2984
e. studies@jesuit.ie
w. www.studiesirishreview.com
■ *Published four times a year by the Irish Jesuits, this journal looks at issues from a Christian viewpoint.*

Subsea Magazine

Irish Underwater Council, 78A Patrick
Street, Dún Laoghaire, Co. Dublin
Editor: Dr Eddie Burke
t. +353 1 284 4601
f. +353 1 284 4602
e. info@scubaireland.com
w. www.scubaireland.com
■ *This quarterly magazine contains features of interest to scuba divers.*

Teacher Magazine

167 Oranmore Road, Dublin 10
Editor: Roddy Peavoy
t. +353 1 410 0266
f. +353 1 410 0228
e. teacher-magazine@impact-press.ie
■ *This magazine covers primary and secondary education and is distributed to all schools and educational organisations.*

Technology Ireland

Enterprise Ireland, Merrion Hall,
Strand Road, Dublin 4
Editor: Mary Sweetman
t. +353 1 206 6337
f. +353 1 206 6342
e. technology.ireland@enterprise-ireland.ie
w. www.technologyireland.ie
■ *This technology and business magazine is published ten times a year, including a yearbook.*

Today's Farm

Teagasc, Oak Park, Carlow
Editor: Jane Kavanagh
t. +353 59 917 0200
■ *This agricultural magazine, published six times a year, is published by the farm organisation Teagasc.*

Today's Grocery Magazine

The Mews, Upper Eden Road, Dún
Laoghaire, Co. Dublin
Editor: Frank Madden
t. +353 1 280 9466
f. +353 1 280 6896
e. fmadden@todaysgrocery.com
w. www.todaysgrocery.com
■ *This is a monthly magazine for the grocery
trade.*

Totally Dublin

HKM Publishing (Ireland) Ltd,
Camden House, 7 Upper Camden
Street, Dublin 2
Editor: Peter Steen-Christensen
t. +353 1 497 1111
e. peter@hkm.ie
■ *This is a free monthly listings and culture
magazine for Dublin.*

Travel Extra

Exhibition House, 6 Sandyford Office
Park, Dublin 18
Managing Editor: Gerry O'Hare
t. +353 1 845 4485
f. +353 1 845 4468
e. gerry@travelextra.ie
■ *This is a free monthly magazine for the
travel trade.*

TV Now!

Minjara Ltd, 2–4 Ely Place, Dublin 2
Editor: Penny Gray
t. +353 1 676 9832
f. +353 1 480 4799
e. info@tvnowmagazine.ie
■ *This is a weekly television listings guide.*

U Magazine

Harmonia, Clanwilliam House,
2 Clanwilliam Square, Dublin 2
Editor: Deirdre O'Keeffe
t. +353 1 240 5300
f. +353 1 661 9486
e. umag@harmonia.ie
w. www.harmonia.ie
■ *This monthly women's magazine features
fashion, beauty and celebrity interviews and is
aimed at the 18–27 age group.*

Unity

7 Bloom Lane, Dublin 1
Editor: James Stewart
t. +353 1 874 7981
e. cpoi@eircom.net
■ *This is a weekly newsletter on political,
economic and cultural issues, published by the
Communist Party of Ireland.*

Village, The

Westland Court, 44 Westland Row,
Dublin 2
Editor: Vincent Browne
t. +353 1 642 5050
f. +353 1 642 5001
e. editor@villagemagazine.ie and
news@villagemagazine.ie
w. www.villagemagzine.ie
■ *This is a weekly politics and current affairs
magazine, launched in October 2004.*

VIP Magazine

Minjara Ltd, 2–4 Ely Place, Dublin 2
Editor: Emer O'Reilly-Hyland
t. +353 1 676 9832
f. +353 1 480 4799
e. info@vipmagazine.ie
■ *This is a monthly life-style and celebrity
magazine. It includes VIP style magazine.*

Visitor Magazine

MAC Communications Ltd, Taney
Hall, Eglinton Terrace, Dublin 14
Editor: Sarah McQuaid
t. +353 1 296 0000
f. +353 1 296 0383
e. info@maccommunications.ie
■ *This is an annual magazine providing
information and features for visitors to Ireland.*

Voice, The

Benedicta Communications, 11
Merrion Square, Dublin 2
Editor: Simon Rowe
t. +353 1 647 5750
e. editor@thevoice.ie
■ *This national weekly compact-format
paper is aimed at Catholic families and
young readers.*

Walking Matters

PO Box 1227, Dublin 8
Editor: Frank Greally
t. +353 1 620 0089
f. +353 1 620 0089
e. editor@irishrunner.ie
■ *This is a bi-monthly magazine for walking enthusiasts.*

Walking World Ireland

PO Box 9543, Rathmines, Dublin 6
Editor: Martin Joyce
t. +353 1 498 2645
f. +353 1 498 3043
e. joycem@iol.ie
■ *This is a bi-monthly magazine for walking enthusiasts.*

Wedding Journal

Penton Publications Ltd, 8 Dawson Street, Dublin 2
Managing Editor: Tara Craig
t. +353 1 433 7610
f. +353 1 240 9334
e. info@pentonpublications.co.uk
w. www.weddingjournalonline.com
■ *This is a quarterly wedding magazine.*

Weddings Irish Style

Zest Publishing Ltd, Unit F5, Bymac Centre, Northwest Business Park, Dublin 15
Managing Editor: Jacinta O'Brien
t. +353 1 822 4477
f. +353 1 822 4485
e. zestpublishing@eircom.net
■ *This is a quarterly wedding magazine.*

White Book, The

Montague Publications Group, 39 Fitzwilliam Street Upper, Dublin 2
Editorial: Siobhán Buchanan-Johnston
t. +353 1 669 2101
f. +353 1 669 2104
e. montaguegroup@eircom.net
w. www.whitebook.net
■ *This interiors and décor magazine is published twice a year.*

Wine Ireland

CPG House, Glenageary Office Park, Dún Laoghaire, Co. Dublin
Editor: John Doyle
t. +353 1 201 3721
f. +353 1 284 7584
e. wine@cpg.ie
w. www.wineireland.ie
■ *This bi-monthly magazine has news and features for wine-lovers.*

Woman's Way

Harmonia, Clanwilliam House, 2 Clanwilliam Place, Dublin 2
Editor: Marie Kelly
t. +353 1 240 5300
f. +353 1 661 9757
e. rmcmeel@harmonia.ie
w. www.harmonia.ie
■ *This is a weekly women's magazine containing human-interest features, regular columns, beauty, food and fashion. It is aimed at the 35–55 age group.*

Word, The

Divine Word Missionaries, Maynooth, Co. Kildare
Editor-in-Chief: Vincent Twomey SVD
t. +353 1 505 4467
f. +353 1 628 9184
e. wordeditor@eircom.net
w. www.theword.ie
■ *This is a monthly magazine discussing ideas and trends from a Christian point of view.*

World of Irish Nursing, The

Medmedia Ltd, 25 Adelaide Street, Dún Laoghaire, Co. Dublin
Editor: Geraldine Meagan
t. +353 1 280 3967
f. +353 1 280 7076
e. mail@medmedia.ie
■ *This is a monthly magazine for the nursing profession.*

Northern Ireland

Telephone numbers in Northern Ireland have the prefix 048 if dialled from the Republic and 004428 if dialled from elsewhere.

Auto Trader

James House, Dargan Crescent, Belfast BT3 9JP
Managing Director: John O'Connell
t. +44 28 9037 0444
e. john.o'connell@autotrader.ie
w. www.autotrader.ie
■ *Motoring magazine and on-line car sales available throughout Ireland.*

Beautiful Irish Homes

Unit 65, Dunlop Commercial Park, 4 Balloo Drive, Bangor, Co. Down BT19 7QY
Editors: Judith Robinson (Homes), Frances Privilege (Features), Samantha Blair (Lifestyle)
t. +44 28 91 473 979
f. +44 28 91 457 226
e. enquiries@ihill.net
■ *This is an annual homes and interiors magazine for readers in the North and the Republic.*

Big Buzz Magazine

96 Duncairn Gardens, Belfast BT15 2GJ
Editor: Barry O'Kane
t. +44 28 9075 7000
e. barry@bigbuzzireland.com
w. www.bigbuzzireland.com
■ *This is a monthly entertainment magazine.*

Big List, The

Flagship Media Group Ltd, 48–50 York Street, Belfast BT15 1AS
Editor: Gavin Bell
t. +44 28 90 319 008
f. +44 2890 727 800
e. listnewscopy@flagshipmedia.co.uk
■ *This is a fortnightly entertainment listings magazine.*

BNIL (Bulletin of Northern Ireland Law)

SLS Legal Publications Ltd, School of Law, Queen's University, Belfast BT7 1NN
Editor: Deborah McBride
t. +44 28 90 273 597
f. +44 2890 326 308
e. d.mcbride@qub.ac.uk
■ *This journal, giving details of legal developments, is published ten times a year.*

Business Eye

Buckley Publications, 20 King's Road, Belfast BT5 6JJ
Editor: Richard Buckley
t. +44 28 9047 4490
f. +44 28 9047 4495
e. info@businesseye.co.uk
w. www.businesseye.co.uk
■ *Business magazine.*

Carsport Magazine

Greer Publications, 5B Edgewater Business Park, Belfast Harbour Estate, Belfast BT3 9JQ
Editor: Patrick Burns
t. +44 2890 783 200
f. +44 2890 783 210
e. patburns@greerpublications.com
■ *This is a monthly motor sport magazine.*

Catering and Licensing Review

Greer Publications, 5B Edgewater Business Park, Belfast Harbour Estate, Belfast BT3 9JQ
Editor: Emma Cowan
t. +44 2890 783 200
f. +4428 9078 3210
e. emmacowan@greerpublications.com
■ *This is a monthly catering and hotel magazine.*

Constabulary Gazette

Ulster Journals Ltd, 39 Boucher Road,
Belfast BT12 6UT
Editor: Bob Catterson
t. +44 2890 681 371
f. +4428 9038 1915
e. info@ulstertatler.com
■ *This is a monthly magazine for the Police
Service of Northern Ireland.*

Emerald Rugby

Office 5A, Legahory Centre,
Craigavon, Co. Armagh
Editor: Manus Lappin
t. +44 28 38 34433
f. +44 28 38 343454
e. editor@emeraldrugby.com
w. www.emeraldrugby.com
■ *This is a monthly all-Ireland rugby magazine for fans, players and clubs.*

Export and Freight

4 Square Media, Old Coach House, 12
Main Street, Hillsborough, Co. Down
BT26 6AE
Managing Editor: Helen Beggs
t. +44 2892 688 888
f. +44 2892 688 866
e. info@4squaremedia.net
w. www.exportandfreight.com
■ *This haulage and freight magazine is published seven times a year.*

Fermanagh Herald

30 Belmore Street, Enniskillen,
Co. Fermanagh BT74 6AA
Editor: Pauline Leary
t. +44 28 66 32 2066
f. +44 28 66 32 5521
e. editor@fermanaghherald.com
w. www.fermanaghherald.com
■ *Weekly paper published each Wednesday
with a circulation of about 12,300 in Co.
Fermanagh.*
Advertising Manager: Ann Mooney

Fortnight

11 University Road, Belfast BT7 1NA
Managing Editor: Malachi O'Doherty
t. +44 28 9023 2353
e. editor@fortnight.org
w. www.fortnight.org
■ *This independent review of politics and the
arts was founded in 1970 and seeks to promote
rational political debate.*

Game, The

All-Star Productions, 51 Gortin Road,
Omagh, Co. Tyrone BT79 7HZ
Editor: Kenny Curran
t. +44 28 82 25 1590
f. +44 28 82 24 6213
e. editor@thegame.ie
w. www.thegame.ie
■ *This is a weekly magazine about the GAA
in Ulster.*

Getting Married

Mainstream Magazines Ltd, 140
Thomas Street, Portadown, Co.
Armagh BT62 3AN
Managing Editor: Catherine McGinn
t. +44 2838 334 272
f. +44 2838 351 046
magazines@mainstreampublishing.co.uk
w. www.mainstreampublishing.co.uk
■ *This is a twice-yearly wedding guide.*

Industrial and Manufacturing Engineer

Greer Publications, 5B Edgewater
Business Park, Belfast BT3 9JQ
Managing Editor: Paul Beattie
t. +44 2890 783 232
f. +44 2890 783 210
e. paulbeattie@greerpublications.com
■ *This is a quarterly publication for engineers.*

Ireland's Equestrian

Mainstream Publications Ltd, 140
Thomas Street, Portadown, Co.
Armagh BT62 3AN
Editor: Diane Wray
t. +44 2838 334272

f. +44 2838 351 046
e. publications@mainstreampublish-
ing.co.uk
w. www.mainstreampublishing.co.uk
■ *This is a quarterly magazine for equestrian enthusiasts.*

Ireland's Homes, Interiors and Living
Unit 65, Dunlop Commercial Park, 4
Balloo Drive, Bangor, Co. Down
BT19 7QY
Publisher: Mike Keenan
t. +44 28 91473 979
f. +44 2891 457 226
e. mkeenan@ihil.net
■ *This is a monthly interior and décor magazine.*

Ireland's Pets
Mainstream Publishing Ltd, 140
Thomas Street, Portadown, Co.
Armagh BT62 3AN
Editor: Debbie Orme
t. +44 2838 334 272
f. +44 2838 351 046
e. publications@mainstreampublish-
ing.co.uk
w. www.mainstreampublishing.co.uk
■ *This is a quarterly magazine for pet-lovers.*

Irish Countrysports and Country Life
PO Box 477, Belfast BT16 2YA
Editor: Albert J. Titterington
t. +44 2890 483 873
f. +44 2890 480 195
e. countrysportsandcountrylife@btin-
ternet.com
w. www.countrysportsandcountrylife.
com
■ *This is a quarterly country life magazine.*

Keystone
Flagship Media Group Ltd, 48–50 York
Street, Belfast BT15 1AS
Editor: Cathy Lang
t. +44 2890 319 008
f. +44 2890 727 800
e. ksnewscopy@flagshipmedia.co.uk

■ *This is a bi-monthly publication for the Northern Ireland construction industry.*

Licensed and Catering News
Ulster Magazines Ltd, 8 Lowes
Industrial Estate, 31 Ballynahinch
Road, Belfast BT8 8EH
Editor: Chris Ayre
t. +44 28 9081 5656
f. +44 28 9081 7481
e. amadden@ulster-magazine.co.uk
■ *This is a monthly trade magazine for the hospitality industry.*

Methodist Newsletter
Edgehill Theological College,
9 Lennoxvale, Belfast BT9 5BY
Editors: George Orr, Lynda Neilands
and Robin Roddie
t. +44 28 9066 5870
f. +44 28 9068 7204
e. newsletter@irishmethodist.org
w. www.irishmethodist.org
■ *This is the monthly newsletter of the Methodist Church.*

Neighbourhood Retailer
Penton Publications Ltd, Penton
House, 38 Heron Road, Sydenham
Business Park, Belfast BT3 9LE
Managing Editor: Des Magee
t. +44 2890 457 457
f. +44 2890 456 611
e. info@pentonpublications.co.uk
w. www.pentongroup.com
■ *This trade magazine for convenience shops is published eleven times a year.*

New Houses
Mainstream Magazines, 140 Thomas
Street, Portadown, Co. Armagh
BT62 3AN
Publisher: Catherine McGinn
t. +44 2838 392 000
f. +44 2838 351 071
e. magazines@mainstreampublishing.
co.uk
w. www.mainstreampublishing.co.uk

■ *This magazine about new housing developments in Northern Ireland is published three times annually.*

Northern Builder Magazine, The

Unit 22, Lisburn Enterprise Centre, Ballinderry Road, Lisburn, Co. Antrim BT28 2BP
Editor: Alan Bailie
t. +44 2892 663 390
f. +44 2892 666 242
e. info@northernbuilder.co.uk
w. www.northernbuilder.co.uk
■ *This is a quarterly magazine for the Northern Ireland construction industry.*

Northern Ireland Legal Quarterly

SLS Legal Publications (NI), Queen's University, Belfast BT7 1NN
Editor: Prof. Sally Wheeler
t. +44 28 9097 5224
f. +44 28 9032 6308
■ *This is a quarterly scholarly journal of Northern Ireland legal issues.*

Northern Ireland Travel and Leisure News

Unit 1, Windsor Business Park, 16–18 Lower Windsor Avenue, Belfast BT9 7DW
Editor: Brian Ogle
t. +44 2890 666 151
f. +44 2890 683 819
e. info@nitravelnews.com
w. www.nitravelnews.com
■ *This is a monthly travel newspaper, with details of holidays and offers.*

Northern Ireland Veterinary Today

Penton Publications Ltd, 38 Heron Road, Sydenham Business Park, Belfast BT3 9LE
Managing Editor: Des Magee
t. +44 2890 457 457
f. +44 2890 456 611
e. info@pentonpublications.com
w. www.pentongroup.com
■ *This is a quarterly veterinary magazine.*

Northern Ireland Visitors' Journal

Penton Publications Ltd, 38 Heron Road, Sydenham Business Park, Belfast BT3 9LE
Managing Editor: Tara Craig
t. +44 2890 457 457
f. +44 2890 456 611
e. info@pentonpublications.co.uk
w. www.pentongroup.com
■ *This is an annual guide for visitors to Northern Ireland.*

Northern Woman

Greer Publications, 5B Edgewater Business Park, Belfast Harbour Estate, Belfast BT3 9JR
Editor: Lyn Palmer
t. +44 28 9078 3200
f. +44 28 9078 3210
■ *This is a monthly magazine aimed at women in Northern Ireland.*

Offshore Investment Magazine

Lombard House, 10–20 Lombard Street, Belfast BT1 1BW
Publisher: Barry C. Bingham
t. +4428 9032 8777
f. +44 28 9032 8777
e. barry@offshoreinvestment.com
w. www.offshoreinvestment.com
■ *This is a financial magazine covering all aspects and trends in offshore investment.*

Pacenotes

Mooney Media Ltd, Unit 45 Banbridge Enterprise Centre, Scarva Road Industrial Estate, Banbridge, Co. Down BT32 3QD
Editor and Publisher: Simon Mooney
t. +44 28 40 660 390
e. editor@pacenotes.net
w. www.pacenotes.net
■ *This is monthly motor sport magazine.*

Plumbing and Heating

Mainstream Magazine, 140 Thomas Street, Portadown, Co. Armagh BT62 3AN

Publisher: Karen McEvoy

t. +44 2838 392 000

f. +44 2838 351 071

e. magazines@mainstreampublishing.co.uk

w. www.mainstreampublishing.co.uk

■ *This is a quarterly trade journal for the plumbing industry.*

Presbyterian Herald

Presbyterian Church in Ireland, Church House, Fisherwick Place, Belfast BT1 6DW

Editor: Rev. Arthur Clarke

t. +44 28 9032 2284

f. +44 28 9041 7307

e. herald@presbyterianireland.org

w. www.presbyterianireland.org

■ *Published ten times a year, this is the official magazine of the Presbyterian Church in Ireland.*

Recruitment

Flagship Media Group Ltd, 48–50 York Street, Belfast BT15 1AS

Editor: Michael Bashford

t. +44 2890 319 008

f. +44 90 727 800

e. recnewscopy@flagshipmedia.co.uk

w. www.jobsnation.net

■ *This is a weekly Northern Ireland jobs magazine.*

Regional Film and Video

Flagship Media Group Ltd, 48–50 York Street, Belfast BT15 1AS

Editor: Stephen Preston

t. +44 2890 319 008

f. +44 90 727 800

e. rfvnewscopy@flagshipmedia.co.uk

w. www.4rfv.co.uk

■ *This is a monthly trade magazine for the film and television industry.*

Retail Grocer

Ulster Magazines Ltd, 8 Lowes Industrial Estate, 31 Ballynahinch Road, Belfast BT8 8EH

Editor: Chris Ayre

t. +44 28 9081 5656

f. +44 28 9081 7481

e. rgrocer@ulster-magazine.co.uk

■ *This is monthly trade magazine for Irish grocers.*

Self Building, Extending and Renovating Homes

Corry Home Building Ltd, 96 Lisburn Road, Saintfield, Co. Down BT24 7BP

Editor: Gillian Corry

t. +44 2897 510 570

f. +44 2897 510 576

e. info@selfbuild.ie

w. www.selfbuild.ie

■ *This is a quarterly specialist magazine for those making house renovations.*

Source

PO Box 352, Belfast BT1 2WB

Editors: John Duncan and Richard West

t. +44 28 9032 9691

f. +44 28 9032 9691

e. info@source.ie

w. www.source.ie

■ *A quarterly magazine for contemporary photography in Britain and Ireland, published by Photo Works North.*

Specify

Greer Publications, 5B Edgewater Business Park, Belfast Harbour Estate, Belfast BT3 9JQ

Manager: Caroline McClean

t. +44 28 9078 3200

f. +44 28 9078 3210

e. carolinemcclean@greerpublications.com

■ *This is a bi-monthly magazine covering the Northern Ireland construction industry.*

Ulster Architect Magazine

182 Ravenhill Road, Belfast BT6 8EE

Editor: Anne Davey Orr

t. +44 2890 731 636

f. +44 2890 738 927

e. info@addemo.com

■ *This is a monthly trade magazine for architects in Northern Ireland.*

Ulster Bride

Ulster Journals Ltd, 39 Boucher Road, Belfast BT12 6UT
Editor: Pauline Roy
 t. +44 2890 681 371
 f. +44 2890 381 915
 e. info@ulstertatler.com
■ *This is a bi-annual magazine for brides-to-be.*

Ulster Business

Greer Publications, 5B Edgewater Business Park, Belfast Harbour Estate, Belfast BT3 9JQ
Editor: Russell Campbell
t. +44 28 9078 3200
 f. +44 28 9078 3210
 w. www.ulsterbusiness.com
■ *This is a monthly business and finance magazine for Northern Ireland.*

Ulster Farmer

Ann Street, Dungannon, Co. Tyrone
Editor: Desmond Mallon
 t. +44 28 8772 2557
 f. +44 28 8772 7334
 e. editor@observernewspapersni.com
■ *This is a weekly farming magazine for Northern Ireland.*

Ulster Grocer

Greer Publications, 5B Edgewater Business Park, Belfast Harbour Estate, Belfast BT3 9JQ
Editor: Kathy Jensen
 t. +44 28 9078 3200
 f. +44 28 9078 3210
 e. kathyjensen@greerpublications.com
■ *This monthly trade magazine covers the grocery trade in Northern Ireland.*

Ulster Tatler

39 Boucher Road, Belfast BT12 6UT
Editor: Richard Sherry
t. +44 2890 681 371
 f. +44 2890 381 915

 e. info@ulstertatler.com
 w. www.ulstertatler.com
■ *This is a monthly life-style magazine for Northern Ireland readers.*

Ulster Tatler Interiors

39 Boucher Road, Belfast BT12 6UT
Editor: Doreen Kelly
 t. +44 2890 681 371
 f. +44 2890 381 915
 e. info@ulstertatler.com
 w. www.ulstertatler.com
■ *This is a quarterly interiors and décor magazine.*

Ulster Tatler Wine and Dine Guide

39 Boucher Road, Belfast BT12 6UT
Editor: Christopher Sherry
 t. +44 2890 681 371
 f. +44 2890 381 915
 e. info@ulstertatler.com
 w. www.ulstertatler.com
■ *This is an annual guide to food, wine and eating out.*

United News

Greer Publications, 5B Edgewater Business Park, Belfast Harbour Estate, Belfast BT3 9JQ
Editor: Kathy Jensen
 t. +44 28 9078 3200
 f. +44 28 9078 3210
 e. kathyjensen@greerpublications.com
 w. www.ulsterbusiness.co.uk/greer/united_news.phtml
■ *This is a monthly magazine for dairy farmers in Northern Ireland.*

Women's News

109–113 Royal Avenue, Belfast BT1 1FF
 t. +44 38 90 322 823
 t. +44 38 90 343 878
 e. womensnews@btconnect.com
■ *A monthly magazine published by a Belfast feminist collective.*

Irish magazines overseas

Irish Connections Magazine

305 Madison Avenue, Suite 1223, New
York, NY 10165, USA
Editor: Tony Quinn
t. +1 212 490 8061
f. +1 212 490 8065
e. editorial@irishconnectionsmag.com
w. www.irishconnectionsmag.com

■ *This is a magazine, published six times a
year, about the achievements of the Irish
around the world.*

Irish Golf Review

World's Fair Ltd, PO Box 57,
Hollingwood Business Centre, Albert
Street, Oldham, Lancs OL8 3WF,
England
Editor: Mike Appleton
t. +44 161 683 8000
f. +44 161 683 8001
e. mike.appleton@worldsfair.co.uk
and irishgolf@worldsfair.co.uk

■ *This is a quarterly magazine reviewing the
Irish golf scene.*

Irish World, The

Irish World Publications, 934 North
Circular Road, London NW2 7RJ,
England
Editor: Tom Griffin
t. +44 208 453 7800
f. +44 208 208 1103
e. donal@theirishworld.com
w. www.theirishworld.com

8

FILM AND AUDIO-VISUAL PRODUCTION: CINEMA HIBERNIA

Helen Shaw

The film landscape

Irish people love films and go to the cinema a lot. According to Arts Council research, cinema-going has increased by 97% in the Republic in the ten-year period from 1991 to 2001. Ireland has the second-highest rate of cinema-going in Europe, surpassed only by Iceland, with each Irish person on average going more than four times a year to a cinema. If video and DVD rentals and purchases are included, as well as digital television film subscriptions, it is plain to see that Ireland enjoys its films.[1]

But while cinema-going is on the rise in Ireland, the number of cinemas has actually fallen, with the local independent screens losing out to the big multiplex operations on the outskirts of cities and towns. The number of screens has gone up by 68%, to a total of 322 at the end of 2001—rising to 328 by 2003—but the number of cinemas had fallen to 64, down 14%. Equally, while screens have multiplied, the number of arts or culture cinemas remains extremely low, with only six describing themselves as cultural or specialist, according to the Arts Council's research.

The top ten films in Ireland in 2004 reflected the power of the sequel, animation and computer-generated images, with blockbusters like *Shrek 2*, *The Day After Tomorrow* and *Harry Potter and the Prisoner of Azkaban*.

---

1. Arts Council, *Cultural and Economic Trends in Cinema in Ireland and Wales*, Inglis Todd Consultants, 2004.

Top ten films in Ireland, 2004

1	Shrek 2	€7.79 m
2	Harry Potter and the Prisoner of Azkaban	€4.28 m
3	Bridget Jones: The Edge of Reason	€4.25 m
4	The Day After Tomorrow	€3.69 m
5	Spider-Man 2	€3.47 m
6	Shark Tale	€3.26 m
7	The Incredibles	€3.26 m
8	The Lord of The Rings: The Return of the Kind	€3.14 m
9	The Passion of the Christ	€2.96 m
10	Troy	€2.83 m

Source: *Irish Times*, 8 January 2005.

Besides our consumption of films, Ireland—both the Republic and Northern Ireland—has also become a vibrant base for film production, with tax incentives, such as section 481 in the Republic, encouraging the development of an Irish film industry over the past twelve years. However, increased competition from new low-cost production zones in Eastern Europe and elsewhere in the last couple of years has reduced Ireland's favoured status as an international film production location. A positive move in 2005 was the increase of 18% in the Irish Film Board's budget.

For international film work in Ireland, 2004 was a difficult year, with only a handful of films being made here, or made partly here. Nevertheless, audiences grew for Irish-made films, with an estimated half a million people turning out for films such as *Man About Dog*, Paddy Breathnach's film, which grossed €2 million at the Irish box office. Irish-made films earned approximately €4.5 million at the box office in 2004, and *Intermission*, the big Irish box-office hit of 2003, continued to break records when it went to DVD and video release. In 2003 two films made in Ireland, Jerry Bruckhemier's *Veronica Guerin* and *Intermission*, made the top ten films.

According to the industry, uncertainty over the continuity of tax incentives at the end of 2003 hit international production schedules in Ireland throughout 2004. While section 481 was retained, the months of debate encouraged Hollywood companies to look elsewhere, particularly to Hungary and the Czech Republic. An equal disincentive for Hollywood was Ireland's higher labour costs and rising production costs, given the highly skilled but low-cost offerings in many of the developed eastern European countries. Other countries, such as New Zealand, which carved its niche with the *Lord of the Rings* trilogy and a new internationally focused tax break, also won out over Ireland.

Production industry and market

Irish directors, such as Jim Sheridan, have been to the forefront of the defence of film tax incentives. Sheridan's film *My Left Foot* broke ground in 1994 and put Ireland on the international film map, winning audiences and an Oscar. According to the industry and the Irish Business and Employers' Confederation's audio-visual analysis, section 481 has been crucial to the growth of the Irish production base, bringing in films such as *King Arthur* and *Evelyn*, which were both made at Ardmore Studios in Bray, Co. Wicklow. Ardmore Studios has more than forty years of history in film-making in Ireland and boasts Ireland's only four-wall studio, with five sound stages. More than a hundred films have been made there. In comparison with some of the international options, such as the new Korda Studio in Budapest, Ardmore's sound stage facilities are small and more suited to drama than big epic productions. In both Budapest and Prague, large-scale studios combined with low costs and great locations have made Hungary and the Czech Republic two of the most attractive tax-break schemes aimed at the international film production business.

IBEC's Audiovisual Federation's annual report put the value of the international film production industry at over €320 million in 2003, with 179 productions, boosted by such major productions as *Laws of Attraction* and *King Arthur*. In the same year the Irish independent production industry's output was valued at nearly €50 million—up from €44 million in 2002; but the changing business climate of the international film and television market made 2004 a more challenging year.

In 2004 the producers behind such blockbusters as *Around the World in 80 Days* considered Ireland but decided against it because the tax breaks were better elsewhere. However, on the positive side, every Hollywood studio has made at least one film in Ireland: Disney, for example, has produced or distributed five major films shot in Ireland in recent years, including *The Count of Monte Cristo* (2000), *Veronica Guerin* (2002) and *King Arthur* (2004). While international production was low generally in Ireland in 2004, it picked up in the second half of the year with

Paramount's *The Honeymooners* and Neil Jordan's filming of the Pat McCabe novel *Breakfast on Pluto* in Belfast. Maeve Binchy's novel *Tara Road* also went to film as a Noel Pearson production but with Dalkey moving to Cape Town, South Africa, as a location.

More than 4,300 people are employed in the production industry in the Republic. Besides the trade in international film there is an emerging school of small-budget independent Irish film-makers who are creating their own space, such as Damien O'Donnell with *Inside I'm Dancing* (2004) and John Crowley with his highly successful *Intermission* (2003). In October 2004 two low-budget Irish-made films made the top ten list: *Inside I'm Dancing* and *Man About Dog*, while Lenny Abrahamson's *Adam and Paul* was a surprise word-of-mouth hit.

Besides tax breaks, grants are available to the audio-visual and film industry through both the Irish Film Board and the European MEDIA fund. These organisations provided grants to Irish audio-visual productions to the tune of €2 million in 2004. The MEDIA fund provides support for production, distribution and training in the sector and has given vital support to many of the small film or documentary-making groups in the country.[2] Another national support to the industry is Screen Training Ireland, which provides quality training to the sector. Screen Producers Ireland (SPI) represents the sector itself.

Incoming foreign production accounts for some 70% of the film industry's revenues in Ireland, and while Ireland is still among the list of top ten preferred external locations for Hollywood it is competing against a growing array of choices for that slice of business. Ireland's edge has been the mix of skills, in both production and creation, aligned with location and cost. Holding this edge will be increasingly challenging for the island of Ireland as even location work in Ireland ends up as post-production work somewhere else, with international operations attempting to benefit from transnational tax breaks and incentives.

Global film production trends

The global film entertainment business is projected to be worth about €90 million by 2008, with Europe, the Middle East and Africa being the areas of fastest growth.[3] The US dominates this market, with a share of approximately 50% in global revenues. Although film piracy has affected

2. See listings in chapter 9.
3. PricewaterhouseCooper, *Global Entertainment and Media Outlook, 2002–2008* (2004).

international on-screen market values, the real drivers for the film business are now DVDs and the growth of the DVD market. DVD is the fastest-growing technology in the world and, linked with the introduction of broadband in the US and Europe, is expected to be the driving force behind film production growth in the coming years.

Digital technology is transforming film production and distribution. Every big-budget film is now being made with digital production in special effects and animation. Along with the on-screen impact, this technology is also changing how we see films. Digital cinema is also part of the industry's future. Digital cinema is a new technology, which uses digital servers and projectors to send film to a network of screens, enabling simultaneous coverage at a lower cost than can be achieved at present. It has dramatic potential for big markets, such as India and China, where cinema is popular but relatively expensive. Digital cinema has the potential to change the distribution business model, for example by reducing the cost of getting a low-budget art film out throughout the UK. This is why the British Film Council is funding the installation of digital cinema, to make it a more attractive proposition for carrying independent films for smaller audiences.

Irish Government support for digital cinema now means that Ireland is likely to be at the forefront of the transition to digital cinema theatres. By the end of 2005, all 515 cinema screens in Ireland will have converted from 35 mm film to digital, at a cost of €40 million. Avica Europe, from its base in Thurles, Co. Tipperary, plans to convert all screens in Northern Ireland and the Republic to digital in an initiative that is being grant-aided in both jurisdictions. Digital cinema in Ireland will reduce the cost of distributing independent and art films and improve the film quality that people see on screens throughout the island.

In Ireland, production companies will be under increased pressure if Ireland continues to lose international film business. This means that the present range of more than two hundred production companies working in broadcast, new media and film production could shrink, reflecting the changing economies of the business, with companies merging or being subject to buy-outs—similar to the transition in the UK over recent years.

For the Irish film industry, strategic alliances will be very important, as companies seeking to maximise their position in the international market will link up with partner companies in the rest of Europe and the US. If the tide of production continues to move east—and into eastern Europe—the best strategy for Irish production interests will be to think international and link with overseas companies to provide pan-European solutions to Hollywood needs. This is why Ealing Studios in the UK headed a consortium to buy out the Bulgarian Boyana Film Studios in 2004, giving it the potential to offer a combined package. It is possible that the best strategy for Irish companies and studios such as Ardmore will be to form similar strategic deals to link the benefits of Ireland—Irish skills and a good track record—with the bigger studios and lower costs found in other European regions. The alternative would be to take a leaf from New Zealand's book and promote national investment in world-class digital studio facilities. This would ensure that both locational and high-end production work stays and grows in Ireland.

Republic of Ireland

2000 AD Productions

Ardmore Studios, Herbert Road, Bray,
Co. Wicklow
Managing Director and Producer:
Adrian Devane
   m. +353 87 297 9131
   e. adrian@2000adproductions.com
   w. www.2000adproductions.com
■ *Produces films and documentaries in
Ireland, the UK and Europe in Irish, French,
German and English.*

A Boy Named Sue Films

1 Brooklawn House, Brooklawn
Wood, Blackrock, Co. Dublin
Managing Director: Michael O'Connell
   t. +353 1 275 5866
   e. abnsf@ireland.com
■ *Produces features, shorts, documentaries and
promotional videos.*

Abú Media

Teach Indreabháin, Indreabhán,
Co. Galway
Managing Director: Pierce Boyce
   t. +353 91 505 100
   f. +353 91 505 135
   e. info@abumedia.com
   w. www.abumedia.com
■ *An audio-visual production and facilities
company, making documentaries, features, com-
edy, news and animation in English and Irish.*
   E-mail addresses for individuals are in
   the format firstname@abumedia.com
Producers: Bríd Seoighe and Eileen
Seoighe
Sound Engineer and Sound Design:
Adrian Ferry
Production Coordinator: Éilís Nic an Rí
Researcher: Alan Ó Laoghaire
Director: Aoife Ní Fhearghusa
Editor: Dáithí Keane
Camera Crew: Dave Fenwick, Pat
Fogarty, Des Carolan, Ivor Carrol and
Com McCaughey.

accessCINEMA

The Studio Building, Meeting-House
Square, Dublin 2
General Enquiries
   t. +353 1 679 4420
   f. +353 1 679 4166
   e. info@accesscinema.ie
   w. www.accesscinema.ie
■ *Supports regional cinema programming in
Ireland on 35 mm, 16 mm and DVD. Members
consist of local film groups promoting and
screening films, both Irish and international,
that would otherwise not be seen by regional
audiences. accessCINEMA maintains contacts
with distributors, block-books and delivers films
and supplies promotional material.*

Adare Productions

Adare House, 35A Patrick Street,
Dún Laoghaire, Co. Dublin
Company Directors and Producers:
Brian Reddin and Brian Graham
   t. +353 1 284 3877
   f. +353 1 284 1814
   e. adare@eircom.net
■ *Produces light entertainment, documentaries
and game shows for television in English and
Irish.*
Producers: Brian Reddin, Brian
Graham, Ciaran Gallagher and Evan
Chamberlain
Editor: Darren Chan

Adsell Productions

Unit 6, The Enterprise Centre,
Bishopsgate Street, Mullingar, Co.
Westmeath
Managing Director: Jim McCartan
   t. +353 44 42 262
   f. +353 44 40 777
   e. jim@adsell.ie
   w. www.adsell.ie
■ *A television and video production company
producing corporate productions, television
advertisements and documentaries in English.*

Aesop Teo

Cill Chiaráin, Co. Galway
Managing Director and Producer:
Eithne Nic Dhonnchadha
t. +353 95 33 604
f. +353 95 33 427
■ *A television production company producing training and corporate films and videos in English, Irish and French.*
Producer and Director: Peadar Mac
Donnacha

Agtel/Independent Pictures

22 Fitzwilliam Street Upper, Dublin 2
Managing Director: John Cummins
t. +353 1 708 8100
f. +353 1 676 6137
e. info@agtel.ie; info@independent-pictures.com
w. www.agtel.ie
■ *A production company producing factual programming in all the documentary, magazine and life-style genres for television and corporate clients in English and Irish.*
Head of Production, Television: Liam
Lavelle
Head of Development, Television:
Conor Moloney
Head of Corporate Division: Michael
Parker
Manager, Corporate Services: Paul
Judge
Office Manager: Pauline Foley
Producer: Clare Pearson
Development Executive: Melanie
Morris
Development Researcher: Helen Earley

Akajava Films

95 Merrion Square, Dublin 2
Managing Director and Producer:
Brendan Culleton
t. +353 1 662 0951
f. +353 1 662 0952
e. akajavafilms@eircom.net
w. www.akajava.ie
■ *Produces documentary films and corporate*

videos in English, Irish, French, German and Italian.

Alchemy Electronic Arts

Schull Road, Ballydehob, Co. Cork
Producer-Director-Editor: David
Bickley
t. +353 1 28 37 714
m. +353 87 698 3033
e. davidbickley@eircom.net
w. www.alchemyelectronicarts.com
■ *Produces documentaries, title sequences, music videos and soundtracks for film and television in English and Irish.*

Algar Productions

10 Crosthwaite Park East, Dún
Laoghaire, Co. Dublin
Producer: Michael Algar
t. +353 1 284 3426
f. +353 1 230 2787
e. algar@ireland.com
■ *Produces television commercials, documentaries and animation and provides line production on features and series as well as consultancy services in scheduling and budgeting.*

A Man & Ink

2nd Floor, 34 Upper Abbeygate Street,
Galway
General Enquiries
t. +353 91 86 5901
e. info@amanandink.com
w. www.amanandink.com
■ *An animation and multimedia company, producing animation, CD ROMs, DVDs, web sites and newsletters.*

Amnesia Film

40 Maylor Street, Cork
Producer-Director: John Richardson
t. +353 87 256 1477
e. johnrichardson@ireland.com
■ *A film, television and multimedia production company producing documentaries and feature dramas.*
Producers: Gerry Breen and Steven
Barber
Producer-Director: Padraig Trehy

Andec Communications Media

19-20 York Road, Dún Laoghaire, Co. Dublin
Managing Director: Annette Kinne
t. +353 1 280 7299
f. +353 1 280 7381
e. info@andec.ie
w. www.andec.ie
■ *Produces broadcast television programmes, educational and training videos and corporate productions in English, Irish and French.*

Animo Television

4 Windmill Lane, Dublin 2
General Enquiries: Adrian Lynch
t. +353 1 671 3004
f. +353 1 679 7046
e. info@animo.ie
w. www.animo.ie
■ *A television production company producing factual television programmes. Animo is Windmill Lane Corporate Communications' broadcast unit.*

Any News

Ashlawn, Wynberg Park, Blackrock, Co. Dublin
Producer-Director: Jerry O'Callaghan
t. +353 1 280 3957
m. +353 87 239 6746
f. +353 1 280 3957
e. anynewsinc@ireland.com
w. www.anynewsinc.com
■ *A film and television production company producing documentaries in English and Irish.*
Cameraman: Jack Sutton
Technical, Web Design and Sales: Denis O'Callaghan

Araby Productions

Apartment 3, 2 Waterloo Road, Dublin 4
General Enquiries: Seán Ó Mórdha
t. +353 1 660 6690
f. +353 1 660 0668
■ *A film production company producing documentaries.*

Áras Telegael

An Spidéal, Co. Galway
Company Director and Executive Producer: Paul Cummins
t. +353 91 553 460
f. +353 91 553 464
e. paul@telegael.com
w. www.telegael.com
■ *A film production company producing animation and films and providing facilities.*
Head of Productions: Siobhán Ní Ghadhra
Head of Development: Micheál Ó Domhnaill
Head of Facilities: Enda Boner

Ardmore Sound

Ardmore Studios, Herbert Road, Bray, Co. Wicklow
General Enquiries
t. +353 1 286 5868
f. +353 1 286 5871
e. info@ardmoresound.ie
w. www.ardmoresound.ie
■ *Provides film sound post-production services.*

Art of Resistance Films

Pramila, Tivoli Road, Dún Laoghaire, Co. Dublin
General Enquiries: Shalini Sinha
t. +353 1 284 2926
f. +353 1 284 2926
e. shalinisinha@eircom.net
■ *A production company producing programmes on anti-racism and equality themes. Shalini Sinha writes a regular column for the* Irish Times.

Association of Film Accountants of Ireland

33 Hillcourt, Highfield Road, Dublin 6
General Enquiries: Miriam C. Kelly
t. +353 1 496 2156
e. miriamk@indigo.ie
■ *Representative body for Irish film accountants.*

Asylum Studios

Abbey Street, Dublin 8
General Enquiries: Jimmy Eadie and
Liam Mulvaney
m. +353 87 980 2878
e. jimbo123@eircom.net
w. www.asylumstudios.org
■ *A sound recording studio.*

Athena Media

Digital Depot, The Digital Hub,
Thomas Street, Dublin 8
Managing Director: Helen Shaw
Contact: Sinead Kennedy and Sarah
Mulkerrins
t. +353 1 488 5850
m. +353 87 675 4375
e. info@athenamedia.ie
w. www.athenamedia.ie
■ *A multimedia production and media con-*
sultancy company that makes radio, television
and on-line content. Athena Media produces
the **Irish Media Handbook** *and specialises*
in using mutlimedia in awareness projects.

Aura Productions/Farm TV

8 William Street, Tullamore, Co. Offaly
Managing Director: Malachy Mangan
t. +353-506 22907
f. +353-506 22908
e. auraproductions@eircom.net
■ *Corporate video and television commercial*
production company producing material in
English and Irish.
Producer-Director: Harry Hill
Scriptwriter-Editor: Lorraine Glennon

AV Edge

The Schoolhouse, St Augustine Street,
Dublin 8
Managing Director: Leo Casey
t. +353 1 646 1180
f. +353 1 646 1181
e. info@av-edge.com
w. www.av-edge.com
■ *A film, video and multimedia production*
company producing material for broadcast and
corporate clients in English and Irish.

Director: Ciaran Casey
Producers and Directors: Sue Russell,
Séamus Hanrahan and Orla Byrne

Tish Barry Productions

33 St Thomas Road, Mount Merrion,
Co. Dublin
General Enquiries: Tish Barry
t. +353 1 288 0461
f. +353 1 283 4548
■ *A production company.*

Beacon Studios

62 Lower Baggot Street, Dublin 2
Senior Engineer and Owner: Noel
Storey
t. +353 1 676 2474
f. +353 1 676 8930
e. info@beaconstudios.net
■ *A sound recording studio providing post-*
production services in sound.
Senior Engineer: Gerard Gogan
Studio Manager: Tara Mullen

Beaufield Productions

24 Beaufield Park, Stillorgan, Co.
Dublin
Managing Director, Producer and
Director: Yvonne McDonald
t. +353 1 278 1990
f. +353 278 1990
e. ymcdonald@eircom.net
■ *Production company producing documen-*
taries, dramas and feature programmes.

Belmont Productions

Stroan, Thomastown, Co. Kilkenny
General Enquiries: John Masterson
t. +353 775 624 598
f. +353 1 668 5696
e. johnmasterson@iol.ie
■ *Production company producing television*
documentaries and entertainment programmes.

Big River

Guinness Enterprise Centre, Taylor's
Lane, Dublin 8
Managing Director, Producer and
Director: Séamus McGrenery

t. +353 1 410 0656
f. +353 1 410 0985
e. info@bigrivertv.com
w. www.bigrivertv.com

■ *Production company producing documentaries, interactive television and corporate videos in English, Irish, French and German.*

Financial Director: David Holmes
Head of Technology: Brian McGrath
Marketing and Business Development: Mary Roche

Blinder Ltd

The Barracks, 76 Irishtown Road, Dublin 4
t: +353 1 6678 068
e: kieron@blinder.ie
Managing Directors: Michael Duffy
General Enquiries: Kieron J. Walsh

Blue Blanket

28 St Alban's Road, Dublin 8
General Enquiries: Dearbhla Walsh
t. +353 1 453 2258
f. +353 1 667 4844
m +353 866046637
e. dearbhlawalsh@ireland.com

■ *A production company headed by the independent director Dearbhla Walsh.*

Blue Monkey Studios

Pilgrims Rest, Ownahincha, Co. Cork
General Enquiries: Michael Carr
m. +353 87 933 5033
e. info@bluemonkeystudio.com
w. www.bluemonkeystudio.com

■ *A sound recording studio providing post-production services in sound.*

Technical Enquiries: Robby Collins
m. +353 86 893 7289

Blueprint Pictures

45 Stephen's Lane, Dublin 2
Producers: David Blake Knox and Hilary Fennell
t. +353 1 611 4989
f. +353 1 611 4986
e. info@blueprintpictures.ie

■ *An independent television production company producing documentaries, music and arts, life-style, drama and entertainment programmes.*

Borderline Productions

Warehouse Studios, 12 Magennis Place, Dublin 2
Managing Director: Tom Maguire
t. +353 1 6725827
m +353862405349
f + 353 1 6790315
e. tom@borderlineproductions.co.uk

■ *A film production company producing feature films, shorts and dramas.*

Bord Scannán na hÉireann/Irish Film Board

Rockford House, St Augustine Street, Galway
Chief Executive: Vacant
t +353 91 561398
f+ 353 91 561405
e info@filmboard.ie
w.www.filmboard.ie

■ *Bord Scannán na hÉireann is a state agency to support the Irish film and audio-visual industry. It was set up in 1993. It provides loans and equity investment to independent film-makers to assist in the production of Irish films. It also funds animation and documentary development, in addition to new talent schemes. These schemes include Short Cuts, Frameworks, Oscailt and Irish Flash. Promotes Ireland internationally as a film location.*

Head of Business Affairs: Teresa McGrane
Head of Production and Development: Brendan McCarthy
Head of Marketing: Moira Horgan
Information Officer: Louise Ryan
Applications and Schemes Co-ordinator: Jill McGregor.
Board members (appointed January 2005 until 2009):
James Morris (Chair), Alan Gilsenan, Margaret McCarthy MacIntyre, Lesley McKimm, Tristan Orpen Lynch, Kevin Moriarty, Kirsten Sheridan.

Boulder Media (see new media listings)

Brother Films

7 Lombard Street East, Dublin 2
Producer: Fiach Mac Conghail
t. +353 1 670 4895
+353 1 670 3881
e. brofilms@eircom.net
■ *Production company producing feature-length and short films, both drama and documentary, in English and Irish.*
Producer-Editor: Cúán Mac Conghail
Writer-Director: Paul Mercier

Brown Bag Films

65 Great Strand Street, Dublin 1
Producer: Cathal Gaffney
t. +353 1 872 1608
f. +353 1 872 3834
e. studio@brownbagfilms.com
w. www.brownbagfilms.com
■ *Production company producing animation, television commercials, television series and feature films and providing on-line editing and compositing for animation and motion graphics.*
Director: Darragh O'Connell
Commercials Producer: Susan Baskett
Facilities Manager and Head of Compositing: Brian Gilmore
Production Manager: Jackie Leonard

Buckshee Films

161 Inchicore Road, Dublin 8
Managing Directors, Producers and Directors: Rachel Moriarty and Peter Murphy
t. +353 1 473 2047
f. +353 1 497 5598
e. buckshee@iol.ie
■ *A production company producing comedy writing and drama for television in English, Irish and French.*

Camel Productions

12 Magennis Place, Dublin 2
Managing Director, Producer and Director: Catherine Lyons
t. +353 1 671 2479
m. +353 87 667 0760
f. +353 1 491 4486
e. camel@ireland.com
■ *Production company making documentary films and multimedia and specialising in deaf drama in English, Irish, French, German and Irish and all international sign languages.*
Producer-Director: John Doherty

The Cartoon Saloon

YIFM, St Joseph's Studios, Waterford Road, Kilkenny
Company Directors: Paul Young, Tommy Moore, Aidan Harte and Nora Twomey
t. +353 56 776 4481
f. +353 56 772 0089
e. info@cartoonsaloon.ie
w. www.cartoonsaloon.ie
■ *An animation production and facilities studio, producing programmes and illustration and animation services for television and cinema in English and Irish.*
Administrator: Ross Murray

Cathal Black Films

161 Monalea Grove, Firhouse, Dublin 24
Managing Director, Producer and Director: Cathal Black
t. +353 1 494 7120
f. +353 1 494 7120
e. cbf@hotmail.com
■ *A film production company producing drama features and documentaries.*
Producer: Darryl Collins

Claddagh Films

Somerset Studios, Aughinish, Co. Clare
Managing Director and Director: Dermot Tynan
t. +353 65 707 8454
f. +353 65 707 8242
e. dtynan@claddagh.ie
w. www.claddagh.ie
■ *An independent production company producing comedy, documentary, drama, feature*

films, multimedia and shorts material for film and television (in English and Irish).
Producer: Bríd Cannon

Coco Television
49–50 Berysteed, Leeson Park, Dublin 6
Managing Director: Stuart Switzer
t. +353 1 497 0817
f. +353 1 497 0796
e. info@cocotelevision.ie
w. www.cocotelevision.ie
■ *A television production company producing television programming in Ireland and internationally. Coco has an animation subsidiary, Rocket Animation.*
Director of Television: Linda Cullen
UK Director: Paul Higgins
Producers: Hilary O'Donovan and Grainne O'Caroll
Production Manager: Suzanne Colwell
Director of Finance: Stephen Kennaugh

Collins Photo Agency
25 Great Strand Street, Dublin 1
Charlie Collins
t. +353 1 873 0011
f. +353 1 873 3391
e. collinsphotoagency@eircom.net
■ *Photographic agency.*

Comet Films and TV Productions
Shamrock Chambers, 1–2 Eustace Street, Dublin 2
Managing Director and Producer: Lesley McKimm
t. +353 1 670 4286
f. +353 1 671 4067
e. cometfilms@eircom.net
■ *A production company producing feature films, televsion programming and dramas in English and French. Lesley McKimm is a member of the Irish Film Board.*
Administrator and Producer: Aisling Ahmed

Cork Film Centre
Emmet House, Emmet Place, Cork
General Enquiries: Chris Hurley
t. +353 21 431 6033
f. +353 21 431 6125
e. info@corkfilmcentre.com
w. www.corkfilmcentre.com
■ *Supports and provides resources for the development, promotion and facilitation of creative work by video artists, animators, film-makers and people using emerging moving-image technologies.*

Cork Film Festival
Emmet House, Emmet Place, Cork
Festival Director: Mick Hannigan
t. +353 21 427 1711
f. +353 21 427 5945
e. info@corkfilmfest.org
w. www.corkfilmfest.org
■ *Provides a mix of international and Irish big-budget pictures, world cinema, independent films, documentaries and short films from all over the globe.*
Festival Manager: Eimear O'Herlihy
Festival Programmer: Una Feely
Festival Administrator: Éanna de Buis

Courtyard Studio, The
The Barracks, 76 Irishtown Road, Dublin 4
Managing Directors, Producers and Directors: John Gleeson and William Dowling
t. +353 1 668 7471
m. +353 87 254 4035
f. +353 1 660 8248
e. info@courtyardstudio.com
w. www.courtyardstudio.com
■ *A film and advertising production company producing corporate videos and providing creative and technical expertise on documentaries, including video playback operators and casting facilities and services.*
Marketing Manager: Robert Coyle

Covert Films
4 Blackhall View, Blackhall Place, Dublin 7
Managing Director and Producer: Richard Carolan

t. +353 1 673 6911

m. +353 86 807 7978

e. richard.carolan@iol.ie

■ *A film and television production company producing documentaries and drama.*

Producers: Jack Field, Paul Murphy and Ronan Burke

Crannóg Films and TV

46 Grafton Street, Dublin 2

Managing Director: Conor Harrington

t. +353 1 671 5677

f. +353 1 671 5678

e. crannogfilms@indigo.ie

■ *A feature film and television drama production company also providing script development and film financing.*

Create

11 Monastery Heath Square, Monastery Road, Dublin 22

Managing Director, Producer and Director: Aine Burke

t. +353 1 403 4984/5

e. createco@eircom.net; burkeaj@eircom.net

w. www.createco.com

■ *An interactive media production company and consultancy in animation, film, television and education in English, Irish and French.*

Administrator: Dawn Burke

Creedo Productions

Bayview, 59 Seacrest, Bray, Co. Wicklow

Writer and Director: Geraldine Creed

t. +353 1 286 8824

e. geraldinecreed@eircom.net

■ *A film production company producing documentaries.*

Crescendo Concepts

88 Leinster Road, Dublin 6

Managing Producer: Louis Lentin

t. +353 1 497 4676

e. lentincrescendo@eircom.net

■ *A film production company producing documentaries and drama for television in English and Irish.*

Crossing the Line Films

Barr an Uisce, Killincarrig Road, Greystones, Co. Wicklow

Managing Director, Producer and Director: John Murray

t. +353 1 287 5394/2910

f. +353 1 287 5394

e. johnmurr@indigo.ie

■ *A film production company specialising in travel, adventure and history documentaries in English, Irish, French, Spanish and Russian.*

Cameraman: Ross Bartley

Cúl a' Tigh

An Chrannóg, Srath na Corca, Doire Beaga, Co. Donegal

Managing Director: Seán Mac Fhionnghaile

t. +353 74 953 2542

■ *A television production company producing dramas and documentaries in English and Irish.*

Directors: Fiona Nic Giolla Bhríde and Treasa Nic Fhionnghaile

Delicious 9

12 Lower Liffey Street, Dublin 1

General Enquiries: Paul Madden

t. +353 878 2026

e. info@delicious9.com

w. www.delicious9.com

■ *An animation production company producing music videos, short films and other media products.*

Denis Desmond Management Productions

Plunkett Chambers, 21–23 Oliver Plunkett Street, Cork

General Enquiries

t. +353 21 427 9680

f. +353 21 427 9690

e. ddmp@eircom.net

■ *An artist and talent agency.*

Dickers Sound Systems

18 Main Street, Bray, Co. Wicklow
General Enquiries: Noel Dicker
t. +353 1 286 5046
m. +353 86 257 3026
f. +353 1 286 5046
■ *A sound post-production studio, providing the hire of sound equipment.*

Distinguished Features

21 Mespil Road, Dublin 4
Producers: David McLoughlin and Clare Scully
t. +353 1 668 2643
f. +353 1 668 2653
e. mail@distinguishedfeatures.com
■ *A film production company producing feature films, television dramas and documentaries.*
Director: Robert Quinn

Dobhar

Áras Teicneolaíochta, Na Forbacha, Co. na Gaillimhe
t: +353 91 592 533
f: +353 91 592 203
e: dobhar@eircom.net
Managing Director and Producer: Máirín Seoighe

Dog House Productions

17 Glendoher Close, Dublin 16
Managing Director: Angela O'Donoghue
t. +353 1 494 1123
f. +353 1 494 5177
e. info@doghouse.ie
■ *A film production company producing feature films and television documentaries.*

Double Z Enterprises

3 Wynnefield Road, Dublin 6
Company Directors: Mick O'Hara, Ciaran Morrison and Ronan McCabe
t. +353 1 497 9737
f. +353 1 497 9515
e. doublez@indigo.ie

■ *A multimedia production company producing comedy, light entertainment and children's programmes.*
Contact: Maia Dunphy

Dublin Institute of Technology, Media Production Unit

Aungier Street, Dublin 2
Media Production Unit: Grainne O'Rourke
t. +353 1 402 3108
f. +353 1 402 3288
e. gorourke@dit.ie
w. www.dit.ie
■ *A media production unit of Dublin Institute of Technology.*

Éamon de Buitléar

Hillside House, Delgany, Co. Wicklow
Managing Director and Director: Éamon de Buitléar
t. +353 1 287 6094
f. +353 1 287 7626
e. eamondebuitlear@ireland.com
■ *A film production company specialising in wildlife filming and documentaries in English and Irish.*
Producers: Laillí de Buitléar and Cian de Buitléar

Early Town Films

180 Merrion Road, Dublin 4
Managing Director, Producer, Line Producer and Production Manager: Patrick O'Donoghue
t. +353 1 269 4197
f. +353 1 269 4197
e. earlyt@indigo.ie
■ *A film and television drama production company producing feature films, shorts, documentaries, dramas and comedy programmes in English, Irish and French.*
Director: Alan Archbold

Earth Horizon Productions

13 Windsor Place, Dublin 2
Managing Director and Producer:
Duncan Stewart
t. +353 1 661 7475
f. +353 1 662 0337
e. info@earthhorizon.ie

■ *A film production company producing environmental programming and documentary series.*

Producers: Suzanne Kelly and
Catherine O'Dowd
Production Co-ordinator and Director:
Ingrid Gargan
Production Assistants: Karen Kennedy
and Jill O'Brien

East Atlantic Productions

Leighcloon, Skibbereen, Co. Cork
Producer: Andrew Carchrae
t. +353 28 38 442
f. +353 28 38 442
e. eastatlantic@eircom.net

■ *An independent production company producing short films, documentaries and children's programmes (in English and Irish) and providing camera and editing facilities and technicians.*

Eclipse Productions

Communications House, 2 Belmont
Court, Donnybrook, Dublin 4
Managing Director: David Harvey
t. +353-1-260 0456
f. +353-1-260 0723
e. info@eclipsetv.com
w. www.eclipsetv.com

■ *A film production company producing television programmes, including documentaries, current affairs, news programmes and corporate videos.*

Producer: Vanessa Kaminski
Senior Editor: Lorcan Maloney
Office Administrator: Gillian Dwyer

Edge Films International

Ground Floor Offices, 95 Haddington
Road, Dublin 4

John Norton

Egg Post Production

35 Lad Lane, Dublin 2
General enquiries
t. +353 1 634 5440
f. +353 1 642 5615
e. eugene@egg.ie
w. www.egg.ie

■ *A sound and multimedia post-production company.*

Element Films

21 Mespil Road, Dublin 4
Company Manager: Jane Roche
t. +353 1 618 5032
f. +353 1 664 3787
e. mail@elementfilms.ie
w. www.elementfilms.ie

■ *A film production company producing feature films.*

Producer: Ed Guiney
Business Executive: Andrew Lowe
Development Consultant: Alan Maher

Element Post Production

16 Fitzwilliam Square, Dublin 2
General Enquiries
t. +353 1 662 1030
f. +353 1 661 5288
e. info@element.ie
w. www.element.ie

■ *Provides a post-production service and produces commercials and animation and computer graphics (CGI).*

Emdee Productions 2000

42 Cross Avenue, Blackrock,
Co. Dublin
Managing Director and Producer:
Larry Masterson
t. +353 1 288 1399
f. +353 1 288 1399
e. emdee@indigo.ie

■ *A film production company producing television documentaries.*

Company Accounts: Hazel Masterson

Entertainment Factory, The

Chevale House, Swords, Co. Dublin
Manager: Fintan Cullen
t. +353 1 813 5070
m. +353 86 340 3232
f. +353 1 890 4679
w. www.ukscreen.com/agent/fintan
■ *A casting company and actors' agency. Also provides professional dancers, DJs, presenters and limousine hire.*

EO Teilifís

Baile Ard, An Spidéal, Co. na Gaillimhe
Managing Director and Producer:
Máire Ní Thuathail
t. +353 91 558 400
f. +353 91 558 470
e. eolas@eoteilifis.ie
w. www.eoteilifis.ie
■ *A television production company producing dramas, documentaries and children's programming (in English and Irish) and providing production facilities.*
Producer: Laura Ní Cheallaigh
Business Development Manager: Orla King

Esperanza Productions

44 Carysfort Avenue, Blackrock,
Co. Dublin
Producers and Directors: Ronan Tynan and Anne Daly
t. +353 1 288 8648
f. +353 1 288 8649
e. info@esperanza.ie
w. www.esperanza.ie
■ *A film and multimedia production company producing documentaries, current affairs and programmes in English, Irish and French. Background in development issues.*

Espresso Films

No. 4, 12 Magennis Place, Dublin 2
Producer and Director: Karen Edmonds
t. +353 1 672 9782
f. +353 1 672 9783
e. espresso@indigo.ie

■ *A film production company producing feature films, shorts, corporate commercials and documentaries.*
Writer and Director: Hugh Farley

Esras Films

43 Mount Merrion Avenue, Blackrock,
Co. Dublin
Managing Director, Producer and Director: Peter Kelly
t. +353 1 288 1939
f. +353 1 283 6253
e. info@esras.com
w. www.esras.com
■ *A media production company producing film and television, including documentaries, multimedia materials and corporate DVDs and videos in English and Irish.*
Producers and Directors: Neal Boyle and Mary Brophy

Fantastic Films

3 Clare Street, Dublin 2
Producer: John McDonnell
t. +353 1 671 3075
f. +353 1 671 3087
e. john@fantasticfilms.ie
w. www.fantasticfilms.ie
■ *A film production company producing feature films and television drama.*

Fastnet Films

15 Albany Road, Dublin 6
Managing Director: Macdara Kelleher
t. +353 1 491 0461
f. +353 1 491 0469
e. info@fastnetfilms.com
■ *An independent film and television production company producing documentaries, feature films and television drama series in English, Irish, French, German and Italian.*
Head of Development: Virginia Gilbert
Development Executives: Morgan Bushe and Michael Kinirons
Writer and Director: Lance Daly
Head of Production: Hughie Kelly
Production Assistant: Gavin Kilduff

Feenish Productions

26 South Frederick Street, Dublin 2
Producer and Director: James Kelly
t. +353 1 671 1166
e. info@feenish.com
w. www.feenish.com
■ *A film production company producing documentaries and animation in English and Irish.*

Ferndale Films

Ardmore Studios, Herbert Road, Bray,
Co. Wicklow
Managing Director and Producer: Noel
Pearson
t. +353 1 276 9666/9350
f. +353 1 276 9557
e. info@ferndalefilms.com
w. www.ferndalefilms.com
■ *A film production company producing feature films and documentaries.*
Head of Production: Anne-Marie
Naughton
Director: James Hickey

Filmbase

Curved Street, Dublin 2
General Enquiries
t. +353 1 679 6716
f. +353 1 679 6717
e. info@filmbase.ie
w. www.filmbase.ie
■ *A support organisation for the independent film and video sector in Ireland. Facilitates training and development, the hire of facilities and information provision and represents members and lobbies for the low-budget film sector in Ireland. Publishes* Film Ireland *and runs two Short Film Award Schemes.*
Administration and Manager: Seamus
Duggan
e. manager@filmbase.ie
Training and Information: Vanessa
Gildea
e. training@filmbase.ie
Training and Information: Jennifer
Killalea
e. info@filmbase.ie

Equipment: Barbara Henkes and Alan
Coleman
e. equipment@filmbase.ie
Final Cut Pro: Vicki Parks
e. finalcutpro@filmbase.ie
Film Ireland Editor: Lir Mac Carthaigh
e. editor@filmbase.ie
Film Ireland Advertising: Maureen Buggy
e. advertising@filmbase.ie
Film Ireland: Esther Terradas
e. esther@filmireland.net
Finance: Ray McKiernan
e. finance@filmbase.ie

Film, Entertainment and Leisure

Liberty Hall, Beresford Place, Dublin 1
t. +353 1 858 6412
f. +353 1 874 3691
e. film.entertainment@siptu.ie
w. www.siptu.ie
■ *A branch of the Services, Industrial, Professional and Technical Union (SIPTU).*

Fishfilms

60 The Coombe, Dublin 8
Managing Director and Producer: Jason
Doyle
t. +353 1 411 3755
f. +353 1 416 6300
e. info@fishfilms.ie
w. www.fishfilms.ie
Production Assistant: Zoe Adamson
■ *A film production company producing commercials and documentaries in English and Irish.*
Directors: Ciaran Donnelly, Gerry
Hoban, Damian Farrell, Orla Walsh,
John Butler and Alan Friel.

Forefront Films

Briarwood, Douglas Road, Cork
Producers and Directors: Tony
McCarthy and Joe McCarthy
t. +353 21 436 6000
f. +353 21 436 0002
e. info@forefront
w. www.forefront.ie

Cameraman and Director: Paschal
Cassidy
■ *A television production company producing*
music and entertainment programmes in
English and Irish.
Editor: Ruaidhrí Kirby
Administration: Jean Hallissey

Four Provinces Films

9 Lower Mount Pleasant Avenue,
Dublin 6
Producer: Redmond Morris
t. +353 1 497 2114
m. +353 87 967 3333
f. +353 1 412 6613
e. fourpfilmsltd@aol.com
■ *A film production company producing fea-*
ture films and television programmes.

Frontier Films

2 Northbrook Road, Dublin 6
Managing Director, Producer and
Director: Gerald Heffernan
t. +353 1 497 7077
f. +353 1 497 7731
e. frontier@indigo.ie
w. www.frontierfilms.ie
■ *A film production company producing docu-*
mentaries and music programmes.
Managing Director and Researcher:
Susan Ebrill
Producer and Head of Development:
Maria Horgan
Production Manager: Jenny McCrohan
Researcher: Bernie Connolly
Production Secretary: Tanya Kavanagh
Trainee Production: Derval Mellett

Fusion Films

The Thatched Cottage, Killarney
Road, Bray, Co. Wicklow
Managing Director, Producer and
Director: Aileen O'Reilly
t. +353 1 284 3139
f. +353 1 284 3139
e. tworoads@indigo.ie
■ *A film production company producing docu-*
mentaries and shorts.

Gabbro Productions

10 Clyde Road, Dublin 4
Producers and Directors: Gay Byrne
and Al Byrne
t. +353 1 668 6276
f. +353 1 668 6858
e. postbox@quinlanprivate.com
■ *A communications consultancy and produc-*
tion company for corporate and broadcast film,
video and radio productions in English, Irish
and French, headed by the legendary broadcast-
er Gay Byrne and his brother Al.

Gael Media

Na Forbacha, Co. Galway
Managing Director and Producer:
Christy King
t. +353 91 592 888
f. +353 91 592 891
e. gaelmed@eircom.net
■ *An independent multimedia production*
company producing light entertainment, music,
sports, educational, children's and documentary
programmes in English and Irish.
Producer: Maria Griffin

Gaelcom

52 Glenageary Park, Dún Laoghaire,
Co. Dublin
Managing Director: Liam Ó Murchú
t. +353 1 285 9606
f. +353 1 285 9606
■ *A film production company producing his-*
torical and cultural documentaries and pro-
grammes in English, Irish and French.
Directors: Denis O'Grady and Justin
Nelson
Researcher and UO: Noelle Gallagher

Gallowglass Pictures

5 Upper Baggot Street, Dublin 4
Managing Director: Eamon McElwee
t. +353 1 667 7050
m. +353 87 260 9288
f. +353 1 667 7051
e. eamon@gallowglasspictures.ie
w. www.gallowglasspictures.ie

■ *An independent production company producing documentaries and industrial videos and CD ROMs and providing editing facilities and camera hire.*

Galway Film Fleadh
Monivea Road, Galway
General Enquiries
t. +353 9 175 1655
f. +353 9 173 5831
w. www.galwayfilmfleadh.com
■ *A film festival, based in Galway.*

Gillian Marsh TV Productions
1 St Patrick Avenue, Crossmolina,
Co. Mayo
Producer and Director: Gillian Marsh
t. +353 96 30 011
f. +353 96 30 011
e. gmarsh@iol.ie
■ *A film production company producing documentaries, popular factual, entertainment and corporate programmes.*
Producer: Aideen Kane
Assistant Producer: Alan Gillespie

Ginty Films
20 Upper Merrion Street, Dublin 2
Producer, Writer and Director: Robert Ginty
t. +353 1 676 1044
f. +353 1 676 2125
e. rwginty@aol.com
w. www.robertginty.com
■ *A film production company producing television series and films for television.*

Glowworm Media
Cornmarket Square, Limerick
Producer: Kieran McConville
t. +353 61 446 044
m. +353 86 241 9211
f. +353 61 446 044
e. kieran@glowworm.ie
w. www.glowworm.ie
■ *A film production company producing news features, current affairs and documentaries. Kieran McConville is an independent television producer based in Limerick.*

Goldfish Films
8a Merton Park, Dublin 8
Writer and Director: Liz Gill
t. +353 1 453 1923
m. +353 87 252 3846
f. +353 1 453 1923
e. info@goldfishmemory.com
■ *A film production company producing feature films. Produced 'Goldfish Memory'*
Producer: Breda Walsh
m. +353 87 262 2584

Gold Star Media
7 Cranford Centre, Stillorgan Road, Dublin 4
Managing Director: Colm Burns
t. +353 1 260 0899
f. +353 1 260 0911
e. drive@indigo.ie
■ *A television and radio production and publishing company, producing motoring programmes, such as RTÉ's 'Drive' programme.*
Producer: Karl Tsigdinos

Grafliks
18 St Lawrence Road, Dublin 3
General Enquiries: Aidan Hickey
t. +353 1 833 1075
m. +353 87 236 1871
f. +353 1 853 1320
e. aidanhickey@eircom.net
■ *A production company specialising in writing scripts for animated series, television specials and education and information films in English and Irish.*

Grand Pictures
44 Fontenoy Street, Dublin 7
Producers: Paul Donovan and Michael Garland
t. +353 1 860 2290
f. +353 1 860 2096
e. paul@grandpictures.ie;
michael@grandpictures.ie
w. www.grandpictures.ie
■ *A film production company producing feature films and television drama. Produced 'Dead Long Enough'.*

Graph Films

4 Windmill Lane, Dublin 2
Producer and Director: Darragh Byrne
t. +353 1 677 7327
f. +353 1 677 7840
e. info@graphfilms.com

■ *A film production company producing documentaries, entertainment and drama programmes in English and Irish.*

Great Western Films

28 Gardiner Place, Dublin 1
Managing Director: Eoin Holmes
t. +353 1 889 8040
f. +353 1 872 8280
e. info@greatwesternfilms.com;
eoin@greatwesternfilms.com
w. www.greatwesternfilms.com

■ *A film production company producing television drama, feature films and short films in English, Irish, French and Spanish.*
Development Director: Niamh Fagan
Head of Business Affairs: Dominic
Hannigan

Grouse Lodge

Rosemount, Co. Westmeath
General Enquiries: Tom Skerritt, Ivan
O'Shea
t. +353 90 643 6175
f. +353 90 643 6131
e. info@grouselodge.com
w. www.grouselodge.com

■ *A residential sound recording studio, providing post-production sound services.*

Guerilla Films

ICC House, 46 Grand Parade, Cork
Producer: Helen Guerin
t. +353 21 427 0833
f. +353 21 427 0833
e. helen.guerin@ucd.ie

■ *A film production company producing short and feature films in English, Irish, French and Italian.*
Director: Chris Hurley

H & H Productions

Merchants' Court, Merchants' Quay,
Dublin 8
Managing Director, Producer and
Director: Bart Daly
t. +353 1 679 0370
f. +353 1 679 0057
e. bartdaly@firstlaw.ie

■ *A film production company.*
Director: Stephanie Daly

Happy Endings Productions

13 Merrion Square, Dublin 2
Producer: Paula Heffernan
t. +353 1 676 4140
f. +353 1 676 4141
e. info@happyendings.ie
w. www.happyendings.ie

■ *A television production company producing the RTÉ show 'The Panel'.*

Harvest Films

Knockeen, Church Cross, Skibbereen,
Co. Cork
General Enquiries: Pat Collins
m. +353 87 225 0945
e. harvestfilms@eircom.net

■ *A television production company producing documentaries.*

Hawkeye Films

Killina, Gort, Co. Galway
Managing Director, Director and
Producer: Donal R. Haughey
t. +353 91 638 219
f. + 353 91 638 048
e. hawkeyefilms@eircom.net

■ *A film production company producing documentaries in English and Irish.*

Hell's Kitchen

21 Mespil Road, Dublin 4
Managing Director and Producer:
Arthur Lappin
t. +353 1 667 5599
f. +353 1 667 5592
e. hellskit@iol.ie

■ *A film production company producing short and feature films. One of the leading Irish film production companies, headed by Jim Sheridan, director of 'In America'.*

Producer and Director: Jim Sheridan

Head of Production: Paul Myler

High Wire

147 Pearse Street, Dublin 2

General Enquiries: Mark Quinn

t. +353 1 671 1010

f. +353 1 671 9194

e. info@highwire.ie

w. www.highwire.ie

■ *Provides post-production services for broadcasting. Founded 1997.*

Hofnaflús Teo

Baile na hAbhann, Co. na Gaillimhe

Managing Director, Producer and Director: Glyn Carragher

t. +353 91 593 800

f. +353 91 593 622

e. hofnanet@iol.ie

w. www.iol.ie/~hofnanet

■ *A film production company producing drama, animation, documentaries and commercials (English, Irish and Italian) and providing studio facilities for film production.*

Producer and Director: Pam Carragher

Administrator: Anne Marie MacDonagh

Horizonline Films

26 South Frederick Street, Dublin 2

Managing Director and Producer: Alan Fitzpatrick

t. +353 1 679 4576

f. +353 1 679 4576

e. horizonline@tinet.ie

w. www.horizonline-films.com

■ *A film production company producing feature films, shorts, documentaries, corporate videos, commercials and multimedia materials in English and Irish.*

Directors: Jim Sperin and Ruari O'Brien

Hummingbird Productions

12 Mountainview Drive, Boghall Road, Bray, Co. Wicklow

Managing Director, Producer and Director: Philip King

t. +353 1 286 8273

f. +353 1 286 8321

e. hummingb@indigo.ie

■ *A film production company producing documentaries and feature films in English and Irish.*

Writer and Producer: Nuala O'Connor

Producer: Tina Moran

Ian Graham Productions

28 Hillcourt Road, Glenageary, Co. Dublin

Managing Director, Producer and Director: Ian Graham

t. +353 1 285 4874

f. +353 1 285 4874

■ *A film production company producing documentaries and television programmes in English and German.*

Icebox Films

8 Herbert Street, Dublin 2

General Enquiries: Clíona Ní Bhuachalla and Charlie McCarthy

t. +353 1 676 7402/3

m. +353 87 838 4500

f. +353 1 676 7412

e. cliona@iceboxfilms.ie

e. Charlie@iceboxfilms.ie

w. www.iceboxfilms.ie

■ *A film production company producing television drama, television studio series, soaps and documentaries in Irish and English.*

Charlie McCarthy

m. +353 86 816 7514

Dee Collier

m. +353 87 968 3132

Igloo

1 Hatch Place, Dublin 2

Managing Director: Jonathan Willis

t. +353 1 662 4624

f. +353 1 676 4022

e. igloo@iol.ie

■ *A film production company producing feature films, shorts and documentaries. Produced the short film 'Sunburn' (2004).*

Producer: Brian Willis

Ikandi Productions

53 Gleann na Coille, Galway
Managing Director: Siún Ní
Raghallaigh
  t. +353 91 590 867
  m. +353 87 248 2681
  e. siun@ikandi.ie
  w. www.ikandi.ie
■ *A film production company producing animations and feature films.*
Creative Director: Maeve McAdam
  m. +353 86 173 8048
  e. maeve@ikandi.ie

Illusion Animated Productions

The Studio, 46 Quinn's Road,
Shankill, Co. Dublin
Director: Gary Blatchford
  t. +353 1 282 1458
  f. +353 1 282 1458
  e. info@illusionanimation.com
  w. www.illusionanimation.com
■ *An animation production company producing animation, direction, design, storyboards, slugging, x-sheets and layouts.*

Imagine Ltd

Ardmore Studios, Herbert Road, Bray,
Co. Wicklow
Producer and Director: Paul Howard
  t. +353 1 286 2971
  m. +353 86 260 0423
  f. +353 1 286 1894
  e. imagine@eircom.net
■ *A film and television production company producing feature films, documentaries and corporate and commercial videos in English, French and Italian.*
Producer: Bernadette Stapleton

Inis Films

64 Lower Gardiner Street, Dublin 1
General Enquiries: Joel Conroy
  t. +353 1 855 6388
  f. +353 1 855 1672
  e. joelconroy@hotmail.com
■ *A film and television production company specialising in underwater photography.*

Irish Film and Television Network (IFTN)

First Floor, Palmerstown Centre,
Kennelsfort Road, Dublin 20
Publisher: Aine Moriarty
  t. +353 1 620 0811
  f. +353 1 620 0810
  e. info@iftn.ie
  w. www.iftn.ie
■ *A film information service. The web site includes a comprehensive directory of the Irish film and television industry, updated daily and providing information about all aspects of the audio-visual industry.*
Editor: Deirdre Hopkins
  e. editor@iftn.ie
Webmaster
  e. webmaster@iftn.ie

Irish Film Board (Bord Scannán na hÉireann)

Rockford House, St Augustine Street,
Galway
Chief Executive: Vacant
  t +353 91 561398
  f+ 353 91 561405
  e info@filmboard.ie
  w.www.filmboard.ie
■ *Bord Scannán na hÉireann/the Irish Film Board is a state agency to support the Irish film and audio-visual industry. It was set up in 1993. It provides loans and equity investment to independent film-makers to assist in the production of Irish films. It also funds animation and documentary development, in addition to new talent schemes. These schemes include Short Cuts, Frameworks, Oscailt and Irish Flash. Promotes Ireland internationally as a film location.*
Head of Business Affairs: Teresa
McGrane
Head of Production and Development:
Brendan McCarthy
Head of Marketing: Moira Horgan
Information Officer: Louise Ryan
Applications and Schemes Co-
ordinator: Jill McGregor.

Board members: (appointed January 2005 until 2009)
James Morris (Chair), Alan Gilsenan, Margaret McCarthy MacIntyre, Lesley McKimm, Tristan Orpen Lynch, Kevin Moriarty, Kirsten Sheridan.

Irish Photographers' Website

8 Kilpedder Grove, Kilpedder, Co. Wicklow
Photographer: Alan Murphy
m. +353 86 266 6260
w. www.irishphotographers.ie

■ *Independent web page providing Irish photographers with industry news, links through a directory and the opportunity to showcase work. The web site also provides a 'pinboard', 'find a photgrapher' and 'find a supplier'.*

Jam Media

Guinness Enterprise Centre, Taylor's Lane, Dublin 8
t: +353 1 617 4816
f: +353 1 677 1558
e: info@jammedia.ie
w: www.jammedia.ie
Company Director: John Rice

■ *JAM Media has produced work for animated features, television series, commercials, short films, multimedia, music videos, title sequences and corporate videos.*

JDM Film and Television Production

4–5 High Street, Galway
Managing Directors and Producers: Mick Ruane and Jonathan White
t. +353 91 564 005
f. +353 91 565 323
e. jdm@iol.ie

■ *A film production company producing documentaries, multimedia materials, corporate and commercial videos and educational materials in English and Irish.*

Neil Jordan

7 Sorrento Terrace, Dalkey, Co. Dublin
■ *International film director and writer.*

Journeyman Productions

Digital Depot, Roe Lane, The Digital Hub, Thomas Street, Dublin 8
General Enquiries: Cóilín Ó Scolaí, Managing Director
t. +353 1 453 7644
f. +353 1 453 4586
e. coilin@journeyman.ie
w. www.journeymanproductions.com

■ *A digital media production company producing digital media content for a range of media. Also provides publishing, editorial content, project management, design and layout, copywriting, audio visual services, scriptwriting, production, off-line editing, directing, a digital media consultancy, project management, production, web, CD ROM and DVD authoring and mobile application development.*

Kairos Communications

Moyglare Road, Maynooth, Co. Kildare
Managing Director: Michael Melvin
t. +353 1 628 6007
f. +353 1 628 6511
e. kairos@iol.ie

■ *A production company producing radio, television and corporate videos and providing media training in English and Irish.*

Producers: Michael Cleere, Henry McNamara and Finbarr Tracey

Kavaleer Productions

The Digital Depot, Roe Lane, Dublin 8
Creative Director: Andrew Kavanagh
t. +353 1 488 5873
e. info@kavaleer.com
w. www.kavaleer.com

■ *A film production company producing feature films, shorts and animation in English and Irish.*

Producer: Paul McGrath
Development: Damien Byrne

Kite Entertainment

4 Windmill Lane, Dublin 2
General Enquiries: Darren Smith
t. +353 1 671 3444
f. +353 1 671 3444

e. darren@kiteentertainment.com
w. www.kiteentertainment.com
■ *A media production company.*

Language

28 Great Strand Street, Dublin 1
Producer and Director: Neasa
Hardiman
t. +353 1 8783300
f. +353 1 878 3301
m. +353 1 877657068
e. neasa@language.ie
w. www.language.ie
■ *A film production company producing dramas and documentaries for television and writing and directing services for films in German, Irish and French.*

Legend Films

Ardmore Studios, Herbert Road, Bray,
Co. Wicklow
Managing Director, Producer and
Director: Gerry Johnston
t. +353 1 276 0590
f. +353 1 286 5923
e. gjohnsto@indigo.ie
■ *A film production company producing feature films, shorts, documentaries and children's programmes in English and Irish.*
Director: Derek Johnston

Liam Quigley Voiceovers

Lucan, Co. Dublin
General Enquiries
t. +353 1 621 4514
f. +353 1 621 4861
w. www.liamquigley.com
■ *A voice-over production company also producing radio commercials.*

Liberty Films

6 Exchequer Street, Dublin 2
General Enquiries: Maria Horgan
t. +353 1 675 3816
f. +353 1 675 3818
e. libertyfilms@eircom.net
■ *A film production company producing documentaries.*

Lifejacket Media Production

66 The Fairways, Monaleen, Castletroy,
Limerick
t: +353 61 340 896
f: +353 41 980 1733
e: wiley@iol.ie
Managing Director: Eddie Wiley

Like It Love It Productions (International)

5 Carysfort Avenue, Blackrock, Co.
Dublin
Managing Director: Andy Ruane
t. +353 1 283 4490
f. +353 1 283 6420
e. mail@likeitloveit.com
w. www.likeitloveit.com
■ *A film production company producing corporate and commercial videos, multimedia materials, dramas, educational programmes and quiz shows in English, Irish, German, French, Spanish, Italian and more.*
Producer and Director: Philip Kampff

Lios na Sí Teoranta

Rinn na Feirste, Co. Donegal
Managing Director: Niall Mac
Eachmharcaigh
t. +353 75 48 605
f. +353 75 48 777
■ *A fim production company producing documentaries, dramas and comedy in English and Irish.*
Producer: Áine Nic Eachmharcaigh

Little Bird

13 Merrion Square, Dublin 1
Chairmen: James Mitchell and Jonathan
Cavendish
t. +353 1 613 1710
f. +353 1 662 4647
e. info@littlebird.ie
w. www.littlebird.ie
■ *A film and television production company producing feature films, documentaries, dramas and music and arts programmes in English, German and French. One of the leading film production companies in Ireland, with a strong international track record.*

Producers: Pascale Lamche and Dixie Linder
Head of Project Development: Lizzie Francke
Development Executive: Nahrein Mirza
Sales and Acquisitions Executive: Karen O'Malley
Financial Director: Frank Lehane
Head of Legal Affairs: Mark Byrne

Lon Dub Teo

Gort na Scairte, Baile Bhuirne, Co. Cork
Managing Director: Gerry Mac Bride
t. +353 26 45 855
m. +353 86 839 8376
f. +353 26 45 855
e. gerymac@eircom.net
■ *A film production company producing documentaries, docusoaps and corporate videos in Irish, French and English.*
Researcher and Presenter: Eibhlín Ní Lionaird

Loophead Studio

Cross, Carrigaholt, Co. Clare
General Enquiries: Naomi Wilson and Brian Doyle
t. +353 65 905 8309
e. loopheadstudio@eircom.net
■ *A film production company producing experimental films, animations and documentaries in English and Irish (and sometimes non-verbally).*

Loopline Film

106 Baggot Lane, Dublin 4
Managing Director: Sé Merry Doyle
t. +353 1 667 6489/6627
f. +353 1 667 6604
e. info@loopline.com
w. www.loopline.com
■ *A film production company producing documentaries, dramas and short films (in English and Irish) and providing post-production services and archive restoration.*
Producer: Martina Durac

Louis Marcus Productions

12 Fortfield Drive, Dublin 6W
Managing Director: Louis Marcus
t. +353 1 490 6723
f. +353 1 490 6723
e. loumarc@indigo.ie
■ *A film production company producing shorts, documentaries, corporate/commercial videos and sports, music and arts, educational and multimedia materials in English, Irish and French.*

Lunah Productions

Old Fintra Road, Killybegs, Co. Donegal
General Enquiries: Declan Hannigan
t. +353 74 973 1379
f. +353 74 973 2245
e. declan@lunah-productions.com
■ *A production company.*

Macalla Teoranta

7 Lombard Street East, Dublin 2
Managing Directors and Producers: Cuán Mac Conghail and Marcus Mac Conghail
t. +353 1 670 3880
f. +353 1 670 3881
■ *A film production company producing short films, multimedia materials and corporate and commercial videos (in English and Irish) and providing dubbing and revoicing services.*
Studio Director: Jane Farley

Magma Films

16 Merchants' Road, Galway
Chairman and Executive Producer: Ralph Christians
t. +353 91 569 142
f. +353 91 569 148
e. info@magmaworld.com
w. www.magmaworld.com
■ *A film production company producing feature films, animation, drama, children's and light entertainment programmes and documentaries in English, Irish, German and French.*
Managing Director: Seamus Mulligan
Artistic Director: Maeve McAdam

Head of Animation: Daina Sacco
Live Action Producers: Clodagh
Freeman and Ann Brehony

Des Martin

8 Orpen Rise, Stillorgan, Co. Dublin
t. +353 86 2679325
f. +353 1 28 38353
Production Manager: Des Martin

Mass Productions

37 Belgium Park, Monaghan
Managing Director: Dara McCluskey
t. +353 47 38 693
e. dara@iol.ie
■ *A film production company producing documentaries, dramas and other programming for television.*

Matheson Ormsby Prentice

30 Herbert Street, Dublin 2
General enquiries: James Hickey
t. +353 1 619 9000
f. +353 1 619 9010
e. james.hickey@mop.ie
w. www.mop.ie
■ *A production company.*

McCamley Entertainment

103 The Woodlands, Ratoath,
Co. Meath
Producer and Director: David
McCamley
t. +353 1 825 7841
f. +353 1 825 7841
e. dmccamley@eircom.net
■ *A production company producing animation for children's television.*

McFilms

15 Vesey Place, Monkstown, Co. Dublin
Managing Director and Producer: Katy
McGuinness
t. +353 1 280 1666
f. +353 1 284 4882
e. goodfilm@indigo.ie
w. www.iftn.ie/production/goodfilm
■ *A film production company producing feature films and drama.*
Producer's Assistant: Geraldine Nolan

Seamus McInerney

Apartment 5, Woodlawn House
Apartments, Lower Mounttown Road,
Dún Laoghaire, Co. Dublin
Production Manager: Seamus
McInerney
t. +353 1 660 7755
f. +353 1 660 7850
e. sci@indigo.ie
e. seamusmcin@eircom.net
■ *A freelance production manager.*

McNamara Films

4 Leeson Walk, Dublin 6
Producer and Director: Ann
McNamara
m. +353 87 243 5498
e. ann@mcnamarafilms.tv
■ *A film production company producing documentaries and music, arts and current affairs programmes.*

McVeigh Broadcast

Porthaw Glen, Buncrana, Co. Donegal
Brian McVeigh
t. +44 780 101 5637
f. +353 776 2723
e. brianmcveigh@eircom.net
■ *Digital filming and editing service for news, documentaries and other programming.*

Mdigginphotography

5 Castle Street, Tralee, Co. Kerry
Photographer: Michael Diggin
t. +353 66 712 2201
f. +353 66 712 2201
w. www.mdigginphotography.com
■ *A photography and production stills company.*

Media Nua

63 Kenilworth Square, Dublin 6
Managing Director and Producer: Roy
Esmonde
t. +353 1 496 7450
f. +353 1 496 7581
e. info@medianua.com
■ *A film production company producing documentaries, music and arts programmes and commercial and corporate materials.*

Mediascapes

58 Percy Lane, Dublin 4
General Enquiries: Brian Nartey
t. +353 1 634 9844
m. +353 86 850 0055
f. +353 1 634 9844
e. brian.nartey@oceanfree.net
■ *Provides post-production sound services to the broadcast, advertising and digital media sectors and produces content for interactive television and webcast and streaming technologies.*

Meem Productions

17a Greenmount Lawns, Dublin 6
Managing Director: Siraj Zaidi
t. +353 1 492 8156
m. +353 87 283 2259
e. szaidi@oceanfree.net; sirajbolly-wood@dublin.ie
w. www.bollywoodireland.com
■ *A film production company producing feature films, documentaries and corporate and commercial materials in English and Spanish.*
Producer-Director: Vivienne Ryan
Directors: John Daly, Noman Mangan, Orla McQuillan and Ruth Roselyn

Merlin Films Group

16 Upper Pembroke Street, Dublin 2
Managing Director: Kieran Corrigan
t. +353 1 676 4373
f. +353 1 676 4368
e. info@merlin.ie
w. www.merlin.ie
■ *A film production company producing documentaries and feature films. A leading international film production company.*
Chairperson: John Boorman
Producers: Jeff Berg and Edgar Gross
Vice President (USA): Norman Siderow
USA Office: 831 Sunset Boulevard, Suite 201, Los Angeles, Calif. 90069, USA
t. +001 310 854 0707
f. +001 310 854 0757

Metropolitan Films

Ardmore Studios, Herbert Road, Bray, Co. Wicklow
Managing Directors and Producers: James Flynn and Juanita Wilson
t. +353 1 276 9528
f. +353 1 276 9471
e. metro@iol.ie
■ *A film production company producing feature films and drama and providing specialist production services.*

Michael O'Connell Productions

10 Herbert Place, Dublin 2
General Enquiries
Managing Director: Michael O'Connell
t. +353 1 662 2500
f. +353 1 662 2531
e. info@promediatv.ie
■ *A television production company producing television life-style programmes.*

Midas Productions

34 Lower Baggot Street, Dublin 2
Managing Director: Mike Keane
t. +353 1 661 1384
f. +353 1 676 8250
e. mike@midasproductions.ie
w. www.midasproductions.ie
■ *A film production company producing documentaries and entertainment programmes and DVDs for films in English and Irish.*
Producer and Director: Billy McGrath and Mark Warren

Midnight Movies

11 Burgh Quay, Dublin 2
General Enquiries: Christopher Wicking and Lily Susan Todd
t. +353 1 670 9221
f. +353 1 670 9221
e. midnightmovies@eircom.net
■ *A film production company producing short films, multimedia productions, dramas, documentaries and comedy and light entertainment programmes.*

Millbrook Studios
Rathfarnham, Dublin 14
Managing Director: Sean Walsh
t. +353 1 493 2147
f. +353 1 493 9241
e. info@millbrook.ie
w. www.millbrook.ie
■ *A production and post-production company producing television programmes and corporate videos in English, Irish, French and German.*
Production Co-ordinator: Sinead Hanna

Mind the Gap Films
22a Fortescue Lane, Dublin 6
Founders, Producers and Directors: Bill Hughes and Bernadine Carraher
t. +353 1 491 3358
f. +353 1 491 1617
e. bernadine@mindthegapfilms.com
■ *A film and radio production company producing music, light entertainment, deaf programming and documentaries in English, Irish, Irish Sign Language and Spanish.*
Producers and Directors: Glen Gorman and Claire Dix

Mint Productions
205 Lower Rathmines Road, Dublin 6
Executive Producer: Steve Carson
t. (Dublin) +353 1 491 3333;
t. (Belfast) + 44 28 9024 0555
f. +353 1 491 3334
e. info@mint.ie
w. www.mint.ie
■ *A film production company producing documentaries and factual entertainment programmes. Mint Productions is now one of Ireland's leading factual television production companies, headed by the RTÉ television presenter Miriam O'Callaghan and her husband, Steve Carson.*
Executive Producer: Miriam O'Callaghan
Head of Production: Niamh Maher
Head of Development: Paula Williams
Researcher: Ailbhe Maher
Executive Producer (Northern Ireland): Jezz Wright

Northern Ireland Office: 13 Fitzwilliam Street, Belfast BT9 6AW

Miss Smith Productions
7 Merton Avenue, Dublin 8
General Enquiries: Lisa Mulcahy
t. +353 1 497 0099
f. +353 1 4548513
e. missmith@eircom.net
m +353872458887
■ *A documentary production company*

Monster Animation and Design
78 Mount Street Crescent, Dublin 2
Producer: Gerard O'Rourke
353 1 603 4980/1
f. +353 1 676 1437
e. gerard@monsteranimation.ie
w. www.monsteranimation.ie
■ *A digital studio and production company producing television specials and commercials, animation and multimedia products in English, Irish, French, German and Spanish.*
Creative Director: Jason Tammemagi

Monster Distributes
The Monster Mews, Rear 51 Merrion Square, Dublin 2
Managing Director: Andrew Fitzpatrick
t. +353 1 611 4934
f. +353 1 611 4935/287 1180
e. andrew@monsterdistributes.com
w. www.monsterdistributes.com
■ *A television distribution company, selling television programmes internationally.*
Producer: Susan Broe
Sales and Acquisitions: Deirdre Barry

Moondance Productions
3 Reilly's Terrace, Dublin 8
Managing Director: Shane Brennan
t. +353 1 473 4599
f. +353 1 473 4598
e. info@moondance.tv
w. www.moondance.tv
■ *A film production company producing corporate and commercial products, documentaries and music and arts programming (in English,*

Irish and French) and providing production crew hire.
Head of Post-Production: Tom Burke

Motive
Unit 18, Guinness Enterprise Centre, Taylor's Lane, Dublin 8
General Enquiries: Cormac Hargaden, Mick Pilsworth and Trisha Canning
t. +353 1 415 1245
f. +353 1 410 0985
e. cormac@motive.ie
w. www.motive.ie
■ *A television production company producing sport, documentaries and life-style programming. Motive was formed following the management buy-out of the production wing of Setanta Television at the end of 2004.*
Cormac Hargaden
m. +353 86 828 3100
Trisha Canning
m. +353 86 821 1595
e. trisha@motive.ie
Mick Pilsworth
e. mick@motive.ie

Moving Still Productions
25 Royal Canal Bank West, Dublin 7
Director: Tim Fernée
t. +353 1 830 0404
e. movingstill@eircom.net
■ *An animation production company producing shorts, corporate and commercial products and children's, educational and drama programming in English and Irish.*

MR Films
1 Westland Square, Pearse Street, Dublin 2
Company Director: Michael Ryan
t. +353 1 881 4010
f. +353 1 881 4011
e. info@mrfilms.ie
■ *A film production, financing and sales company.*
Producer: Emma Scott
Financial Administrator: Mary Sweeney
Sales Executive: Mary Clare Curran

Production and Administration: Patrick O'Neill
Sales Consultant: Will Machin

Multi Media Arts Ireland
125 Lower Baggot Street, Dublin 2
Producer: Marion Cullen
t. +353 1 639 1233
f. +353 1 639 1102
e. safinia_mma@yahoo.com
w. www.mmarts.com

Múnla
34 Lower Baggot Street, Dublin 2
Managing Director and Producer: Mike Keane
t. +353 1 661 1384
f. +353 1 676 8250
e. munla@eircom.net
■ *A film production company producing documentaries in English and Irish.*
Managing Director: Aidan Sheeran
Producer and Director: Rosie Nic Cionnaith

Jimmy Murakami Film Production
2A Cliff Terrace, Sandycove, Co. Dublin
Producer and Director: Jimmy T. Murakami
t. +353 1 280 6301
f. +353 280 9385
e. murakami@iol.ie
■ *A film production company producing animation, children's programmes, feature films and shorts in English, Irish, French and Japanese.*
Production Co-ordinator: Ethna Murakami

Musketeer Productions
Currahy, Barryroe, Clonakilty, Co. Cork
Producer-Director: Niall Mahoney
t. +353 23 53 974
m. +353 87 681 4256
f. +353 23 53 974
e. muskateerproductions@eircom.net
■ *A production company producing drama, entertainment and documentaries.*

Nelvana International

228–230 Airport House, Shannon Free
Zone, Shannon, Co. Clare
Managing Director: Dale R. Hancocks
t. +353 61 474 244
f. +353 61 474 233
e. daleh@irl.nelvana.com
w. www.nelvana.com

■ *The Irish subsidiary of Nelvana Limited,*
an animation production and distribution com-
pany producing feature films, children's and
educational programming in Chinese, English,
French, Spanish, German, Italian and
Japanese.

Financial Controller: Patrick Lynch
Legal Counsel: William Crean
PA to Managing Director: Mairéad
Bermingham
Accounts Assistant: Sheila O'Doherty
Supervisor, Compositing: Liam
Hannan
Compositor: Carol Hannan
Systems Administrator: Alun Warner
Supervisor, Digital Ink and Paint:
Kathy Carter Costello

Nemeton

An Rinn, Co. Waterford
Managing Director: Irial Mac Murchú
t. +353 58 46 499
f. +353 58 46 208
e. info@nemeton.ie
w. www.nemeton.ie

■ *A film production company producing*
sport, health, historical, marine and biographi-
cal documentaries in English, Irish, German
and Spanish.

Finance Manager: Tadhg Ó Maoileoin
Technical Manager: Tomás Mac Craith
Production Manager: Paula Uí
Uallacháin
Head of Sports: Gearóid Mac Donncha
Head of Development and Executive
Producer: Larry Masterson

New Decade TV and Film

25 South Frederick Street, Dublin 2
Managing Director: Ciaran O'Connor
t. +353 1 679 3282
f. +353 1 679 3336
e. info@newdecade.ie
w. www.newdecade.ie

■ *A film and television production company*
producing feature films, shorts, documentaries,
current affairs and news programming, internet
digital production and corporate and commercial
products and providing crew hire and off-line
and digital on-line post-production facilities.

Producer and Director: Nuala
Cunningham

Newgrange Pictures

49–50 Berystede, Leeson Park, Dublin 6
t. +353 1 4970817
f. +353 1 4970817
e. info@newgrangepictures.com
w. www.newgrangepictures.com

Chief Executive Officer: Jackie Larkin

Newsfile

1 Millmount Abbey, Drogheda, Co.
Louth
Fran Caffrey
t. +353 41 987 1200
f. +353 41 987 1010
e. newsfile@eircom.net

■ *Photographic agency.*

Nomad

39 Upper Fitzwilliam Street, Dublin 2
Managing Director: Brian Raftery
t. +353 1 661 0220
f. +353 1 661 0027
e. production@nomad.ie
w. www.nomad.ie

■ *A film production company producing fea-*
ture films, commercials and documentaries.

Directors: Richie Smith, Conor
Horgan, Kieron J. Walsh, Luca Maroni,
Lloyd Stein and Nic Wickham.

Ocean Film Productions

Castleview House, 22 Sandymount
Green, Dublin 4
Producer: Catherine Tiernan
t. +353 1 663 0036
f. +353 1 663 0036
e. ocean@indigo.ie
■ *A film production company producing feature films, television documentaries and television drama in English and Irish.*
Director: Frank Stapleton

Octagon

Ardmore Studios, Herbert Road, Bray,
Co. Wicklow
Managing Directors and Producers:
Morgan O'Sullivan and James Flynn
t. +353 1 276 9528
f. +353 1 276 9471
e. octagon@iol.ie
■ *A film production company producing feature films and television drama.*
Producers: Catherine Tiernan and
Juanita Wilson
Production Finance Executive: Nessa
King

Oscarina Ltd

118 South Park, Foxrock, Dublin 18
Managing Director: Angie Mezzetti
t. +353 1 289 5264
e. mezzetti@iol.ie
■ *A film production company producing documentaries.*

Pace Entertainment Productions

8 Herbert Road, Dublin 4
Managing Directors and Producers:
Triona Campbell and Marcus Lynch
t. +353 1 660 9265
f. +353 1 660 4305
e. info@pace-entertainment.com
w. www.pace-entertainment.com
■ *A film production company producing films, documentaries and drama and children's programming in English and Irish and providing script development services.*
Project Co-ordinator: Erika Csibi
e. erika@pace-entertainment.com

Palomino Pictures

322 Harold's Cross Road, Dublin 6W
Managing Directors: David Heffernan
and Bous de Jong
t. +353 1 492 9809
f. +353 1 492 9809
e. info@palominopictures.ie
■ *A film production company producing documentaries, films and television programmes in English and Irish.*
Producer: Tina Heffernan

Paradise Pictures

44 Westland Row, Dublin 2
Managing Director: Colin Cowman
t. +353 1 661 0234
f. +353 1 661 0108
e. info@paradisepictures.ie
w. www.paradisepictures.ie
■ *A film and multimedia production company producing documentaries, shorts and corporate and commercial productions in English, Irish, French and German.*
Company Director: Natasha O'Connor
Production Manager: Liz Kinsella

Paradox Pictures

26 South Frederick Street, Dublin 2
Managing Director: Liam O'Neill
t. +353 1 670 6883
f. +353 1 670 6889
e. paradoxp@iol.ie
■ *A film production company producing films, documentaries, shorts and animations.*
Producer: Nuala Carr
Director: Declan Recks

Parallel Film Productions

Columbia Mills, 14–15 Sir John
Rogerson's Quay, Dublin 2
Managing Directors and Producers:
Alan Moloney and Tim Palmer
t. +353 1 671 8555
f. +353 1 671 8242
e. pfp@iol.ie
■ *A film production company producing films and television drama.*
Managing Director: Justin Keating

Enquiries: Orla Bleahen and Susan Mullen

Parzival Productions

4–5 High Street, Galway
Managing Director and Producer:
Tomás Hardiman
 t. +353 91 569 109/520 592
 f. +353 91 562 202
 e. thc@iol.ie
 w. www.parzival.ie
■ *A film production company producing features, shorts, documentaries and corporate videos in English and Irish.*

Patrick M. Verner Photography

25 Springhill Park, Killiney, Co. Dublin
Photographer: Patrick Verner
 t. +353 1 285 3463
 m. +353 87 234 4922
 f. +353 1 285 3463
■ *A photography company, photographing music, arts and fashion events, celebrity portraiture and performance.*

Peer Pressure

46 Upper Baggot Street, Dublin 2
Company Director: Aileen McDonagh

Pegasus Productions

1 Diamond Terrace, Bray, Co. Wicklow
Managing Director: Howard Gibbins
 t. +353 1 204 2949
 m. +353 86 5255 3051
 e. howardg@indigo.ie
■ *A film production company producing feature films, shorts and comedy/light entertainment and drama programming in English and French.*

Peripheral Vision

Coronea Studios, Skibbereen, Co. Cork
Managing Director: Stephen Bean
 t. +353 28 22 087
 f. +353 28 22 028
 e. ctnbean@iol.ie
■ *A video production company producing documentaries, current affairs and news, children's, corporate and commercial and life-style programming in English, Irish and German. Along with multimedia productions provides studio facilities, research and digital editing with digital effects.*
Technical Director: Uwe Schiller
Design and Graphics: Bronwyn Wright
Producers: Eamon Lankford and Dick Hill
Editor: Darragh Murphy

Photocall Ireland

Unit 14, Docklands Innovation Park, 128–130 East Wall Road, Dublin 3
 t. +353 1 887 5945
 e. photoire@indigo.ie
 w. www.photocallireland.com
■ *Photographic agency, providing images of all aspects of Irish life from 1980 onwards.*

Pictia Productions

33 Thornbury Road, Raheen, Limerick
Managing Director: Dan Dwyer
 t. +353 87 816 8629
 e. pictia@eircom.net
■ *A film production company producing documentaries in English, Irish, French and Catalan.*

Piranha Bar

37 Fitzwilliam Square, Dublin 2
Managing Director: Dave Burke
 t. +353 1 605 3739
 e. marc@piranhabar.ie
■ *A post-production house providing a digital media facility and expertise in post-production on television programmes and commercials.*
Creative Director: Gavin Kelly
Facility Director: Marc Long
Post-Producer: Peter Green

Planet Rock Profiles

The Monster Mews, Rear 51 Merrion Square, Dublin 2
Director and Producer: Susan Broe
 t. +353 1 611 4933/4934
 f. +353 1 611 4935
 e. susan@planetrock.net
 w. www.planetrock.net

■ *A production company producing programmes that are profiles of music performers,
available for television, video-on-demand and
internet broadband and on airline media and
radio.*

Planet Television UK and Ireland

2 St John's Square, Limerick
General Enquiries: Ian Moriarty
t. +353 61 468 476
f. +353 61 481 527
e. planttv@iol.ie
w. www.planet-television.com
■ *Provides post-production services and dupli-
cation and standards conversion.*

Poolbeg Productions

Killalane, Laragh, Co. Wicklow
Managing Director: Donald Taylor Black
t. +353 40 445 909
f. +353 40 445 893
e. info@poolbeg.ie
■ *A film production company producing feature films, shorts, drama and documentaries.*
Executive Producer: James Hickey
Producer (Belfast): Ivan Martin

Post IT

8 Appian Way, Dublin 6
t +35316672703
f +35316676446
e info@postit.ie
w. www.postit.ie
Contact: Richard Callaghan
■ *A post-production facility for the broadcast
video and film industry, specialising in digital
technology editing and processing.*

Power Pictures

4–5 High Street, Galway
Managing Director: David Power
t. +353 91 569 707
f. +353 91 562 202
e. powerpix@iol.ie
■ *A production company producing documentaries and fiction films in English, Irish and
French.*
Company Director: Paul Power

Powertrip Productions

11 Grangemore Rise, Dublin 13
Managing Directors: Graham Cantwell
and Patrick Wickham
m. +353 86 374 7974
e. powertrip@ireland.com
w. www.powertriphome.com
■ *A production company producing feature
films, shorts and animations.*

Press 22

11–12 Nicholas Street, Limerick
Manager and Chief Photographer: Liam
Burke
t. +353 6 120 4222
f. +353 6 140 1306
e. photos@press22.com
w. www.press22.com
■ *Photographic agency.*

Prime Productions

Belville Mews, Stillorgan Road,
Donnybrook, Dublin 4
General Enquiries: David Harvey
t. +353 1 260 0456
f. +353 1 260 0723
e. dharvey@eclipsetv.com
w. www.eclipsetv.com

ProMedia (see Michael O'Connell Productions)

10 Herbert Place, Dublin 2
Managing Director: Michael O'Connell
t. +353 1 662 2500
f. +353 1 662 2531
e. info@promediatv.ie
■ *A production company producing feature
films, documentaries, corporates and current
affairs and news programmes.*

PúCán Films

12 Magennis Place, Dublin 2
Managing Director and Producer:
Brendan Goss
t. +353 1 672 7244
m. +353 86 827 6706
f. +353 1 671 9481
e. pucan@indigo.ie

■ *A film production company producing feature films, shorts, documentaries and corporate and commercial products.*

Purple Productions Teoranta
91 Leopardstown Avenue, Blackrock, Co. Dublin
Producer: Aprile Blake
  m. +353 86 350 2426
  e. aprile@eircom.net;
  w. www.purpleproductions.net
■ *A video production company producing documentaries and corporate videos in English, Irish and Spanish.*
Director: Dearbhla Glynn

Quin Films
Knockinglass, Coalbrook, Thurles, Co. Tipperary
Managing Director: David Quin
  t. +353 52 54 309
  f. +353 52 54 309
■ *A production company producing computer-animated series for television in English and Irish.*
Producer and Director: James Quin

Rapid Film
10 Ballymun Road, Dublin 9
General Enquiries
Gerry McColgan and Patrick Bergin
  t. +353 1 857 0866
  f. +353 1 857 0867
  e. info@rapidfilm.com
  w. www.rapidfilm.com
■ *A film and television production company producing feature films and television documentaries and dramas.*

Ravel Productions
52 Mount Pleasant Square, Dublin 6
Managing Director: Michael O'Sullivan
  t. +353 1 496 2096
  f. +353 1 496 2355
  e. ravona@eircom.net.
■ *A film production company producing feature films, multimedia products, documentaries, drama and educational programming.*
Producer: Brian Palfrey

Realt Entertainment
26 Rochestown Park, Dún Laoghaire, Co. Dublin
Managing Director: Brian Eustace
  t. +353 1 285 0621
  e. realtent@eircom.net
■ *A film production company producing documentaries and music programming in English and Irish.*
Production Manager: Lisa McDonnell

Red Lemonade Productions
10 Larkfield Grove, Dublin 6W
Producer and Director: Liam Wylie
  t. +353 1 492 0965
■ *A film production company producing documentaries.*

Red Pepper Productions
Shamrock Chambers, 1–2 Eustace Street, Dublin 2
Producers: Máire Kearney and Marie Toft
  t. +353 1 670 7277
  m. +353 87 918 5940
  f. +353 1 670 7278
  e. info@redpepper.ie
  w. www.redpepper.ie
■ *A film production company producing documentaries and series for television in English, Dutch and French.*
Director: Martin Danneels
Post-Production Supervisor: Laura Cranley

Reel Fishy
53 Park Street, Dundalk, Co. Louth
Directors and Producers: Martin Connolly and Philip McGarrity
  t. +353 86 258 4857
  f. +353 42 935 2516
  e. reelfishy@oceanfree.net
  w. www.reelfishylive.com
■ *A film production company producing television documentaries about fishing and fishing destinations around the world, and corporate videos.*
Business Development and Secretary: Susan Connolly

River Films (see also Tyrone Production listing)

23 Mary Street Little, Dublin 7
Executive Producers: Moya Doherty,
John McColgan and Joan Egan
t. +353 1 889 4900
f. +353 1 889 4991
e. rheayberd@riverfilms.ie;
smcauley@riverfilms.ie
■ *A film production company producing feature films.*
Creative Director and Producer: Roy
Heayberd
Business and Finance Executive:
Suzanne McAuley

Rocket Animation (see Coco Television)

19 Creighton Street, Dublin 2
Creative Directors: Caroline Dunn and
Owen Fitzpatrick
t. +353 1 617 0480
f. +353 1 617 0481
e. info@cocotelevision.ie
w. www.rocketanimation.com
■ *A film production company producing short films, commercials and opening titles. A subsidiary of Coco Television.*

Ronan O'Leary Productions

23 Upper Mount Street, Dublin 2
Producer: Ronan O'Leary
t. +353 1 676 6831
f. +353 1 661 8551
e. redhen@iol.ie
■ *A film production company producing feature films, dramas and documentaries.*

Rosg

An Spidéal, Co. na Gaillimhe
Managing Director: Ciarán Ó Cofaigh
t. +353 91 55 3951
f. +353 91 55 8491
e. eolas@rosg.ie
■ *A film and television production company producing documentaries, drama and animation in Irish, English and French.*

Director: Darach Ó Scolaí
Production Manager: Eilís Ní
Cheallaigh

Rough Magic Film Productions

7 South Great George's Street, Dublin 2
Managing Director: Siobhan Bourke
t. +353 1 672 5464
f. +353 1 670 4272
e. rmfilms@iol.ie
■ *A multimedia production company producing feature films, television drama and multimedia software.*
Producer: Kathryn Lennon
Multimedia: John Gerrard, Jobst Graeve
and Stephen O'Reilly

Russell Avis Productions

The White House, Strawberry Beds
Road, Dublin 20
Managing Director: Russ Russell
t. +353 1 820 5318
f. +353 1 820 5946
e. russavis@iol.ie
■ *A film production company producing commercials and television programming.*
Producer: Anne Marie Curran
Production Co-ordinator: Lizzie Turvey
Directors: Colum Maguire, Dominic
Murgia, John Moore, Syd Macartney,
Damien O'Donnell, Enda Hughes,
Rory Kelleher and Mitch Walker

Saffron Pictures

First floor, 7 South Great George's
Street, Dublin 2
Contact: Siobhan Bourke

Safinia Productions (see Multi-Media Arts Ireland listing)

37 Fitzwilliam Square, Dublin 2
Managing Director: Shay Healy
e. safinia_mma@yahoo.com
■ *A film production company*
Company Director: Declan Farrell
Producers: Marion Cullen and Maria
Gardiner

Joe St Leger
33 Ashton Park, Monkstown,
Co. Dublin
Producer: Joe St Leger
t. +353 1 284 1677
e. joest@indigo.ie
w. www.joestleger.com
■ *A freelance television documentary producer.*

Samson Films
The Barracks, 76 Irishtown Road,
Dublin 4
Managing Director: David Collins
t. +353 1 667 0533
f. +353 1 667 0537
e. info@samsonfilms.com
■ *An independent film and television production company producing feature films, television drama, series and light entertainment.*
Development Executive: Hilary Kehoe
Head of Development: Lorianne Hall
Production Assistant: Creona O'Connor
Producer: Martina Niland
Production Assistant: Lisa Byrne

Scannáin Dobharchú
Áras Teicneolaíochta, Na Forbacha, Co.
na Gaillimhe
Managing Director: Máirín Seoighe
t. +353 91 592 533
f. +353 91 592 203
e. dobhar@eircom.net
■ *A film production company producing documentary and music and arts productions for television in English, French and Irish.*
Producer and Director: Stiofán Seoighe

Scannáin Lugh
Pier Head, Tory Island, Co. Donegal
Company Director: Loïc Jourdain
t. +353 74 953 2026
e. lughfilms@eircom.net
w. www.lughfilm.com;
w. w.scannainlugh.com
■ *A film production company producing documentaries and feature films and providing a production service in English and Irish.*

Secretary, Director and Producer: Anne
Marie Nic Ruaidhrí

Screen Directors' Guild of Ireland
18 Eustace Street, Dublin 2
General Enquiries: Catherine Punch
t. +353 1 6337433
f. +353 1 478 4087
e. info@sdgi.ie
■ *A representative body for Irish directors.*

Screen Producers Ireland
Studio Building, Meeting-House
Square, Dublin 2
General Enquiries
Director: David McLoughlin
Chair: Ronan McCabe
Information: Niamh Boylan and Jimmy
Healy
t. +353 1 676 0168/+353 1 671 3525
f. +353 1 671 4292
e. info@screenproducersireland.com
w. www.screenproducersireland.com.
■ *The representative and lobbying body for Irish independent film and broadcast producers. Four sub-committees—Broadcasting, Labour Relations, Film and Animation—deal with specific issues. The group has more than two hundred company members. It produces strategy and policy submission documents on the industry and seeks to enhance and support the audio-visual sector in Ireland.*

Screen Scene
30 Upper Mount Street, Dublin 2
General Enquiries
t. +353 1 676 3522
f. +353 1 661 1494
e. brooks@screenscene.ie
w. www.screenscene.ie
■ *A sound recording studio, providing post-production sound services.*

Screentime ShinAwiL
The Digital Depot, The Digital Hub,
Thomas Street, Dublin 8
Chief Executive Officer: Larry Bass
t. +353 1 488 5855

f. +353 1 488 5871
e. info@shinawil.ie
w. www.shinawil.tv

■ *A film production company producing documentaries, commercials and live-event programming in English and Irish.*
Head of Production and Development: Lynda McQuaid
Head of Finance: Jim Gilmartin
Head of Drama: Mark Kenny
Administration: Nikki Ryan
Production Assistant: Eileen McGee
Researcher: Eugenia Cooney

Scun Scan

Ráth Cairn, Co. na Mí
Managing Director: Dónall Ó Maolfabhail
t. +353 46 943 0392
m. +353 87 234 2039
f. +353 46 943 2381
e. info@scunscan.ie
w. www.scunscan.ie

■ *A film production company producing documentaries and corporate and commercial products in English and Irish.*
Chairperson: Pádraic Mac Donncha

SháineFilms

12 Marie Place, Windmill Road, Cork
Managing Director and Producer: Annmarie Cotter
t. +353 21 431 9320
f. +353 21 431 9320
e. samcotmc@gofree.indigo.ie

■ *A film production company producing feature films, drama series and serials and documentaries in English, Irish and German.*
Development: Seán McCarthy

Shine On Productions

An Tigín Bán, Ballyguile Mór, Wicklow
Managing Director and Producer: Kathrina Shine
t. +353 40 469 414
m. +353 86 602 5065
f. +353 40 469 414
e. tiginban@iol.ie

■ *A film production company producing films and animations (in co-production) in English and Irish.*

The Shortt Comedy Theatre Co/Warehouse TV

Unit D1A, Eastway Business Park, Ballysimon Road, Limerick
General Enquiries: Pat Shortt
t. +353 61 423 934
f. +353 61 423 928
e. amanda@patshortt.com

■ *A production company specialising in comedy.*

Sin Sin! Teo

An Caorán Beag, An Cheathrú Rua, Co. na Gaillimhe
Managing Director and Producer: Trevor Ó Clochartaigh
t. +353 91 595 655
f. +353 91 595 655
e. trevoroc@indigo.ie

■ *A television production company producing drama and arts programming and providing training and development services in Irish and English.*

SMIRSH Films

Corlisheen, Riverstown, Sligo
Managing Director and Producer: Colum Stapleton
t. +353 71 65 994
f. +353 71 65 930
e. smirsh@eircom.net
w. www.smirsh.com

■ *A film production company producing documentaries and films on religious, spiritual and paranormal subjects in Arabic, English, Irish, Italian, French, German, Spanish and Turkish.*
Producer: Noirin Hennessy

Solo Too

Eblana House, Eblana Avenue, Dún Laoghaire, Co. Dublin
Managing Director and Producer: Ned O'Hanlon
t. +353 1 230 3375
f. +353 1 230 3350

e. info@solotoo.com

w. www.dreamchaser.ie

■ *A multimedia production company producing pop promotional videos and documentaries and multimedia installations for museums.*

Director: Maurice Linnane

Line Producer: Tara Mullen

Production Co-ordinator: Vanessa Moss

SOL Productions

Quarantine Hill, Wicklow

Managing Director, Producer and Director: Kevin Jacobsen

t. +353 40 467 270

f. +353 40 467 153

e. sol@eircom.net

■ *A film production company producing dramas, documentaries, shorts and videos.*

Producer: Veronica O'Reilly

Directors: Seamus Byrne, Gay Kirby and Bernard Kirby.

Sorrento Pictures

49 Tudor Lawns, Foxrock, Dublin 18

Managing Directors and Producers: Paul Munn and Carmel Munn

t. +353 1 289 8361

f. +353 1 289 8361

e. pmunn@eircom.net

■ *A film production company producing feature films and television films and dramas.*

Speers Films

66 Fitzwilliam Square, Dublin 2

Managing Director and Producer: Johnny Speers

t. +353 1 662 1130

f. +353 1 662 1139

e. peers@speers.ie

■ *A film production company producing commercials and drama*

Producer: Catherine Magee

Directors: Lenny Abrahamson ('Adam and Paul'), Stephen St Leger, Dave Campbell and Ruan Magan

SP Films

Unit F5, Riverview Business Park, Nangor Road, Dublin 12

Producers and Directors: Brendan Muldowney and Conor Barry

t. +353 1 460 4760

f. +353 1 460 4770

e. spfilms@eircom.net

■ *A film production company producing features films, shorts, commercials and music videos.*

Stoney Road Films

11 Burgh Quay, Dublin 2

Directors and Producers: Roger Hudson and Simon Hudson

t. +353 1 677 6681

f. +353 1 670 9764

e. stoneyroadfilms@ireland.com

■ *A film and television production company producing documentaries, short dramas, features and commercial and corporate materials.*

stop.watch television

Guinness Enterprise Center, Taylor's Lane, Dublin 8

General Enquiries: Tom Johnson, Mary Murphy, Aisling Milton and Kathriona Deveraux

t. +353 1 410 0845

f. +353 1 410 0826

e. info@stopwatch.ie

■ *A film and television production company producing documentaries and corporate materials.*

Stray Dog Films

53 Heytesbury Lane, Dublin 4

Producer: Jackie Larkin

t. +353 1 660 6293

f. +353 1 660 6293

e. straydog@indigo.ie

■ *A television and film production company producing drama and documentaries.*

Writer and Director: John O'Donnell

Subotica Entertainment

55 Fitzwilliam Square, Dublin 2
Company Directors: Tristan Orpen
Lynch, Dominic Wright and Paul
Moore
t. +353 1 662 2226
f. +353 1 662 2227
e. subotica@indigo.ie
■ *A film and television production company*
producing feature films and television drama.
Producers: Tristan Orpen Lynch and
Dominic Wright
Head of Development: Aoife
O'Sullivan

Telegael Media Group

Áras Telegael, An Spidéal, Co. Galway
Group Managing Director: Paul
Cummins
t. +353 91 553 460
f. +353 91 553 464
e. eolas@telegael.com
w. www.telegael.com
■ *A production company producing films and*
television programmes and providing financing,
animation, production and post-production
facilities, digital outside broadcasting and
subtitling.
Operations Manager: Enda Boner
Head of Production: Siobhán
Ní Ghadhra
Head of Development: Micheál
Ó Domhnaill
Head of Outside Broadcast: Billy Keady
Head of Finance: Caitlín Gavin

Telwell Productions

77 Christ Church View, Dublin 8
Producer and Director: Barrie Dowdall
t. +353 1 454 8790
f. +353 1 454 8790
e. telwell@iol.ie
■ *A film and television production company*
producing documentaries, corporate videos and
children's television and drama programming
in English and Irish (all languages considered).

Temple Bar Music Centre

Curved Street, Dublin 2
General Enquiries
t. +353 1 677 0647
f. +353 1 677 7106
e. info@tbmc.ie
w. www.tbmc.ie
■ *Provides broadcasting facilities and sound*
recording studios.

Terraglyph Productions

8 Grant's Row, Dublin 2
Managing Directors and Producers:
Gerry Shirren and Russell Boland
t. +353 1 678 7990
f. +353 1 678 7993
e. info@terraglyphproductions.ie
■ *A production company producing animated*
feature films, shorts and television programmes.
Directors: Deane Taylor, Paul Bolger
and Maurice Joyce

Tile Films

13 Windsor Place, Dublin 2
Managing Director: Stephen Rooke
t. +353 1 611 4646
m. +353 87 221 5435
f. +353 1 611 4647
e. tilefilms@eircom.net
■ *A film and television production company*
producing documentaries and dramas in
English, Irish and Welsh.
Company Director: Marie Rooke
Development Director: Dave Farrell
Production Manager: Rachel Towell

Time Horizon Productions

13 Windsor Place, Dublin 2
General Enquiries: Duncan Stewart and
Maria Ismair
t. +353 1 662 1082
f. +353 1 661 6644
e. timehorizon@tinet.ie
■ *A television production company producing*
home building and renovation television series
and environmental programmes.

Toytown Films

4 Windmill Lane, Dublin 2
Managing Director: Celine Cawley
t. +353 1 671 1326
f. +353 1 671 1057
e. celine@toytownfilms.com
w. www.toytownfilms.com
■ *A television production company producing television commercials and providing broadcasting facilities.*
Producers: Eamonn Lillis and Andy Bradford

Translucid Media Ireland

24 Mount Prospect Park, Dublin 3
General Enquiries: Ben Murry and Alan Maloney
m. +353 86 897 7451
e. info@translucidireland.tk
w. www.translucidireland.net
■ *A voice-over production company providing voice-over artists and radio imaging.*

Treasure Films

Shamrock Chambers, 1–2 Eustace Street, Dublin 2
Managing Director: Robert Walpole
t. +353 1 670 9609
f. +353 1 670 9610
e. info@treasure.ie
w. www.treasurefilms.com
■ *A film, television and animation production company producing feature films, documentaries and animation.*
Producer and Director: Paddy Breathnach (*Man and Dog*)
Manager Television Division: Justin Moore Lewy
Head of Business Affairs and Producer: Paddy McDonald
Production and Development Executive and Associate Producer: Katie Holly

Trigger Productions

2 Mount Verdon Terrace, Wellington Road, Cork
General Enquiries: Gerard Crowley, Avril O'Brien, Paul O'Brien and Stephen O'Connell
t. +353 21 455 0728
e. x@triggerproductions.com
■ *A digital film production company producing animation films, programmes and commercials.*

Tyrone Productions

27 Lower Hatch Street, Dublin 2
Group Executive Chairman: Joan Egan
t. +353 1 662 7200
f. +353 1 662 7217
e. info@tyrone productions.ie
w. www.tyroneproductions.com
■ *A television production company producing entertainment programmes, drama, documentaries, children's and life-style programmes in English and Irish. Directors: Moya Doherty and John McColgan.*
General Manager: Patricia Carroll
Executive Assistant to Joan Egan: Caroline O'Keefe
Executive Assistant to Patricia Carroll: Deborah French
Head of Documentaries: Jimmy Duggan
Head of Entertainment: Mary Richmond
Producer and Director: Teresa Smith
Producer: Pauline McNamara
Head of Corporate and Producer: Joanne McGrath
Director: Claire Wilde
Writer: Michael Scott
Drama Development Executive: Dearbhla Regan
Sales and Marketing Executive: Judy Forde
Media, Press and Publicity Officer: Clare Ridge

Vedanta Productions

25 Sans Souci Wood, Bray, Co. Wicklow
Producer and Director: Pat Shine
t. +353 1 286 8790

m. +353 87 260 2998

f. +353 1 286 8790

e. vedanta@iol.ie

■ *A film production company producing documentaries and educational and corporate programmes in English, Irish, French and Spanish.*

Producer: Audrey McMahon

Venus Film and Television Productions

7 South Great George's Street, Dublin 2

Producers: Anna Devlin and Marina Hughes

t. +353 1 670 4274

f. +353 1 670 4275

e. venus.productions@ireland.com

■ *A film production company producing feature films, dramas and documentaries.*

Vico Films

1 Convent Road, Dalkey, Co. Dublin

Company Directors: Michael Doherty, Cormac Fox and Peter Foott

t. +353 1 253 1680

f. +353 1 676 7734

e. info@vicofilms.com

w. www.vicofilms.com

■ *A production company producing short and feature films, music videos and corporate productions.*

Vinegar Hill Productions

Príomhshráid, Gort an Choirce, Co. Donegal

Managing Director and Producer: David Rane

t. +353 74 918 0730

m. +353 86 811 8112

f. +353 74 918 0732

e. info@vinegarhill.com

w. www.vinegarhill.com

■ *A film production company producing feature films, shorts, documentaries, animation and television programmes (in English, Irish and French) and providing facilities for editing and dubbing, with or without a picture and sound editor.*

Director: Neasa Ní Chianáin

m. +353 87 278 5216

Vitel Productions

Unit 3, John's Street, Limerick

Managing Director: Ian Hourigan

t. +353 61 312 900

m. +353 87 236 2929

f. +353 61 317 567

e. vitel@eircom.net

w. www.vitel.ie

■ *A television production and facilities company, producing sports programmes, features and documentaries.*

Producer: Errol Reeves

Voicebank

The Barracks, 76 Irishtown Road, Dublin 4

General Enquiries

t. +353 1 668 7234

f. +353 1 660 7850

e. enquiries@voicebank.ie

w. www.voicebank.ie

■ *Provides voice-overs and other sound services.*

Wallslough Studios

Danville Lodge, Kilkenny

Managing Director, Producer and Director: Kevin Hughes

t. +353 56 71 071

f. +353 56 71 070

e. hughesarts@eircom.net

■ *A film production company producing feature films, documentaries and dramas.*

WalshCreative

Jane Harder Films, 11 Killarney Street, Dublin 1

Managing Director: Sinead Walsh

t. +353 1 887 8973

e. shootnscore@indigo.ie

■ *A film and television production company producing documentaries, features, educational programming and commercials.*

Producer: Fiona Walsh

Web4mations

St Paul's Church, North King Street,
Dublin 7
Managing Director: Mark Cumberton
t. +353 1 617 4816
m. +353 87 927 4842
e. studio@web4mations.com
w. www.web4mations.com
■ *A multimedia production company
producing animation features, shorts and
commercials.*
Producer: John Rice
Director: Alan Shannon

Wide Eye Films

30 Herbert Street, Dublin 2
General Enquiries: Nathalie
Lichtenthaeler and David Gleeson
t. +353 1 678 7930
f. +353 1 678 7930
e. mail@wideeyefilms.com
■ *A film production company producing feature films.*

Wider Vision Productions

Danganella, Cooraclare, Co. Clare
Producer and Director: Deirdre Noonan
t. +353 65 905 9460
f. +353 65 905 9916
e. info@widervision.ie
w. www.widervision.ie
■ *A television production company producing
documentaries, dramas and commercials and
providing broadcast production and post-production facilities.*
Producer and Editor: Ann Blake

Wildfire Films and Television Production

Olympia House, Suite 2B, 61–63
Dame Street, Dublin 2
Company Directors and Producers:
Martha O'Neill and Adrian McCarthy
t. +353 1 672 5553
f. +353 1 672 5573
e. info@wildfirefilms.net
w. www.wildfirefilms.net

■ *A film production company producing feature films, television drama and documentaries
in English, Irish and German.*
Project Co-ordinator and
Administrator: Laura McCahill

Wonderland

Coolure House, Coole, Co. Westmeath
Producer and Director: Ruán Magan
t. +353 44 62 820
f. +353 44 62 899
e. ruanmagan@eircom.net
■ *A subsidiary of Create One, a television
production company producing documentaries
in English, Irish and French.*

Woodend Films Teo

Gortanachra, Baile Mhic Íre, Macroom,
Co. Cork
Managing Director, Producer and
Director: Peter Carr
t. +353 26 45 702
f. +353 26 45 702
e. woodend@indigo.ie
■ *A television production company producing
documentaries.*
Director: Victoria Carr

World 2000 Entertainment

Ardmore Studios, Herbert Road, Bray,
Co. Wicklow
Managing Directors: Morgan
O'Sullivan, Tom Palmieri, Bernard
Somers and Marguerite Somers
t. +353 1 276 9672
f. +353 1 286 6810
e. info@world2000.ie
w. www.world2000.ie
■ *A film production company producing fea-
ture films and television programmes.*
Executive Assistant: Auveen
O'Sullivan
Project Co-ordinator: Gráinne Dunne

X:Stream Pictures

12 Moyville Lawn, Dublin 14
Producers and Directors: Jason Forde
and Paul Tully
   t. +353 1 495 4359
   f. +353 1 495 4359
   e. info@xstream pictures.com
   w. www.xstream pictures.com
■ *A film production company producing television drama and documentary feature films and shorts, and music-based visual events.*

Yellow Asylum Films

28 South Frederick Street, Dublin 2
General Enquiries: Martin Mahon
   t. +353 1 679 0427
   f. +353 1 672 7452
   e. yasylum@eircom.net
■ *A film production company producing documentaries.*

Young Irish Film Makers

St Joseph's Studios, Waterford Road,
Kilkenny
Artistic Director: Mike Kelly
   t. +353 56 64 677
   f. +353 56 51 405
   e. mike@yifm.com
   w. www.yifm.com
■ *A film training and production company producing youth and children's products and providing training to 14 to 18-year-olds.*
Administrator and Public Relations
Officer: Angela Walsh
Directors: Jon McGuinness and Keith
Bohanna

Zanita Films

Ardmore Studios, Herbert Road, Bray,
Co. Wicklow
Managing Director and Producer:
Seamus Byrne
   t. +353 1 286 2971
   f. +353 1 276 0020
   e. seamus@zanita.ie
   w. www.zanitafilms.com
■ *A production company producing commercials and music videos.*

Zanzibar Productions

12 Magennis Place, Dublin 2
Managing Directors: Edwina Forkin
and Chris Roche
   t. +353 1 671 9480
   f. +353 1 671 9481
   e. zanzibarfilms@eircom.net
   w. www.zanzibarfilms.net
■ *A film production company producing short and feature films in English and Irish.*
Producer: Edwina Forkin
Directors: Shimmy Marcus, Pearse
Lehane, Audrey O'Reilly, Colette
Cullen, Jacqueline O'Neill, Mary
Mullan, Chris Roche, Lionel Mill,
Enda McCallion, Cashell Horgan,
Neasa Hardiman
Development Officer: Mark Harley
Production Assistant: Marlyn Gelsing

Zink Films

The Digital Depot, Thomas Street,
Dublin 8
Producer and Director: Gary O'Neill
   t. +353 1 488 5845
   f. +353 1 488 5801
   e. gary@zinkfilms.com
   w. www.zinkfilms.com
■ *A film production company producing animated television series and features in any language.*
Associate Producer: Sinead Sarsfield
Artistic Director: Martin Fagan

Northern Ireland

Telephone numbers in Northern Ireland have the prefix 048 if dialled from the Republic and 004428 if dialled from elsewhere.

About-Face Media Productions
Townsend Enterprise Park, Townsend Street, Belfast BT13 2ES
Managing Director, Producer and Director: Anthony Rowe
   t. +44 028 9089 4555
   f. +44 028 9089 4502
   e. production@about-face.co.uk
■ *Produces television documentaries and entertainment programmes in English.*
Producer and Director: Michael Appleton
Unit Manager: Lily McKee
Assistant Producers: Jennifer Waugh and Tracie McKee

Besom Productions
26–28 Bishop Street, Derry BT48 6PP
Managing Director: Margo Harkin
   t. +44 28 71 370 303
   f. +44 28 71 370 728
   e. margo@besomproductions.co.uk
   w. www.besomproductions.co.uk
■ *Production company producing programming in documentary, arts and educational programming and drama in English and Irish.*
Productions Co-ordinator: Morag Tinto
Secretary: Tracey O'Kane

Blue Sphere Productions
11 Slieve Crescent, Dromintee, Newry, Co. Down BT35 8UF
Managing Director, Producer and Director: George Kingsnorth
   t. +44 28 3088 9263
   f. +44 28 3088 9032
   e. george@bluesphere.co.uk
   w. www.bluesphere.co.uk
■ *A film and television production company producing feature films, documentaries and drama.*
Administrator: Patricia Kingsnorth

Borderline Productions
62 Donegall Pass, Belfast BT7 IBU
General Enquiries: Patrick FitzSymons
   t. +44 28 9033 3360
   f. +44 28 9033 3660
   e. info@borderlineproductions.co.uk
■ *A production company with offices in Belfast and Dublin producing drama.*

Brian Waddell Productions
Strand Studios, 5–7 Shore Road, Holywood, Co. Down BT18 9HX
Managing Director: J. Brian Waddell
   t. +44 28 9042 7646
   f. +44 28 9042 7922
   e. jbw@bwpltv.co.uk
   w. www.bwpltv.co.uk
■ *A television production company producing children's programmes, comedy, documentaries, drama, educational programmes, feature films, life-style and music and arts programmes.*
Executive Producer: Richard Williams
Drama Development Editor, Press and Public Relations: Jane Coyle
Producers and Directors: Tracie O'Neill and Sarah Redding
Head of Development: David Cumming
Executive Producer: Jon-Barrie Waddell
Production Manager: Gillian Hammill
Facilities Manager: Mark McMaster
Company Secretary: Irene Boyd

Clanvisions
1 Sullivan Place, Holywood, Co. Down BT18 9DQ
Managing Director and Producer: Patrick Fitzsymons
   t. +44 28 9042 2492
   e. clanviz@gofree.indigo.ie
■ *A production company producing drama, documentaries and multimedia.*

Address in the Republic: 12 Magennis Place, Dublin 2
Producer and Finance: Donna Fitzsymons

De Facto Films

30 Chamberlain Street, Derry BT48 6LR
Managing Director: Tom Collins
t. +44 28 7126 0714
f. +44 28 7126 0714
e. defactofilms@eircom.net
w. www.defactofilms.co.uk
■ *A film production company producing shorts, dramas, documentaries and feature films in English, Irish, French, German and Derryese.*
Producer: Fergal McGrath

Double Band Films

Crescent Arts Centre, 2–4 University Road, Belfast BT7 1NH
Contact: Michael Hewitt
t. +44 28 9024 3331
e. mhewitt@doublebandfilms.com
w. www.doublebandfilms.co.uk

Extreme Production

1 Church View, Holywood, Co. Down BT18 9DP
Managing Director: David Malone
t. +44 28 9080 9050
f. +44 28 9080 9051
e. extreme@extremeproduction.com
w. www.extremeproduction.com
■ *A media production company producing television and new media content (English, Irish and French), including popular factual programming, docusoaps, sports events and music videos.*
Senior Researcher: Michelle O'Dowd
Head of Production: Susan Malone

Green Inc Productions

47a Botanic Avenue, Belfast BT7 1JL
Managing Directors: Stephen Stewart, Patrick Kielty and Harry Carvill
t. +44 28 90 57 3000
f. +44 28 9057 0057
e. tv@greeninc.co.uk
■ *A media production company producing television programmes and multimedia materials.*
Head of Development: Deborah Bennett
Head of Factual: Alison Millar
Producer: Mark Benson

Moondog Productions

The Old Gasworks, 8 Cromac Avenue, Belfast BT7 2JA
Managing Director: Jackie Hamilton
t. +048 90 594 444
f. +048 90 585 751
e. production@moondog.co.uk
w. www.moondog.co.uk
■ *A production company producing multimedia products, comedy and light entertainment programmes, radio programmes, and management of live events.*
Production Associate: Colin McQuaid
Administrator: Maria Hamilton

The Nerve Centre

7–8 Magazine Street, Derry BT48 6HJ
General Enquiries: Pearse Moore
t. +44 28 7126 0562
f. +44 28 7137 1738
e. p.moore@nerve-centre.org.uk
w. www.nerve-centre.org.uk
■ *A production company.*

Northern Ireland Film Commission

21 Ormeau Avenue, Belfast BT2 7HD
t. +44 28 9023 2444
f. +44 28 9023 9918
w. www.nifc.co.uk

Nua Media

79 Chichester Street, Belfast BT1 4JE
Producer and Director: Una Murphy
t. +44 28 9039 4052

m. +44 776 026 1693
e. mail@nuamedia.com
w. www.nuamedia.com

■ *A film production company producing documentaries and current affairs and factual programmes in English and Irish.*
Researcher: Brian Phelan

Raw Nerve Productions

7–8 Magazine Street, Derry BT48 6HJ
General Enquiries: Pearse Moore
t. +44 28 7126 0562
f. +44 28 7137 1738
e. p.moore@nerve centre.org.uk

■ *A film, animation and multimedia production company producing feature films and drama for television.*

Stirling Film and Television Productions

137 University Street, Belfast BT7 1HP
Managing Director: Anne Stirling
t. +44 28 9033 3848
f. +44 28 9043 8644
e. anne@stirlingtelevision.co.uk
w. www.stirlingtelevision.co.uk

■ *A film production company producing films and television programmes and providing production facilities.*
Production Manager: Alison Carr
Producers and Directors: Jackie Newell and Grainne McCotter
Editor: Declan McCann

Straight Forward Film and Television Productions

Building 2, Lesley Office Park, 393 Holywood Road, Belfast BT4 2LS
Managing Director: John Nicholson
t. +44 28 9065 1010
f. +44 28 9065 1012
e. enquiries@straightforwardltd.co.uk
w. www.straightforwardltd.co.uk

■ *A television production company producing documentaries and current affairs and news programming.*
Chairman and Producer: Ian S. Kennedy
Development Producer: Jane Kelly
Producer: Andrea McCartney
Production Manager: Joy Hines

TVD

6 Clooney Terrace, Waterside, Derry BT47 6AR
Managing Director, Producer and Director: Chris Orr
t. +44 28 71 593 503
f. +44 28 71 783 343
e. chrisorrtvd@hotmail.com

■ *A film and television production company producing documentaries.*

9

EDUCATION, CAREERS AND TRAINING: WORKING IN THE MEDIA

Dr Mark O'Brien

Media education has come a long way over the last twenty years. Until the 1980s, media education usually meant securing a position in a local paper or pirate radio station and building up experience, skills and contacts before graduating to a national title or, if you were lucky, to the national broadcaster, RTÉ. Given the limited media environment of the day (this was before the advent of local radio or the internet) and the relatively limited opportunities available in the media, this 'apprenticeship' system served its purpose. Today's media students still appreciate the value of 'hands-on' practical experience, and employers look for people with a mix of both skills and experience.

Nowadays the media sector is one of the most dynamic and constantly changing sectors of the work force. There are two core reasons for this media market revolution. Firstly, deregulation of the media sector has resulted in a multitude of new media companies. This opening up of the media led to the arrival of local radio from 1988, the appearance of a new national television station, TV3, in 1998 and the setting up of an Irish-language television station, TG4, in 1996. State and European incentives have also promoted competition, for example a requirement that RTÉ spend a certain percentage of its annual budget on the independent production sector, and tax incentives for film production. Equally, the introduction of competition in the mobile telephone market has boosted the media jobs market.

Secondly, the development of new media technologies, such as the mobile phone and the internet, and their increased proliferation in everyday life have given media companies the ability to supply content in ways not thought possible previously. Digital services and applications have become increasingly central to the media sector and, as the full potential of digital technology continues to be harnessed, future innovations are inevitable. All these developments have resulted in the demand for highly qualified graduates and a constant re-skilling of media employees. This has led to a substantial increase in the number of courses at all educational levels and of varying durations to meet the demands of students and the market.

Education and training

The extensive range of media-specific and media-related courses (media studies with another subject) on offer north and south is detailed here. Most courses offer an interdisciplinary mixture of what might be termed the theory and the practical elements of media education. This mixture provides students with an understanding of the social contexts in which the media operate, as well as offering opportunities for them to develop essential professional skills appropriate to the work-place. Some courses provide work placement as part of their programme. These tend to be popular with students and are good ways for employers to 'test-drive' graduates. In recent years there has been a huge growth in student interest in, and the provision of, multimedia courses. As digital and multimedia technologies are increasingly adopted for the creation and production of material in many of the traditional media and communication fields, students and industry alike are demanding courses in the creative use or development of multimedia products, such as digital text, image and sound manipulation and multimedia authoring.

Media education began in the early 1980s. In Northern Ireland the University of Ulster (Coleraine) pioneered the development of under-graduate courses in media studies. In 2003 it received £3 million in exchequer funding for a new Centre for Media Research, which will facilitate research into film and photography history and archives, media policy, cultural issues and emerging digital issues. In the Republic the College of Commerce (Rathmines) was the first institution since independence to offer a recognised qualification in journalism. Its two-year diploma in journalism has since become a four-year degree course taught by Dublin Institute of Technology's School of Media. In 1979 DIT launched the first two-year diploma course of its kind in film and broad-casting, later a degree in media arts. This school now offers three under-graduate and four postgraduate media degrees and has approximately 450 students. Dublin City University (formerly the National Institute of Higher Education) is still the only university with a communications department. It initially offered a bachelor of arts degree in communications studies and a higher diploma in journalism (the first graduates came out in 1983) but has since expanded to offer three undergraduate and six postgraduate courses. The School of Communications at present has approximately 690 students.

Since 1992 the University of Limerick (through Mary Immaculate College) has offered a bachelor of arts degree in which media and communications studies may be taken as a subject. Dún Laoghaire Institute of Art, Design and Technology opened in 1997, and it now has approxi-mately 1,500 undergraduate students. Recent developments in third-level education include the creation of a Media Studies Department in the National University of Ireland, Maynooth. It now offers a bachelor of arts degree in media studies, has approximately 120 students and will shortly launch a postgraduate course. In addition, the National University of Ireland, Galway, which formally offered a postgraduate diploma in journalism, now offers a master's in journalism. At present it has 16 students.

The post-Leaving Certificate (PLC) sector is also notable in its pro-vision of media courses, with most Colleges of Further Education (run by regional Vocational Education Committees) offering students courses in media production. In recent years links have been established between Colleges of Further Education and third-level institutions to allow students who perform well to progress to third-level courses. The private sector also offers degree-standard media courses, with Griffith College's Faculty of Journalism and Media Communications in particular earning a reputation for its courses.

The numerous courses offered by universities, institutes of technology, colleges of further education and private colleges are taught at master's, primary degree, higher diploma, diploma and certificate levels. Among the diverse media courses on offer are courses in radio production and broadcasting, television production and broadcasting, journalism, com-munications, multimedia, film studies, screenwriting, media studies, cultur-al studies, performing arts, visual art, theatre studies, computer game design, photography, web design, video production, music production, animation, fine art, art and design, marketing, advertising, public relations, political communication, science communication and health communication.

In addition, a number of professional and governmental organisations provide media training. The Irish Management Institute offers degrees and diplomas in marketing and also offers short courses in personal communication skills. The Irish Academy of Public Relations offers courses in public relations, journalism, marketing and advertising. The Broadcasting Commission of Ireland offers a Community Radio Support Scheme. MEDIA Desk Ireland offers a number of professional training courses in scriptwriting, screenwriting and the financial and legal aspects of media production. The Northern Ireland Film and Television Commission offers similar workshops.

Employment

The media sector is a highly competitive one, and academic achievement alone by no means guarantees success. Personal characteristics such as curiosity, determination, tenacity and creative thinking are required. It is worth remembering that the great majority of media professionals work behind the scenes, putting media products such as newspapers, magazines, radio and television programmes together, and are not necessarily in the public eye. Also, much of the media sector, particularly the independent production sector, is characterised by high levels of contract employment and freelance work.

Like any other industry, the number of people employed in the media fluctuates from time to time. The National Union of Journalists has 4,300 members north and south at present and the Audiovisual Federation (which represents all sections of the audio-visual industry in Ireland) estimates that in any given year the industry has approximately 17,000 workers.

Over the last ten years the collapse of the Irish Press Group and the restructuring of both RTÉ and the *Irish Times* have resulted in a number of media professionals changing ship. The BBC's announcement that its planned restructuring will cut four thousand jobs may also see a movement of staff to the independent production market.[1] The demand for college places on media courses is still extremely high, showing that employment in the sector is buoyant. Graduates with a good qualification in media studies are well qualified to undertake employment in any information-related work, and many flourish in the business environment. It is this flexibility that makes a media education a much sought-after commodity, and the future promises more growth.

1. *Financial Times*, 22 March 2005.

Republic of Ireland

American College, Dublin
2 Merrion Square, Dublin 2
General Enquiries
t. +353 1 676 8939
f. +353 1 676 8941
e. degree@amcd.ie
w. www.amcd.ie
■ *A private college, providing modules in e-commerce and internet marketing, marketing research and marketing communications within a bachelor's degree programme.*

Ballsbridge College of Further Education
Shelbourne Road, Dublin 4
General Enquiries
t. +353 1 668 4806
f. +353 1 668 2361
e. info@ballsbridge.cdvec.ie
w. www.ballsbridgecollege.com
■ *A college of further education, providing professional qualifications certified and accredited by nationally and internationally recognised examining and professional bodies.*
  The following courses are offered:
English as a foreign language and media studies
Marketing, advertising and management
Web authoring and multimedia

Ballyfermot College of Further Education
Ballyfermot Road, Dublin 10
General Enquiries
t. +353 1 626 9421
f. +353 1 626 6754
e. info@bcfe.cdvec.ie
w. www.bcfe.ie
■ *A college of further education, providing professional qualifications certified and accredited by nationally and internationally recognised examining and professional bodies.*
  The following courses are offered:
Classical animation

Film operations and production
Interactive multimedia production
Media
Media production and management
Presentation and performance
Print journalism
Radio production
Television and film
Television operations and production

Ballymun Comprehensive Adult Education Centre
Ballymun Comprehensive School,
Ballymun Road, Dublin 9
Co-ordinator: Joan Cristie
t. +353 1 842 0654
f. +353 1 842 5828
e. bvtos.ias@tinet.ie
■ *Provides an adult education course on newspapers, radio and television.*

Broadcasting Commission of Ireland
2–5 Warrington Place, Dublin 2
General Enquiries
t. +353 1 676 0966
f. +353 1 676 0948
e. info@bci.ie
w. www.bci.ie
■ *The broadcasting regulator of Ireland. Provides a Community Radio Support Scheme (Scéim Thacaíochta do Raidió Pobail).*

Burren College of Art
Newtown Castle, Ballyvaughan,
Co. Clare
General Enquiries
t. +353 65 707 7200
f. +353 65 707 7201
e. admin@burrencollege.ie
w. www.burrencollege.com
■ *A private college providing short courses on photography and portfolio preparation.*

Carlow Vocational School (Carlow Institute of Further Education)

Kilkenny Road, Carlow
General Enquiries
t. +353 913 1187
e. homepage.eircom.net/~carvoc
■ *A college of further education, providing professional qualifications certified and accredited by nationally and internationally recognised examining and professional bodies.*
The following courses are offered:
Marketing
Media production and photography
Multimedia production

Cavan College of Further Studies

Main Street, Cavan
General Enquiries
t. +353 49 433 2633
f. +353 49 436 1933
e. ccfs@iol.ie
w. www.iol.ie/~ccfs
■ *A college of further education, providing professional qualifications certified and accredited by nationally and internationally recognised examining and professional bodies.*
The following courses are offered:
Multimedia and web design
Performing arts—theatre and media

Coláiste Dhúlaigh College of Further Education

Barry's Court Road, Dublin 17
General Enquiries
t. +353 1 848 1337
f. +353 1 847 4294
e. info@cdc.cdvec.ie
w. www.colaistedhulaigh.ie
■ *A college of further education, providing professional qualifications certified and accredited by nationally and internationally recognised examining and professional bodies.*
The following courses are offered:
Communications and media production
Film production
Journalism
Marketing, advertising and language
Multimedia

Coláiste Stiofáin Naofa (College of Further Education, Cork)

Tramore Road, Cork
General Enquiries
t. +353 21 496 1020
f. +353 21 496 1320
e. info@csn.ie
w. www.csn.ie
■ *A college of further education, providing professional qualifications certified and accredited by nationally and internationally recognised examining and professional bodies.*
The following courses are offered:
Media production
Multimedia computing
Music management and sound
Radio broadcasting

Davis College

Mallow, Co. Cork
General Enquiries
t. +353 222 1173
f. +353 222 2524
e. davisoff.ias@eircom.net
w. daviscollege.ie
■ *A college of further education, providing professional qualifications certified and accredited by nationally and internationally recognised examining and professional bodies.*
The following course is offered:
Multimedia

Dublin Business School

13–14 Aungier Street, Dublin 2
General Enquiries
t. + 353 1 417 7500
f. +353 1 417 7543
e. admissions@dbs.edu
w. www.dbs.edu
■ *A private college providing the following programmes:*
BA (hons) business management
BA (hons) business studies
BA (hons) journalism
BA (hons) marketing
BA (hons) media and marketing studies
BA (hons) media studies

Diploma in marketing, advertising and public relations

Dublin City University

Collins Avenue Extension, Dublin 9
Registry
t. +353 1 700 5000
f. +353 1 836 0830
e. registry@dcu.ie
w. www.dcu.ie

■ *Courses available:*
BA in communication studies
BA in journalism
BSc in multimedia
MA in communication and cultural studies
MA in film and television studies
MA in journalism
MA in political communication
MSc in multimedia
MSc in science communication

■ *The following courses offer one or more communications or media modules:*
BSc i bhfiontraíocht le ríomhaireacht agus Gaeilge fheidhmeach
GDip in applied languages and intercultural studies
GDip in translation studies
MBS in marketing
MSc/Dioplóma do chéimithe i ngnó agus i dteicneolaíocht an eolais

Dublin Institute of Technology

Admissions Office, Fitzwilliam House, 30 Upper Pembroke Street, Dublin 2
General Enquiries
t. +353 1 402 3000
f. +353 1 402 3399
e. admissions@dit.ie
w. www.dit.ie

Other DIT colleges in the city centre:

Aungier Street
Bolton Street
Cathal Brugha Street
Chatham Row
Kevin Street
Mountjoy Square
Pembroke Street
Portland Row
Rathmines Road
Temple Bar

■ *The following degree courses are offered:*
BA in design (visual communications)
BA in journalism
BA in media arts
BA in photography
BSc in marketing
BSc in printing management
BSc in tourism (marketing)
MA in digital media technologies
MA in design (digital media)
MA in journalism
MA in media studies
MA in public relations

■ *The following diploma and certificate courses are offered:*
Certificate in business studies
Certificate in design (display)
Certificate in marketing
Diploma in marketing and e-business

Dún Laoghaire Institute of Art, Design and Technology

Kill Avenue, Dún Laoghaire, Co. Dublin
General Enquiries
t. +353 1 214 4600
f. +353 1 214 4700
e. info@iadt.ie
w. www.iadt.ie

■ *The following courses are offered:*
BA in animation
BA in business studies with arts management
BA in English, media and cultural studies
BA in film and television production
BA in photography
BA in visual arts practice (fine art)
BA in visual arts practice (fine art) ACCS
BA/BDes in film and video studies/design

Bachelor of business studies
BDes in interactive media
BDes in production design
BDes in visual communication
BSc in computing in multimedia systems
MA in scriptwriting
MA in visual arts practice (ACCS)
MA Visual Arts Practice
Nat. cert. in design in make-up for film/television and theatre
Nat. cert. in humanities in radio broad-casting
Nat. cert. in technology in audiovisual media technology
Nat. cert. in television and video pro-duction
Nat. dip. in computing in multimedia programming
Nat. dip. in model making and design for film and media
Nat. dip. in technology in digital media technology
Nat. diploma in business studies
Nat. diploma in technology in photog-raphy

Further Education Centre

Bandon Road, Kinsale, Co. Cork
General Enquiries
  t. +353 21 477 2275
  f. +353 21 477 2446
  e. kinsalefurthered@eircom.net
  w. www.kinsalefurthered.ie
■ *A college of further education, providing professional qualifications certified and accred-ited by nationally and internationally recog-nised examining and professional bodies.*
  The following courses are offered:
Print journalism
Television, film and multimedia production

Galway-Mayo Institute of Technology

Dublin Road, Galway
General Enquiries
  t. +353 91 75 3161
  f. +353 91 75 1107

  e. info@gmit.ie
  w. www.gmit.ie
■ *The following courses are offered:*
Bachelor of business studies
Nat. cert. in business studies
Nat. dip. in art and design
Nat. dip. in business studies
Nat. dip. in business studies in marketing
Nat. dip. in business studies in tourism and services marketing
Nat. dip. in humanities in film and television

Griffith College

South Circular Road, Dublin 8
General Enquiries
  t. +353 1 415 0400
  f. +353 1 454 9265
  e. admissions@gcd.ie
  w. www.gcd.ie
■ *A private college providing the following full-time and part-time courses in the Faculty of Journalism and Media Communications:*
BA in journalism and media communi-cations
Certificate in photography
Diploma in media techniques: television and video
Music recording and sound techniques
National diploma in journalism
The diploma in marketing, advertising, PR and sales is offered as a professional course.
The graduate diploma in journalism and media communications is offered as a postgraduate course.
Various short courses are also provided.

Institute of Public Administration

51–61 Lansdowne Road, Dublin 4
General Enquiries
  t. +353 1 240 3600
  f. +353 1 668 9135
  e. information@ipa.ie
  w. www.ipa.ie
■ *A state-sponsored body providing modules in marketing.*

Institute of Technology, Athlone

Dublin Road, Athlone, Co. Westmeath
General Enquiries
t. +353 90 642 4400
w. www.ait.ie
■ *The following courses are offered:*
Bachelor of business studies
Bachelor of design (visual communi-
cations)
Bachelor of design in multimedia studies
National diploma in business studies in
marketing
National diploma in design (communi-
cations)

Institute of Technology, Blanchardstown

Blanchardstown Road North, Dublin 15
General Enquiries
t. +353 1 885 1000; +353 1 244 9300
f. +353 1 885 1001
e. info@itb.ie
w. www.itb.ie
■ *The following courses offer media or com-*
munications modules:
BA in applied social studies in social care
Bachelor of business in information
technology
Higher certificate in business

Institute of Technology, Carlow

Kilkenny Road, Carlow
General Enquiries
t. +353 59 917 0400
f. +353 59 917 0500
e. info@itcarlow.ie
w. www.itcarlow.ie
■ *A BA in communications and public*
relations is offered, along with the following
courses providing communications or media
modules:
Bachelor of business studies—services
marketing
Nat. cert. in business studies
Nat. dip. in business studies—
marketing
Nat. dip. in fine art

Institute of Technology, Cork

Rossa Avenue, Bishopstown, Cork
General Enquiries
t. +353 21 432 6100
f. +353 21 454 5343
e. admissions@cit.ie
w. www.cit.ie
■ *The following courses are offered:*
BA (hons) in multimedia
BA (hons) in visual communi-cations
BA in design communication
Bachelor of business (hons) in inform-
ation systems

Institute of Technology, Dundalk

Dublin Road, Dundalk, Co. Louth
General Enquiries
t. +353 42 933 3505
e. laura.mckenna@dkit.ie
w. www.dkit.ie
■ *The following courses are offered:*
BA in humanities (cultural resource
studies)
Bachelor of business studies in marketing and French
Bachelor of business studies in marketing and e-business
Bachelor of business studies
Master of business studies in entrepre-
neurship and marketing
Nat. cert. in business studies (marketing
with language)
Nat. cert. in office information systems
(public relations)
Nat. dip. in applied cultural studies
(film studies option)
Nat. dip. in business studies (international marketing)
Nat. dip. in business studies (marketing
with language)
Nat. dip. in communications (creative
multimedia)
A MSc in future communications in
creative technology and a certificate in
creative media/multimedia production
may be attended here, run by the
Digital Diversity Project.

Institute of Technology, Letterkenny

Port Road, Letterkenny, Co. Donegal
General Enquiries
  t. +353 74 918 6000
  f. +353 74 918 6005
  e. info@lyit.ie
  w. www.lyit.ie
■ *Offers a bachelor's degree in design and digital media. Offers communication or marketing modules in bachelor of business degrees and continuing education courses in photography and multi-media information systems.*

Institute of Technology, Limerick

Moylish Park, Limerick
General Enquiries
  t. +353 61 20 8208
  f. +353 61 20 8209
  e. information@lit.ie
  w. www.lit.ie
■ *Provides modules in photography, marketing and event management and a bachelor of science (hons) degree in multimedia computing with design.*

Institute of Technology, Sligo

Ballinode, Sligo
General Enquiries
  t. +353 71 915 5222
  f. +353 71 9 6 0475
  e. info@itsligo.ie
  w. www.itsligo.ie
■ *The following courses include communications or media modules:*
BA in fine art
Bachelor of business studies
Nat. cert. in business studies
Nat. cert. in business studies with
  French, German or Spanish
Nat. dip. in business studies in international marketing
Nat. dip. in fine art

Institute of Technology, Tallaght

Dublin 24
General Enquiries
  t. +353 1 404 2000
  f. +353 1 404 2700
  w. www.it-tallaght.ie

■ *The following courses are offered:*
BA (audio/visual media)
Nat. cert. in humanities (audio/visual media)
Nat. dip. in humanities (audio/visual media)
The nat. cert. in business studies (marketing) includes communications/media modules.
The BA (applied languages) includes marketing modules.
The BA (European studies) includes modules exploring advertising, media representations and cinema in Europe.

Institute of Technology, Waterford

Cork Road, Waterford
General Enquiries
  t. +353 51 30 2000
  f. +353 51 30 2800
  w. www.wit.ie
■ *The following courses are offered:*
BA in languages and marketing
National diploma in design in communications

Irish Academy and Irish Academy of Public Relations, The

Academy House, 1 Newtown Park,
Blackrock, Co. Dublin
General Enquiries
  t. +353 1 278 0802
  f. +353 1 278 0251
  e. info@irishacademy.com
  w. www.irishacademy.com
■ *A private body offering the following public relations courses:*
Advanced certificate in public relations and PR writing skills
Certificate in marketing and advertising
Certificate in public relations and PR writing skills
Certificate in television, video and print techniques
Diploma in public relations
Diploma in public relations, advertising and marketing

Higher diploma in arts in public relations
Introduction to public relations
Advanced certificate in journalism and
  broadcast media
Certificate in journalism and print pro-
  duction
Diploma in journalism
Grammar by distance learning
Legal and political studies for journalists
Practical journalistic writing skills

Irish Management Institute
Sandyford Road, Dublin 16
General Enquiries
  t. +353 1 207 8400
  f. +353 1 295 5150
  e. reception@imi.ie
  w. www.imi.ie
■ *A private college providing degrees and
diplomas in marketing and short courses on
personal communication skills.*

Killester College of Further Education
Collins Avenue East, Dublin 5
General Enquiries
  t. +353 1 833 7686
  f. +353 1 830 0348
  e. info@kcfe.cdvec.ie
  w. www.killestercollege.ie
■ *A college of further education, providing
professional qualifications certified and accredited by nationally and internationally recognised examining and professional bodies.*
  The following courses are offered:
Commercial photography
Marketing

Kilroy's College
25 Kingram Place, Dublin 2
General Enquiries
  t. +353 1 662 0538; (free in RoI)
  1850 700 700
  f. +353 1 662 0539
  e. homestudy@kilroyscollege.ie
  w. www.kilroyscollege.ie
■ *A private college providing distance learning
courses in freelance journalism.*

Liberties College
Bull Alley Street, Dublin 8
General Enquiries
  t. +353 1 454 0044
  f. +353 1 454 6348
  e. info@liberties.cdvec.ie
  w. www.libertiescollege.ie
■ *A college of further education, providing
professional qualifications certified and accredited by nationally and internationally recognised examining and professional bodies.*
  The following courses are offered:
Broadcast media production
Media production development
Media production foundation

Marino College Further Education Centre
Connolly House, 171 North Strand
Road, Dublin 1
General Enquiries
  t. +353 1 855 7116
  f. +353 1 855 4064
  e. marinofe@eircom.net
  w. www.marinocollege.com
■ *A college of further education, providing
professional qualifications certified and
accredited by nationally and internationally
recognised examining and professional bodies.*
  The following courses are offered:
Advanced broadcasting
Introduction to broadcast media
Photography and photo journalism

MEDIA Antenna Galway
Monivea Road, Galway
General Enquiries: Eibhlín Ní
Mhunghaile
  t. +353 91 77 0728
  f. +353 91 77 0746
  e. mediaant@iol.ie
  w. www.media-antenna.com
■ *Provides professional training courses (and
support to trainers) in the following areas:*
Scriptwriting for film and television,
  screenwriting and story editing.
Financial, legal and management aspects
  of film and television production, film

marketing and multimedia management.

Animation, and interactive multimedia and writing.

MEDIA Desk Ireland

6 Eustace Street (IFI), Dublin 2
General Enquiries: Siobhan
O'Donoghue and Cáit Barden
t. +353 1 679 1856
f. +353 1 670 9608
e. info@mediadesk.ie
w. www.iftn.ie/*mediadesk*
■ *Provides professional training courses (and support to trainers) in the following areas:*
Scriptwriting for film and television, screenwriting and story editing.
Financial, legal and management aspects of film and television production, film marketing and multimedia management.
Animation, and interactive multimedia and writing.

National College of Art and Design

100 Thomas Street, Dublin 8
General Enquiries
t. +353 1 636 4200
f. +353 1 636 4207
e. fios@ncad.ie
w. www.ncad.ie
■ *The following courses are provided, along with studio-based postgraduate studies:*
BA in fine art
BA in history of art and fine art
MA in virtual realities

National College of Ireland

Mayor Street, Dublin 1
General Enquiries
t. (free RoI) 1850 221 721; +353 1 406 0500
f. +353 1 497 2200
e. info@ncirl.ie
w. www.ncirl.ie
■ *A private college providing modules in e-marketing and strategy and multimedia in the School of Business and Humanities.*

National Training and Development Institute (NTDI)

Beach Road, Dublin 4
General Enquiries
t. +353 1 205 7200
f. +353 1 205 7202
e. info@rehab.ie
w. www.rehab.ie/ntdi/index.htm
■ *Provides training for people at a disadvantage in the labour market to learn career skills. The following courses are offered in the arts and media sector:*
Art link
Digital photography and photographic assistant
Graphic design
Performing arts

National University of Ireland (Central Office)

49 Merrion Square, Dublin 2
General Enquiries
t. +353 1 439 2424
f. +353 1 439 2477
e. registrar@nui.ie
w. www.nui.ie
■ *The National University of Ireland comprises four universities and five colleges. Enquiries about admissions and specific courses of study should be made to the Admissions Offices of the individual institutions.*

National University of Ireland, Cork

Cork
General Enquiries
t. +353 21 490 3571
f. +353 21 490 3233
e. admissions@ucc.ie
w. www.ucc.ie
■ *The following courses are offered:*
The Faculty of Arts offers an MA degree in American literature and film and an MA in sociology (including modules in sociology of the mass media and communication and bio-philosophy: contending paradigms in contemporary sociology).

National University of Ireland, Dublin

Stillorgan Road, Dublin 4
General Enquiries
t. +353 1 716 7777
f. +353 1 269 4409
w. www.ucd.ie

■ *The following courses are offered:*

The Centre for Film Studies offers a
BA modular (evening) degree and an
MA degree in film studies.

The Adult Education Centre offers a
short course in media studies.

The Faculty of Law offers a media law
module.

The Department of Sociology offers an
MA in media and cultural studies.

The Michael Smurfit Graduate School of
Business offers modules in marketing.

National University of Ireland, Galway

University Road, Galway
General Enquiries
t. +353 91 524 411
f. +353 91 495 566
e. info@nuigalway.ie
w. www.ucg.ie

■ *The Huston School of Film and Digital Media has the following courses:*

MA in film studies (film, culture and
society)

MA in screenwriting

The Department of Marketing includes
a marketing communications module
in undergraduate courses.

National University of Ireland, Maynooth

Maynooth, Co. Kildare
General Enquiries
t. +353 1 628 5222
f. +353 1 628 9063
e. admissions@may.ie
w. www.may.ie

■ *The following courses are offered:*

The Centre for Media Studies offers a
BA in media studies.

The Sociology Department provides
the following second-year modules:
media and society; and state, market
and the broadcast media; and the following third-year module: media,
technology and social change.

New Media Technology College

13 Harcourt Street, Dublin 2
General Enquiries
t. +353 1 478 0905
f. +353 1 478 0922
e. info@hypermedia7.ie
w. www.nmtc.ie

■ *A private college providing the following full-time and part-time courses:*

Certificate in digital photography (leading to a FETAC award in media production, NCVA level 2)

Certificate in film production (leading
to a FETAC award in television and
film production, NCVA level 2)

Certificate in interactive media production (leading to a FETAC award in
multimedia production, NCVA level 2)

Certificate in music technology (leading
to a FETAC award in radio production, NCVA level 2)

Certificate in performing arts (leading
to an award made by FETAC, NCVA
level 2)

Diploma in electronic media (interactive television track or web design
track, with the European Broadcasting
Union)

Short courses are offered on the following topics:

3D Studio Max
Active Server Pages (ASP)
Adobe Photoshop
Digital Video Production
HTML
JavaScript, CGI, CSS
Macromedia Director
Macromedia Dreamweaver
Macromedia Flash

Open University (Dublin)

Holbrook House, Holles Street, Dublin 2
Enquiry and Advice Centre
t. +353 1 678 5399
f. +353 1 678 5442
e. ireland@open.ac.uk
w. www.open.ac.uk/ireland
■ *The following undergraduate courses are offered:*
Language studies
Social sciences
Sociology
The following postgraduate courses are offered:
MA in cultural and media studies
MA in humanities
MA in popular culture
Social sciences

Pearse College

Clogher Road, Dublin 12
General Enquiries
t. +353 1 453 6661/454 1544
f. +353 1 4541060
e. information@pearse.cdvec.ie
w. www.pearsecollege.cdvec.ie
■ *A college of further education, providing professional qualifications certified and accredited by nationally and internationally recognised examining and professional bodies.*
The following course is offered:
Media techniques

Portobello College

South Richmond Street, Dublin 2
General Enquiries
t. +353 1 475 5811
f. +353 1 475 5817
e. admin@portobello.ie
w. www.portobello.ie
■ *A private college providing a BA and a National Certificate in Business Studies and Marketing.*

Rathmines College

Town Hall, Rathmines Road, Dublin 6
General Enquiries
t. +353 1 497 5334
f. +353 1 497 9678
e. info@rsc.cdvec.ie
w. www.rathmines-college.com
■ *A college of further education, providing professional qualifications certified and accredited by nationally and internationally recognised examining and professional bodies.*
The following courses are offered:
Journalism and public relations
Media (journalism)
Public relations

Ringsend Technical Institute

Cambridge Road, Dublin 4
General Enquiries
t. +353 1 668 4498
f. +353 1 668 4437
e. info@ringtec.cdvec.ie
w. www.ringtec.ie
■ *A college of further education, providing professional qualifications certified and accredited by nationally and internationally recognised examining and professional bodies.*
The following course is offered:
Multimedia studies

Saor-Ollscoil na hÉireann (Free University of Ireland)

55 Prussia Street, Dublin 7
General Enquiries
t. +353 1 868 3368
e. saorollscoil@eircom.net
w. homepage.eircom.net/~saorollscoil
■ *Offers a course in media studies.*

Screen Training Ireland

Adelaide Chambers, Peter Street, Dublin 8
General Enquiries
t. +353 1 483 0840
f. +353 1 483 0842
e. film@fas.ie
w. www.screentrainingireland.ie
■ *A state-supported industry body offering the following short courses:*
Advanced screenwriting: scene types and character transformation
Format creation for television programming

Legal workshop: co-productions and
sales and distribution agreements
Lighting drama for digital
Post-production supervisors
Script analysis
Television format rights protection,
exploitation and the global market
The business of film scoring
The mechanics of film scoring
Visual structure for directors
Visual structure for film and television

Senior College Dún Laoghaire (SCD)

Eblana Avenue, Dún Laoghaire,
Co. Dublin
General Enquiries
t. +353 1 280 0385; (free RoI) 1800
265 5343
f. +353 1 280 0386
e. info@scd.ie
w. www.scd.ie
■ *A college of further education, providing
professional qualifications certified and accredited by nationally and internationally recognised examining and professional bodies.*
The following courses are offered:
Business studies (including international
communications and marketing
subjects)
Marketing (including marketing communications)
Multimedia
Theatrical and media make-up artistry

St John's Central College of Further Education

Sawmill Street, Cork
General Enquiries
t. +353 21 427 6410
f. +353 21 431 4681
■ *A college of further education, providing
professional qualifications certified and accredited by nationally and internationally recognised examining and professional bodies.*
The following courses are offered:
Advanced video production
Computer game design and development

Multimedia
Photographic studies
Video production film-making
Visual media communications

St Kevin's College

Clogher Road, Dublin 12
General Enquiries
t. +353 1 453 6397
f. +353 1 473 0868
e. info@stkevins.cdvec.ie
w. www.daycourses.com/profile/
stkevins
■ *A college of further education, providing
professional qualifications certified and accredited by nationally and internationally recognised examining and professional bodies.*
The following courses are offered:
Media production
Media production (moving image)
Photography (digital imaging, print
production)

Stillorgan College of Further Education

Old Stillorgan Road, Stillorgan,
Co. Dublin
General Enquiries
t. +353 1 288 0704
f. +353 1 283 2207
e. admissions@stillorgancollege.ie
w. www.stillorgancollege.ie
■ *A college of further education, providing
professional qualifications certified and accred-
ited by nationally and internationally recog-
nised examining and professional bodies.*
The following courses are offered:
Design for digital media
Journalism
Media
Media foundation
Photography

Tipperary Institute

Nenagh Road, Thurles, Co. Tipperary
General Enquiries
t. +353 50 42 8000
f. +353 50 42 8001

e. info@tippinst.ie

w. www.tippinst.ie

■ *A private institute providing a bachelor of science (hons) degree in information technology (multimedia and communication studies).*

Trinity College, Dublin (University of Dublin)

College Green, Dublin 2

General Enquiries

t. +353 1 608 1000

e. info@tcd.ie

w. www.tcd.ie

■ *A degree in music technology is offered by the School of Music, with the emphasis on recording and production.*

University of Limerick

Moylish Park, Limerick

Admissions Office

t. +353 6120 2700

f. +353 6133 0316

e. admissions@ul.ie

w. www.ul.ie

■ *Courses offered:*

BA in history, politics, sociology and social studies

BA in language and cultural studies

BA (offered at Mary Immaculate College)

BA in new media and English

Graduate diploma or MA in technical communication

MA in cultural theory and textual practice

MA in e-learning design and development

MA in sociology (applied social research)

The following degree courses offer communication or media modules:

BA in economics and sociology

Bachelor of business studies

Bachelor of business studies with a modern language (French, German, Spanish or Japanese)

University of Limerick (Mary Immaculate College of Education)

South Circular Road, Limerick

General Enquiries

t. +353 61 20 4929

f. +353 61 20 4348

e. admissions@mic.ul.ie

w. www.mic.ul.ie

■ *The Department of Media and Communication Studies and Department of Theology and Religious Studies jointly offer a BA degree in media and communication studies.*

Postgraduate research options include: television drama, Irish film industry, radio studies, gender and popular culture, media construction and representation, public opinion formation, forces shaping media content, media sociology, Irish-language media, television and radio production, sport in media and popular culture, media audiences and cultural consumption.

In partnership with Limerick Institute of Technology sponsors Wired FM, a student radio station.

Westmoreland College of Management and Business

Westmoreland Street, Dublin 2

t. +353 1 679 5324 / 679 7266

f. +353 1 679 1953

e. info@westmorelandcollege.ie

w. www.westmorelandcollege.ie

■ *A private college offering the following courses:*

Diploma in journalism and media studies

Diploma in marketing, advertising and public relations

Northern Ireland

Armagh College

College Hill, Armagh BT61 7HN
General Enquiries
t. +44 28 3752 2205
f. +44 28 3751 2845
e. enquiries@armaghcollege.ac.uk
w. www.armaghcollege.ac.uk
■ *Offers the following courses:*
Art and design (EDEXCEL)
AVCE double award in information
and communication technology
AVCE single award in information and
communication technology
BTEC first diploma in e-media
BTEC national certificate in e-media
BTEC national diploma in design crafts
BTEC national diploma in e-media

Belfast Institute of Further and Higher Education

College Square East, Belfast BT1 6DJ
General Enquiries
t. +44 28 9026 5000
f. +44 28 9026 5001
e. information_services@belfastinsti-
tute.ac.uk
w. www.belfastinstitute.ac.uk
■ *The following courses are offered:*
AVCE in media
BTEC GNVQ intermediate art and
design
BTEC HNC in multimedia
BTEC HND in media (moving image)
BTEC HND in media (writing)
BTEC HND in multimedia
Foundation degree in science,
multimedia
Newspaper journalism: writing NVQ 4
VTCT L III diploma in theatrical and
media make-up

Castlereagh College

Montgomery Road, Belfast BT6 9JD
General Enquiries
t. +44 28 9079 7144
f. +44 28 9040 1820
w. www.castlereagh.ac.uk
■ *The following courses are offered:*
AVCE media double award
AVCE media single award
BTEC first diploma in e-media
BTEC national diploma in e-media
Media GNVQ intermediate

Causeway Institute

Union Street, Coleraine, Co. Derry
BT52 1QA
General Enquiries
t. +44 28 7035 4717
f. +44 28 7035 6377
e. admissions@causeway.ac.uk
w. www.causeway.ac.uk
■ *The following courses are offered:*
AS level film studies
BTEC first diploma in performing arts
BTEC national diploma in e-media
BTEC national diploma in media
(moving image)
BTEC national diploma in performing
arts
CIM advanced certificate in marketing
CIM certificate in marketing
The music business uncovered

East Antrim Institute of Further and Higher Education

400 Shore Road, Newtown Abbey,
Co. Antrim BT37 9RS
General Enquiries
t. +44 28 9085 5000
f. +44 28 9086 2076
e. info@eaifhe.ac.uk
w. www.eaifhe.ac.uk

■ *The following courses are offered:*
BTEC GNVQ intermediate (media production and communications)
BTEC higher national diploma in computing
BTEC national diploma in media (e-media)
BTEC national diploma in media (moving image)
National diploma in media (publishing)

East Down Institute of Further and Higher Education
Market Street, Downpatrick, Co. Down BT30 6ND
General Enquiries
  t. +44 28 4461 5815
  f. +44 28 4461 5817
  e. admin@edifhe.ac.uk
  w. www.edifhe.ac.uk
■ *The following course is offered:*
BTEC first diploma in media

East Tyrone College of Further and Higher Education
Circular Road, Dungannon, Co. Tyrone BT71 6BQ
General Enquiries
  t. +44 28 8772 2323; (text) +44 18002 28 8772 0625
  f. +44 28 8775 2018
  e. info@etcfhe.ac.uk
  w. www.etcfhe.ac.uk
■ *The following courses are offered:*
AVCE in media: communication and production (double award)
BTEC national diploma in art and design (multimedia)

Limavady College of Further and Higher Education
Main Street, Limavady, Co. Derry BT49 0EX
General Enquiries
  t. +44 28 7776 2334
  f. +44 28 7776 1018
  w. www.limavady.ac.uk

■ *Offers the following courses:*
BTEC advanced diploma in e-media
BTEC diploma foundation studies in art and design
BTEC national diploma in media (e-media)
Foundation degree in computing with e-media (FDSc)/certificate in computing

Lisburn Institute of Further and Higher Education
39 Castle Street, Lisburn, Co. Antrim BT27 4SU
  t. +44 28 9267 7225
  f. +44 28 9267 7291
  e. admissions@liscol.ac.uk
  w. www.liscol.ac.uk
■ *The following courses are offered:*
AVCE art and design, graphic design (double award)
AVCE in information and communication technology
BTEC diploma in foundation studies in art and design
BTEC national certificate in graphic design
CIM advanced certificate in marketing
Short courses are offered in the following subjects:
Intermediate web design
Principles of marketing
Shorthand

Newry Institute
Patrick Street, Newry, Co. Down BT35 8DN
General Enquiries
  t. +44 28 3026 1071
  f. +44 28 3025 9679
  e. admissions@nkifhe.ac.uk
  w. www.nkifhe.ac.uk
■ *Offers the following courses:*
BTEC first diploma in media
BTEC national award in media (video—includes sound)
BTEC national diploma in media (moving pictures and sound)

BTEC national diploma in multimedia design

Foundation degree in interactive multimedia

Higher national diploma in software development

■ *Part-time and short courses are offered in*

Introduction to digital photography and Photoshop

Photography

North Down and Ards Institute (NDAI)

Castle Park Road, Bangor, Co. Down BT20 4TF

General Enquiries

t. +44 28 9127 6600

f. +44 28 9127 6601

w. www.ndai.ac.uk

■ *The following courses are offered:*

AVCE media studies

GNVQ level 2 intermediate media studies

HNC media (moving image)

National award, music technology (music for media)

Single award, media (radio and journalism)

The following multimedia and web development courses are offered:

OCN digital photography

OCN digital photography advanced

OCN digital and computer imaging

OCN introduction to Photoshop

OCN making web sites with Dreamweaver

Northern Ireland Film and Television Commission (NIFTC)

Alfred House, 21 Alfred Street, Belfast BT2 8ED

General Enquiries

t. +44 28 9023 2444

f. +44 28 9023 9918

e. info@niftc.co.uk

w. www.niftc.co.uk

■ *The following skills and development courses and workshops are offered:*

Basic skills for television researchers

Casting: Doing the deal

Co-producing feature films

Digital video post-production

FILM (film industry locations manager)

Health and safety

Health and safety for film and television

Legal and copyright for film workshop

Movie magic scheduling and budgeting

Production accounting and cost reports

The art of negotiating for producers

The black art of completion guarantees

The business of writing

Writing a treatment

Northern Visions

23 Donegall Street, Belfast BT1 2FF

General Enquiries

t. +44 28 9024 5495

f. +44 28 9032 6608

e. info@northernvisions.org

w. www.northernvisions.org

■ *Offers training, access and media production in radio and video to people marginalised by mainstream media or denied self-expression or collective expression. Participants are able to become involved in broadcasting through NvTv.*

North West Institute of Further and Higher Education (NWIFHE)

Strand Road, Derry BT48 7AL

General Enquiries

t. +44 28 7127 6000

f. +44 28 7126 0520

e. annette.odoherty@nwi.ac.uk

w. www.nwifhe.ac.uk

■ *Offers the following courses:*

BTEC higher national diploma in media (moving image)

BTEC national diploma in media (audio and moving image)

Newspaper journalism (NCTJ-validated), NVQ level 4

Omagh College

Mount Joy Road, Omagh, Co. Tyrone
BT79 7AH
General Enquiries
t. +44 28 8224 5433
f. +44 28 8224 1440
e. ann.brogan@omagh.ac.uk
w. www.omagh.ac.uk
■ *The following courses are offered:*
Certificate in creative computing for
web designers
Certificate in software development
Digital photo shoot, retail and fashion
design (first diploma level II)
Introduction to Flash and Dreamweaver
Media (first diploma level II)
Media, music, art and design (NQF
level III awards and certificates)
Media, music, art and design (NQF
level III awards and certificates)
Web site design with Frontpage

Open University (Belfast)

40 University Road, Belfast BT7 1SU
Director: Dr Rosemary Hamilton
t. +44 28 9024 5025
f. +44 28 9023 0565
e. ireland@open.ac.uk
w. www.open.ac.uk/ireland
■ *The following undergraduate courses are*
offered:
Language studies
Social sciences
Sociology
The following postgraduate courses are
offered:
MA in cultural and media studies
MA in humanities
MA in popular culture
Social sciences

Queen's University

University Road, Belfast BT7 1NN
General Enquiries
t. +44 28 9024 5133
f. +44 28 9024 7895
e. admissions@qub.ac.uk

w. www.qub.ac.uk
■ *The following courses are offered:*
BA in film studies
MA in film and visual studies

Synergy Learning

1 Millennium Way, Springvale Business
Park, Belfast BT12 7AL
General Enquiries
t. +44 28 9028 8830
f. +44 28 9028 8850
e. info@synergy-learning.com
w. www.synergy-learning.com
■ *A private organisation offering the follow-*
ing courses:
BTEC first certificate in media
BTEC first diploma in media
BTEC national certificate in media
(e-media production)
BTEC national certificate in media
(games production)
BTEC national diploma in media
(e-media)
BTEC national diploma in media
(games)
Courseware is also provided for post-
primary, further and higher education
and in the areas of recreational, vocational and continuing professional
development.

University of Ulster

York Street, Belfast BT15 1ED
General Enquiries
t. +44 87 0040 0700
f. +44 28 7032 4964
w. www.ulst.ac.uk

Other University of Ulster colleges:

Coleraine: Cromore Road, Coleraine
BT52 1SA
Jordanstown: Shore Road, Newtown
Abbey, Co. Antrim BT37 0QB
Magee College: Northland Road,
Derry BT48 7JL
■ *The University of Ulster's media pro-*
grammes are now being clustered at the

Coleraine college. The following degree courses are offered:

BA hons combined arts—media studies

BA hons design for visual communication

BA hons European studies with media studies

BA hons history with media studies

BA hons media arts

BA hons media studies

BA hons media studies and Spanish, German, Irish or French

BA hons media studies with film studies

BA hons media studies with journalism and publishing studies

BA hons media studies with psychology

BA hons visual communication

BSc hons business with media studies

BSc hons communication with advertising

BSc hons communication with health communication

BSc hons communication with public relations

BSc hons communication, advertising and marketing

BSc hons computing with media studies

BSc hons politics with communication

MSc in future communications

Postgraduate diploma or MA media studies

Postgraduate diploma or MSc political communication and public affairs

A MSc degree in future communications in creative technology may be attended at the Belfast college, run by the Digital Diversity Project.

Upper Bann Institute

Castlewellan Road, Banbridge,
Co. Down BT32 4AY
General Enquiries
t. +44 28 3839 7700
f. +44 28 3839 7701
e. quinnj@ubi.ac.uk
w. www.ubi.ac.uk

■ *Offers the following courses:*

Advanced VCE full award in media, communications and production

BA (hons) creative imaging

C&G media techniques—journalism and radio competences

C&G media techniques—television and video competences

GNVQ intermediate award in media, communications and production

Higher national certificate in media, communication and production

Higher national certificate/diploma in multimedia

Higher national certificate/diploma in photography

HND in photography (with multimedia modules)

NCFE NVQ level 4 in newspaper writing

NVQ level 4 journalism

10

ADVERTISING, PUBLIC RELATIONS AND MARKETING: THE HARD SELL

Cariona Neary

The number of advertising messages that are beamed into our homes every day or that we encounter as we go about our daily lives is so great that, as consumers, we filter out most of the messages.

The days of mass advertising are long over, brought to an end by the ever-increasing range of media available to advertisers. Ten years ago it was possible to achieve national coverage by running a campaign across the main Irish media, including television, press and radio. Today these media swim in a much larger media pool, including satellite and cable channels, six daily newspaper titles and a host of radio stations. This range of media poses a real problem for advertisers who seek to run major campaigns. Marketers refer to *fragmentation* in the media, where consumers read, watch and listen to an ever-increasing number of media.

The worldwide spending in this sector, according to ZenithOptimedia, grew in 2004, with an estimated $350 billion being spent on media advertising and marketing, between television, radio, newspapers, magazines, cinema, outdoor and the internet.

The Irish advertising market is difficult to measure because of the increased media fragmentation. There is no single agreed figure for the value of the industry; however, it was estimated to be worth over €1,145 million in 2004, up 9% from 2003. The industry is expected to continue growth into 2005, with a projected growth of a further 6% in the sector.[1] The year 2003 was a relatively poor one, with only 2% growth, again reflecting the general downturn in the economy.

1. Mediaworks estimates.

The advertising landscape

Newspapers absorb the lion's share of advertising expenditure. The national press takes 52% of all advertising budgets, while the regional press takes a further 13%, so that almost two-thirds of all advertising expenditure in Ireland goes to the newspaper industry. This reflects the fact that Ireland has one of the highest newspaper readership rates in Europe. 2004 saw advertising in the press grow by 23%.[2]

Despite the fact that television is the strongest medium in impact, it attracts only 17% of the total advertising budget, while national radio holds 4% of advertising share, just ahead of local radio at 3%.[3] Broadcasting advertising revenue was up 21% in 2004 with local radio and television.

Outdoor advertising, which includes poster sites and transport advertising such as buses and trains, is growing more slowly, up just 4% in 2004. According to the Outdoor Media Association, the sector is worth some €80 million in the Republic.

Profile of media expenditure, January–December 2004

MEDIUM	Expenditure 2004 January–December € (m)	Profile % 2004	Profile % 2003
Press	928.6	68	66
Television	236.2	17	17
Radio*	90.6	7	8
Outdoor	105.8	8	9
Cinema	10.0	1	1
Total	1,371.2	100	100

Source: IAPI BASE, Adspend 2004, Medialive.

*Independent analysis of the radio market suggests that these figures under-report the radio share of advertising. The Ox Report (July 2004) reports radio advertising share as 9%—one of the highest in Europe.

The Irish advertising market is largely owned by international media organisations. Of the forty significant advertising agencies in Ireland, some thirty-five are owned by larger advertising groups whose head office is in

2. BASE (Breakdown of Advertising Share and Expenditure) 2004 (www.iapi.ie).
3. Ox Report, 2004, gives the radio share as 9%.

New York, Paris or London. This reflects the fact that many of the advertisers represent global brands and prefer to control global campaigns through a network of agencies around the world. The largest independent Irish agency is McConnells Advertising.

In the past, agencies were 'full service', carrying out all the functions, from creating ads to media buying. The lucrative media-buying aspect of an agency's work was used to cross-subsidise other functions, in particular the creative work associated with producing an advertisement. Media buying is now seen as a separate function, and so there are media-buying specialists who have expertise in rolling out an advertisement campaign across the full range of media. Many of these media specialists are also owned by international advertising agencies but work independently of the advertising agency. Interestingly, one of the largest Irish advertisers, Ryanair, has a policy of not using advertising agencies or media-buying specialists. The company believes it gets better value by creating its own advertisements and buying media space, mainly with the press, directly.

From an advertiser's perspective, fragmentation in the market can dilute the effectiveness of an advertising campaign. Advertising effectiveness is achieved through reaching a target audience and exposing that audience to an advertising message a number of times. In the past, this could be achieved by placing an advertisement on the two major Irish stations, RTÉ1 and RTÉ2. Today there are fourteen channels watched by Irish consumers—most coming from outside the state. Ireland has a very open media market. An advertiser has to place an advertisement on a whole range of channels and in a wide number of newspapers in order to reach an audience and to make sure the advertising message registers with a target audience.

However, fragmentation is not all bad. For some highly specialised products, there are also specialised media. For example, for mountain-climbers there is a specialist magazine called *Outsider*.

Many of the channels beamed into Ireland from abroad are able to run Irish ads. It is estimated that approximately €20 million worth of advertising revenue is going out of the Republic to such channels as UTV, Sky and Nickelodeon. Equally, in the newspaper sector we are seeing more Irish editions of British newspapers, such as the *Sunday Times*, carrying Irish-focused adverts.

Diageo Ireland, with major drinks brands such as Guinness and Baileys Irish Cream, is the biggest advertiser, followed by the concert promoter MCD, Proctor and Gamble and Vodafone. However, Coca-Cola, the world's no. 1 brand, is ranked thirteenth as an advertiser in Ireland. None of the other top ten brands, which include Microsoft, McDonald's, Nokia and Toyota, can be found among the top twenty Irish advertisers. In fact retailers such as Tesco, Dunnes, Lidl and Aldi are the biggest advertisers in Ireland by category.

The BASE figures do not include so-called 'below the line' advertising, that is, advertising that does not use the mass media of television, radio, outdoor advertising or print. Sponsorship is becoming a very powerful ingredient in brand development. Often associated with major sporting events, there are simply not enough high-quality sponsorship properties to meet the demand by advertisers. Sponsorship is valued at €67 million[4] and is growing at the rate of about 5–7% per year.

In recent years there has been a growing requirement for firms to become accountable and transparent in how budgets are spent. Advertisers have traditionally been reluctant number-crunchers and the old adage 'I know half my advertising budget is working, I just don't know which half!' comes to mind when one is trying to find ways to test the effectiveness of advertising spending. Normal advertising using mass media is a one-way form of communication. The advertisement is placed on television and the consumer watches it. The advertiser cannot know that an advertisement campaign has led directly to a particular action. However, direct market-ing methods, which incorporate two-way communication between the consumer and advertiser, is claimed to be the most measurable and accountable form of advertising.

Direct marketing uses a number of media, which makes possible a direct response, including direct-response television, direct mail, the internet and telephone marketing. In 2004 the direct marketing sector was estimated to be worth €575 million.[5] The Irish Direct Marketing Association (IDMA) predicts that the sector will grow by another 30% by 2006, bringing it to a value of approximately €575 million.

The breakdown of the direct marketing expenditure is estimated by the IDMA as follows:

4. *Sponsorship in Ireland: Outlook for 2004*, Amárach Consulting.
5. Source: Irish Direct Marketing Association.

Direct mail (including postage)	€275 million
Telemarketing bureaus	€240 million
On-line marketing (domestic)	€10 million
Customer relationship management	€50 million
Total	€575 million

Future trends

The growing trend in advertising is to link up with interactive technologies, such as the internet and mobile devices, in order to have both greater consumer information and more feedback from the consumer. Advertisements can be tailored to the profile of the user and sales can be made on the basis of a promotion through interactive television, radio or mobile wireless devices.

For television, the challenge is the development of personal video recorders, which will allow people to download television programmes, films and music without the advertisements. Almost 70% of American consumers said, not surprisingly, that they would pay for products to avoid advertisements.[6] While this may cause the advertising industry to shiver, the reality is that content-providers and broadcasters will work to find solutions, such as product placement and sponsorship, to get products into the consumer's face. Without advertising revenue, the business model for content provision is too fragile. Internet-based sales are set to grow and grow as more homes go on line. The mobile phone, being the most ubiquitous communications tool in the developed world, will become a critical platform for multimedia advertising content. In Ireland, the choice for advertisers will get bigger, with more digital television stations offering Irish advertising space, but this will lead to an even greater fragmentation in the market.

6. The *Economist*, 26 June 2004, 'Special report: The future of advertising.'

PR and marketing: The professional soft sell!

The role of public relations is to facilitate communications between an organisation and its stakeholders or public. According to industry experts, independent coverage by a journalist is considered seven times more credible than advertising. A company may wish to influence its customers, the local community in which it operates, the media or policy-makers at a local, national or EU level. The public relations profession divides its activities according to the stakeholders it is seeking to address. Some public relations agencies specialise in consumer public relations, while others deal with public affairs, corporate or business-to-business (B2B) public relations. The biggest specialisation is product-related public relations, aimed at the consumer sector. Public affairs is ranked no. 2 in importance and includes such activities as lobbying.

While it is impossible to get an accurate figure for the value of public relations in Ireland, the Public Relations Institute of Ireland estimates the industry to be worth about €50 million. There are some forty recognised public relations consultancies in Ireland, the largest of which are Fleishman-Hillard Saunders, Murray Consultants, Edelman Public Relations, Drury Communications and Weber Shandwick FCC. Of the top five companies only Murray Consultants is wholly Irish-owned. Some new Irish companies like Q4, with two ex Government spin doctors at the helm, have managed to take a slice of the PR pie in its first two years.

Market research

According to the Association of Irish Market Research Organisations (AIMRO), market research was valued at €51.4 million in 2003. Some ten years earlier, market research was valued at €17 million. The sector has grown dramatically, for two reasons. Like advertising and public relations, market research growth tends to mirror general growth in the economy. The second reason is that management thinking has changed in the ten years from 1993 to 2003. Gut instinct and intuition are not good enough as a justification for a market spending. Marketing and advertising budgets are also much bigger than they were ten years ago, and marketeers are expected to be able to justify objectively market spending on new product development and brand-building campaigns. Today research is used before, during and after marketing and advertising activities.

Marketing

While central marketing functions such as advertising, public relations and market research are often handled by third-party specialists external to an organisation, the market function itself is almost always managed from within an organisation. With regard to power within the organisation, the marketing function has seen its position eroded in recent years as more organisations are run by accountants. In the UK, only eight of the FTSE 100 companies have board-level marketing positions.[1] While similar research is not available for Ireland, there is much debate in the marketing community about the marketing profession's lack of influence within organisations. One of the criticisms levelled at marketing is the lack of transparency about the impact of marketing performance on profitability. Many marketers are woolly about accountability. Yet marketing-related expenditure tends to be one of the most significant line items in the total company budget, typically accounting for 8% to 15% of revenue. PA Consulting in the UK queried 100 senior marketing managers about their role in organisations in 2003 and found that 85% could not allocate costs fairly and more than 90% lacked robust data sources. On a more positive note, research published by the Irish Management Institute (IMI) and the University of Limerick found that Irish marketers compared very positively with their international counterparts: 65% of Irish companies surveyed were classed as highly market-oriented[2]—above the international average and well ahead of poorer performers, which included the UK and Hong Kong.

One of the most significant changes in marketing practice in recent years has been the impact of technology on how marketers communicate with customers. In the early days of the internet, banner advertising was seen as the most effective means of advertising on the web. Media-savvy companies are now investing in search engine marketing to make sure their companies are highly visible on the web when potential customers use a search engine to find information about their business sector. Up to 80% of all traffic comes through commercial search engines, such as Google. To achieve a high ranking in a search, companies use interventions, such as buying up key words, and work with sponsored links or advertise on high-profile sites. In reality, the one thing that raises the ranking of your site in internet searches is the number of other sites linked to yours; so media-savvy companies aim to get their clients linked to them.

1. 'Why Marketing is not at the Board Table', Alternative View e-zine, April 2004.
2. IMI/UL (2004), *Marketing in the 21st Century: A Study of Marketing Practice and Performance in Ireland.*

Republic of Ireland

141/Red Cell
9 Upper Pembroke Street, Dublin 2
Managing Director: Mark Skinner
t. +353 1 676 0527
f. +353 1 676 5201
w. www.hunter-redcell.ie
■ *A marketing communications agency and part of the Red Cell Network, providing direct marketing, database management, sales promotion, design and print management, SMS and e-marketing, point of sale, customer relationship management and event management services.*
Creative Director: Joe Clancy
Deputy Creative Director: Mike Mesbur
Account Director: Barry Kennedy

A1 Advertising and Marketing
Unit 13, Melbourne Business Park,
Model Farm Road, Cork
Managing Director: Ray Walsh
t. +353 21 434 7123
f. +353 21 434 7128
e. rwa@eircom.net
w. www.rwamarketing.com
■ *An advertising agency and subsidiary of Ray Walsh Associates, providing strategy development, market research, corporate identity development, sales and promotional activity, direct mail campaigns, design and print services, web site development, event management, sponsorships and public relations services.*

A & D
Envision House, Flood Street, Galway
Managing Directors: Larry Hynes and Ide Deloughry
t. +353 91 561 370
e. eolas@a-and-d.ie
w. www.a-and-d.ie
■ *A graphic design and advertising agency, providing graphic design for print, branding and corporate and recruitment advertising services.*

Adapt Marketing Services
1a Coolamber Park, Dublin 16
Managing Director: Mark Kerr
t. +353 1 493 9511
f. +353 1 494 7711
e. markkerr@eircom.net
■ *An advertising agency, providing exhibition and event management services.*

Adept Creative Facilities
1 Kingram Place, Dublin 2
Joint Managing Directors: Adrian Van Der Lee and Denis Goodbody
t. +353 1 662 4767
f. +353 1 662 4793
e. adrian@adept.ie; denis@adept.ie
■ *An advertising agency, providing strategic planning services.*

Adhouse
22 Crosthwaite Park,
Dún Laoghaire, Co. Dublin
General Enquiries: Louise O'Connor
t. +353 1 230 4577
f. +353 1 230 4597
e. info@adhouse.ie
w. www.adhouse.ie
■ *An advertising agency.*

Adimpact Media
Unit 2, Brewery Court, Brewery Road, Stillorgan, Dublin 18
Sales Director: Niall McConnell
t. +353 1 210 3868
f. +353 1 278 9181
e. info@adimpact-media.com
w. www.adimpact-media.com
■ *An advertising agency, providing vehicle branding, signage and graphics, display units and materials, and window films and graphics.*

AdSat

62 Lower Mount Street, Dublin 2
Chief Executive Officer: John O'Connor
t. +353 1 662 9557
f. +353 1 662 9148
e. info@imdadsat.com
w. www.imdadsat.com
■ *An advertising agency, distributing audio and text advertising copy to television stations throughout the UK and Ireland.*

Advertising Standards Authority

IPC House, 35–39 Shelbourne Road, Dublin 4
General Enquiries and Complaints
t. +353 1 660 8766
f. +353 1 660 8113
e. info@asai.ie
w. www.asai.ie
■ *An independent self-regulatory body set up and financed by the advertising industry to promote good standards in advertising and sales promotion.*

Members of the Board:
Edward McCumiskey, Jennifer Balfe, Shane Lynch, Terry Buckley, Michael Caraher, Ruth Payne, J. P. Cusack, Dennis Henderson, Steve Shanahan, Brendan McCabe, Deirdre Keogh, Yvonne Tuohy, Paul Mulligan, Kieran Killeen and Eamonn Buttle

Members of the Complaints Committee:
Bairbre Redmond (Chairperson), Margaret Beaumont, Michael Higgins, Emer McLeavey, Anne Marie Lenihan, Brian Martin, Tom Morgan, Bill Moss, Michael O'Keeffe, Brian Pierce, Josephine Garry, Ken Kilbride, Mary McLoughlin and Leonie Lunny

Adworks

A12 Greenogue Square, Greenogue Business Park, Newcastle, Co. Dublin
Managing Director: Maria O'Brien
t. +353 1 458 7800
f. +353 1 458 7986
e. adworks@eircom.net
■ *An advertising agency.*

AE Consulting

Unit 1A, Glenageary Office Park, Dún Laoghaire, Co. Dublin
General Enquiries: Aileen Eglington
t. +353 1 284 7796
f. +353 1 284 7618
e. post@aeconsult.ie
w. www.aeconsult.ie
■ *A public relations company.*

AFA O'Meara Advertising

46 St James's Place, Dublin 2
t. +353 1 676 2500
f. +353 1 676 2506
e. media@afaom.com
w. www.afaomeara.com
■ *An advertising agency, providing advertising and marketing and media, public relations and promotional services.*
Managing Director: Stuart Fogarty
Deputy Managing Director: Shane Lynch
Creative Director: John Walsh
Media Director: Philip Bergin
Head of Direct Marketing: Heather Kennedy
Client Services: Feargal Jennings, Ruth Allen, Gareth O'Gorman, Shane Lynch, Michael Mackey and Stuart Fogarty
Production Managers: Denise Waters and Emer O'Reilly
Studio Manager: Deirdre Riordan
Financial Controller: Olive Cronin

All Media Matters

17 Idrone Park, Dublin 16
General Enquiries: Frank McGouran
t. +353 1 494 1071
m. +353 86 811 1567
f. +353 1 494 1071
e. frank@allmediamatters.com
■ *An advertising agency, providing marketing strategies, advertising sales, planning, publicity and corporate communications services.*

Amárach Consulting

37 Northumberland Road, Dublin 4
Chief Executive: Gerard O'Neill
t. +353 1 660 5506
f. +353 1 660 5508
e. info@amarach.com
■ *A market research company, providing market research, consumer trend analysis and business forecasting services.*
Director: Michael McLoughlin
Senior Research Manager and Director of Research: Corona Naessens
Field Director: Mary Mulcahy

artdirector.ie

6 Kent Terrace, Barnhill Road, Dalkey, Co. Dublin
General Enquiries: Tony Purcell
t. +353 1 285 1209
m. +353 87 224 2905
e. tpurcell@iol.ie
w. www.artdirector.ie
■ *An advertising agency, providing art direction and design services.*

Atomic

27–28 Great Strand Street, Dublin 1
General Enquiries
t. +353 1 878 2418
f. +353 1 878 2419
e. info@atomic.ie
w. www.atomic.ie
■ *An advertising agency, providing advertising, design and marketing services.*

Banahan McManus

32 Morehampton Road, Dublin 4
Director: Thomas Banahan
t. +353 1 668 9322
f. +353 1 668 9367
e. bma@indigo.ie
w. www.banahanmcmanus.ie
■ *An advertising agency, providing advertising and design services.*

Bell Advertising and Employee Communications

6 Ely Place, Dublin 2

Account Manager: Deirdre Kelly
t. +353 1 669 0004
f. +353 1 669 0049
w. www.ogilvy.ie
■ *The Dublin office of the worldwide Ogilvy marketing communications network, providing design, research, public relations, identity, retail marketing, sales promotion and new media services.*

Bill O'Herlihy Communications Group

40 Eastmoreland Lane, Dublin 4
General Enquiries: Bill O'Herlihy
t. +353 1 660 2744
f. +353 1 660 2745
e. boherlihy@ohcpr.ie
■ *A public relations company.*

Birchall Company, The

57 Waterloo Road, Dublin 4
Managing Director: Richard A. Birchall
t. +353 1 668 3993
f. +353 1 668 3991
e. info@birchall.ie
■ *An advertising agency.*
Directors: Fionnuala Hickland, A. M. Birchall and F. Hickland

Bloom

The Black Church, St Mary's Place, Dublin 7
General Enquiries
t. +353 1 860 0007
f. +353 1 860 0008
e. info@bloom.ie
w. www.bloom.ie
■ *An advertising agency, providing sales promotion, direct mail, point of sale, design, copywriting and branding services.*

Bofin Byers Company/BBC Advertising

Apex Building, Blackthorn Road, Sandyford, Dublin 18
Managing Director: Conor Bofin
t. +353 1 293 0999
f. +353 1 293 2056
e. info@advertising.ie
w. www.advertising.ie

■ *An advertising agency, providing advertising, print, radio, television, outdoor, web design, interactive new media, promotions, corporate identity, branding, corporate literature and packaging services.*
Account Directors: Enda Murphy and Una Kelly
Media Buyer: Johnny Ross

Bonfire
3 Wellington Quay, Dublin 2
General Enquiries: Sean Hynes and Ian Doherty
t. +353 1 677 0376
f. +353 1 677 1139
e. thebrandignitors@bonfire.ie
w. www.bonfire.ie
■ *An advertising and communications agency, providing strategic planning, creative development and campaign production services.*

Bracken Public Relations
11 Inns Court, Winetavern Street, Dublin 8
Managing Director: Brendan Bracken
t. +353 1 677 3277
f. +353 1 677 3257
e. info@brackenpr.com
w. www.brackenpr.com
■ *A public relations company, providing financial services and education public relations.*

Brian Wallace Advertising
122 Lower Baggot Street, Dublin 2
Managing Director: Brian Wallace
t. +353 1 639 1470
f. +353 1 639 1122
e. info@brianwallace.ie
w. www.brianwallace.ie
■ *An advertising agency, providing advertising, promotions, public relations, direct marketing and web design services. Associated with the Anderson Spratt Group.*
Creative Director: Seán A. McDermott
Production Manager and Account Executive: Sarah McDevitt
Senior Art Director: Martin Gleeson
Financial Controller: Gerard Morris

Brindley Advertising
Brindley House, 17 Mount Street Upper, Dublin 2
Managing Director: Basil Brindley
t. +353 1 676 7467
f. +353 1 676 7108
e. info@brindleyadv.ie
Directors: Bernice Brindley, Donald Brindley, Michael McCabe and Eileen Byrne
■ *An advertising agency, providing sales promotion and public relations services.*

Cabvertise
20 Lower Stephen Street, Dublin 2
Managing Director: Peter Maguire
t. +353 1 475 2134
w. www.cabvertise.ie
■ *An advertising agency, offering advertising space on rear windows and 'super rears' of taxis.*

Campaign HTDS
37 Leeson Close, Dublin 2
Managing Director: Brendan Bonass
t. +353 1 662 2333
f. +353 1 662 2359
e. info@campaign.ie
w. www.campaign.ie
■ *An advertising and marketing agency, providing creative, media, print and internet services.*
Director of Client Services: Gavin McAuliffe
Account Manager: Gail Mahon
Account Manager: Yvonne Gordon
Client Services Executive: Suzanne Magnier
Non-executive Director: Alexis O'Shea

Captive Advertising
56 Fitzwilliam Square, Dublin 2
Manager: John Teahon
t. +353 1 661 0383
f. +353 1 661 2284
e. info@captive.ie
w. www.captive.ie
■ *An advertising agency, providing washroom advertising.*

Sales and Marketing Manager: Shauna McClafferty

Cara Gregg Creative Consultancy

28 St Vincent's Park, Blackrock,
Co. Dublin
General Enquiries
t. +353 1 280 6769
f. +353 1 280 6779
e. caragregg@eircom.net
■ *An advertising agency, providing creative and corporate advertising, and design services.*

Carat Ireland

Carat House, 16A The Crescent,
Monkstown, Co. Dublin
Chairman: Pat Donnelly
t. +353 1 271 2100
f. +353 1 271 2111
e. alan@carat.ie; ciaran@carat.ie
w. www.carat.com
■ *An advertising agency, providing advertising and public relations services.*
Chief Executive Officer: Liam McDonnell
Managing Directors: Ciaran Cunnigham and Alan Cox
Financial Director: Arthur Byrne

Carival Advertising and Design

Keane House, 93–95 Oliver Plunkett Street, Cork
Consultant: Owen O'Kelly
t. +353 21 427 3660
f. +353 21 425 1762
e. advertising@carival.ie
w. www.carival.ie
■ *An advertising agency, providing advertising, brand identity and promotional services, and leaflets and brochure production.*

Carr Communications

4 Bracken Business Park, Bracken Road, Sandyford, Dublin 18
General Enquiries: Dermot McCrum
t. +353 1 278 5000
f. +353 1 278 5001
e. info@carrcommunications.ie
w. www.carrcommunications.ie
■ *A public relations company, providing public relations, event management, design, sponsorship, lobbying, corporate affairs, internal communications and crisis management services.*

Casey Communications

8 Sheares Street, Cork
General Enquiries: Patrick Casey
t. +353 21 427 2224
f. +353 21 427 1830
e. info@caseycommunications.ie
w. www.caseycommunications.ie
■ *A public relations company, providing media relations, corporate communications, crisis management, community relations and event management services.*

Cawley Nea/TBWA

41a Blackberry Lane, Dublin 6
Founding Partner and CEO:
Chris Cawley
t. +353 1 496 6920
f. +353 1 496 6923
e. post@cawleynea-tbwa.ie
w. www.cawleynea-tbwa.ie
■ *An advertising agency, providing print, television and radio advertising services.*
Director: Brian Swords
Media Director: Debbie Owens
Creative Directors: Pearse McCaughey and Martin Cowman

Chemistry Strategic Communications

14 Leeson Park, Dublin 6
Managing Director: Ray Sheerin
t. +353 1 498 8800
f. +353 1 497 1857
w. www.chemistry.ie
■ *An advertising agency, providing television, radio, press, outdoor, ambient and on-line advertising and direct mail services.*
E-mail addresses for individuals are in the format firstname.lastname@chemistry.ie
Client Service Director: Fintan Cooney
Creative Director: Mike Garner
Media Director: Jarlath Naughton

CMB Designs

7 St Stephen's Green, Dublin 2
 t. +353 1 679 9906
 f. +353 1 679 9873
 w. www.cmbdesign.ie
■ *A graphic design company.*

Comit Marketing

126 Ranelagh, Dublin 6
Managing Director: Allan Chapman
 t. +353 1 498 4640
 f. +353 1 498 4644
 e. emailus@comitmarketing.com
 w. www.comitmarketing.com
■ *A public relations and marketing agency, providing public relations, advertising, direct mail, event management, brochures and web site services.*
Project Manager: Barry Chapman

Concept Advertising and Design

15 Bridge Street, Cork
General Enquiries
 t. +353 21 450 3600
 f. +353 21 450 3446
 e. info@conceptads.ie
 w. www.conceptads.ie
■ *An advertising agency, providing print, radio, television and internet advertising services, graphic design and new media authoring.*

Convenience Advertising

2nd Floor, 5–6 Lombard Street East, Dublin 2
Managing Director: Cathy Ward
 t. +353 1 672 5444
 f. +353 1 675 9840
 e. sarah@conads.com
 w. www.conads.com
■ *A public health communications agency and part of the worldwide Convenience Advertising International group, providing services on issues such as sexual health, drug education, teenage smoking, and men's and women's health.*
Marketing Manager: Sarah Spencer

Copper Reed Studio

94 Henry Street, Limerick
Director of Design: Michelle McInerney
 t. +353 61 400 620
 f. +353 61 400 511
 e. design@copperreed.com
■ *An advertising and design agency, providing market and competitor analysis, project management, design and art direction, copywriting and photography.*
Project Manager and Technical Director: Gary MacMahon
Senior Designer, Interface Design and Production: Tim Harrington
Senior Designer, Interface Design and Production: Con Ryan

Copy Desk, The

93A Monkstown Road, Blackrock, Co. Dublin
Copywriter: Shane Harrison
 t. +353 1 230 4286
 f. +353 1 284 6929
 e. shane@copydesk.ie
■ *A copywriting service.*

Corporate Connections

12 Windsor Place, Dublin 2
General Enquiries
 t. +353 1 644 9500
 f. +353 1 644 9501
 e. info@corporateconnections.ie
■ *An advertising agency, providing corporate communications services.*

CP&A

106 Upper Leeson Street, Dublin 2
Managing Director: John Dick
 t. +353 1 660 4644
 f. +353 1 660 4497
 e. johndick@eircom.net
Production Manager: Neil Rooney
■ *An advertising agency.*

Creative Works

1 Argyle Square, Morehampton Road,
Dublin 4
General Enquiries
t. +353 1 664 3341
f. +353 1 664 3302
e. info@creativeworks.ie
w. www.creativeworks.ie
■ *An advertsing agency.*

CSL Associates

6 Lower Mount Street, Dublin 2
General Enquiries
t. +353 1 676 6650
f. +353 1 662 1181
e. info@cslassociates.ie
w. www.cslassociates.ie
■ *An advertising, sponsorship and event agency.*

Cullen Communications

Clyde Lodge, 15 Clyde Road, Dublin 4
General Enquiries: Frank Cullen
t. +353 1 668 9099
f. +353 1 668 9872
e. fcullen@cullencommunications.ie
w. www.cullencommunications.ie
■ *A public relations company, providing public relations and marketing services.*

Cyberline

3 Waldemar Terrace, Dublin 14
Managing Director: Chris Craig
t. +353 1 205 1485
w. www.cyberline.ie
■ *An advertising agency, providing digital screen advertising in shops.*
Operations Manager: Triona Byrne

DDFH&B Advertising

3 Christ Church Square, Dublin 8
Managing Director: Jeremy Crisp
t. +353 1 410 6666
f. +353 1 410 6699
e. jeremy.crisp@ddfhb.ie
w. www.ddfhb.ie
■ *An advertising agency.*

DHR Communications

157 Thomas Street, Dublin 8
General Enquiries: Paul Daly, Catherine
Heaney and Dermot Ryan
t. +353 1 707 1929
e. info@dhr.ie
w. www.dhr.ie
■ *A public relations company, providing media management, public affairs, campaign management, advocacy strategies, crisis management, event management, communications reviews, media training and project proposal development services.*

Dialogue—The Direct Response Brand Agency

2–5 Wellington Quay, Dublin 2
Managing Director: Michael Killeen
t. +353 1 662 2277
f. +353 1 662 2278
e. mkilleen@dialogue.ie
w. www.dialogue.ie
■ *Dialogue is a direct response branding agency, providing strategic planning, relationship, management programme management, database consultancy and on-line strategy services. Also provides direct response advertising and direct mail campaigns.*

DMA

Burlington House, Waterloo Lane,
Dublin 4
General Enquiries
t. +353 1 667 1144
f. +353 1 660 2204
e. dma@dma.ie
w. www.dma.ie
■ *A direct marketing agency, providing direct marketing and project management services.*

dpdesign

42 The Stables, Kill, Co. Kildare
General Enquiries: David Peckett
t. +353 86 892 5129/458 2152
e. david@dpdesign.bz
w. www.dpdesign.bz
■ *An advertising and design agency, providing coporate identity, campaigns, brochures and direct mail services.*

Drury Communications

1 Richview Office Park, Clonskeagh,
Dublin 14
Managing Director: Pauric McKeown
Public Affairs Director: Tim Collins
  t. +353 1 260 5000
  f. +353 1 260 5066
  e. tcollins@drurycom.com
  w. www.drurycom.com
■ *A public relations company, providing
strategic and tactical advice and implementation
services, specifically corporate public relations,
financial communications, internal communications, market research, public affairs, marketing
communications and presentation skills training services.*

Eason Advertising

66 Middle Abbey Street, Dublin 1
Director and General Manager: Marcus
McQuiston
Director: Rosanne Clarke
  t. +353 1 873 0477
  f. +353 1 873 0620
  e. executive@easonadvert.ie
  w. www.easonadvert.ie
E-mail addresses for individuals are in
the format firstname_lastname@eason-
advert.ie
■ *An advertising agency, specialising in
recruitment advertising, and including press,
print, radio, internet, outdoor, television and
brochure advertising services.*

Edelman

5th Floor, Huguenot House, 37 St
Stephen's Green, Dublin 2
General Manager (Dublin): Hugh
Gillanders
  t. +353 1 678 9333
  f. +353 1 661 4408
  e. dublin@edelman.com
  w. www.edelman.com/offices/
  europe/dublin
■ *A public relations company and part of the
worldwide Edelman Public Relations, providing
consumer marketing, corporate, financial,
health and technology communications services.*

Ergo Advertising Marketing

11 Northumberland Avenue, Dún
Laoghaire, Co. Dublin
General Enquiries
  t. +353 1 280 6630
  f. +353 1 280 6992
  e. ergoad@indigo.ie
■ *An advertising and marketing agency.*

Financial Dynamics Ireland

10 Merrion Square, Dublin 2
Paul McSharry
  t. +353 1 663 3600
  f. +353 1 663 3601
  e. paulmc@fdireland.ie
  w. www.fdireland.com
■ *A public relations company and part of the
FD International communications network,
providing corporate and financial public
relations, public affairs, crisis management,
consumer and brand communications, ICT
communications and community and social
responsibility.*

Fleishman-Hillard

15 Fitzwilliam Quay, Dublin 4
General Enquiries
  t. +353 1 618 8444
  f. +353 1 660 2123
  e. info@fleishmaneurope.com
  w. www.fleishmaneurope.ie
■ *A public relations company, providing marketing, technology, one-to-one, corporate and
financial, public affairs and health-care public
relations services.*

Focus Advertising

The Warehouse, 26A Mount Eden
Road, Dublin 4
General Enquiries: Daragh Cafferky
  t. +353 1 269 3322
  f. +353 1 269 3404
  w. www.in-advertising.com
■ *An advertising agency, providing advertising
and marketing services.*

Folio

9 Upper Mount Pleasant Avenue,
Dublin 6
General Enquiries: Eric Beasley and
Richard Callanan
t. +353 1 497 2741
f. +353 1 496 4032
e. info@folio.ie
w. www.folio.ie
■ *A copywriting agency, providing copy-writing, editing, proof-reading, ghost-writing and technical writing services.*

Gaffney McHugh Advertising

6 Lower Mount Street, Dublin 2
Managing Director: David McHugh
t. +353 1 676 4034
f. +353 1 661 3469
e. david@gaffneymchugh.ie
w. www.gaffneymchugh.ie
■ *An advertising agency in partnership with CSL Associates.*

Generator Marketing

Denshaw Marketing, Deshaw House,
121 Baggot St, Dublin 2
General Enquiries: Chris Small
t. +353 1 659 9403
e. coffee@generatormarketing.ie
w. www.generatormarketing.ie
■ *A marketing agency, providing strategy, creative, production, television, press, radio, direct mail and point-of-sale services.*
Team: Judith Gilsenan and John
Watson

Gibney Communications

Newmount House, 22–24 Lower
Mount Street, Dublin 2
General Enquiries: Ita Gibney
t. +353 1 661 0402
f. +353 1 661 0284
e. info@gibneycomm.ie
w. www.gibneycomm.ie
■ *A public relations company, providing corporate, technology and financial public relations services.*

Grey Helme

44 Serpentine Avenue, Dublin 4
Managing Director: Philip Sherwood
t. +353 1 634 9200
f. +353 1 660 7372
e. info@greyhelme.ie
■ *An advertising agency affiliated with Grey Worldwide, providing artwork studio, market research, marketing and public relations facilities, and television, press and media planning services.*
Chairman: Donald Helme
Media Director: Maureen Carrigan
Creative Director: John Carvill

GT Media (Dublin)

Castle House, Main Street,
Rathfarnham, Dublin 14
Joint Managing Directors: John
Gallagher and Liam Pender
CEO: Graham Taylor
t. +353 1 492 5515
f. +353 1 492 5521
e. jgallagher@gtmedia.ie
■ *An advertising agency, providing media advertising services.*
Directors: Jenny Taylor and Nicky
Sherry
Finance Controller: Noel Davey

Heneghan PR

54 Pembroke Road, Dublin 4
General Enquiries: Nigel Heneghan
t. +353 1 660 7395
f. +353 1 660 7588
e. info@hpr.ie
w. www.hpr.ie
■ *A public relations company, providing corporate, financial, ICT, telecommunications, environmental and industrial relations PR services, new company launches and plant openings, media relations, crisis and incident management, internal communications and community relations.*

Hibernia Advertising

The Graphics House, 12–17 Mark
Street, Dublin 2
Managing Director: Philip Nutley
t. +353 1 672 7533
f. +353 1 672 7520
w. www.hibernia-advertising.com
■ *An advertising agency, providing advertising
and public relations services.*

Hill and Knowlton

7 Fitzwilliam Street Lower, Dublin 2
General Enquiries: Kieran O'Byrne
t. +353 1 662 6930
f. +353 1 662 6944
e. kobyrne@hillandknowlton.com
w. www.hillandknowlton.com
■ *A public relations company and part of the
worldwide Hill and Knowlton group, providing
corporate and financial communications, consumer public relations, technology communications, environmental public relations and crisis
management services.*

HMG Advertising and Marketing

HMG House, 51 Clontarf Road,
Dublin 3
Contact: Bob McMahon
t. +353 1 853 1400
f. +353 1 853 1401
e. info@hmgadv.ie
■ *An advertising agency, providing advertising
and public relations services.*

Hopkins Communications

42 Patrick Street, Cork
Managing Director: Mark Hopkins
t. +353 21 427 2200
f. +353 21 427 1625
e. sales@hopkinscommunications.ie
w. www.hopkinscommunications.ie
■ *An advertising agency, providing advertising, public relations, design and event management services.*
Chairperson: Mary Hopkins
Account Manager: Niamh O'Sullivan
Graphic Designer: Claire Kerney

ICAN Interactive

The Malt House North, Grand Canal
Quay, Dublin 2
Managing Director: Shenda Loughnane
t. +353 1 677 0440
f. +353 1 677 0349
e. interact@ican.ie
w. www.ican.ie
■ *An advertising agency, providing media
planning, buying tracking and reporting, strategy
and concept development, design, copywriting,
art direction and web site design services.*
Creative Director: Flick Henderson
Business Development Director:
Siobhan Lavery
Account Director: Arlene Hanratty
Media Analyst: George Thomas
Web Developer: Torlogh O'Boyle
Web Designer: Alan Currie

ICE Cool

Fr Griffin Road, Galway
General Enquiries
t. +353 91 546 700
f. +353 91 585 070
e. icecool@icegroup.ie
w. www.icecool.ie
■ *An advertising and design company and
part of the ICE Group, providing graphic
design, web site development, advertising, logo
design, corporate identity, brand development
and integrated advertising campaigns.*

IDEA

5 Clarendon Mews, Lad Lane, Dublin 2
Managing Director: Ciaran Flanagan
t. +353 1 250 0050
f. +353 1 250 0087
e. info@idea.ie
w. www.idea.ie
■ *A marketing and communications agency,
providing marketing audits, focus group
research, survey research, strategic marketing
planning and project management services.*
Director: Hilary Morgan
Creative Director: Leon Gruizinga
Studio Manager: Barry O'Connor

Senior Creative Designer: Clare Hogan
Account Manager: Grace Kiernan

IMM Public Relations

278 Ryevale Lawns, Leixlip, Co. Kildare
Managing Director: Oisin O'Briain
t. +353 1 624 5640
m. +353 86 257 2497
e. imm@indigo.ie

■ *A public relations consultancy, specialising in motorsport public relations services.*

Impact Media

Unit 1, 1st Floor, Oranmore Business Park, Galway
Directors: Niall McGarry and Tom Lynskey
t. +353 91 788 370
f. +353 91 788 371
e. info@impactmedia.ie
w. www.impactmedia.ie

■ *An advertising agency, providing advertising, graphic design and corporate identity services.*

Account Manager: Helen Faherty
Graphics Manager: Mary O'Malley
Graphic Designers: Diarmuid McCormack and Sheila Flaherty
Information Technology and Technical Support: Emmet Macken

Info TV

Kilmacthomas Business Park, Union Road, Kilmacthomas, Co. Waterford
t. +353 51 294 900
m. +353 86 365 6972
f. +353 51 294 901
e. infotv@eircom.net
w. www.infotv.ie

■ *An advertising agency, providing plasma and LCD screens in shops and credit unions.*

Operations Manager: David Ridguard
Marketing Manager: Helen Ridguard
Graphic Designer: Brian Buckley

Initiative Dublin

7th Floor, Iveagh Court, 6–8 Harcourt Road, Dublin 2
General Enquiries: David Harland

t. +353 1 475 1895
f. +353 1 478 5226
e. dave.harland@ie.initiative.com
w. www.initiativemedia.com

■ *A media management company and part of Initiative Worldwide, providing advertising and public relations services.*

Interactive Return

5 Citygate, Bridge Street, Dublin 8
General Enquiries: Martin Murray
t. +353 1 672 9022
f. +353 1 679 2396
e. info@interactivereturn.com
w. www.interactivereturn.com

■ *An on-line marketing agency, providing search engine marketing, e-mail marketing, internet advertising, usability studies, web site design and development, and traffic analysis services.*

Irish International Group

17 Gilford Road, Sandymount, Dublin 4
Managing Director: Ian Young
t. +353 1 260 2000
f. +353 1 260 2111
w. www.iibbdo.com

■ *An advertising and marketing agency and part of BBDO Worldwide, providing advertising, design, direct marketing, integrated marketing communications, media, production, relationship marketing and sales promotion services.*

Email addresses for individuals are in the format firstnamefirstinitialoflastname@iibbdo.com

Account Director: Justin Cullen

Javelin/Young and Rubicam

Dawson House, 55 Dawson Street, Dublin 2
Managing Director: Joe Dobbin
t. +353 1 679 8770
f. +353 1 679 8798
e. info@javelin.ie
w. www.javelin.ie

■ *An advertising and marketing agency, providing advertising and marketing services.*

Creative Director: Conor Kennedy
Chairman: Paul Myers
Media Director: Ruth Payne
Client Services Director: Ken Ivory

JH Parker and Company

Parker House, 13 Adelaide Road,
Dublin 2
Managing Director: Kingsley Dempsey
  t. +353 1 478 3044
  f. +353 1 478 3862
  e. info@parker.ie
  w. www.parker.ie
■ *An advertising agency, providing advertising, marketing, media, design, promotions, direct mail and internet services.*
Director: Fiona Dempsey
Media Director: Elaine Shoebridge
Creative Director: John Feehan

Keating and Associates

19 Fitzwilliam Place, Dublin 2
General Enquiries: Pat Keating
  t. +353 1 662 0345
  f. +353 1 662 0346
  e. pat@keating.ie
  w. www.keating.ie
■ *A public relations company, providing corporate communications services.*

Larkin Partnership, The

23 Fitzwilliam Place, Dublin 2
Managing Director: Martin Larkin
  t. +353 1 611 0604
  f. +353 1 667 4270
  e. info@larkin.ie
  w. www.larkin.ie
■ *An advertising and strategic communications agency.*
Client Service Director: Niamh Kelly

Leo Burnett Associates

46 Wellington Road, Dublin 4
Managing Director: Shane McGonigle
  t. +353 1 668 9627
  f. +353 1 668 1341
  e. info@leoburnett.ie
  w. www.leoburnett.com

■ *An advertising agency and part of Leo Burnett Worldwide, providing market research, brand planning, brand idea development, multimedia campaign development and content creation, futures planning, and direct, interactive, promotional and shop marketing services.*
Client Service Director: Killian Flanagan
Creative Director: John Flynn

Lime Media Solutions

Pembroke House, 2 Pembroke Street,
Cork
General Enquiries
  t. +353 1850 272 829
  e. info@lime.ie
  w. www.lime.ie
■ *A strategic advertising and design company, providing corporate branding and literature design, web site development, web editing software, concept advertising, and advertising placement and production services.*

Louis Knowles and Associates

15 Willow Court, Cabinteely, Dublin 18
Managing Director: Louis Knowles
  t. +353 1 272 1419
  f. +353 1 272 1421
  e. louisknowles@eircom.net
■ *An advertising agency.*
Media Director: Anita Meehan

Marketing Works

Unit 7, Village Court, Portmarnock,
Co. Dublin
Managing Director: Brendan Hickey
  t. +353 1 846 1888
  f. +353 1 846 1901
  e. micworks@indigo.ie
■ *An advertising agency, providing radio and print advertising services.*
Creative Director: S. O'Connell
Direct Mail: W. Horkan
Media: B. Hickey

Marley Media

22 Ely Place, Dublin 2
Managing Director: Philip Marley
  t. +353 1 676 5884
  f. +353 1 662 2496

e. info@marleymedia.com
w. www.marleymedia.com

■ *A marketing and promotions agency.*

Account Manager: Audrey Mills
Creative Director: Paul Fox

Mary Crotty Public Relations

18 Clanwilliam Square, Dublin 2
General Enquiries: Mary Crotty and
Derek Sherwin

  t. +353 1 661 8777
  f. +353 1 661 9138
  e. pr@marycrottypr.ie
  w. www.marycrottypr.ie

■ *A public relations company, providing consumer services, tourism and film industry public relations and event management services.*

McCann Erickson

Hambleden House, 19–26 Lower
Pembroke Street, Dublin 2
Managing Director: Orlaith Blaney

  t. +353 1 676 6366
  e. firstname.lastname@europe.
mccann.com
  w. www.mccann-erickson.ie

■ *An advertising agency and part of McCann Erickson Worldwide Advertising (see Universal McCann listing).*

McConnells Advertising Service

McConnell House, Charlemont Place,
Dublin 2
Chairman: John Fanning

  t. +353 1 478 1544
  f. +353 1 478 0544
  e. info@mcconnells.ie
  w. www.mcconnells.ie

■ *An advertising agency, providing advertising, direct marketing, sales promotion, public relations, recruitment advertising, multimedia and production services.*

Managing Director: Jarlath Jennings
Deputy Managing Director: Greg Jones
Media Director: Fiona Scott
Creative Director: Gerry Kennedy
Account Directors: Gareth Kinsella,
Margaret Gilsenan and Pardaic Burns

MCM Communications

McConnell House, Charlemont Place,
Dublin 2
General Enquiries: Fiona Scott

  t. +353 1 417 7689
  e. fiona.scott@mcmcommunications.ie
  w. www.mcmcommunications.ie

■ *A media agency and part of McConnells Advertising Service, providing media planning services.*

Media Bureau

Nutley, Merrion Road, Dublin 4
Managing Director: Michael Bowles

  t. +353 1 283 8933
  f. +353 1 283 8260
  e. info@mediabureau.ie
  w. www.mediabureau.ie

■ *An advertising agency, providing advertising and public relations services.*

Directors: Martin Cody, John Priestly
and Ann Bowles

Mediacom

44 Serpentine Avenue, Dublin 4
Managing Director: Maureen Carrigan

  t. +353 1 634 9280
  f. +353 1 660 5309
  w. www.mediacomeurope.com

■ *An advertising agency, providing advertising planning and purchasing services.*

mediaedge:cia Ireland

6 Ely Place, Dublin 2
Joint Managing Directors: David Hayes
and Michael Quilty

  t. +353 1 669 0090
  f. +353 1 669 0099
  e. info.emea@mecglobal.com
  w. www.mediaedgecia.com

■ *An advertising agency and part of the worldwide mediaedge:cia network, providing communication channel planning and implementation, econometric modelling, research and consumer insight, strategic media planning, implementational planning, media investment management, digital consultancy and client management services.*

Account Executives: Erin Quinn and
Dave Bruen
Finance: Jane McAleese

Media Link

15 Windsor Place, Dublin 2
Managing Director: John Patten
  t. +353 1 662 2444
  f. +353 1 676 2242
  e. joe@medialink.ie
■ *An advertising agency, providing advertising sales services.*

Mediaworks

37 Fitzwilliam Place, Dublin 2
Managing Director: Paul Moran
  t. +353 1 661 0161
  f. +353 1 662 1208
  e. paul.mediaworks@owensddb.com
■ *An advertising agency.*
Account Director: Fiona O'Regan

Mercury Media

13 Meadow Court, Stepaside Park,
Stepaside, Dublin 18
General Enquiries: Sharon Lawless
  t. +353 1 294 5847
  e. sharon@mercurymedia.ie
  w. www.mercurymedia.ie
■ *An advertising agency.*

MindShare

3 Christ Church Square, Dublin 8
Chief Executive Officer: Bill Kinlay
  t. +353 1 415 0300
  f. +353 1 415 0333
  e. bill.kinlay@mindshareworld.com
  w. www.mindshareworld.com
■ *A full-service media company and part of the worldwide MindShare group, providing media investment management.*

Montague Communications

2–3 Prospect House, Prospect Road,
Dublin 9
General Enquiries: Patrick Montague
  t. +353 1 837 7960
  f. +353 1 837 7962

  e. info@montaguecomms.ie
  w. www.montaguecomms.ie
■ *A public relations company.*

MRM Design

Cloughvalley Industrial Estate,
Carrickmacross, Co. Monaghan
General Enquiries
  t. +353 42 969 2550
  f. +353 42 966 3933
  e. info@mrmdesign.net
  w. www.mrmdesign.net
■ *An advertising agency.*

MRPA Consultants

Barclay House, 6 Pembroke Place,
Dublin 2
General Enquiries: Ray Gordon
  t. +353 1 678 8099
  f. +353 1 678 8103
  e. mail@mrpa.ie
■ *A public relations company, providing corporate media relations and public affairs campaigns.*

MRPA Kinman

13 Lower Pembroke Street, Dublin 2
Directors: Tim Kinsella, Laurie
Mannix, Stephen O'Byrnes and Ray
Gordon
  t. +353 1 678 8330
  f. +353 1 678 8331
  e. info@mrpakinman.ie
  w. www.mrpakinman.ie
■ *A public relations company, providing strategic programme development, media relations, event management, public information programmes and lobbying services.*

Murray Consultants

Dartmouth House, 1 Grand Parade,
Dublin 6
Directors: Bláithín Boylan and Pauline
McAlester and Pat Walsh
  t. +353 1 498 0300
  f. +353 1 498 0344
  e. pr@murrayconsult.ie
  w. www.murrayconsult.ie

■ *A public relations company, providing media relations, financial public relations, public affairs, crisis management, event management, marketing communications and internal communications services.*

Neworld Group

9 Greenmount Avenue, Dublin 12
General Enquiries
t. +353 1 4165 600
f. +353 1 4165 621
e. post@neworld.ie
w. www.neworld.ie
■ *An advertising agency and part of the Neworld Group, providing design, promotional and marketing, strategic branding and product development, multimedia and web site development, and publishing and sales services.*
Design: Pat Kinsley
    e. pat@neworld.ie
Design and brand: Gary Gartland
    e. garyg@neworld.ie
Vision: David Jordan
    e. davidj@neworld.ie
Vision: Sabina Bonnici
    e. sabina@neworld.ie
Image: Rosemary Delaney
    e. rosemary@neworld.ie

Niamh Lehane Design and Advertising

17 Amiens Square, Dublin 1
General Enquiries: Niamh Lehane
t. +353 1 855 0857
f. +353 1 855 0857
e. nlehane@iol.ie
■ *An advertising and design agency.*

N Power PR International

1st floor, 10 Drogheda Street,
Balbriggan, Co. Dublin
General Enquiries: Nadia Power
t. +353 1 843 0380
f. +353 1 843 0381
■ *A public relations agency.*

Ocean Brand Opportunities

Garden Level, 56 Leeson Street Upper,
Dublin 4
Managing Director: Doug Baxter

t. +353 1 667 7000
f. +353 1 667 7007
e. info@oceangroup.ie
w. www.oceangroup.ie
■ *An advertising and marketing agency, providing branding, research, advertising, publishing, promotions, direct mail, event, sponsorships and digital services.*
Creative director: Roddy O'Leary

Ogilvy and Mather Advertising

6 Ely Place, Dublin 2
General Enquiries
t. +353 1 669 0000
f. +353 1 669 0019
w. www.ogilvy.com
■ *An advertising agency and part of Ogilvy and Mather Worldwide.*
Chair: J. P. Donnolly

O'Leary PR and Marketing

James House, 50 James's Place East,
Dublin 2
General Enquiries: Mari O'Leary
t. +353 1 678 9888
f. +353 1 676 5570
e. info@olearypr.ie
w. www.oleary.ie
■ *A public relations company, providing public relations and communications services.*

One Productions

3 Clare Street, Dublin 2
t. +353 1 678 4077
f. +353 1 678 4070
e. info@oneproductions.com
w. www.oneproductions.com
■ *A communications and digital media production agency, providing advertising, marketing and design, strategic planning and consultancy services.*

O'Sullivan Public Relations

Maryborough Lodge, Maryborough
Hill, Douglas, Cork
General Enquiries: Robin O'Sullivan
t. +353 1 21 489 1100
f. +353 1 21 489 1102

e. info@osullivanpr.ie
w. www.osullivanpr.ie
■ *A public relations company, providing community relations, internal and employee relations and media relations, particularly in the area of environmental planning permissions.*

O'Sullivan Ryan Advertising

23 Seapoint Avenue, Blackrock,
Co. Dublin
Managing Director: Ted O'Sullivan
　t. +353 1 663 6305
　f. +353 1 663 6312
　e. info@osr.ie
　w. www.osr.ie
■ *An advertising agency.*
Media Director: Bill Davis
Creative Director: Rachel Rowan

Outhouse Advertising

1 Potato Market, Carlow
Managing Director: Aoife Corcoran
　t. +353 59 913 7232
　f. +353 59 913 3449
　e. info@outhouseadvertising.net
　w. www.outhouseadvertising.net
■ *An advertising agency, providing washroom advertising services.*

Owens DDB

38 Fitzwilliam Place, Dublin 2
Managing Director: Mark Hogan
　t. +353 1 676 1191
　f. +353 1 676 1042
　e. info@owensddb.com
　w. www.owensddb.com
■ *An advertising agency, providing advertising, public relations and marketing services.*
Media Director: Paul Moran
Creative Director: Colin Murphy
Finance Director: Sean O'Sullivan

Padbury Advertising

105 Lower Baggot Street, Dublin 2
Managing Director: Mark Beggs
　t. +353 1 676 4001
　f. +353 1 676 7072
■ *An advertising agency.*

Paddy Meegan

Hollywood, Co. Wicklow
Writer, Composer and Producer: Paddy
Meegan
　t. +353 45 864 174
　f. +353 45 864 174
　e. pmeegan@indigo.ie
■ *A copywriter and music composer for radio, television and outdoor advertising.*
Personal Assistant: Libby Van
Cauwelaert

Paragon Design and Image Consultants

15 Oxford Lane, Dublin 6
General Enquiries
　t. +353 1 496 6004
　f. +353 1 498 2985
　e. paragon@clubi.ie
　w. www.paragondesign.ie
■ *A graphic design and advertising agency and part of Paragon Design International.*

Park Communications

85 Merrion Square, Dublin 2
General Enquiries: Seán O'Riordáin,
and Catherine Carey
　t. +353 1 676 5297
　f. +353 1 661 0028
　e. soriordain@parkpr.ie
　w. www.parkcommunications.com
■ *A public relations company and associate of Burson-Marsteller, providing corporate, technology, health-care, consumer and leisure sector public relations services.*

Paul Allen and Associates PR

4 Upper Mount Street, Dublin 2
Paul Allen
　t. +353 1 676 9575
　f. +353 1 676 9518
　e. info@prireland.com
　w. www.prireland.com
■ *A public relations company, providing reputation management, corporate public relations, consumer public relations, parliamentary affairs, ICT communications and event management services.*

Pearl and Dean

Bridgewater House, Islandbridge,
Dublin 15
Sales: Kathy O'Meara
t. +353 1 820 8896
m. +353 86 242 9901
e. kathy.omeara@pearlanddean.com
w. www.pearlanddean.com/ireland/home.html
■ *Provides cinema advertising sales.*

Pembroke Communications

16 Sir John Rogerson's Quay, Dublin 2
General Enquiries: Colm Cronin
t. +353 1 649 6486
f. +353 1 649 6487
e. firstname.lastname@pembrokec.com
w. www.pembrokec.com
■ *A public relations company and partner of Manning Selvage and Lee, providing a full range of communications services.*

Pierce Media and Advertising

The Black Church, St Mary's Place,
Dublin 7
Managing Director: Peadar Pierce
t. +353 1 830 0501
f. +353 1 830 0532
e. piercem@iol.ie
■ *An advertising agency.*
Media Director: Shane Casey

Power of Seven

17 Clyde Road, Dublin 4
General Enquiries
t. +353 1 667 1323
f. +353 1 667 1321
e. info@powerof7.com
w. www.powerof7.com
■ *A marketing and advertising agency, providing communications services.*
Creative Director: Phil Walsh
Client Services and Strategy: Carol Shaw and Jody Rolandson
Art Directors: Ben Dolan and John Fitzpatrick

New Media and Information
Technology: Robert Farrell

Primus Advertising and Marketing

Main Street, Fethard, Co. Tipperary
General Enquiries
t. +353 52 31 877
f. +353 52 31 483
e. rhenry@primus.ie
■ *An advertising and marketing agency.*

Proactive Group

Unit 3, Liosban Business Park, Tuam
Road, Galway
General Enquiries
t. +353 91 565 154
f. +353 91 569 008
e. info@proactive.ie
w. www.proactive.ie
■ *An advertising and marketing agency, providing branding and internet services.*
Internet Services
Branding: marketing@proactive.ie

Public Communications Centre

22 South Great George's Street,
Dublin 2
General Enquiries
t. +353 1 679 4173
f. +353 1 679 5409
e. info@pcc.ie
w. www.pcc.ie
■ *A national non-profit communications agency, assisting non-profit organisations with campaigning and communications in the areas of strategic communications, research, public education, public advocacy, fund-raising, and design and print.*

Pulse Group Ireland

25 Temple Lane, Dublin 2
Chief Executive: Ciaran O'Reilly
t. +353 1 633 0300
f. +353 1 633 0301
e. info@pulsegroup.com
w. www.pulsegroup.com
■ *An advertising agency and member of the Pulse Group, providing advertising,*

promotions, direct marketing, web design and management, events, design for print and brand and corporate identity services.
Head of Client Services: Richard Johnson
Account Director: Graham Nolan

Purple

27 Fitzwilliam Street Upper, Dublin 2
General Enquiries: Eoin Byrne and Karl Smyth
t. +353 1 632 8604
f. +353 1 632 8654
e. info@purpledesign.ie
w. www.purpledesign.ie
■ *An advertising agency, providing advertising and design services for all media.*

Q4 Public Relations

88 St Stephen's Green, Dublin 2
Directors: Jackie Gallagher, Angie Kinane, Martin Mackin and Gerry O'Sullivan
t. +353 1 475 1444
f. +353 1 475 1445
e. info@q4pr.ie
w. www.q4pr.ie
■ *A public relations and communications service company, established in June 2003 by the four directors.*

QMP Publicis (QMP D'Arcy)

16 Sir John Rogerson's Quay, Dublin 2
Managing Director: Tom Doherty
t. +353 1 649 6400
f. +353 1 649 6401
e. qmp-info@qmpdarcy.ie
w. www.qmppublicis.ie
■ *An advertising agency and part of D'Arcy Worldwide.*
Media Director: Richard Law
Creative Directors: Carol Lambert and Anton McClelland
Production Director: Dave Wright
Directors: Padraig Moran and Mike Keely

Quantum Advertising Group International

Mespil House, 37 Adelaide Road, Dublin 2
General Enquiries: Marion Mulhall
t. +353 1 231 4600
m. +353 86 819 0785
f. +353 1 231 5202
e. info@quantum-ad.com
w. www.quantum-ad.com
■ *An advertising agency catering to the Catholic Church, providing a range of advertising, design, production and communication services.*

Quantum Communications

20 Knocknacree Park, Dalkey, Co. Dublin
General Enquiries
t. +353 1 284 8933
f. +353 1 284 8932
■ *An advertising agency and part of Quantum Communications Group.*

Rapport Marketing Communications

49 Morehampton Road, Dublin 4
Managing Director: Tom Power
Director: Andrew Watchorn
t. +353 1 667 5666
f. +353 1 667 5587
e. info@rapport.ie
w. www.rapport.ie
■ *An advertising agency.*

Rational Decisions

44 Serpentine Avenue, Dublin 4
Managing Director: Philip Sherwood
t. +353 1 634 9200
f. +353 1 660 7372
■ *An advertising agency and part of the Helme Partnership, providing strategic services in direct marketing, CRM, internet design, virtual site hosting and web advertising.*

Reality Design and Marketing Consultants

Moycullen, Co. Galway
General Enquiries
t. +353 91 555 055
f. +353 91 555 515
e. info@realitydesign.ie
w. www.realitydesign.ie
■ *An advertising agency, providing graphic design, marketing and advertising services.*

Regional Advertising Associates

Hardiman House, 5 Eyre Square, Galway
General Enquiries
t. +353 91 569 094
■ *An advertising agency.*

Rothco

8 Castlewood Place, Rathmines, Dublin 6
General Enquiries
t. +353 1 491 4200
f. +353 1 491 4201
e. info@rothco.ie
w. www.rothco.ie
■ *A marketing and communications agency.*

Rubicon Advertising

22 Fitzwilliam Place, Dublin 2
Chief Executive Officer: Des O'Meara
t. +353 1 500 0680
f. +353 1 661 4779
e. firstinitiallastname@rubicon.ie
w. www.rubicon.ie
■ *An advertising agency, providing strategic planning, creative development, account management, media planning, web site advice and design and artwork services.*
Business Development Manager: Anne Marie English
Account Manager: Eoghan O'Meara

Setanta Communications

6 Fitzwilliam Street Lower, Dublin 2
General Enquiries: Michael Moloney
t. +353 1 676 2429
f. +353 1 676 2399

e. mail@setanta.ie
w. www.setanta.ie
■ *A public relations company and member of Europe on Line, providing media relations, crisis management and editorial services and the design and production of corporate web sites.*

Simpson Financial and Technology PR

Seafield House, 23 Seafield Road, Blackrock, Co. Dublin
General Enquiries: Ronnie Simpson
t. +353 1 260 5300
f. +353 1 260 5305
e. ronnie@simpsonftpr.ie
w. www.simpsonftpr.ie
■ *A public relations company, specialising in the high-tech sector and with a business, financial and media focus.*

Sites Media

26 Fitzwilliam Street Upper, Dublin 2
t. +353 1 662 6926
f. +353 1 662 8484
e. info@sitesmedia.ie
w. www.uniqueperspectives.ie
■ *Advertising panels.*

Slattery Communications

22 Merrion Square, Dublin 2
General Enquiries
Padraig Slattery
t. +353 1 661 4055
f. +353 1 661 4106
e. p.slattery@slatterycommunications.ie
w. www.slatterycommunications.ie
■ *A public relations company, providing corporate public relations, ICT, financial public relations, consumer public relations, sponsorship and sports management services.*

Southern Advertising and Marketing (Cork)

9 East Gate Avenue, East Gate Business Park, Little Island, Cork
Managing Director: Manus O'Callaghan
t. +353 21 431 3744
f. +353 21 431 3365

e. info@southernad.ie
w. www.southernad.ie

■ *An advertising agency. Also has an office in Limerick.*

Southern Advertising and Marketing (Limerick)

Killoran House, Catherine Place, Limerick
Account Directors: Kay McGuinness and Dave O'Hora
t. +353 61 310 286
f. +353 61 313 013
e. info@southernadlimk.com
w. www.southernad.ie

■ *An advertising agency. Also has an office in Cork.*

Account Executive: Brendan Doran

Spark Marketing Communications

100 O'Connell Street, Limerick
Marketing Director: Deirdre Corbett
t. +353 61 409 251
f. +353 61 409 270
e. info@sparkmarketing.ie
w. www.sparkmarketing.ie

■ *An advertising agency, providing media advertising, branding, direct mail, web design and project management services.*

Account Executive: Laura Carney

Spokesman Advertising Company

20 Lentisk Lawn, Dublin 13
General Enquiries
t. +353 1 847 7511

■ *An advertising agency.*

Stacey Marketing Services

27 Upper Fitzwilliam Street, Dublin 2
Managing Director: Ciaran Stacey
t. +353 1 274 2957
f. +353 1 632 8654
e. info@stacey.ie

■ *An advertising agency, providing advertising and marketing, and print and design services.*

Starcom-MediaVest Group

16 Sir John Rogerson's Quay, Dublin 2
Managing Director: Richard Law

t. +353 1 649 6445
f. +353 1 649 6446
e. media-info@mediavest.ie

■ *An advertising agency, providing media planning and buying services.*

Directors: Eddie O'Mahony, Cormac O'Shea, Padraig Moran, Aidan Greene and Nick Fletcher

Starfish

9 Semple Court, Capel Street, Dublin 1
General Enquiries
t. +353 1 878 8006
f. +353 1 872 9694
e. PROD33@icpc.ie
w. www.notlimitednyc.com/folio/starfish/resource.html

■ *A communications and media company, providing writing and editing, press releases, marketing and advertising copy, résumés, political and corporate literature, and academic reports.*

Stratus Marketing and Development

Unit 21, Waterford Business Park, Cork Road, Waterford
Managing Director: Johnathan Torrie
General Enquiries
t. +353 51 351 325
f. +353 51 351 326
e. stratus@iol.ie

■ *An advertising agency.*

Stuart Kenny Associates

Coolbracken House, Church Terrace, Bray, Co. Wicklow
Chief Executive: Stuart Kenny
t. +353 1 286 9138
f. +353 1 286 9138
e. skenny@indigo.ie

■ *An advertsing and marketing agency, providing planning, product development, advertising, public relations, promotions and direct response services.*

Student Link

22 Ely Place, Dublin 2
Managing Director: Philip Marley
t. +353 1 676 5884
f. +353 1 662 2496

e. slink@iol.ie
w. www.studentlink.ie

■ *A marketing and promotions company, specialising in the student market.*

Account Manager: Cher Engerer
Production Manager: Jean Slattery
Creative Director: Peter Queally
Account Manager: Audrey Mills

The Swift Agency

10 Orwell Road, Dublin 6
Managing Director: Donal Swift
t. +353 1 496 2788
f. +353 1 496 4491
e. swift@indigo.ie

■ *An advertising agency.*

Media Director: Graham Taylor
Creative Director: Pete Price

Text 100 International

PO Box 9410, Dublin 15
General Enquiries: Dan Halliwell
t. +353 1 815 4744
m. +353 86 859 3376
e. dan.halliwell@text100.com
w. www.text100.ie

■ *A public relations company, providing public relations and communications services, including corporate and product public relations, marketing communications, community relations, crisis management, internal communications and event management services.*

TMP Worldwide Advertising and Communications (Cork)

5 Albert Street, Cork
General Enquiries:
t. +353 21 431 8204
w. www.tmpw.ie

TMP Worldwide Advertising and Communications (Dublin)

Hillview House, Gilford Road, Dublin 4
t. +353 21 431 8204
w. www.tmpw.ie

■ *An advertising agency and part of TMP Worldwide, providing recruitment advertising,*

interactive communications and employer branding services.

Unique Perspectives Advertising

26 Fitzwilliam Street Upper, Dublin 2
General Enquiries
t. +353 1 662 6926
f. +353 1 662 8484
e. info@uniqueperspectives.ie
w. www.uniqueperspectives.ie

■ *An advertising and marketing agency, providing research, marketing and strategic consultancy services.*

Universal McCann

Hambledon House, 19–26 Lower Pembroke Street, Dublin 2
General Enquiries: Martina Stenson
t. +353 1 676 7393
f. +353 1 676 7117
e. martina_stenson@europe.mccann.com
w. www.universalmccann.com

■ *A media-buying agency and part of the worldwide Universal McCann group.*

Vision Advertising

108 Upper Leeson Street, Dublin 4
Managing Director: Michael Shannon
t. +353 1 667 1511
f. +353 1 667 1256
e. vision@indigo.ie

■ *An avertising agency.*

Account Executive: Emer Mordaunt

Walsh Public Relations

Huband House, 16 Upper Mount Street, Dublin 2
General Enquiries: Jim Walsh
t. +353 1 661 3515
f. +353 1 661 4769
e. info@walshpr.ie
w. www.walshpr.ie

■ *A public relations company, providing media relations and monitoring, sponsorship, marketing communications and crisis management services.*

Weber Shandwick Ireland

2–4 Clanwilliam Terrace, Grand Canal
Quay, Dublin 2
Joint Managing Directors: Mary
McCarthy and Siobhán Molloy
  t. +353 1 676 0168
  t. +353 1 676 5241
  e. smolloy@webershandwick.com
  w. www.webershandwick.ie
■ *A public relations company and part of
Weber Shandwick Worldwide, providing corporate, financial, technology, public affairs, consumer and health-care public relations services.*

Wilson Hartnell Public Relations

5 Ely Place, Dublin 2
General Enquiries: Roddy Guiney
  t. +353 1 669 0030
  f. +353 1 669 0039
  e. roddy.guiney@ogilvy.com
■ *A public relations company, providing
strategic communications, consumer public relations, financial public relations, corporate communications, public affairs, government relations, sponsorship, media relations planning,
product launches, crisis management, event
management, research and monitoring, food
and health public relations and technology
public relations services.*

Young Euro RSCG

64 Lower Leeson Street, Dublin 2
Managing Director: Brian Hayes
  t. +353 1 614 5300
  f. +353 1 661 1992
  e. info@youngeuroscg.ie
  w. www.youngeuroscg.ie
■ *An advertising agency, providing advertising
and direct marketing services.*
Finance Director: Peter O'Brien
Creative Director: Tony St Ledger
Media Director: Conor Murphy
Account Director: Tony Caravousanos

Zebedee Marketing

1 Coachhorse Lane, The Square, Main
Street, Midleton, Co. Cork
General Enquiries
  t. +353 21 463 3777
  f. +353 21 463 3056
  e. enquiries@zebedeemarketing.com
  w. www.zebedeemarketing.com
■ *A design, advertising and marketing company.*

ZenithOptimedia Ireland

3rd Floor, Molyneaux House, Bride
Street, Dublin 8
Chairman: Claire Nardone
  t. +353 1 480 4444
  f. +353 1 480 4455
  w. www.zenithoptimedia.ie
■ *An advertising and communications agency
and part of ZenithOptimedia media services
group, providing advertising and communication services.*
  firstname_lastname@zenithmedia.ie
Managing Director: Shay Keany
Director: Larry Neary

Northern Ireland

Telephone numbers in Northern Ireland have the prefix 048 if dialled from the Republic and 004428 if dialled from elsewhere.

Affinity

mxbrandcom, 9 Upper Crescent, Belfast BT7 1NT
Account Director: Karen Brady
t. +44 28 9031 2948
f. +44 28 9023 1777
e. info@affinitycreative.co.uk
w. www.affinitycreative.co.uk
■ *An advertising and marketing agency.*
Creative Director: Kevin McAllister

AndersonSprattGroup (Belfast Office)

Anderson House, Holywood Road, Belfast BT4 2GU
General Enquiries
t. +44 28 9080 2000
f. +44 28 9080 2001
e. info@andersonspratt.com
w. www.andersonspratt.com
■ *An advertising agency, providing advertising, design, public relations, new media, direct marketing, research and consultancy services, and a recruitment advertising practice.*

AndersonSprattGroup (Holywood Office)

Holywood House, Innis Court, Holywood, Co. Down BT18 9HF
General Enquiries
t. +44 28 9042 3332
f. +44 28 9042 7730
e. info@andersonspratt.com
w. www.andersonspratt.com
■ *An advertising agency, providing advertising, design, public relations, new media, direct marketing, research and consultancy services, and a recruitment advertising practice.*

AV Browne Advertising

46 Bedford Street, Belfast BT2 7GH
Managing Director: George Lavery
t. +44 28 9032 0663
f. +44 28 9024 4279
e. info@avb.co.uk
w. www.avb.co.uk
■ *An advertising agency, providing advertising, media placement, interactive media, event management, recruitment advertising and public relations services.*
Client Services and Media Director: Sam McIlveen
Senior Advertising Executive: Michael Stewart
Creative Director: Mike Fleming

Citigate Smarts

Citigate House, 157–159 High Street, Holywood, Co. Down BT18 9HU
General Enquiries: Leontia Fetherston and Pippa Arlow
t. +44 28 9039 5500
f. +44 28 9039 5600
e. hello@citigatesmartsni.co.uk
w. www.citigatesmartsni.co.uk
■ *A public relations company and part of Incepta, providing corporate relations, public affairs and public issue management, reputation management, crisis management, consumer public relations, publications and design, event management, sponsorship and new media services.*

Coey Advertising Company

Victoria Lodge, 158 Upper Newtownards Road, Belfast BT4 3EQ
Managing Director: Ivor Coey
t. +44 28 9047 1221
f. +44 28 9047 1509
e. info@coeyadvertising.co.uk
w. www.coeyadvertising.co.uk
■ *An advertising agency, providing corporate identity, graphic design, exhibition design, art direction, print buying, television concepts, illustration, photography, planning and event management services.*
Studio Manager: Sean Hartey

Des Bingham Associates

3 Windslow Gardens, Carrickfergus,
Co. Antrim BT38 9AU
Managing Director: Des Bingham
t. +44 28 9336 8157
f. +44 28 9336 8157
e. info@desbinghamassociates.com
w. www.desbinghamassociates.com
■ *An advertising agency and contact for
PrimairSites, a specialist airport advertising
specialist company.*
Director: Chris Bingham

FireIMC

10 Dargan Crescent, Duncrue Road,
Belfast BT3 9JP
Joint Chief Executive Officers
Tim McKane and David Mackey
t. +44 28 9077 4388
f. +44 28 9077 6906
e. info@fireimc.com
w. www.fireimc.com
■ *An advertising agency, providing advertis-
ing, public relations and design services.*
Operations Director: Andy Rice
Media Director: Stephen Lamb
Public Relations Director: Andrew
McAteer
Creative Director: Adrian Power

Future Image

26 Church Road, Holywood,
Co. Down BT18 9BU
Chairman: Rosemary Hamilton
t. +44 28 9042 3314
f. +44 28 9042 4773
e. newsdesk@futureimage.co.uk
w. www.futureimage.co.uk
■ *A public relations agency, providing press
and media liaison, business-to-business, crisis
management and training, event management
and lobbying services.*
Managing Director: Sally Gardiner

GCAS Group

Russell Court, 38–52 Lisburn Road,
Belfast BT9 6AA

General Enquiries
t. +44 28 9055 7700
f. +44 28 9024 5741
e. advertising@gcasgroup.com
w. www.gcasgroup.com
■ *A group with separate advertising, design,
networks, public relations and sales promotions
agencies.*

Genesis Advertising

7 Crescent Gardens, Belfast BT7 1NS
Chairman: Bill Trimble
t. +44 28 9031 3344
f. +44 28 9031 2245
e. info@genesis-advertising.co.uk
w. www.genesis-advertising.co.uk
■ *An advertising, marketing and communications agency and part of the McConnell Group.*
Managing Director: Peter Stark
Media Coordinator: Clare Daly

GM Consultants

26 Banbridge Road, Dromore,
Co. Down BT25 1NE
Chief Executive: Lorraine Curran
t. +44 28 9269 8505
f. +44 28 9269 9997
e. info@gmconsultants.co.uk
w. www.gmconsultants.co.uk
■ *An advertising and corporate communications agency, providing corporate recruitment
and human resource, planning and strategic,
sales and lobbying services.*

Jelly Communications

24 College Gardens, Belfast BT9 6BS
General Enquiries: Keith Murray
t. +44 28 9066 3663
f. +44 28 9066 3600
e. info@jellycommunications.com
w. www.jellycommunications.com
■ *An advertising and communications agency,
providing planning, design, television, radio,
print and digital services.*

Levy McCallum Advertising Agency

22 Great Victoria Street, Belfast
BT2 7BA
Managing Director: John McCallum

t. +44 28 9031 9220
f. +44 28 9031 9221
e. levymccallum.bel@dnet.co.uk
w. www.levymccallum.co.uk
■ *An advertising agency, providing mixed media campaigns and post-campaign analysis services. Offices are in Belfast, Glasgow and Edinburgh.*

Lyle Bailie International
31 Bruce Street, Belfast BT2 7JD
David Martin and Robert Lyle
t. +44 28 9033 1044
f. +44 28 9033 1622
e. directors@lylebailie.com
w. www.lylebailie.com
■ *Specialists in attitude and behaviour change monitoring, providing research to pinpoint the psychological triggers needed to influence attitudes and perceptions.*

McCann Erickson
31 Bruce Street, Belfast BT2 7JD
General Enquiries
t. +44 28 9033 1044
f. +44 28 9033 1622
e. infobelfast@europe.mccann.com
w. www.mccann-belfast.com
■ *An advertising agency and part of McCann Erickson Worldwide Advertising.*

Morrow Communications
Hanwood House, Pavilions Office Park, Kinnegar Drive, Holywood, Co. Down BT18 9JQ
General Enquiries: Peter Morrow
t. +44 28 9039 3837
f. +44 28 9039 3830
e. mail@morrowcommunications.co.uk
w. www.morrowcommunications.co.uk
■ *A public relations company, providing business-to-business public relations, marketing communications, public affairs, lobbying, and sponsorship management and crisis management services.*

PrimairSites
3 Windslow Gardens, Carrickfergus, Co. Antrim BT38 9AU

General Enquiries
t. +44 28 9336 6999
f. +44 28 9336 8157
e. info@primairsites.com
w. www.primairsites.com
■ *An advertising agency, specialising in airport advertising.*

RLA Group
86 Lisburn Road, Belfast BT9 6AF
CEO: Simon Dodd
t. +44 28 9066 4444
f. +44 28 9068 3497
e. info@rla.co.uk
w. www.rla.co.uk
■ *An advertising agency.*
Managing Director: David McIlwaine

TDP Advertising
76 University Street, Belfast BT7 1HE
Chairman: Robert S. Hood
t. +44 28 9032 2882
f. +44 28 9033 2727
e. mail@tdpadvertising.co.uk
w. www.tdpadvertising.co.uk
■ *An advertising agency, providing advertising, design, media and marketing services.*
Media Director: Joanne Brown

Walker Communications
The Old Post Office, 43 High Street, Holywood, Co. Down BT18 9AB
General Enquiries: Catherine McKeown
t. +44 28 9042 5555
f. +44 28 9042 1222
e. mail@walkercommunications.co.uk
w. www.walkercommunications.co.uk
■ *An advertising agency, providing advertising, design, event management and web services.*

Weber Shandwick Northern Ireland
425 Holywood Road, Belfast BT4 2GU
Managing Director: Brenda Boal
t. +44 28 9076 1841
e. bboal@webershandwick.com
w. www.webershandwick.co.uk

11

MEDIA INSTITUTIONS, SERVICES AND PROFESSIONAL ORGANISATIONS: REGULATING FOR CHOICE

Helen Shaw

One of the hot topics in the media world is regulation. It may not sound exciting, but regulation can be a make-or-break issue. In the newspaper sector, the debate has centred on the creation of a Press Council. In broadcasting, major changes are ahead with the creation of the proposed Broadcasting Authority of Ireland (BAI), which was announced at the end of 2002. The BAI will replace the present broadcasting regulator, the Broadcasting Commission of Ireland (BCI), and is expected to combine its regulatory role over the independent broadcasting sector with the duties of the RTÉ Authority, the government-appointed non-executive board that regulates the public broadcasting company, RTÉ. RTÉ has opposed the change and continues to lobby against it.

In Ireland, media regulation has traditionally focused on the broadcasting sphere. This reflects the fact that the spectrum carrying radio and television programmes is limited and belongs to the public. While spectrum limitations are not so much an issue in a digital age, Ireland is still a long way behind its European partners in terrestrial digital broadcasting. After a failed attempt to introduce digital terrestrial television (DTT) in 2001, Ireland now has the second-highest penetration of digital television in Europe, but it is broadcast via satellite and cable, rather than through a national DTT network. The Government has now moved to create a digital TV pilot in Dublin.

Media policy in Ireland has traditionally dealt with content regulation. As the airwaves belong to the public, public service duties and obligations apply, even to commercial broadcasters. From the Broadcasting Act (1988), which broke the RTÉ monopoly and introduced a framework for independent television and radio (although independent television took more than ten years to appear), commercial broadcasters have received their broadcasting licence free of charge, but with defined obligations (such as a requirement to broadcast 20% news and current affairs on commercial radio). The initial independent regulator, the Independent Radio and Television Commission (IRTC), became the BCI following the broadcasting legislation of 2001, which also gave the BCI expanded powers in regulating advertising code among all broadcasters, including RTÉ.

By the end of 2002, following the Forum on Broadcasting (a government-appointed ad hoc body of experts that reported on the future of Irish broadcasting), the then Minister for Communications, Dermot Ahern, announced the creation of a new regulator—the BAI—which would integrate content regulation in both the independent and the public sector. This new body is intended to replace the BCI and to increase powers over the regulation of broadcasting, making it more accountable to the public. The creation of the BAI will mean a consolidation in broadcasting legislation (from the 1960 RTÉ legislation to the Broadcasting Acts of 1988 and 2001) and the formation of a regulatory framework for future digital media, as well as for the existing structures of public and independent radio and television. RTÉ's Director-General, Cathal Goan, has expressed opposition to the BCI becoming the new regulator and RTÉ maintains that public and private broadcasting should be regulated separately.

The issues behind regulation: citizens and consumers

At the BCI annual conference at the end of 2004, a leading advertiser stood up and called for an end to both regulation and regulators. What had particularly irked the advertising industry was the BCI's new code on advertising aimed at children. The Broadcasting Act (2001) had directed the BCI to develop the code, and, after lengthy and detailed consultation, the BCI introduced it. The advertising industry was obviously not keen on this attempt to curb its business, but the issue that was raised was a difficult one: the Children's Advertising Code and a future code for 'taste and decency' set content regulation on a national basis, yet the media in Ireland offer global choices. Although the BCI code was the result of extensive consultation, in reality it affects only terrestrial broadcasters and has no direct impact on transnational television. Some 80% of Irish homes receive transnational television. While Irish channels, from RTÉ to TV3, do extremely well in audience figures, half the television market is with transnational television.

The issue of regulation in a global environment requires pan-European if not international responses in order to set minimum standards and requirements. National regulators need to have more co-ordinated actions throughout Europe in order to affect content. For advertisers or others who are anti-regulation, the issue of content regulation is seen as over-interference in the market. Yet state media policy and regulation strives for a balance between the interests of the publics and the interests of the consumer and the market. A healthy competitive market can provide better choices for consumers, but in entertainment and information there is the added issue of public interest. For this to be served, diversity (a wide range of content) and plurality (a wide range of suppliers) are required.

Another contentious issue is that of media ownership. Many business interests see no need for ownership regulation, but in Europe most states apply some form of control of media ownership. This reflects the view that diversity and plurality are often best provided by ensuring that there are at least three major media competitors in any market. The development of digital technology and the opportunity for new choices has, in some cases, been seen as the end of regulation. It was certainly used to justify deregulation measures in both the UK and US media markets. However, the digital arena and new media sphere opens up just as much potential for media monopolies as traditional broadcasting and press does. In Ireland, both the BCI and the Competitions Authority have a role in media ownership controls, as media mergers are required to pass through the Competitions Authority. Here the view has been that some level of ownership concentration may have a positive factor on the quality of the independent media market. However, Irish audiences need to receive diverse choices that reflect their own culture, rather than simply getting repackaged offerings made by global markets.

The integrated regulator in the UK (Ofcom), which was created in 2003, states that it serves the interests of the 'citizen-consumer'—as if the interests of both are the same. The delicate work of regulating the media shows that not only can the interests of citizens and consumers be different but also they may be in conflict. Citizen interests are often long-term and reflect an attempt to be of benefit to a whole community (as with the

Children's Advertising Code). Consumer interests are usually short-term and driven more by individuals or single organisations. There is a great Irish example of where the interests of the two differ: the plastic bag levy. When the levy was introduced some years ago, both consumers and retailers resisted it, yet who could deny that the levy was in the long-term not in the best interests of both parties? In broadcasting regulation, putting the citizen first should mean that the lowest level of the marketplace does not dominate.

Regulating broadcasting and new media

The idea of having the regulation of broadcasting separate from the regulation of new media and the internet now seems out of date. In Australia the broadcasting and internet regulation bodies have been combined, and in other countries broadcasting content and film classification regulations have been merged. Content regulation needs to reflect how life and technology are changing in a world where television is as likely to be delivered to mobile hand-held sets as it is to a flat screen in the corner. While tight controls may be more difficult in a new media environment, a holistic approach to regulation should see content as the focus of regulation, regardless of how and where it is delivered. It seems strange, for example, that we can have tight controls on television advertisements aimed at children but little or no controls on internet advertisements or online content aimed at children. Children are as likely to be found in front of a web browser as a television set. The trend in regulation is towards integration. As convergence really begins to hit home, the limits of regulation may become apparent. Still, it is essential that we adopt transnational and multimedia approaches to regulation and media literacy.

The public and media institutions

The Department of Communications, Marine and Natural Resources is the government authority for media policy in the Republic, with responsibility for broadcasting and telecommunications. The department maintains an excellent web site, with all reports and public consultation processes available on line (see www.dcmnr.gov.ie). Telecommunications regulation and spectrum management are covered by Comreg, which also has an excellent, informative web site, with lots of up-to-date data on telecommunications, including digital television and broadband (see www.comreg.ie).

The public has access to several accountability mechanisms, including the Broadcasting Complaints Commission (BCC), which is an independent, statutory body handling the public interest in broadcasting content and advertising. RTÉ has its own complaints process and established an Audience Council in January 2004—an appointed audience body that advises the RTÉ Authority and is designed to improve RTÉ's accountability to the public. The concept of audience councils is becoming popular, not just in Ireland but throughout Europe, as both states and the electronic media seek ways of improving relationships with the public. Complaints relating to independent broadcasters can now be referred to the BCI, which is responsible for the monitoring of that sector's adherence to codes. A new European initiative, the European Association for Viewers' Interests (EAVI; see www.eavi.org) is designed to promote the public's interest in the electronic media. If anything, media public interest groups are likely to grow and develop in the future.

Then there is the office of the Ombudsman, which regulates the Freedom of Information Act and ensures that the public has access to information and redress from public and statutory bodies. While the Freedom of Information legislation has been a welcome development, putting the public's right to know on the policy agenda, the Government's decision in 2003 to introduce charges for queries has led to a dramatic reduction in the public's use of the legislation. In RTÉ the recorded use of such queries fell by 70% in the six months following the charges; and while there has been a marked increase by the public in the use of the BCC procedures it is clear that the levy on Freedom of Information queries, at present €7 per query, has reduced the impact of the legislation.

In late June 2005, the Minister for Justice, Michael McDowell, promised the long-awaited Defamation Bill by the autumn. He confirmed that the new bill, aimed at reforming Irish libel law (see the background in Chapter 2 Newspapers), would also establish a Press Council, a Press Ombudsman and a Press Code of Standards. He maintained that the new council would be independent and a 'poodle' of neither the media nor the State. But according to Mark Brennock in *The Irish Times*, 25 June 2005, many Government ministers want a privacy protection law before they will concede ground to newspapers on libel reform, reflecting the level of bitterness many of them hold towards the Irish tabloids.

A&L Goodbody International

Financial Services Centre, North Wall,
Dublin 1
Contact: Paul White
t. +353 1 649 2000
f. +353 1 649 2649
e. law@algoodbody.ie or
p.white@algoodbody.ie
w. www.algoodbody.ie
■ *This international law firm has represented several Irish newspapers. It provides a wide range of legal services to individuals, production companies and Government and industry bodies.*

Actors and Movers

13 Ballyfermot Drive, Dublin 10
Halina Frodist
t. +353 1 625 9760
e. actorsandmovers@iol.ie
■ *This is a casting agency.*

AIB Investment Managers

AIB Investment House, Percy Place,
Dublin 4
Brian Morrison
t. +353 1 661 7077
f. +353 1 660 2278
e. brian.g.morrison@aib.ie
w. www.aib.ie
■ *This division of AIB provides investment service and advice for the film industry.*

Anglo Irish Bank Operation

18–21 St Stephen's Green, Dublin 2
Michael O'Sullivan
t. +353 1 616 2170
f. +353 1 631 0096
e. michaelosullivan@angloirishbank.ie
w. www.angloirishbank.com
■ *This bank provides financial services and business advice to companies in the film industry.*

Arthur Cox

Earlsfort Centre, Earlsfort Terrace,
Dublin 2
Media Lawyers: Colin Kavanagh and
Mary Swords

t. +353 1 618 0000
e. colin.kavanagh@arthurcox.com;
mary.swords@arthurcox.com
w. www.arthurcox.com
■ *This large firm is one of the specialist teams of media lawyers in Ireland. The group advises on the full range of issues governing all aspects of content provision for the media and entertainment industry, including films, television, music, radio, production finance, distribution, licensing, talent, advertising and publishing law, defamation and broadcasting regulation.*

Assets

28 The Basement, Lower Leeson
Street, Dublin 2
Derek Daniels
t. +353 1 676 0443
f. +353 1 661 5104
e. assetsagency@eircom.net
w. www.assetsmodels.com
■ *This is an agency for actors and models.*

BOI Business Banking

40 Mespil Road, Dublin 4
Manager (Tax Unit): Andrew Cullen
t. +353 1 665 3400
f. +353 1 665 3481
e. andrew.cullen@boimail.com
w. www.bankofireland.ie
■ *This firm can help media companies with taxation issues.*

Broadcasting Commission of Ireland (BCI)

2–5 Warrington Place, Dublin 2
Chief Executive: Michael O'Keeffe
t. +353 1 676 0966
f. +353 1 676 0948
e. mokeeffe@bci.ie
w. www.bci.ie
■ *This statutory body is responsible for enforcing several areas of broadcasting legislation, including licensing independent broadcasting services and developing codes and rules for programming and advertising. The BCI also monitors broadcasting institutions to ensure*

that licence-holders comply with their contracts. It also undertakes research in the broadcasting field.

Director of Broadcasting and Deputy Chief Executive: Celene Craig
e. ccraig@bci.ie
Executive Officer, Secretarial: Sinéad Owen
e. sowens@bci.ie
Executive Officer, Broadcasting: Brian Furey
e. bfurey@bci.ie
Executive Officer, Broadcasting: Patricia Kelly
e. pkelly@bci.ie
Executive Officer: Joe Lynch
e. jlynch@bci.ie
Research Officer: Ruth-Blandina Quinn
e. rquinn@bci.ie
Broadcasting Standards Officer: Margaret Tumelty
e. mtumelty@bci.ie
Senior Executive Engineer: Roger Woods
e. rwoods@bci.ie
Director of Engineering: Neil O'Brien
e. nobrien@bci.ie
Director of Corporate Services: Bernard Mullarkey
e. bmullarkey@bci.ie
Head of Broadcasting: Ciarán Kissane
e. ckissane@bci.ie
Executive Officer, Information: Andrew Robinson
e. arobinson@bci.ie
Broadcasting Fund Scheme Officer: Stephanie Comey
e. s.comey@bci.ie
Information Officer: Aoife Clabby
e. a.clabby@bci.ie
Chairman of the Board (Senior Counsel): Conor J. Maguire
Board Member (Journalist): John Waters

Board Member (Director, Ashfield College): Joe Griffin
Board Member (Chairman, Dublin South Community Radio, and National President, Credit Union Managers' Institute): John O'Brennan
Board Member (Director, Dundalk Institute of Technology): Tom Collins
Board Member (Chairperson, National Disability Authority and Director, Rehab Group): Angela Kerins
Board Member (CEO, 2003 Special Olympics World Summer Games): Mary Davis
Board Member (Director, Southern Advertising Agency): Kay McGuinness
Board Member (Senior Partner, Accenture): Vivenne Jupp
Board Member (Journalist, Barrister): Mary Kerrigan

Broadcasting Complaints Commission (BCC)

2–5 Warrington Place, Dublin 2
Chairperson: Oonah McCann
t. +353 1 676 1097
f. +353 1 676 0948
e. info@bcc.ie
w. www.bcc.ie

■ *This independent statutory body considers and adjudicates on complaints from viewers or listeners about programmes and advertisements broadcast on radio or television. It deals with complaints about, among other things, current affairs impartiality, taste and decency, law and order, privacy and slander.*

Board Members: Joseph Brady, Kay Cogan-Daly, Gerry Collison, Christy Cooney, Elizabeth Linnane, David Main, Brenda O'Hanlon and Pierce O'Malley.

Castaway Actors' Agency

30–31 Wicklow Street, Dublin 2
Chairman: Steve Blout
t. +353 1 671 9264
f. +353 1 671 9133
e. castaway@clubi.ie

w. www.irish-actors.com

■ *This is a non-profit organisation aimed at increasing the influence of individual actors over the professional management of their careers.*

Commission for Communications Regulation (ComReg)

Abbey Court, Irish Life Centre, Lower Abbey Street, Dublin 1

Commissioner: Isolde Goggin

t. +353 1 804 9600
f. +353 1 804 9680
e. info@comreg.ie
w. www.comreg.ie

■ *This regulatory authority is responsible for the electronic communications industry, which includes telecommunications, radiocommunications and broadcasting transmission, and the postal service.*

Public Affairs Manager: Tom Butler

t. +353 1 804 9639
f. +353 1 804 9680
e. tom.butler@comreg.ie

Competition Authority

Parnell House, 14 Parnell Square, Dublin 1

Chair: John Fingleton

t. +353 1 804 5400
f. +353 1 804 5401
e. chair@tca.ie and info@tca.ie
w. www.tca.ie

■ *This statutory body's remit is to ensure that competition works well for consumers throughout the economy. It also has powers to enforce competition law as well as to adjudicate on mergers.*

Press and Communications Officer: Mark Garrett

t. +353 1 804 5406
e. mg@tca.ie

Department of Communications, Marine and Natural Resources

29–31 Adelaide Road, Dublin 2

Secretary General: Brendan Tuohy

t. +353 1 678 2000
f. +353 1 678 2449

e. brendan.tuohy@dmcr.ie
w. www.marine.gov.ie

■ *This Government department is responsible for policy and legislation regarding communications and broadcasting.*

Deputy Secretary-General: Sara White

e. sara.white@dmcr.ie

Minister: Noel Dempsey TD

e. minister@dmcr.ie

Assistant Principal (Broadcasting): Sheila Clifford

t. +353 1 678 2123
e. Sheila.Clifford@dmcr.ie

Assistant Secretary (Communications Sector): Eamonn Molloy

e. eamonn.molloy@dmcr.ie

Principal Officer (Communications): Niall O'Donnchu

t. +353 1 678 3171
e. niall.odonnchu@dmcr.ie

Enterprise Ireland

Glasnevin, Dublin 9

Chief Executive Officer: Frank Ryan

t. +353 1 808 2000
f. +353 1 808 2802
w. www.enterprise-ireland.com

■ *This national organisation is responsible for Ireland's industry and driving the country's economic development.*

European Journalism Centre

Avenue Céramique 50, 6221 KV Maastricht, Netherlands

t. +31 43 325 40 30
f. +31 43 321 26 26
e. eu4journalists@ejc.nl
w. wwweu4journal.com

■ *This is a comprehensive information resource for journalists.*

Farrell Grant Sparks

Molyneux House, Bride Street, Dublin 8

General Enquiries

t. +353 1 418 2000
f. +353 1 418 2044
w. www.fgs.ie

■ *An accountancy, finance and insurance company, with media clients.*

Forfás

Wilton Park House, Wilton Place,
Dublin 2
Enterprise Division Head: Brian Cogan
t. +353 1 607 3000
f. +353 1 607 3030
e. info@forfas.ie
w. www.forfas.ie
■ *This statutory body deals with enterprise, trade, science, technology and innovation.*

Institute of Advertising Practitioners in Ireland

8 Upper Fitzwilliam Street, Dublin 2
Information Manager: John Holohan
t. +353 1 676 5991
f. +353 1 661 4589
e. john@iapi.com
w. www.iapi.com
■ *This is the representative body for the advertising industry in Ireland.*

Irish Business and Employers' Confederation (IBEC)

Confederation House, 84–86 Lower
Baggot Street, Dublin 2
Director General: Turlough O'Sullivan
t. +353 1 605 1500
f. +353 1 638 1647
e. info@ibec.ie
w. www.ibec.ie
■ *This national employers' body comprises ICT Ireland and the Telecommunications and Internet Federation, which cover the audio-visual sector.*

Irish Recorded Music Association

IRMA House, 1 Corrig Avenue, Dún
Laoghaire, Co. Dublin
Gaelle Corley
t. +353 1 280 6571
f. +353 1 280 6579
e. info@irma.ie
w. www.irma.ie
■ *This is a non-profit association set up by record companies and companies carrying on associated trades in the Republic. Among its roles are lobbying the Government and fighting piracy.*

Irish Small and Medium Enterprises Association (ISME)

17 Kildare Street, Dublin 2
Chief Executive: Mark Fielding
t. +353 1 662 2755
f. +353 1 661 2157
e. info@isme.ie
w. www.isme.ie
■ *This body represents small and medium-sized enterprises.*

Mason, Hayes and Curran

6 Fitzwilliam Square, Dublin 2
John Kettle and Kevin Hoy
t. +353 1 614 5000
f. +353 1 614 5001
e. jkettle@mhc.ie; khoy@mhc.ie
w. www.mhc.ie
■ *This legal practice, with business, governmental and institutional clients, has particular expertise in advising regulated industries, including the media.*

Matheson Ormsby Prentice

30 Herbert Street, Dublin 2
Head, Entertainment Law Group:
James Hickey
t. +353 1 619 9000
f. +353 1 619 9010
e. james.hickey@mop.ie
w. www.mop.ie
■ *This firm has extensive international expertise in giving legal advice to the film and entertainment industries.*

McCann Fitzgerald

2 Harbourmaster Place, International
Financial Services Centre, Dublin 1
Partner: David Clarke
t. +353 1 829 0000
f. +353 1 829 0010
e. david.clarke@mcannfitzgerald.ie
w. www.mccannfitzgerald.ie
■ *This firm provides legal services to the entertainment sector, particularly the film industry. It advises many Irish and international film and television production companies about producing and financing their projects in Ireland.*

Media Monitors Ireland

230 Harold's Cross Road, Dublin 6
Managing Director: Michael Riordan
t. +353 1 491 1930
f. +353 1 491 1936
e. info@mediamonitors.ie
■ *This company supplies press-cutting and broadcast monitoring services to clients. It also undertakes special projects as requested.*

Merrion Capital Group

Block C, Sweepstakes Centre, Merrion
Road, Dublin 4
Contact: Cathal Friel
t. +353 1 240 4100
f. +353 1 240 4101
e. cathal.friel@merrion-capital.com
w. www.merrion-capital.com
■ *This venture capital company is involved in several media merger deals.*

Millar McCall Wylie

Eastley House, 396 Upper
Newtownards Road, Belfast BT4 3EY
Damien McParland
t. +44 2890 200050
f. +44 2890 200051
e. mmw@mmwlegal.com
w. www.mmwlegal.com
■ *This firm provides expert advice to the film industry.*

Moiselle Casting

7 Corrig Avenue, Dún Laoghaire,
Co. Dublin
Nuala Moiselle and Frank Moiselle
t. +353 1 280 2857
f. +353 1 280 3277
■ *This is a firm of casting directors.*

Movie Extras

140 Terenure Road West, Dublin 6W
Derek Quinn
t. +353 1 492 7640
e. support@movieextras.ie
w. www.movieextras.ie
■ *The company provides a casting database of background actors and extras for films, television and advertising.*

National Newspapers of Ireland

Clyde Lodge, 15 Clyde Road, Dublin 4
Chairman: Gavin O'Reilly
t. +353 1 668 9099
f. +353 1 668 9872
e. nni@cullencommunications.ie
w. www.nni.ie
■ *This is the representative body of nine newspaper publishers which produce twelve titles. It was founded to promote newspaper advertising, but it now campaigns on problems facing the Irish newspaper industry.*

National Union of Journalists

9th Floor, Liberty Hall, Beresford
Place, Dublin 1
Irish Secretary: Séamus Dooly
t. +353 1 805 3258
f. +353 1 874 9250
e. liberty.hall@nuj.ie
w. www.nuj.org
■ *This is the main trade union for print and broadcast journalists in Ireland.*

News Extracts

7 Ely Place, Dublin 2
Managing Director: Stephen Cousins
t. +353 1 661 6966
f. +353 1 661 5361
e. cuttings@newsextracts or broadcast@newsextract.ie
■ *This company monitors press, radio and television as well as providing media analysis and evaluation.*

News Monitoring Services

5 St Andrew's Street, Dublin 2
Irene Scott (press) or Susan Murphy
(broadcast)
t. +353 1 679 9488
f. +353 1 679 9559
e. info@newsmonitoring.ie
■ *This company provides press cutting and broadcast monitoring and information services.*

Northern Ireland Press Photographers' Association (NIPPA)

c/o Brian Thompson Photography, 72
High Street, Belfast BT1 2BE

Chairman: Mervyn Dowling
m. +44 777 054 2294
www.n-ippa.org
■ *This is the association for press photographers working in Northern Ireland.*
Chairman: Mervyn Dowling
e. chairman@n-ippa.org
Vice Chairman: Stephen Davison
e. vicechairman@n-ippa.org
t. +44 28 9066 3191
m. +44 78 3114 1272
Secretary: Trevor Martin
e. secretary@n-ippa.org
t. +44 28 9026 4000
Treasurer: Brian Thompson
e. treasurer@n-ippa.org
t. +44 28 9024 2898
m. +44 78 5041 0909

Ofcom (Belfast Office)

Landmark House, The Gasworks,
Ormeau Road, Belfast BT7 2JD
General Enquiries
t. +44 28 9041 7500
f. +44 28 9041 7533
w. www.ofcom.org.uk
■ *Ofcom is the independent regulator and
competition authority for the UK communications industries, with responsibility for television, radio, telecommunications and wireless
communications services. The regional offices
represent Ofcom's needs and interests to people
and organisations in the nations and regions
but do not handle consumer complaints.*

Ombudsman

18 Lower Leeson Street, Dublin 2
Ombudsman: Emily O'Reilly
t. +353 1 678 5222
f. +353 1 661 0570
e. ombudsman@ombudsman.gov.ie
w. www.ombudsman.gov.ie
■ *The Ombudsman examines complaints
from members of the public who feel they have
been unfairly dealt with by public bodies. She is
also the Information Commissioner, providing
an independent review of decisions relating to
the right of access by a person' to records held
by public bodies.*

Philip Lee Solicitors

Fitzwilton House, Wilton Place,
Dublin 2
General Enquiries: Jonathan Kelly
t. +353 1 609 9500
f. +353 1 662 8290
e. jkelly@plee.ie
w. www.plee.ie
■ *A legal company handling media issues.*

Pricewaterhouse Coopers

Wilton House, Dublin 2
Senior Partner: Donal O'Connor
t. +353 1 678 9999
f. +353 1 662 6200
w. www.pwc.com/ie
■ *This leading professional services firm offers
media analysis as part of its business and
financial advisory services.*

Regional Newspapers Association of Ireland

Sheridan House, 33 Parkgate Street,
Dublin 8
Administrator: Barbara Sheridan
t. +353 1 677 9112
f. +353 1 677 9144
e. barbara@rnan.ie
■ *This is an association of regional weekly
newspapers.*

Research and Markets

Guinness Centre, Taylor's Lane, Dublin 8
Press Officer: Laura Wood
f. +353 1 410 0980
e. laura.wood@researchandmarkets.com
w. www.researchandmarkets.com
■ *A comprehensive resource for international
market research and market data, providing
information about markets, industries and
companies.*

Services, Industrial, Professional and Technical Union (SIPTU)

Liberty Hall, Beresford Place, Dublin 1
General President: Jack O'Connor
t. +353 1 858 6300
f. +353 1 874 9466
e. genpress@siptu.ie
w. www.siptu.ie

12

GLOBAL MEDIA: FEWER OWNERS, MORE CHOICE?

Helen Shaw

Globalisation, the interconnectedness of our world through technology, economics and trade, has transformed the media landscape. In Ireland we are now used to hearing that we are 'the most globalised' country in the world, based on international indexes, and that, combined with our use of the English language, which has rapidly become the language of globalisation, this has brought the fruits of global media to our living-rooms.

In real terms when we talk about global media we often mean the impact of the US hegemony in media content, distribution and influence. The world media landscape is dominated by fewer than ten conglomerates, mostly US, but probably the most powerful person in global media is an Australian by birth, Rupert Murdoch, whose company News Corporation has a vast transnational life in newspapers, television, radio, publishing and satellites. News Corporation is now a US-registered conglomerate, and Murdoch himself took up US citizenship in order to enhance his ability to increase his US media ownership. Murdoch's media strength has been the combination of content and distribution—what is called vertical and horizontal integration.

In vertical expansion, for example, a film production company moves into distribution and cinema theatres—like Warner Brothers. In horizontal expansion, one record company buys another, as when Sony Music merged with the German music giant BMG, or, to give an Irish example, Scottish Radio Holdings bought Today FM and FM 104 to expand its core radio interests. This spread creates a concentration of ownership, which is usually regulated both for the public interest, in maintaining diversity, and for market competition, to protect consumers' interests.

A third form of media market expansion is diagonal or cross media integration—the classic example being the megamedia AOL Times Warner deal in 2000, which married internet, cinema, television and publishing and cost the company dearly. Merger mania peaked in the run-up to the dot-com crash in 2001, but relaxed ownership regulations in both the US and the UK, through the UK's Communications Act (2003), has increased the scope and interest in media merger deals. Many merger deals now reflect all three forms of integration, as with the purchase by Sony Pictures of MGM studios in Los Angeles in mid-2004, in which Comcast, the cable television and broadband distribution giant, was one of Sony's partners.

'The media battlefield', according to Ken Auletta of the *New Yorker*, 'today resembles Europe in the 19th century where there were potent nation states but no single super power'.[1] Media conglomerates battle for an edge, and many are now re-embracing the concept of convergence and undertaking on-line mergers for their content products by partnering with technology giants, like Microsoft, to produce games consoles and interactive mobile entertainment. The big media empires are marked by dozens of leading brands interwoven under each umbrella, and increasingly interwoven between each conglomerate, like the Sony-BMG (Bertelsmann) merger, to maximise their combined resources and carve out even larger slices of the world for their brands.

Global players

The world's biggest and most powerful media mega-companies are listed below.[2] (While GE is by far the most valuable of the companies in the list, a higher percentage of its business is non-media. The ranking reflects not their present market value, but the global nature of their businesses and the diversity of their media ownership.)

1. **Viacom**—led by Sumner Redstone, an American mega-company (formed through a merger of CBS and Westinghouse) and described by the *Financial Times* as 'the world's largest media company'. Viacom's stable includes CBS, MTV, Nickelodeon and a range of genre channels. It owns 183 radio stations, 39 television stations, outdoor advertising,

1. *Irish Times*, 11 January 2005.
2. See www.mediaowners.com for a detailed listing of all holdings in the US.

Paramount film studios, the Blockbusters video chain, and Simon and Schuster books, to name but a few. Nearly 400 million people watch MTV channels in 166 countries and MTV is one of Viacom's strongest profit-earners, pushing its non-US turnover to more than a billion dollars.

2. **General Electric**—a pre-eminent US industrial conglomerate, with 20% of its $182 billion value coming from its telecommunications and finance interests. GE stretches back to Thomas Edison and the light bulb, owns US television network NBC, and runs a joint cable news venture with Microsoft MSNBC. It has cable television interests, including the History Channel and Bravo, which are carried in Ireland on digital television packages.

3. **Time Warner**—a US media giant, described as the 'largest communications company in the world' following its ill-fated and expensive merger with AOL in 2000. Time Warner owns CNN, the HBO cable channels, film studios and theatres, among other interests.

4. **Disney Corporation**—a US public company with extensive cinema, entertainment, television and radio interests. It owns Walt Disney Motion Pictures, Disney Entertainment, the ABC television network, Miramax (until September 2005), Touchstone, a host of radio stations in the US and a range of interactive and on-line businesses.

5. **News Corporation**—Murdoch's empire, with interests in the US, Canada, the UK, Australia, India, Latin America and the Pacific Basin. Its television and satellite businesses include BskyB and Fox Broadcasting Company, which includes the controversial Fox News channel in the US, Star TV in Asia and Stream TV in Italy. It owns 175 newspapers around the world, including *The Times*, *Sunday Times*, the *Sun* and *News of the World* in the UK and the *New York Post*. It owns the HarperCollins publishing company and DirecTV—the US television satellite company, previously owned by GE (see Box: Round the World in Eighty Seconds: Murdoch's Global Empire).

6. **Sony**—Japanese media, music, electronics and games conglomerate, with a growing basket of interests from electronic goods to content through its music, film and games businesses. Sony was behind two of the big media business stories in 2004 with its acquisition of MGM studios and the merger of its music business with BMG—which has created the second-largest music production company in the world.

7. **Bertelsmann**—a 172-year-old private German company that is considered the third-largest global media conglomerate, with cross-

media ownership in 55 countries. It owns RTL, the number one pan-European television and radio chain, with 23 television and 14 radio companies, Random House, the world's biggest book publishing company, with 10% of all English-language sales globally, and a host of magazine and book interests. Its music business BMG has now merged with Sony, creating a solid block of conglomerate power in music publishing.

In the film industry the world's dominant players are most of those listed above: Warner Brothers (Time Warner), Paramount (Viacom), Columbia/Sony/MGM (Sony Corporation), 20th Century Fox (News Corporation) and Universal Pictures (Vivendi). Vivendi, originally a French utilities company, was built into a global media corporation during the late 1990s by the flamboyant Jean-Marie Messnier, but following major losses caused by over-expansion it was forced to break up and sell parts of its global media interests. Messnier was ousted and blamed for the debacle.

Other US global corporations in the top ten include Clear Channel, which owns hundreds of US regional radio stations and outdoor advertising interests, and which has interests in both the UK and Ireland, and Comcast, the US cable and broadband giant. The UK Communications Act (2003) allows companies like Viacom and Clear Channel to buy into the UK broadcast market, subject to the 'public interest test' which the Labour peer and film director Lord Puttnam lobbied for to protect the diversity and plurality of the British radio and television market.

Around the world in 80 minutes: Murdoch's global empire

News Corporation, the media company run and controlled by Rupert Murdoch, boasts that it touches someone every minute of the day, in every time zone in the world. 'The only vertically integrated media company on a global scale,' its web site proclaims, adding that it spans the five continents. 'More than any other figure Murdoch has been the visionary of a global corporate media empire,' according to US media analyst Robert McChesney, whose book *Rich Media, Poor Democracy* (1999) charted the impact of the growing global concentration of media ownership and its impact on information diversity. Through BskyB, Murdoch has approximately 70% of the UK pay television market.

Through the Fox network in the US, which remains its biggest market, the STAR pan-Asian satellite network and FOXTEL channel in Australia, News Corporation spans the globe. Add his broadcasting interests in Europe, particularly Germany and Italy, in Latin America and the Middle East, and Murdoch can claim the greatest gateway to the world's television screens and eyeballs. Murdoch's own shareholding in News Corporation is 29%.[1]

Murdoch, whose media empire began in newspapers, has skilfully played the deregulation trends in media ownership in the UK and the US. He recognised the potential for satellite television at a time when few were prepared to risk capital on it. Murdoch is a media baron with a knack for understanding popular media and what drives audiences— like sport. In the UK, BSkyB made money buying up the rights to broadcast live football matches and creating pay-per-view sports television, which has, for good or evil, changed the face of television and sports in general.

In January 2005, News Corporation spent €182 million on a share buy-back plan, increasing its stake in BSkyB from 35 to 37%. At the same time it acquired full control of Fox Entertainment, its US television and studio affiliate, by offering shares to Fox shareholders in order to consolidate its US media holdings.

News Corporation's interests include newspapers, book publishing, radio, television, satellite networks and interactive broadcasting.[2] In the US it acquired DirecTV, a television satellite company, from GE in 2003 and it is now attempting to create its BSkyB model of vertically integrated digital television network in the US, taking on the cable giants that dominate television delivery there.

In late 2004, News Corporation re-incorporated, moving its base from Australia to Delaware in the US—a final recognition that a global media empire has to be registered on Wall Street. In September, at the time of the re-incorporation, News Corporation was valued at $52 billion, with total annual revenue of $22 billion—the bulk of that coming from the US Fox television network, which now boasts of being the most popular network with young Americans. Fox News, the right-wing news channel,

[1] Quoted in Peter Steven (2003), The *No Nonsense Guide to Global Media*, Verso (p. 45).

[2] Sources are company web sites, the *Financial Times*, the *Economist* and Helen Shaw (July 2003), 'The Age of McMedia', Harvard University.

which came to the fore during the Iraq War in 2003, has long overtaken CNN as the most popular 24-hour news channel.

What has shaped this global empire is not just Murdoch's vision and knack for the popular but also a canny awareness of the potential of new technologies, from digital television to interactive home shopping channels. Equally, Murdoch's empire has developed by playing politics—particularly in the US and UK—and putting political and business interests above content: after the Chinese Government criticised the BBC, the BBC World Service was withdrawn from his STAR network. For those opposed to the growing concentration of media power in a few hands, Rupert Murdoch embodies the enemy. He is the visible head of an empire created, built and still led by him and now his family—an achievement that distinguishes News Corporation from many of the other global media empires. His son, James Murdoch, heads BSkyB, which the Murdoch family has a 35% stake in, and another son, Lachlan Murdoch, is Deputy Chief Executive Officer at News Corporation.

Love him or hate him, Murdoch has changed the face of global media and shaped the media world we live in. The writer Dennis Potter called the cancer that killed him 'Rupert', after Murdoch, reflecting his hatred for the Murdoch empire, which had been behind the crushing of the Wapping Strike in the 1980s. For others he is a modern-day Citizen Kane. In the business world, though, he remains something of a living legend, a media Houdini who has managed, so far, to ride the tidal waves of change and come back stronger every time. The question is, how much of the personal Murdoch empire and reign can and will survive his inevitable demise?

Future trends

Convergence is back—and this time it is serious! Today, the focus for the media business market, in terms of delivery, is less the computer and television set and more the handset or mobile phone. The concept of convergence, that digital technology is a means of supplying interactive multimedia content, hit a reality wall with the dot-com collapse in 2000–2001. Back then the focus was on using the internet and personal computers and televisions as the vehicle. Today the introduction of broadband and the availability of mobile applications that can be delivered to the mobile phone have brought new life to convergence and to global media ambitions. The present global corporations are set to expand, with both Viacom and News Corporation looking at Asia for new growth. Further consolidations are expected in both the UK and Irish radio markets, with some of the US players like Viacom, looking for new business interests here. Media mergers have returned to centre stage and the big media corporations are once again lining up for a round of acquisitions.

With the growth of new media opportunities, cross-media will become more crucial to survival. All forms of content will be contained within media business plans. This is, in a sense, how the BBC operates. Although it is a non-profit public broadcaster, the BBC is one of the most influential and powerful global media brands in the world. It is the BBC's combination of television and radio, and of course its brand reputation, that has ensured that its web site remains one of the most popular sources in the world for information and news. For the media behemoths, the future will see content forms converging in new digital and mobile packages so while media ownership is consolidating, the potential for audiences to 'be their own media' and create content will grow.

The big race for the global media future will be in Asia, with its vast populations in China and India. While the digital divide remains an important barrier to media penetration, the ability of digital technologies to provide services across vast territories, and relatively cheaply compared with analogue technologies, will have a transformational impact in all forms of society. For those entering the media industry today, the essential tip is: think digital and think global.

Further reading:

Farrel Corcoran, *RTÉ and the Globalisation of Irish Television*, Bristol: Intellect, 2004.

Daya Kishan Thussu, *International Communications: Continuity and Change*, London: Arnold, 2000.

Peter Steven, *The No Nonsense Guide to Global Media*, Oxford: Verso, 2003.

Don Tapscott, *Growing Up Digital*, New York: McGraw-Hill, 1998.

Republic of Ireland

Agence France Press (Dublin Correspondent)
41 Belgrave Square, Dublin 6
Dublin Correspondent: Andrew Bushe
t. +353 1 497 5638
f. +353 1 496 6723
e. abushe@indigo.ie
■ *This is the Irish correspondent for the French global news agency.*

ANSA (Dublin Correspondent)
56 Greenfield Park, Dublin 24
Bureau Chief: Dr Enzo Farinella
t. +353 1 494 1389
f. +353 1 494 1389
e. enzo@iol.ie
■ *This is the Dublin bureau of the Italian news agency.*

Associated Press (Dublin Correspondent)
146 Chapelgate, St Alphonsus's Road, Dublin 9
Correspondent: Shawn Potatchnik
t. +353 1 882 8281
f. +353 1 882 8146
e. spogatchnik@ap.org
■ *This is the Dublin correspondent of the international wire service news agency.*

Bloomberg News
Regus House, Harcourt Road, Dublin 2
Dublin Correspondent: Brian O'Neill
t. +353 1 402 9442
f. +353 1 475 4289
e. bjoneill@bloomberg.net
■ *This is a global financial news and information agency.*

Dow Jones Newswires
Executive Suites, Block 3, Harcourt Centre, Harcourt Road, Dublin 2
Chief Correspondent: Quentin Fottrell
t. +353 1 676 2189
e. quentin.fottrell@dowjones.com

■ *This is the Dublin bureau of the global financial information provider.*

EFE News Agency (Dublin Correspondent)
158 Monalea Grove, Dublin 16
Dublin Correspondent: Paloma Santolaria Sabio
t. +353 1 494 6254
w. palomassabio@eircom.net
■ *This is the Dublin correspondent for the Spanish news agency.*

Financial Times
20 Upper Merrion Street, Dublin 2
Ireland Correspondent: John Murray Brown
t. +353 1 676 2071
f. +353 1 676 2125
e. johnmurraybrown@ utvinternet.com
■ *This is the Ireland correspondent for the London financial and business paper.*

Ireland International News Agency
51 Wellington Quay, Dublin 2
Managing Director: Diarmaid MacDermott
t. +353 1 671 2442
f. +353 1 679 6586
e. iina@eircom.net
■ *This news agency covers news and court sittings for its media clients.*

ITAR Tass
16 Foxrock Wood, Dublin 18
Ireland Correspondent: Eugen Ikachev
t. +353 1 289 8266
f. +353 1 289 8091
e. eugen@indigo.ie
■ *This is the Ireland correspondent for the Russian news agency.*

New York Times (Dublin Correspondent)
13 Newgrove Avenue, Dublin 4
Dublin Correspondent: Brian Lavery
t. +353 872 411 514
e. lavery@dna.ie
■ *This is the Dublin correspondent of the US paper.*

Press Association (Belfast Office)
Scottish Providence Building,
7 Donegall Square West, Belfast
BT1 1DB
Ireland Editor: Deric Henderson
t. +44 2890 245 008
f. +44 2890 439 246
e. derich@pa.press.net
■ *This is the Belfast office of the international news agency.*

Press Association (Dublin)
80 Harcourt Street, Dublin 2
News Editor: Kieran McDaid
t. +353 1 605 6330
f. +353 1 405 3630
e. dublin@pa.press.net and
kieran.mcdaid@pa.press.net
■ *This is the Dublin office of the international news agency.*

Reuters (Dublin Office)
12–13 Exchange Place, IFSC, Dublin 1
Chief Correspondent: Jodie Ginsberg
t. +353 1 500 1504
f. +353 1 500 1551
e. dublin.newsroom@reuters.com
w. www.reuters.com
■ *This is the Dublin office of the international news agency, which specialises in financial news*

United Kingdom

(00 is dialled before international numbers.)

Agence France Presse, UK
78 Fleet Street, London EC4Y 1NB,
England
Photo Editor: Joshua Roberts
t. +44 207 7353 7461
e. london.bureau@afp.com
w. www.afp.com
■ *This is the London bureau of the French news agency, which claims it is the oldest in the world, founded in 1835.*

BBC Radio
Broadcasting House, Portland Place,
London W1A 1AA, England
Director of Radio and Music: Jenny
Abramsky
t. +44 207 765 4561
e. press.office@bbc.co.uk
w. www.bbc.co.uk/radio
■ *The national public broadcaster, BBC radio has five national stations. Radio 1 has popular music. Radio 2 features music for older listeners.*

Radio 3 broadcasts classical music, world music and the arts. Radio 4 is speech-based and has the station's flagship news programme, 'Today', while 'Five Live' has rolling news and sport.
The BBC World Service is an international news station funded by the UK's Foreign Office.

BBC Television
Television Centre, Wood Lane,
London W12 7RJ, England
Director of Television: Jana Bennett
t. +44 208 743 8000
e. press.office@bbc.co.uk
w. www.bbc.co.uk/television
■ *The UK's public broadcaster runs two national terrestrial channels, BBC 1 and BBC 2. It also has two free digital channels, BBC 3 and BBC 4, as well as a rolling news service, BBC 24.*

BBC World Service
Bush House, Strand, London WC2B
4PH, England

Director: Nigel Chapman
t. +44 207 557 2941
e. press.office@bbc.co.uk
w. www.bbc.co.uk/worldservice
■ *This arm of BBC radio features 24-hour news and information from around the world, in English and 42 other languages. It is funded by the UK's Foreign Office.*

BBC World Service Trust
Bush House, Strand, London WC2B 4PH, England
Chair: Nigel Chapman
Director: Stephen King
t. +44 207 557 2941
e. press.office@bbc.co.uk
w. www.bbc.co.uk/worldservice/trust
■ *This was set up in 1999 as an independent charity within the BBC world service. It aims to reduce poverty through the innovative use of the media in developing countries and countries in transition and to help build media expertise within those countries.*

Daily Express
Express Newspapers, Northern & Shell Building, 10 Lower Thames Street, London SE3R 6EN, England
Editor: Peter Hill
t. +44 87 0062 6620
e. peter.hill@express.co.uk
w. www.express.co.uk
■ *This is a daily mid-market paper owned by Northern and Shell group, with executive control in the hands of Richard Desmond. It has a circulation of 892,000.*

Daily Mail
Associated Newspapers, Northcliffe House, 2 Derry Street, Kensington, London W8 5TT, England
Editor: Paul Dacre
t. +44 20 7938 6000
e. paul.dacre@dailymail.co.uk
w. www.dailymail.co.uk
■ *This mid-market compact paper has the second-highest circulation in the UK, at 2,322,970, and is owned by the Daily Mail and General Trust.*

Daily Mirror
Trinity Mirror, 1 Canada Square, Canary Wharf, London E13 5AP, England
Editor: Richard Wallace
t. +44 207 293 3000
e. richard.wallace@mirror.co.uk
w. www.mirror.co.uk
■ *This traditionally left-wing popular tabloid with a circulation of 1,883,000 is owned by the media group Trinity Mirror.*

Daily Star
Express Newspapers, Northern & Shell Building, 10 Lower Thames Street, London SE3R 6EN, England
Editor: Dawn Neesom
t. +44 87 0062 6620
e. dawn.neesom@dailystar.co.uk
w. www.dailystar.co.uk
■ *This is a downmarket tabloid with a circulation of 898,000 and is owned by the Northern and Shell Group. Richard Desmond has executive control.*

Daily Star Sunday
Express Newspapers, Northern & Shell Building, 10 Lower Thames Street, London SE3R 6EN, England
Editor: Gareth Morgan
t. +44 87 0062 6620
e. gareth.morgan@dailystar.co.uk
w. www.megastar.co.uk
■ *This is a downmarket tabloid Sunday paper with a circulation of 515,000 and is owned by the Northern and Shell Group, which is ultimately controlled by Richard Desmond.*

Daily Telegraph
Telegraph Group, 1 Canada Square, Canary Wharf, London E14 5DT, England
Editor: Martin Newland
t. +44 207 538 5000
e. martin.newland@telegraph.co.uk
w. www.telegraph.co.uk
■ *This conservative paper is the UK's highest-selling daily broadsheet, with a circulation of*

878,030. It is owned by Telegraphy Group, controlled by the Barclay brothers.

Financial Times

The Financial Times Group, 1
Southwark Bridge, London SE1 9HL,
England
Editor: Andrew Gowers
  t. +44 207 873 3000
  e. andrew.gowers@ft.com
  w. www.ft.com
■ *This is a daily financial and business newspaper with a circulation of 414,000, owned by the Pearson group.*

News of the World

News Group Newspapers, 1 Virginia
Street, London E98 1NW, England
Editor: Andy Coulson
  t. +44 207 782 4000
  e. andy.coulson@notw.co.uk
  w. www.thenewsoftheworld.co.uk
■ *This popular Sunday tabloid is the highest-selling Sunday paper in the UK, with a circulation of 3,840,000 and is owned by Rupert Murdoch's News International.*

Newsquest Media Group

58 Church Street, Weybridge, Surrey
KT13 8DP, England
Chief Executive Officer: Paul Davidson
  t. +44 193 2821 212
  w. www.newsquest.co.uk
■ *This subsidiary of the American media giant Gannett is the second-largest regional newspaper publisher in the UK, with interests in more than 300 titles. This includes 17 daily papers.*

OneWorld International Foundation

2nd Floor, River House, 143–145
Farringdon Road, London EC1R 3AB,
England
Director: Anuradha Vittachi
  t. +44 207 7239 1400
  e. foundation@oneworld.net
  w. www.oneworld.net
■ *This network is governed by the OneWorld International Foundation, the governing body of the OneWorld network, which is dedicated to harnessing the democratic potential of the internet to promote human rights and sustainable development.*

Panos Media London

9 White Lion Street, London N19 PD,
England
Executive Director: Mark Wilson
  t. +44 207 278 1111
  f. +44 207 278 0345
  e. mark.wilson@panos.org.uk
  w. www.panos.org.uk
■ *Panos Media is a non-profit organisation that aims to foster debate about important development issues to foster sustainable development.*

Press Association (PA)

292 Vauxhall Bridge Road, London
SW1V 1AE, England
Editor-in-Chief: Paul Potts
  t. +44 207 963 7000
  e. information@pa.press.net
  w. www.pa.press.net
■ *This is the national news agency of the UK, providing news and sports information.*

Reuters

85 Fleet Street, London EC4P 4AJ,
England
Editor-in-Chief: Geert Linnebank
  t. +44 207 250 1122
  e. robert.woodward@reuters.com
  w. www.reuters.com
■ *This is a global news service, specialising in financial information to companies and clients. It was founded in London in 1851.*

Reuters Foundation

85 Fleet Street, London EC4P 4AJ,
England
Chief Executive Officer: Tom Glocer
  t. +44 207 250 1122
  e. foundation@reuters.com
  w. www.foundation.reuters.com
■ *This educational trust was created in 1982 to support journalists from developing countries. It sponsors a wide range of educational, humanitarian and environmental causes and projects.*

Scottish Radio Holdings

Clydebank Business Park, Glasgow
G81 2RX, Scotland
Chief Executive: David Goode
t. +44 141 565 2200
f. +44 141 565 2202
e. radio@srh.co.uk
w. www.srhplc.com
■ *This international media group now owns a large share of the Irish newspaper and radio market. It grew from a consortium in Glasgow in the early 1970s that won the third commercial radio licence offered in the UK. Now it has interests throughout Ireland and owns Morton Newspapers.*

Sunday Mirror

Trinity Mirror, 1 Canada Square,
Canary Wharf, London E14 5AP,
England
Editor: Tina Weaver
t. +44 207 293 3000
e. tina.weaver@mirror.co.uk
w. www.mirror.co.uk
■ *This Sunday tabloid, a sister to the Daily Mirror, is owned by the media group Trinity Mirror and has a circulation of 1,940,000.*

Sunday Telegraph

Telegraph Group, 1 Canada Square,
Canary Wharf, London E14 5DT,
England
Editor: Dominic Lawson
t. +44 207 538 5000
e. dominic.lawson@telegraph.co.uk
w. www.telegraph.co.uk
■ *This conservative Sunday broadsheet, a sister to the Daily Telegraph, has a circulation of 672,550. It is owned by the Telegraph Group.*

The Business

Sunday Business Publishing, PA News
Centre, 292 Vauxhall Bridge Road,
London SW1V 1AE, England
Deputy Editor: Ian Watson
t. +44 207 961 0000
e. iwatson@thebusiness.press.net
w. www.thebusinessonline.com

■ *This is a weekly business paper with a circulation of 61,100, owned by the Telegraph Group.*

The Guardian

Guardian Media Group, 119
Farringdon Road, London EC1R 3ER,
England
Editor: Alan Rusbridger
t. +44 207 278 2332
e. alan.rusbridger@guardian.co.uk
w. www.guardian.co.uk
■ *This daily left-wing newspaper, ultimately controlled by the Scott Trust, has a circulation of 358,000, and its web site is one of the most popular in the UK.*

The Independent

Independent News and Media (UK),
Independent House, 191 Marsh Wall,
London E14 9RS, England
Editor: Simon Kelner
t. +44 207 005 2000
e. simon.kelner@independent.co.uk
w. www.independent.co.uk
■ *This liberal compact paper has a circulation of 224,000 and is owned by Tony O'Reilly's Independent News and Media.*

The Independent on Sunday

Independent News and Media (UK),
Independent House, 191 Marsh Wall,
London E14 9RS, England
Editor: Tristan Davies
t. +44 207 005 2000
e. t.davies@independent.co.uk
w. www.independent.co.uk
■ *A sister Sunday to the Independent, this is owned by Tony O'Reilly's Independent News and Media and has a circulation of 174,000.*

The Mail on Sunday

Associated Newspapers, Northcliffe
House, 2 Derry Street, London
W8 5TT, England
Editor: Peter Wright
t. +44 20 7938 6000
e. peter.wright@mailonsunday.co.uk
w. www.mailonsunday.co.uk

■ *Sister Sunday paper to the* **Daily Mail,** *this paper has a circulation of 2,269,271 and is owned by the* **Daily Mail** *and* **General Trust.**

The Observer

Guardian Media Group, 119 Farringdon Road, London EC1R 3ER, England
Editor: Roger Alton
t. +44 207 278 2332
e. roger.alton@observer.co.uk
w. www.observer.co.uk

■ *This liberal broadsheet Sunday, sister paper to the* **Guardian,** *has a circulation of 425,000 and is owned by the Guardian Media Group.*

The People

MGN, 1 Canada Square, Canary Wharf, London E14 5AP, England
Editor: Mark Thomas
t. +44 207 293 3000
e. mark.thomas@people.co.uk
w. www.people.co.uk

■ *This Sunday tabloid, owned by Trinity Mirror, has a circulation of 1,029,000.*

The Sun

News Group Newspapers, 1 Virginia Street, London E98 1SN, England
Editor: Rebekah Wade
t. +44 207 782 4000
e. rebekah.wade@the-sun.co.uk
w. www.thesun.co.uk

■ *This conservative popular tabloid has the highest circulation in the UK, with 3,365,000. It is ultimately owned by Rupert Murdoch's News International.*

The Sunday Express

Express Newspapers, Northern & Shell Building, 10 Lower Thames Street, London SE3R 6EN, England
Editor: Martin Townsend
t. +44 87 0062 6620
e. martin.townsend@express.co.uk
w. www.express.co.uk

■ *This Sunday mid-market paper, a sister to the* **Daily Express,** *is owned by Northern and Shell group, with executive control in the hands of Richard Desmond. It has a circulation of 889,000.*

The Sunday Times

Times Newspapers, 1 Pennington Street, London E98 1TT, England
Editor: John Witherow
t. +44 207 782 5000
e. john.witherow@Sunday-times.co.uk
w. www.Sunday-times.co.uk

■ *This is the UK's best-selling Sunday broadsheet, with a circulation of 1,347,000. A sister to the* **Times,** *it is owned by Rupert Murdoch's News International. It has an Irish edition, produced by journalists in its Dublin office.*

The Times

Times Newspapers, 1 Pennington Street, London E98 1TT, England
Editor: Robert Thomson
t. +44 207 782 5000
e. robert.thompson@thetimes.co.uk
w. www.timesonline.co.uk

■ *This is a conservative compact UK paper with a circulation of 616,000 and is owned by Rupert Murdoch's News International.*

Europe

(00 is dialled before international numbers.)

Corriere della Sera
Via Solferino 28, Milano, Italy
Editor: Paolo Mieli
t. +39 02 6339
w. www.corriere.it
■ *This is a quality Italian centre-right daily.*

Cyprus Broadcasting Corporation
Cybc Street, Nicosia 2120, Cyprus
Director-General: Marios Mavrikios
t. +357 22 86 2000
f. +357 22 31 4050
w. www.cybc.com
■ *The Cyprus Broadcasting Corporation is Cyprus's public broadcasting service, transmitting throughout the country on three radio and two television channels.*

Cyprus Mail
24 Vassiliou Voulgaroctonou Street,
PO Box 21144, 1502 Nicosia, Cyprus
Editor: Kista Pavlowitch
t. +357 22 818 585
e. editor@cyprusmail.com
w. www.cyprus-mail.com
■ *This is a Cypriot English-language daily.*

Czech Radio
Vinohradska 12, 120 99 Prague, Czech Republic
Director-General: Jiri Holac
t. +420 22 155 1250
e. online@rozhlas.cz
w. www.rozhlas.cz
■ *This is public service radio for the Czech Republic.*

Czech Television
Kavci Hory, 140 70 Prague, Czech Republic
t. +420 261 131 111
e. info@czech-tv.cz
w. www.czech-tv.cz
■ *This is the public service television channel for the Czech Republic.*

De Telegraaf
Post Bus 376, Amsterdam, Netherlands
Editor: J. Olde Kalter
t. +31 20 585 9111
e. redactie@telegraaf.nl
w. www.telegraaf.nl
■ *This mid-market paper is the Netherlands' largest-selling national daily.*

Der Standard
Schenkenstrasse 4–6, 1010 Vienna, Austria
Editor: Gerfried Sperl
t. +43 431 53 1700
e. chefredaktion@derStandard.at
w. www.derstandard.at
■ *An Austrian liberal daily.*

DR—Denmark Broadcasting Corporation
TV Byen, 2860 Soborg, Denmark
Acting Director-General: Lars Vesterlokke
t. +45 352 03019
e. drkommunikation@dr.dk
w. www.dr.dk
■ *DR (Danish Broadcasting Corporation) is Denmark's oldest and largest electronic media enterprise. It was founded in 1925 as a public service organisation. It has four radio channels and two television channels. DR is now creating a multimedia content centre, maximising its use of new technologies.*

Deutsche Welle
Kurt-Schumacher Strasse 3, 53113 Bonn, Germany
Director-General: Erik Bettermann
t. +49 228 429 0
w. www.dw-world.de
■ *This German public television and radio broadcaster provides international news from a European viewpoint.*

Diario de Noticias

Avenida da Liberdade 226, 1250–149
Lisboa, Portugal
Editor: Miguel Coutinho
t. +351 2131 87500
e. dnot@dn.pt
w. www.dn.pt
■ *This is an elite Portuguese daily, regarded as a paper of record.*

El Mundo

Calle Pradillo 42, 28002 Madrid, Spain
Editor: Pedro J. Ramírez
t. +34 91 586 4800
e. cartas.director@elmundo.es
w. www.elmundo.es
■ *This is a Spanish quality daily, respected for its high-profile investigations.*

El País

Miguel Yuste 40, Madrid 28037, Spain
Managing Editor: Diego Martínez Lloreda
t. +34 91 337 8200
e. redaccion@prisacom.com
w. www.elpais.es
■ *This is Spain's biggest-selling general information paper.*

EuroNews

BP 131, 60 Chemin de Mouilles,
69131 Lyon Ecully, France
Sales Director for UK and Ireland:
Justin Davison
t. +33 47 218 8000
e. info@euronews.net
w. www.euronews.net
■ *This is a pan-European television news network, covering international news in seven languages, which is carried in Ireland on RTÉ television.*

European Broadcasting Union

Ancienne Route 17, 1218 Grand-
Saconnex, Switzerland
Secretary-General: Jean Réveillon
t. +41 22 717 2111
f. +44 22 747 4000
e. ebu@ebu.ch
w. www.ebu.ch
■ *Founded in 1950, the European Broadcasting Union (EBU) is the largest professional association of national broadcasters in the world, having 72 active members in 52 countries of Europe, North Africa and the Middle East and 50 associate members.*

European Journalism Centre

Sonneville-lunet 10, 6221 KT
Maastricht, Netherlands
Director: Raymonde Griswold
t. +31 433 254 030
f. +44 3143 321 2626
e. secr@ejc.nl
w. www.ejc.nl
■ *The European Journalism Centre (EJC) is an independent non-profit institute dedicated to high journalism standards, primarily through the further training of journalists and media professionals. It produces quality research on European media.*

Frankfurter Allgemeine

Postfach 6, 60267 Frankfurt am Main,
Germany
Editor-in-Chief: Peter Beck
t. +49 69 75910
e. reduktion@faz.de
w. www.faz.de
■ *This is a right-of-centre German quality daily.*

Gazeta Wyborcza

8–10 Czerska Street, Warsaw, Poland
Editor-in-Chief: Adam Michnik
t. +48 22 555 4000
e. postmaster@gazeta.pl
w. www.gazeta.pl
■ *This is Poland's most popular daily newspaper.*

International Herald Tribune

6 bis, rue des Graviers, 92521 Neuilly
Cedex, France
Publisher: Michael Golden
t. +33 1 4143 9322
e. iht@iht.com
w. www.iht.com

■ *This is an English-language daily newspaper specialising in international events. It is owned by the New York Times company.*

Kathimerini

D Falireos and E Makariou St 2,
185-47 N Faliron, Piraeus, Greece
Chief Editor: Nikos Konstandaras
t. +30 210 480 8000
e. editor@ekathimerini.com
w. www.ekathimerini.com
■ *This is a Greek English-language daily available inside the* International Herald Tribune *in Greece and Cyprus.*

La Repubblica

Piazza Indipendenza 11/b, Roma
00185, Italy
Editor-in-Chief: Loreduna Bartoletti
t. +39 06 49 821
e. larepubblica@repubblica.it
w. www.repubblica.it
■ *This is a left-wing quality newspaper in Rome.*

Le Figaro

37 Rue du Louvre, 75002 Paris, France
Editor-in-Chief: Nicolas Beytout
t. +33 1 5865 0101
e. n.beytout@lefigaro.fr
w. www.lefigaro.com
■ *This is a French right-wing quality daily.*

Le Monde

80 Boulevard Auguste Blanqui, 75707
Paris Cedex 13, France
Editor: Gérard Courtois
t. +33 1 572 8200
e. mail@mondepub.fr
w. www.lemonde.fr
■ *This is a French quality left-leaning daily.*

Libération

11 Rue Béranger, 75154 Paris Cedex
03, France
Managing Editor: Antoine de
Gaudemar
t. +33 0142 761789
w. www.libe.com

■ *This is a French left-leaning quality newspaper.*

ORF (Austrian Broadcasting Corporation)

Würzburggasse 30, 1136 Vienna,
Austria
Director-General: Dr Monika Lindner
t. +43 1 878 7814515
w. www.orf.at
■ *This is Austria's public service broadcaster, which broadcasts two television channels (ORF 1 and ORF 2) and has nine regional stations throughout Austria, in addition to 13 radio stations.*

Prague Post

Stepanska 20, 110 00 Prague, Czech
Republic
Managing Editor: Will Tizard
t. +42 029 633 4400
e. wtizard@praguepost.com
w. www.praguepost.com
■ *This is the Czech Republic's largest-selling newspaper.*

Radio France Internationale

116 Avenue du President Kennedy,
Paris 75016, France
English Service Editor: John Maguire
t. +33 1 443 08996
e. www.john.maguire@rfi.fr
w. www.rfi.fr
■ *This is a French equivalent of the BBC's world service, with 30 million overseas listeners.*

Radio Netherlands

Box 222, 1200 JG Hilversum,
Netherlands
Deputy Director-General: Jan Hoek
t. +31 35 672 4211
e. marjolein.hulst@rnw.nl (press)
w. www.rnw.nl
■ *This is a Dutch English-language public broadcaster that is publicly funded.*

RTBF (Belgium)

52 Boulevard August Reyes, 1044
Bruxelles, Belgium
Controller: Jean Gerardy
t. +32 2 737 2551
f. +44 2 737 4210
w. www.rtbf.be
■ *This is a Belgian public-service broadcaster for the country's French-speaking community.*

Sagasnet

Bayerisches Filmzentrum,
Bavariafilmplatz 7, 82031 München-
Grümwald, Germany
t. +49 89 649 811 29
e. sagasnet@sagasnet.de
w. www.sagasnet.de
■ *Sagasnet is an organisation building a network for European professionals engaged in content development for the audio-visual and digital media. It works to support the European MEDIA framework for the audio-visual sector. It provides European-funded training and development.*

Süddeutsche Zeitung

Sendlinger Strasse 8, 80331 Munich,
Germany
Science Editor: Jeanne Rubner
t. +49 89 21830

e. redaktion@sueddeutsche.de
w. www.sueddeutsche.de
■ *This is a quality liberal national newspaper based in the south of Germany.*

VRT (Belgium's Flemish public broadcaster)

VRT Reyerslaan 52, 1043B Brussels,
Belgium
Managing Director: Tony Mary
t. +32 274 1 3111
e. info@vrt.be
w. www.vrt.be
■ *Vlaamse Radio- en Televisieomroep is the public broadcaster of the Flemish community in Belgium.*

YLE (Finland)

Radio and TV Centre, Yleisradio,
00024 Helsinki, Finland
Director-General: Mikael Jungner
t. +358 9 148 01
w. www.yle.fi
■ *YLE is Finland's national public service broadcasting company, operating five national television channels and thirteen radio channels and services, complemented by 25 regional radio programmes. Mikael Jungner was appointed DG in May 2005 and moved to YLE from Microsoft.*

International

(00 is dialled before international numbers.)

Al-Jazeera

PO Box 22300, Doha, Qatar
Marketing Director: Ali Kamal
t. +974 438 2777
e. info@aljazeera.net.qa
w. www.english.aljazeera.net
■ *This Arabic satellite channel has more than thirty bureaus around the world.*

Bloomberg

731 Lexington Avenue, New York,
NY, USA
Director: Peter Grauer
t. +1 212 318 2000
f. +1 917 369 5000
w. www.bloomberg.com
■ *This is a global financial information services company that operates in 26 countries.*

CBS Broadcasting Inc.
51 West 52nd Street, New York, NY
10019, USA
t. +1 212 975 4321
w. www.cbs.com
■ *This major news network is owned by the international media conglomerate Viacom.*

CNN
One CNN Centre, Atlanta, Georgia
30348, USA
President overseeing News: Johnathan
Klein
t. +1 404 827 1500
e. cnn@cnn.com
w. www.cnn.com
■ *This is one of the best-known US 24-hour news networks launched by the media mogul Ted Turner but now owned by Time Warner.*

Daily Mail and Guardian
PO Box 91667, Auckland Park,
Johannesburg 2006, South Africa
Editor: Ferial Haffajee
t. +44 27 11 727 7000
e. newsdesk@mg.co.za
w. www.mg.co.sa
■ *This is a quality South African weekly paper, which played a key role in the maintainence of the free press in South Africa.*

Jerusalem Post
Jerusalem Post Building, PO Box 81,
Jerusalem 91000, Israel
Editor: David Horovitz
t. +972 2 531 5666
e. editors@jpostmail.com
w. www.jpost.com
■ *This is a conservative English-lanuage daily in Jerusalem.*

LA Times
202 W 1st Street, Los Angeles,
California 90012, USA
Editor: John S. Carroll
t. +1 213 237 5000
e. national@latimes.com
w. www.latimes.com
■ *This is the biggest west-coast daily paper.*

Media Access Project
1625, K Street NW, Suite 1000,
Washington, DC 20006, USA
President: Andrew Jay Schwartzman
t. +1 202 232 4300
f. +1 202 466 7656
e. info@mediaaccess.org
w. www.mediaaccess.org
■ *Media Access Project (MAP) is 30-year-old non-profit public-interest telecommunications law firm, which promotes the public's right to hear and be heard on the electronic media, as enshrined in the US Constitution's First Amendment. MAP successfully challenged the US Federal Communications Commission (FCC) on its relaxation of cross-media ownership in 2004.*

Middle East Times
12 rue Mohamed Bayoumi, Ard El
Golf, Heliopolis, Cairo, Egypt
Editor: Grahame Bennett
t. +357 2 245 4757
e. editor@metimes.com
w. www.metimes.com
■ *This quality English-language daily deals with the Middle East and is based in Egypt.*

Moscow Times
Building 4, Ulitsa Vyborgskaya 16,
125212 Moscow, Russia
Editor: Lynn Berry
t. +7 095 937 3399
e. moscowtimes@imedia.ru
w. www.moscowtimes.ru
■ *This is an English-language daily in Moscow.*

New York Times
229 West 43rd Street, New York, NY
10036, USA
Executive Editor: Bill Keller
t. +1 212 556 1234
e. editoral@nytimes.com
w. www.nytimes.com
■ *This is the influential national paper of record. It is owned by the New York Times Company, which publishes the* **Boston Globe**

and the **International Herald Tribune** *and fifteen smaller US newspaper. It also operates eight television and two radio stations.*

South African Broadcasting Corporation (SABC)

Private Bag X1, Auckland Park 2006, South Africa
Chief Executive: Peter Matlare
t. +44 2711 714 9111
e. comments@sabc.co.za
w. www.sabc.co.za
■ *This South African public broadcaster has a radio network listened to by 19 million adults each day and three free-to-air television channels.*

South China Morning Post

16F Somerset House, Taikoo Place 979, King's Road, Quarry Bay, Hong Kong, China
Editor-in-Chief: David Armstrong
t. +852 2565 2222
w. www.scmp.com
■ *This is a daily English-language paper for Hong Kong.*

Sydney Morning Herald

201 Sussex Street, GPO Box 506, Sydney, NSW 2000, Australia
Editor-in-Chief: Greg Hywood
t. +61 2 9282 2833
e. newsdesk@smh.com
w. www.smh.com.au
■ *This is a quality Australian daily paper.*

The Age

250 Spencer Street, Melbourne 3000, Australia
Editor: Andrew Jaspan
t. +61 3 9601 2250
e. newsdesk@theage.com.au
w. www.theage.com.au
■ *This is a 150-year-old quality daily paper for the Melbourne and Victoria area of Australia.*

The Associated Press

450 W 33rd Street, New York, NY 10001, USA
Chief Executive: Tom Curley
t. +1 212 621 1500
e. info@ap.org
w. www.ap.org
■ *This is a major global newswire agency, founded in the US in 1848 and now having 242 bureaus around the world.*

Wall Street Journal

200 Liberty Street, New York, NY 10281, USA
Managing Editor: Ned Crabb
t. +1 800 568 7625
e. wsj.ltrs@wsj.com
w. www.wsj.com
■ *This is a conservative financial daily that provides detailed business and stock exchange news.*

Washington Post

1150 15th Street NW, Washington, DC 20071, USA
Executive Editor: Leonard Downie Jnr
t. +1 202 334 6000
w. www.washingtonpost.com
■ *This influential paper is the main east-coast competitor to the* **New York Times.** *The Post was home to the Watergate exposé journalists Bob Woodward and Carl Bernstein.*

Global media companies

(00 is dialled before international numbers.)

Bertlesmann

Carl-Bertelsmann-Strasse 270, 33311
Gütersloh, Germany
Chief Executive Officer: Gunter
Thielen
  t. +49 5241 800
  e. info@bertlesman.com
  w. www.bertlesman.com
■ *This international media company has a
range of interests, including television and radio
stations, television production companies, print
service providers, magazines, music companies
and book publishers. The company is structured
into six corporate divisions.*

Clear Channel

200 East Basse Road, San Antonio,
Texas 78209, USA
Chief Executive Officer: Mark Mays
  t. +1 210 822 2828
  e. lisacdollinger@clearchannel.com
  w. www.clearchannel.com
■ *This is the dominant radio station owner in
the US, owning, operating, programming or
selling air time for about 1,270 radio stations.
It also has interests in 240 radio stations
around the world. The company owns or managers more than 30 US television stations and
has a global outdoor media business.*

ComCast

1500 Market Street, Philadelphia,
Pennsylvania 19102, USA
Chief Executive Officer: Brian Roberts
  t. +1 215 665 1700
  w. www.comcast.com
■ *This is the world's largest cable television
operator, primarily broadband communications
in the US. At the end of 2003 it had 21.5 million subscribers. It gets more than 95 per cent
of its revenue from cable operations.*

Gannett

7950 Jones Branch Drive, McLean,
Virginia 22107, USA
Chief Executive Officer: Douglas H.
McCorkindale
  t. +1 703 854 6000
  w. www.gannet.com
■ *This is among the largest US newspaper
groups, owning 101 daily newspapers with a
combined circulation of 7.6 million. It owns
USA Today, the country's largest-selling daily
paper. The company also owns and operates 21
television stations in the US.*

General Electric/NBC

3135 Easton Turnpike, Fairfield,
Connecticut 06828, USA
Executive Officer: Bob Wright
  t. +1 203 373 2039
  w. www.ge.com/en
■ *General Electric is the parent company of
the global media company NBC. It owns 11
broadcast stations, as well as having interests in
the cable, international and multimedia
markets. Internationally, NBC owns NBC
Europe, CNBC Europe, and NBC Asia.*

NewsCorp

1211 Avenue of Americas, 8th Floor,
New York, NY 10036, USA
Chief Executive: Rupert Murdoch
  t. +1 212 852 7000
  e. abutcher@newscorp.com (press)
  w. www.newscorp.com
■ *This international media, news and
entertainment company has operations in
eight main areas: films (20th Century Fox),
television (Fox and Sky), cable, network programming, satellite television (BSkyB) magazine, newspapers (including the Times,
Sunday Times, and News of the World)
and book publishing. (See 'Around the world in
80 minutes: Murdoch's Global Empire' at the
beginning of the listings.)*

Sony

550 Madison Avenue, New York, NY 10022, USA
Chief Executive Officer (Sony Corporation in America): Howard Stringer
t. +1 212 833 8000
w. www.sony.com and www.sony.co.uk

■ *One of the biggest entertainment companies in the world, Sony Corporation of America is the US subsidiary of Sony Corporation, Tokyo. The company is a leading manufacturer of audio, video, communications and information technology.*

Time Warner

1 Time Warner Centre, 58th Street and 8th Avenue, New York, NY 10019, USA
Chief Executive Officer: Richard D. Parsons
t. +1 212 484 8600
w. www.timewarner.com

■ *This global media and entertainment company has interests in films, television networks, cable systems and publishing. It owns America Online, Time Inc., Time Warner Cable, HBO, New Line Cinema and Warner Brothers.*

Viacom

1515 Broadway, New York, NY 10036, USA
Chief Executive Officer: Sumner Redstone
t. +1 212 258 6000
w. www.viacom.com

■ *This is a leading global media company with extensive interests in broadcast and cable television, radio, advertising and the internet. Its best-known brands are CBS, MTV, Nickelodeon, VH1, and Paramount Pictures. Its revenue in 2003 was $26.6 billion.*

Walt Disney Company

500 South Buena Vista Street, Burbank, California 91521, USA
Chief Executive Officer: Michael D. Eisner
t. +1 818 560 1000
w. www.disney.go.com

■ *Founded in 1923, this global entertainment company is divided into four major business areas: studio entertainment, parks and resorts, consumer products and media networks. It owns ABC News in the US.*

Vivendi Universal

42 Avenue de Friedland, 75380 Paris Cedex 08, France
President: Jean-René Fourtou
t. +33 1 7171 1000
w. www.vivendiuniversal.com

■ *This is a global media and telecommunications conglomerate with activities in television, music, gaming and fixed and mobile telecommunication. The French company has interests in the Canal+ Group, a major digital and pay TV company in France.*

13

MEDIA AWARDS, FESTIVALS AND COMPETITIONS: ONE FOR EVERY-ONE IN THE AUDIENCE!

Helen Shaw

In Ireland it used to be that you did not get any recognition until you were well dead, but now there is an award scheme for just about everything you can imagine, and the media and entertainment industry like to lead the pack.

There are the PPI Radio Awards every autumn, a new radio-only awards scheme just reaching its fifth year, the classic National Media Awards (previously sponsored by the ESB), which covers journalism in all media, and the glittering new Irish Film and Television Awards, which attempt to bring a touch of the Oscars to Ireland, along with a host of new schemes for specialist content, like the Metro Eireann Media and Multicultural Awards (MAMA), aimed at recognising content with a multi-cultural theme, and new media awards, like the Digital Media Awards, which are growing annually.

Awards, as we all know, are generally to be sniffed at until you win one, and then you call the mammy, clear a place on your mantelpiece and put 'award-winning . . .' before yourself for the rest of your life. The plethora of black-tie dinners may block the media schedule in the autumn, but for many people starting out, the awards schemes are ways of getting useful cash prizes and can open lots of windows and a few doors. Equally impor-tant in the start-up years are grant schemes, scholarships and fellowships, which can help fund creative ambitions when no-one else is offering.

Most of the awards schemes in recent years have grown from one sector's desire to raise its own profile and improve public relations. The PPI Radio Awards (sponsored by the Phonographic Performance Institute and the Broadcasting Commission of Ireland) grew from the independent, commercial radio sector's desire to mark its coming of age in the industry, and from the view that the journalist-focused National Media Awards had no place for a gong for radio music and entertainment stations. The PPI Radio Awards have become an established part of the Irish radio calendar and have successfully raised the profile of both the industry and radio programme-makers at the local and national level. Photographers have the long-established Irish Press Photographers Association (IPPA) Awards, which also have a Northern chapter (NIPPA) and are well respected.

But awards are also a way of creating recognition for output that is not produced for the mass market, such as the Celtic Film and Television Festival, which rewards quality programming from the pan-Celtic region in defined categories, including radio and the web.

More challenging for documentary and film-makers though is trying to get the funding to make the type of programmes that might win a competition like the Celtic Film and Television Festival. The new Broadcast Funding Scheme, which is derived from 5% of the annual television licence fee revenues, will provide welcome additional funding for programming in genres such as history, heritage, Irish language and culture. That fund, which is worth over €8 million a year, becomes available for the first time in late 2005, through the broadcast regulator BCI, but its impact, in programming and content, will be felt in the coming years.

In the UK the most prestigious radio award scheme is still the Sony Radio Academy Awards, held every May in London, which sees the BBC battle it out against the independent sector. In television and film the BAFTAs (British Academy of Film and Television Arts awards) are the industry's Oscars, while the Royal Television Society awards are seen as peer recognition. New awards take years to gain the kind of prestige, credibility and respect that the Sony and BAFTA have, and an important aspect is how successfully they hold on to awards sponsors from year to year. What makes the sponsor stay is how seriously the industry treats the awards; so the awards schemes that are run as public relations back-slapping events tend not to last the distance. Once the awards become a self-serving joke, the sponsors, not surprisingly, get cold feet and think their marketing budget can be best spent elsewhere.

The more successfully grounded awards schemes are those that are industry-led, like the BAFTAs, which are not dependent on one sponsor and which have gained legitimacy through the buy-in of the targeted sector.

For the Irish film and independent production sector, the new Irish Film and Television Awards have provided a good showcase for talent. The fact that there are both judged and public voting awards creates a sense of difference and occasion. The new talent award, sponsored by the Irish Film Board, which in 2004 went to John Simpson, writer-director of *Freeze Frame*, is a great entry point for newcomers in an industry in which it is often extremely difficult to get a break. For factual film documentary makers, the round of festivals and awards is often the only way to get recognition and further funding, given the low value that television broadcasters place on documentaries, both in the budgets and in the schedule.

The phenomenal success of *Chavez: The Revolution Will Not Be Televised*, which picked up awards for the film-makers Kim Bartley and Donnacha Ó Briain at Irish and international film and media festivals, illustrated that often fragile balance. Among its many prizes, from the Prix Italia documentary award and the Celtic Film and Television Festival to the Banff Television Festival in Canada, was the prestigious and elite Grierson 2004 (the British Documentary Awards) in London. For both Bartley and Ó Briain, winning awards have made it easier to get commissioning editors to take their calls.

In television, everyone wants an award-winner, but not everyone is ready to fund distinctive programmes when reality television is holding audiences every night. TG4, the Irish-language television channel, has done remarkably well in recent years, and its commissioned documentary of the Irish artist Harry Clarke won at the Celtic Film and Television Festival in 2004.

In new media, the Golden Spider Awards, presented in part by the Department of Communications, Marine and Natural Resources, celebrates excellence in the internet and on-line sector; RTÉ won the Best Media Service category in 2004. The Golden Spider Award is in its ninth year now; the event takes place in November, with entry opening from October. The Digital Media Awards take place in February and are entering their fifth year in 2006. For Irish-language media, Oireachtas na Gaeilge in May is the highlight. In Northern Ireland, beyond the plethora of awards in all these sectors, there are the new Northern Ireland Arts and Business Creativity Awards, which seem ideal for digital media innovation concepts and businesses.

Peer recognition is all-important in awards, so long-established schemes generally have a high level of respect. For the newcomers and schemes that appear to reflect how many black-tie dinner tables are booked, peer recognition and industry respect can take years to build. This is why awards can come and go like fashions, particularly in the non-content areas of the media, such as marketing, sales and advertisement.

ESB National Media Awards winners, 2004

Overall Journalist of the Year Award	Primetime Investigates	RTÉ
Scoop of the Year	Deirdre Tynan	*Ireland on Sunday*
Young Journalist	Michael Brennan	*Irish Examiner*
Iriseoir na Bliana	Rónán Mac Con Iomaire	Nuacht TG4
Political and Current Affairs	Carole Coleman	RTÉ
Arts	T. J. Flynn	*Clare Champion*
Features	Mary Carr	*Ireland on Sunday*
Television Documentary	Paul Loughlin and Rita O'Reilly	RTÉ
Radio Documentary	Karen Coleman	Newstalk
Special Judges' Award	Vinnie Doyle	*Irish Independent*
Opinion	Liam Fay	*Sunday Times*
Business Features	Bill Tyson	*Irish Independent*
Business News	Conor Keane	*Irish Examiner*
Sport Print	Keith Duggan	*Irish Times*
Sport Broadcast	Conor Moloney, Karen McGrath and Paul Giles	Independent Pictures
Provincial and Regional Sport	Jonathan Mullin	*Athlone Voice*
Provincial and Regional Broadcast	Fran McNulty	Shannonside Northern Sound
Provincial and Regional News	Chris Thornton	*Belfast Telegraph*

Note: The National Media Awards will have a new sponsor in 2005 as ESB has withdrawn, but a new sponsor had not been announced by June 2005, and the future of the awards obviously depends on finding sponsorship.

Irish Film and Television Awards winners, 2004

People's Choice

Siemens Television Personality of the Year	Claire Byrne
AIB Best Irish Film Song	For a Raggy Boy

Jury Award

Best Irish Film	Omagh
Best Actor	Gerard McSorley
Best Actress	Eva Birthistle, Ae Fond Kiss
Best Film Director	Lenny Abrahamson
Best Editing	Emer Reynolds
Best Cinematography	Mark Garrett
Best Production Design	Ashleigh Jeffers
Best Music	Ray Harman
Best Script	Jeffrey Caine
Best Short Film	Undressing My Mother
Best Animation	The Boy Who Had No Story
Best Television Drama or Drama Series or Soap	Holy Cross
Best Current Affairs/News Programme	Prime Time: Intellectual Disability
Best Entertainment Programme	The Bronx Bunny Show
Best Lifestyle Programme	Show Me the Money
Best Documentary	Battle of the Bogside
Best Children's or Youth Programme	The Boy Who Had No Story
Best Actor in a Television Drama	Ciarán Hinds
Best Actress in a Television Drama	Anne Marie Duff
Best Supporting Actor in Film or Television	Peter O'Toole
Best Supporting Actress in Film/TV	Susan Lunch, 16 Years of Alcohol
Best Irish-Language Short or Animated film or Programme	Yu Ming Is Ainm Dom
Best New Talent	John Simpson, Freeze Frame

Special Award Recipients

Outstanding Irish Contribution to Cinema	Pierce Brosnan
Lifetime Achievement Award	Maureen O'Hara

PPI Radio Award winners, 2004

Local Station of the Year, Full Service	Newstalk 106 FM (Dublin)
Local Station of the Year, Music-Driven	FM 104 (Dublin)
National Stations of the Year	RTÉ Lyric FM
Overall Station of the Year	Newstalk 106 FM (Dublin)

Republic of Ireland

All-Ireland Agricultural Journalism Awards

Irish Guild of Agricultural Journalists, c/o IFP Media, 31 Dean's Grange Road, Blackrock, Co. Dublin
General Enquiries: David Markey
t. +353 1 289 3305
f. +353 1 289 6406
e. david@ifpmedia.com
■ *Annual awards in the categories of national radio and television, national press, provincial and local media, targeted communications and Young Agricultural Journalist (under 28), for reporters, photographers and agricultural communicators.*

Bill Naughton Short Story Competition

Aghamore, PO Box 2005, Ballyhaunis, Co. Mayo
General Enquiries: Paul Rogers
t. +353 94 936 7016
e. paulwdr@gofree.indigo.ie
w. www.aghamoregaa.com/society/shortstory.htm
■ *An annual short story competition.*

Bisto Book Awards

Children's Books Ireland, 17 North Great George's Street, Dublin 1
Bisto Administrator: Liz Marshall
t. +353 1 872 7475
f. +353 1 872 7476
e. bistoawards@childrensbooksireland.com
w. www.childrensbooksireland.com/bisto_book_awards/index.shtml
■ *Annual awards for children's books. Open to any author or illustrator of children's books born or resident in Ireland.*

Clones Film Festival

Shambles Lane, Clones, Co. Monaghan
General Enquiries
t. +353 47 52309
e. info@clonesfilmfestival.com
w. www.clonesfilmfestival.com
■ *An annual art house and non-commercial cinema festival. The festival is held in October.*

Cork Film Festival

Emmet House, Emmet Place, Cork
Festival Director: Mick Hannigan
t. +353 21 427 1711
f. +353 21 427 5945
e. info@corkfilmfest.org
w. www.corkfilmfest.org
■ *An annual film festival with a mix of big-budget pictures, world cinema, independent films, documentaries and short films from all over the globe. The festival is a showcase for Irish film production and is held in October.*
Festival Manager: Eimear O'Herlihy

Cork Youth International Film and Video Arts Festival

Croppy Boy House, Fairhill, Cork
General Enquiries: Helen Prout
t. +353 21 430 6019
e. hprout@europe.com
■ *An international annual film, video and arts festival aimed at creating an awareness and involving young people in film making and the arts. The festival is held in May.*

Darklight Festival

69 Dame Street, Dublin 2
General Enquiries
t. +353 1 670 9017
e.info@darklight-filmfestival.com
w. www.darklight-filmfestival.com
■ *An annual festival aimed at presenting Irish and international film-making, video, graphic design, post-production, art, music and animation. The festival is accompanied by an exhibition and seminar programme and is held in November.*

Digital Media Awards

Digital Media Intelligence, Digital
Media House, 9 Baggot Court, Dublin 2
Awards Director: Helen Connolly
t. +353 1 669 1750
e. hconnolly@digitalmedia.ie
w. www.digitalmedia.ie
■ *Awards are open to Irish and international
companies and are divided into the following
categories: Education, Digital Media
Innovation, Web sites, Wireless, Content,
Business, Creativity, Special Award and Grand
Prix Award.*
*The last ceremony was held at the Burlington
Hotel in Dublin on Wednesday 2 February
2005. Deadline for entries: late December 2005
(finalists announced mid-January).*
Head of Production: Ailbhe O'Donnell
aodonnell@digitalmedia.ie

Dublin International Film Festival

13 Merrion Square, Dublin 2
Contact: Rory Concannon
t. +353 1 661 6216
f. +353 1 661 4418
e. info@dubliniff.com
w. www.dubliniff.com
■ *An annual festival of contemporary Irish
and international cinema. The festival is held
in February.*

Dublin Lesbian and Gay Film Festival (Outlook)

c/o Glen, Fumbally Court, Fumbally
Lane, Dublin 8
Director: Brian Sheehan
t. +353 1 415 8414; +353 86 233 0417
f. +353 1 473 0597
e. dlgff@ireland.com
w. www.gcn.ie/dlgff
■ *An annual film festival showcasing Irish
and international gay films and documentaries.
The festival is held over the August holiday
weekend.*
Programmers: Deborah Ballard and
Paul Connell

Dublin Writers' Festival

Dublin City Council Arts,
10 Cornmarket, Dublin 8
Director: Jack Gilligan
t. +353 1 671 3639
e. office@dublinwritersfestival.com
w. www.dublinwritersfestival.com

Fish International Short Story Prize

Durrus, Co. Cork
General Enquiries
t. +353 27 55 645
e. info@fishpublishing.com
w. www.fishpublishing.com
■ *An annual prize for new literary short
stories.*

Fresh Film Festival

Belltable Arts Centre, 69 O'Connell
Street, Limerick
Festival Director: Jayne Foley
t. +353 61 319 555/+353 87 218 0033
f. +353 61 319 555
e. info@freshfilmfestival.com
■ *An annual contemporary film and video
festival for young people. The festival is held in
April.*
Festival Co-ordinator: Tim O'Mullane
Features Programmer: Brendan Maher

Galway Film Fleadh

Cluain Mhuire, Monivea Road, Galway
Managing Director: Miriam Allen
t. +353 91 751 655
f. +353 91 735 831
e. gafleadh@iol.ie
w. www.galwayfilmfleadh.com
■ *An annual international film festival catering for film-makers and attracting directors,
actors, cinematographers and artists. The festival is held in July.*
Programme Director: Sally Ann O'Reilly

Golden Spider Awards

General Enquiries: Alan Ryan and
Tracy Mongan
t. +353 1 416 7809; +353 1 416 7836
e. info@goldenspiders.ie
w. www.goldenspiders.ie

■ *Annual awards open to Irish companies and divided into the following categories:*

1 The Prosperity (Best Financial Web Site)
2 Best Travel and Tourism Web Site
3 The Last Minute.com (Best On-Line Search Engine Portal)
4 The FÁS Best On-Line Recruitment Web Site
5 The IACT Best SME Web Site
6 Best International Web Site
7 IrishJobs.ie (Best E-Commerce Web Site Award)
8 Entertainment Sports and Leisure Web Site Award
9 The RTÉ Best Community, Charity or Special Interest Award
10 Best Information Excellence Award
11 The Department of Communications, Marine and Natural Resources Best Educational Institution or Schools Web Site
12 The Tourism Ireland On-Line/Marketing Advertising Award
13 Best E-Business Consultancy Award
14 The Argus Car Rental.com Best On-Line Logistical Web Award
15 Media Service Web Site of the Year Award
16 Web Design Development Agency of the Year Award
17 The Business and Finance Business Person's Contribution to Irish Internet Industry Award
18 The Domain.ie web site of the year
19 Overall web site of the year award
20 Best Motoring Category

The ceremony is held in November.

GSK Irish Medical Media Awards

GlaxoSmithKline, Stonemason's Way, Dublin 16
General Enquiries
  t. +353 1 495 5000
  f. +353 1 495 5105
■ *Annual awards for medical journalism.*

IIA & MSN Net Visionary Awards

Irish Internet Association, The Digital Hub, 10–13 Thomas Street, Dublin 8
General Enquiries
  t. +353 1 453 5707
  e. info@iia.ie
  w. www.iia.ie
■ *Annual internet awards, honouring individuals for their contribution to the Irish internet industry, with the following categories: Social Contribution, Innovation, Technology Journalist, E-government, Internet Marketing, Web Designer Excellence, Web Developer Excellence, Online Trader, New Entrepreneur, Education Contribution, Mobile Internet Contribution, Special IIA Contribution and the Net Visionary Award. The awards ceremony is held in November.*

International IMPAC Dublin Literary Award

Dublin City Library and Archive, 138–144 Pearse Street, Dublin 2
General Enquiries: Clare Hogan
  t. +353 1 674 4802
  f. +353 1 674 4879
  e. literaryaward@dublincity.ie
  w. www.impacdublinaward.ie
■ *An award open to works of fiction written in, or translated into, English, published within a specified period, and nominated by selected libraries in cities throughout the world.*

Irish Film and Television Awards (IFTA)

Irish Film and Television Network, First Floor, Palmerstown Centre, Kennelsfort Road, Dublin 20
General Enquiries
  t. +353 1 620 0811
  f. +353 1 620 0810
  e. info@iftn.ie
  w. www.iftn.ie
■ *Annual awards organised by the Irish Film and Television Network (IFTN), by jury and people's choice, and for lifetime achievement and outstanding contribution to Irish film or television. The awards ceremony is held in October.*

Irish Professional Photographers Association Awards

General Enquiries

e. president@ppai.ie

w. www.ppai.ie

■ *Annual awards, showcasing Irish press photography through a traveling exhibition.*

Kerry Film Festival

The Boatyard, Blennerville, Tralee, Co. Kerry

Director: Maurice Galway

t. +353 66 712 9934

f. +353 66 712 0934

e. samhlaiocht@indigo.com

w. www.samhlaiocht.com

■ *An annual film festival showcasing Irish and international films. The festival is held in October.*

Law Media Awards

Law Society of Ireland, Blackhall Place, Dublin 7

General Enquiries

t. +353 1 672 4800

f. +353 1 672 4801

w. www.lawsociety.ie

■ *Awards for excellence in journalism dealing with legal issues.*

Listowel Writers' Week

24 The Square, Listowel, Co. Kerry

t. +353 68 21074

f. +353 68 22893

e. writersweek@eircom.net

w. www.writersweek.ie

■ *Long-established writers' festival with competitions and awards for fiction, short-story, poetry and drama. 2005 boasted a prize fund of €30,000, with €10,000 for the top Irish Fiction Award. The Listowel Writers' Week honours the legacy of local writers, the late Bryan MacMahon, a school-teacher and fiction writer, and the late John B. Keane, the celebrated dramatist.*

Meteor Ireland Music Awards

General Enquiries

w. meteor.webhost.ie/html/home.html

■ *Annual awards for music, with categories including Best Irish DJ, Best Irish Band, Best Irish Male Artist, Best Irish Female Artist and Best Irish Pop Band. The awards ceremony is held in February.*

Metro Eireann Media and Multicultural Awards (MAMA)

Metro Eireann, The Mews, 213 North Circular Road, Dublin 7

General Enquiries

t. +353 1 869 0670

f. +353 1 868 9142

e. awards@metroeireann.com

w. www.metroeireann.com/awards

■ *Annual awards recognising and celebrating outstanding contributions of individuals and groups to creating cross-cultural understanding and co-operation in Ireland and initiatives that promote and celebrate cultural diversity in Ireland.*

National Media Awards

New contact details not available at time of going to press.

■ *Annual awards aimed at promoting excellence in journalism in the Republic and Northern Ireland and divided into the following categories: Journalist of the Year, Young Journalist of the Year (under 25 at closing date), Political and Current Affairs Journalist of the Year, Arts Journalist of the Year, Irish-Language Media Journalist of the Year and Scoop of the Year.*

The closing date in 2004 was Friday 13 August.

Oireachtas na Gaeilge

6 Harcourt Street, Dublin 2

General Enquiries

t. +353 1 475 3857

f. +353 1 475 8767

e. eolas@antoireachtas.ie

w. www.antoireachtas.ie

■ *A celebration of Irish culture that moves location each year around Ireland. Includes a media awards ceremony, competitions, singing, dancing, storytelling, sessions, seminars, exhibitions, book launches, CDs, games, craft, drama, table quizzes, debates, a young people's parade and concerts.*

The communication awards ceremony is held in May.

Picture Editors' Awards

General Enquiries
e. administrator@pictureawards.net
w. www.pictureawards.net
■ *Annual awards, open to photographic journalists living in the UK or Ireland and British and Irish photographers wherever they reside. There is also a student award. The awards ceremony is held in May.*

PPA Ireland Magazine Awards

Periodical Publishers' Association of Ireland (PPA Ireland), c/o 18 Upper Grand Canal Street, Dublin 4
General Enquiries: Grace Aungier
t. +353 1 668 2056
e. aungierg@eircom.net
w. www.ppa.ie
■ *Annual awards recognising and rewarding the best Irish magazines in a number of categories, including: Consumer Magazine of the Year, Publisher of the Year, Consumer Specialist Magazine of the Year, Business to Business Magazine of the Year, Business to Business Specialist Magazine of the Year, Editor of the Year, Designer of the Year, Customer Magazine of the Year, Annual of the Year, Interactive Magazine of the Year and Religious Magazine of the Year. The awards ceremony is held in December.*

PPI Radio Awards

PPI House, 1 Corrig Avenue, Dún Laoghaire, Co. Dublin
Event Manager: Sean Murtagh
t. +353 1 280 5977
e. info@ppiradioawards.com
w. www.ppiradioawards.com
■ *Annual awards for radio production and programming in the areas of Music Programming, News and Sports Programming, Speech Programming, General Programming, Personality and Station of the Year. The award ceremony is held in October.*

Rooney Prize for Irish Literature

Strathin, Templecarrig, Delgany, Co. Wicklow
General Enquiries
t. +353 1 287 4769
f. +353 1 287 2595
e. rooneyprize@ireland.com
■ *An annual award for Irish writers under the age of 40 and who are published.*

RTÉ Awards

Contact information office, RTÉ, Donnybrook, Dublin 4
t. +353 1 208 3434
e. press@rte.ie
w. www.rte.ie
■ *RTÉ, the public broadcasting company, runs a number of awards schemes, including;*
RTÉ Radio
The P. J. O'Connor Radio Drama Awards
The Francis MacManus Short Story Competition
The RTÉ 2FM/Jacob's Song Contest
RTÉ also sponsors the MAMA awards, and RTÉ television broadcasts many of the main Irish media awards, including the Irish Film and Television Awards, the Meteor Awards and highlights of the National Media Awards.

Stranger Than Fiction Documentary Festival and Market

Irish Film Institute, 6 Eustace Street, Dublin 2
Director: Grainne Humphreys
t. +353 1 679 5744
f. +353 1 677 8755
e. stf@irishfilm.ie
w. www.irishfilm.ie
■ *An annual documentary film festival and audience award and Irish short documentary film competition. The festival is held in October, usually centred around the Irish Film Institute in Temple Bar, and the market is organised by Screen Producers Ireland (SPI)— the audio-visual sector's representative body.*

Strokestown Poetry Competition
Strokestown, Co. Roscommon
General Enquiries
t. +353 66 947 4123; +353 71 963 8540
e. pbushe@eircom.net
w. www.strokestownpoetryprize.com
■ *Annual poetry festival and competition. The festival is held in May.*

Tiernan MacBride International Screenwriting Award
Irish Film Institute, 6 Eustace Street, Dublin 2
General Enquiries
t. +353 1 679 5744
■ *An annual award aiming to encourage and develop new Irish screen-writing talent and open to all Irish-born writers, Irish citizens or Irish residents. Submission date: Friday 1 October.*

West Cork Literary Festival
27 June to 3 July 2005

13 Glengarrif Road, Bantry, Co. Cork
t. +353 27 52788
f. +353 27 52797
w. www.fishpublishing.com
Contact: Festival Director, Clem Cairns.
■ *The West Cork Literary Festival aims to bring the best and most inspiring literary figures to West Cork and to make their talents and knowledge accessible to the audience and participants. The festival runs concurrently with the Cork Chamber Music Festival and has workshops on all forms of writing, from films to poetry for children. Workshops are run by established writers, from Eoghan Harris to Mary Morrissey. Events take place at Bantry library.*

Wexford Book Festival
12–17 April 2005
t. +353 53 22226
e. wexfordbookfestival@eircom.net
w. www.wexfordbook.com
■ *Literary festival currently sponsored by Eircom.*

United Kingdom

(00 is dialled before international numbers.)

Belfast Film Festival
Exchange Place Building, 23 Donegall Street, Belfast BT1 2FS
General Enquiries: Michele Devlin
t. +44 28 9032 5913
f. +44 28 9032 9397
e. info@belfastfilmfestival.org
w. www.belfastfilmfestival.org
■ *An annual film festival, including European and international premieres, a shorts competition, classics, musicals, animation and a programme of music and film events. The festival is held in April.*

British Academy of Film and Television Arts (BAFTA)
195 Piccadilly, London W1J 9LN, England
General Enquiries
t. +44 20 7734 0022

f. +44 20 7734 1792
w. www.bafta.org
■ *An organisation promoting and rewarding the best in films, television and interactive media. The BAFTA runs awards schemes, including the Orange British Academy Film Awards, the BAFTA Television Awards, the BAFTA Television Craft Awards, the BAFTA Children's Film and Television Awards, the BAFTA Games Awards, and the BAFTA Interactive Awards.*

Celtic Film and Television Festival
249 West George Street, Glasgow G2 4QE, Scotland
General Enquiries: Frances Hendron
t. +44 141 302 1737
f. +44 141 302 1738
e. mail@celticfilm.co.uk
w. www.celticfilm.co.uk

■ *A film and television festival promoting the cultures and languages of Brittany, Cornwall, Ireland, Scotland, Wales and the Isle of Man on screen, radio and new media. The festival is held in April.*

Cinemagic

49 Botanic Avenue, Belfast BT7 1JL
Chief Executive: Joan Burney
t. +44 28 9031 1900
f. +44 28 9031 9709
e. info@cinemagic.org.uk
w. www.cinemagic.org.uk
■ *A world screen festival for young people.*
Festival Programmer: Chris Shaw
Press and Marketing Manager: Maria McAlister
Project Co-ordinator: Laura Carlisle

Institute of Internal Auditors (IIA) Award for Business Journalism

13 Abbeville Mews, 88 Clapham Park Road, London SW4 7BX, England
Competition Secretary: Victoria Sutton
t. +44 20 7819 1917
e. victoria.sutton@iia.org.uk
w. www.iia.org.uk
■ *Annual award for excellence in business writing, with regard to the presentation of issues and practices of internal auditing. Open to staff journalists, freelance writers and academics, published in any UK-based or Irish publication.*

Northern Ireland Arts and Business Creativity Awards

Arts and Business Northern Ireland, 53 Malone Road, Belfast BT9 6RY
General Enquiries
t. +44 28 9066 4736
f. +44 28 9066 4500
e. northern.ireland@aandb.org.uk
w. www.aandb.org.uk
■ *An annual awards scheme, with categories including: Arts, Business and Brand Identity; Arts, Business and Sustainability; Arts, Business and Community; Arts, Business and Young People; Arts, Business and the Individual; Arts, Business and Employees; The DCAL Unlocking Creativity; and the Legal*

and General Group PLC Arts Award. The awards ceremony will be held in January.

Royal Television Society (RTS)

Holborn Hall, 100 Gray's Inn Road, London WC1X 8AL, England
General Enquiries
t. +44 20 7430 1000
f. +44 20 7430 0924
e. info@rts.org.uk
w. www.rts.org.uk
■ *A forum for discussion and debate on all aspects of the television community, recognising and rewarding excellence, providing opportunities for people in television to get together, and promoting professional development. Provides an awards scheme (the RTS Awards), including the categories of Programme, Television Journalism, Television Sports, Craft and Design, Technical Innovation, Educational Television and Student Television.*

Seagate Foyle Film Festival

The Nerve Centre, 7–8 Magazine Street, Derry BT48 6HJ
General Enquiries
t. +44 28 7126 7432
w. www.foylefilmfestival.com
■ *An annual film festival providing screenings, competitions, workshops, education programmes and special events. The festival is held in November.*

Sony Radio Academy Awards

c/o ZAFER Associates, 47–48 Chagford Street, London NW1 6EB, England
General Enquiries
t. +44 20 7723 0106
f. +44 20 7724 6163
e. info@radioawards.org
w. www.radioawards.org
■ *An annual award for radio, with categories including music and entertainment, news and speech, station and special awards. The awards are organised by a committee representing the landscape of radio, whose chairman and mem is in January, and the awards ceremony is held in May.*

INDEX

(Note: where there is more than one reference, the directory entry is indicated by bold type)

A & A Farmar, 127
A & D, 264
A & L Goodbody International, 294
A1 Advertising and Marketing, 264
AA Motoring, 144
Abbey Press, 137
ABC (Audit Bureau of Circulation), 14, 20, 140
ABC television, 302
Ability, 144
About-Face Media Productions, 233
Abroad, 144
Abú Media, 195
accessCINEMA, 195
Accountancy Ireland, 144
Accountancy Plus, 144
AC Nielson, 2
Actors and Movers, 294
Adapt Marketing Services, 264
Adare Productions, 195
Adept Creative Facilities, 264
Adhouse, 264
Adimpact Media, 264
Adleader Publications, 137
AdSat, 265
Adsell Productions, 195
Advance Publications (APL Group), 127
advertising, 10, 257–63
    advertisers, 259–60
    agencies, 258–9
    expenditure, 257–8
    internet, 10, 261, 263
    magazines and periodicals, 140, 142
    marketing, 260–61, 262–3
    media buying, 259
    newspapers, 13, 17, 18, 19–20, 258
    outdoor, 258
    radio, 76, 78, 258
    sponsorship, 260
    standards and code, 265, 290–91
    television, 10, 62, 66, 258, 290–91
    trends, 261
Advertising Standards Authority, 265
Adworks, 265
AE Consulting, 265
Aesop Teo, 196
AFA O'Meara Advertising, 265
Affinity, 286
Afloat, 144
Age, The, 318
Ageing Matters in Ireland, 144
Agence France Press
    Dublin correspondent, 307
    London bureau, 308
Agtel/Independent Pictures, 196
Ahern, Dermot, 80, 290
AIB Investment Managers, 294
Aís, 6
Aisling Quarterly, 144
Akajava Films, 196
Alchemy Electronic Arts, 196
Algar Productions, 196
Al-Jazeera, 316
All-Ireland Agricultural Journalism Awards, 327
All-Ireland Kitchen Guide, 145
All Media Matters, 265
Alpha Newspapers Group, 15, **46**
Amárach Consulting, 112
AMAS, 112
Amazon, 112
American College, Dublin, 240
Amnesia Film, 196
Amnesty International, 145

Andec Communications Media, 197
AndersonSprattGroup
  Belfast office, 286
  Holywood office, 286
Andersonstown News, 46
Andersonstown News Group, 46
Anglo-Celt, The, 21
Anglo Irish Bank Operation, 294
Animo Television, 197
ANSA, 307
Antrim Guardian, 46–7
Antrim Hospital Radio, 103
Anvil Books, 127
Any News, 197
AOL Time Warner, 301, 302
Apple, 111
Appletree Press, 137
Aquaculture Ireland, 145
Araby Productions, 197
Áras Telegael, 197
Archaeology Ireland, 145
Architecture Ireland, 145
Ardmore Sound, 191, 194, **197**
Argus, The, 21
Arlen House, 127
Armagh College, 252
Armagh-Down Observer, 47
Armagh Observer, 47
artdirector.ie, 266
Arthur Cox, 294
Art of Resistance Films, 197
Arts Ireland, 145
Ashville Media Group, 127
Assets, 294
Associated Press, 318
  Dublin correspondent, 307
Association of Film Accountants of Ireland,
  197
Association of Freelance Editors,
  Proofreaders and Indexers (AFEPI), 127
Astronomy and Space, 145
Asylum Studios, 198
Athena Media, 112, 198
Athlone Institute of Technology, 244
Athlone Observer, 21
Athlone Topic, 21
Athlone Voice, 21
Atomic, 266
Attic Press, 127–8
audience councils, 293
audio-visual *see* film and audio-visual pro-
  duction

Audiovisual Federation, 191, 239
Audit Bureau of Circulation (ABC), 14, 20,
  140
Auletta, Ken, 301
Aura Productions/Farm TV, 198
Auto Ireland, 145–6
Auto Trade Journal, 146
Auto Trader, 182
Autowoman, 146
AV Browne Advertising, 286
AV Edge, 198
Avica Europe, 193
Avondhu, The, 21
awards and competitions, 321–6

Baby & Child, 146
Backpacker Ireland, 146
Backspin, 146
BAFTA (British Academy of Film and
  Television Arts) awards, 322, **332**
Ballincollig Newsletter, The, 21
Ballsbridge College of Further Education, 240
Ballyfermot College of Further Education,
  240
Ballylough Books, 128
Ballymena Guardian, 47
Ballymena Times, 47
Ballymoney and Moyle Times, 47
Ballymun Comprehensive Adult Education
  Centre, 240
Banahan McManus, 266
Banbridge Chronicle, 48
Banbridge Leader, 48
Banff Television Festival, 323
Banking Ireland, 141
BBC, 60, 239
  global influence, 306
  market share, 63
  Radio, 78, **308**
  Radio Foyle, **100**
  Radio Ulster, 5, 10, **100**
  Television (London), **308**
  Television (N. Ireland), 3, 7, 60, **72–3**
  World Service, 305, **308–9**
  World Service Trust, **309**
BCI *see* Broadcasting Commission of Ireland
Beacon Studios, 198
Beat 102–103 FM, 77, 79, **86**
Beaufield Productions, 198
Beaumont Hospital Radio, 99
Beautiful Irish Homes, 182
Belfast Film Festival, 332

Belfast Institute of Further and Higher
Education, 252
Belfast News, 17, **48**
Belfast Telegraph, 15, 17, **48–9**
Bell Advertising and Employee
Communications, 266
Belmont Productions, 198
Bertelsmann, 302–3, **319**
Besom Productions, 233
Beyond International, 112
BFBS Radio 1, 102
Big Buzz Magazine, 182
Big List, The, 182
Big River, 198–9
Big Top Multimedia, 112
Bill Naughton Short Story Competition, 327
Bill O'Herlihy Communications Group, 266
Birchall Company, 266
Bisto Book Awards, 327
Blackhall Publishing, 128
Blackstaff Press, 121, **137**
Blackwater Press, 128
Blanchardstown Institute of Technology, 244
Blanch Gazette, 22
Blinck Mobile Ltd, 112
Blinder Ltd, 199
Blockbusters, 302
Bloom, 266
Bloomberg, 316
Dublin office, 307
Blue Blanket, 199
Blue Monkey Studios, 199
Blueprint Pictures, 199
Blue Sphere Productions, 233
BMG, 300, 302, 303
BNIL (Bulletin of Northern Ireland Law),
182–3
Bofin Byers Company/BBC Advertising,
266–7
BOI Business Banking, 294
Bonfire, 267
book publishing, 121–6
best-sellers, 125–6
Irish language, 6
libel and, 124, 293
market, 122–4
trends, 124–5
Books Ireland, 146
Bookview Ireland, 146
Borderline Productions
Belfast office, 233
Dublin office, 199

Bord Scannán na hÉireann (Irish Film
Board), 190, 192, **199**, 323
Boulder Media, 112
A Boy Named Sue Films, 195
Bracken Public Relations, 267
Bradshaw Books, 128
Brandon Books, 128
Bravo, 302
Bray People, 22
Breacadh, 128
Breaking Ball, 141
Brennock, Mark, 293
Brian Waddell Productions, 233
Brian Wallace Advertising, 267
Brindley Advertising, 267
British Academy of Film and Television Arts
(BAFTA) awards, 322, **332**
broadband, 1, 2, 108, 110, 143, 305
Broadcast Funding Scheme, 322
Broadcasting Act (1988), 290
Broadcasting Act (2001), 8, 9, 70, 290
Broadcasting Authority of Ireland (BAI),
289, 290
Broadcasting Commission of Ireland (BCI),
9, 10, 62, 79, 289, 293, **294–5**, 322
advertising code, 290–91
Broadcasting Complaints Commission
(BCC), 293, **295**
Broadcasting Funding Scheme, 9
Brother Films, 200
Brown Bag Films, 200
Browne, Vincent, 139–40
BSkyB, 8, 10, 11, 60, 61, 259, 303, 304
Sky News (Belfast Bureau), **74**
Sky News (Ireland), **70**
Buckshee Films, 200
Build Your Own House and Home, 146
Burren College of Art, 240
Business, The, 311
Business & Finance, 141, **147**
Business Eye, 182
Business Plus, 141, **147**
Business2Arts, 147
Business World, 147
Buy and Sell
Belfast office, 49
Dublin office, 22
Buyer's Guide to Irish Art, 147

Cable and Wireless Ireland Ltd, 112
Cablelink, 61
Cabletext Waterford, 71

Caboom, 113
Cabvertise, 267
Calico Media, 113
Cambridge Animation Systems, 113
Camel Productions, 200
Campaign HTDS, 267
Cancerwise, 147
CanWest, 8, 61
Capiche Design, 113
Captive Advertising, 267–8
Cara, 147
Cara Gregg Creative Consultancy, 268
Carat Ireland, 268
careers in media, 3–4, 239
Carival Advertising and Design, 268
Carlow Advertiser, 22
Carlow Institute of Technology, 244
Carlow Nationalist, 22
Carlow People, 22
Carlow Times, 22
Carlow Vocational School, 241
Carr Communications, 268
Carrickfergus Advertiser, 49
Carrick Times, 49
Carrigdhoun Newspaper, 22
Carsport Magazine, 182
Cartoon Saloon, 200
Casey, Norah, 139
Casey Communications, 268
Cashel and District Community Radio, 95
Castaway Actors' Agency, 295–6
Castlereagh College, 252
Catering and Licensing Review, 182
Cathal Black Films, 200
Causeway Coast Radio, 102
Causeway Institute, 252
Cavan College of Further Studies, 241
Cawley Nea/TBWA, 268
CBS Broadcasting Inc., 301, **317**
Celtic Film and Television Festival, 322,
   323, **332–3**
Celtic Media Group, 19, **22**
Celtic Publications, 128
censorship, 7–8
Centre for Media Research, 237
Certification Europe, 113
Channel 6, 67
Channel 9 TV (c9tv), 73
Checkout, 147
Chemistry Strategic Communications, 268
Childnames.net, 128
Children's Advertising Code, 290, 292

Children's Press, 129
Children's Wear in Ireland, 147
Chorus, 11, 61, **113**
Church of Ireland Gazette, 49
Church of Ireland Publishing, 129
Cibenix, 113
Cinemagic, 333
cinemas, 189
Circa Art Magazine, 148
Citigate Smarts, 286
Citybeat 96.7 FM, 100–101
City Channel, 62, **71**
City News, 50
City Tribune, 23
Citywide News, 23
Claddagh Films, 200–201
Clanvisions, 233–4
Clare Champion, 23
Clare County Express, 23
Clare FM, 86
Clár na nÓg, 148
Classmate, 148
Clé (Irish Book Publishers' Association),
   122, **130**
Clear Channel, 303, **319**
Cló an Rátha Bháin, 135
Cló Iar-Chonnachta, 6, **129**
Clones Film Festival, 327
CMB Designs, 269
CNN, 302, 305, **317**
Coca-Cola, 259–60
Coco Television, 201
Coey Advertising Company, 286
Cois Life, 6, **129**
Coiscéim, 6, **129**
Coláiste Dhúlaigh College of Further
   Education, 241
Coláiste Stiofáin Naofa, 241
Coleraine Chronicle, 50
Coleraine Times, 50
Colleges of Further Education, 238
Collins Photo Agency, 201
Collins Press, 129
ColourBooks, 129
Colourpoint Books, 137
Columba Press, 129–30
Columbia, 303
Comcast, 301, 303, **319**
Comet Films and TV Productions, 201
Comhar, 6
Comit Marketing, 269
Commercial Interiors of Ireland, 148

Commercial Law Practitioner, 148
Communications Act 2003 (UK), 301, 303
Communications, Marine and Natural
    Resources, Dept of, 292, **296**, 323
Communicorp Group, 10, 78, 79
Community Radio Castlebar, 95
Community Radio Youghal, 95
Competition Authority, 291, **296**
competitions and awards, 321–6
complaints process, 293
Computerscope, 148
ComReg (Irish Commission for
    Communications Regulation), 2, 11,
    292, **296**
Concept Advertising and Design, 269
Confetti, 148
Connacht Sentinel, 23
Connacht Tribune, 23
Connaught Telegraph, 23
Connemara Community Radio, 95–6
Constabulary Gazette, 183
Constitution of Ireland, 7–8
Construction, 148
Construction and Property News, 148–9
Construction Information Service (CIS)
    Report, 149
Construct Ireland, 149
Consumer Choice, 149
Convenience Advertising, 269
Conveyancing and Property Law Journal,
    149
Cool FM, 101
Copper Reed Studio, 269
Copy Desk, The, 269
Cork 96FM/103FM County Sound, 10,
    86–7
Cork Campus Radio, 96
Cork College of Further Education, 241
Cork Film Centre, 201
Cork Film Festival, 201, 327
Cork Institute of Technology, 244
Corkman, The, 23
Cork Now, 149
Cork University Press, 122, **130**, 149
Cork Youth International Film and Video
    Arts Festival, 327
Corporate Connections, 269
Corriere della Sera, 313
Cosantór, An, 149
County Sound, 10, **86–7**
Courtyard Studio, 201
Covert Films, 201–2

CP&A, 269
Craigavon Echo, 50
Cranagh Press, 137
Crannóg Films and TV, 202
Create, 202
Creative Inputs, 113
Creative Works, 270
Credit Union Review, 149
Creedo Productions, 202
Crescendo Concepts, 202
Crossing the Line Films, 202
CSL Associates, 270
CUH FM Hospital Radio, 99
Cúl a' Tigh, 202
Cullen Communications, 270
Cumann Leabharfhoilsitheoirí Éireann (Clé),
    122, **130**
Cumhacht, 149
Currach Press, 130
Cyberline, 270
Cyesta, 114
Cyprus Broadcasting Corporation, 313
Cyprus Mail, 313
Czech Television, 313

DAB (digital audio broadcasting), 11, 80
Daft.ie, 114
Daily Express, 309
Daily Ireland, 4, 14, **50**
Daily Mail, 309
Daily Mail and Guardian (S. Africa), 317
Daily Mirror, 309
Daily Star, 309
Daily Star Sunday, 309
Daily Telegraph, 309–10
Dara Creative Communications, 114
Dare to be Digital, 108
Darklight Festival, 107, **327**
Davis College, 241
DDFH&B Advertising, 270
de Buitléar, Éamon, 203
Decision, 141, **149–50**
Dedalus Press, 130
Deering, Mark, 10
De Facto Films, 234
Defamation Bill (2005), 293
Delicious 9, 202
Dempsey, Noel, 62
Denis Desmond Management Productions,
    202
Dept of Communications, Marine and
    Natural Resources, 292, **296**, 323

deregulation, 236, 291
Derry Journal, 50
Derry Journal Newspapers Group, 50–51
Derry News, 51
Derry on Monday, 51
Des Bingham Associates, 287
Deutsche Welle, 313
DHR Communications, 270
Diabetes Ireland, 150
Diabetes Wise, 150
Diageo Ireland, 259
Diageo Learning Liberties Initiative, 108
Dialogue – The Direct Response Brand
    Agency, 270
Diario de Noticias, 314
Dickers Sound Systems, 203
Digital Animation Media, 113
Digital Hub Development Agency, 107–8, **114**
Digital Media Awards, 321, 323, **328**
Digital Media Centre, 105
Digital Media Forum, 114
Digital Media Services Directory, 150
digital technology
    digital content companies, 106
    digital divide, 1, 104, 306
    education and employment, 237
    films, 193
    global trends, 305–6
    radio, 8, 11, 80
    television, 1, 8, 10, 11, 60, 61–2, 289
direct marketing, 260–61
DirecTV, 302, 304
Disney, 191, 302, **320**
'disruptive technologies', 110–11
Distinguished Features, 203
DMA, 270
Dobhar, 203
Doctor's Deskbook, 150
Doctrine and Life, 150
Dog House Productions, 203
Donegal Democrat, 23
Donegal News, 24
Donegal on Sunday, 24
Double Band Films, 234
Double Z Enterprises, 203
Dow Jones Newswires, 307
Down Democrat, 51
Down Recorder, 51
Downtown Radio, 101
dpdesign, 270
DR – Denmark Broadcasting Corporation,
    313–14

Drinks Industry Ireland, 150
Drive, 150
Drogheda Independent, 24
Drogheda Leader, 24
Dromore Leader, 51
Drumlin Publications, 130
Drury Communications, 262, **271**
Drystock Farmer, 150
DTT (digital terrestrial television), 61–2, 289
Dublin Business School, 241–2
Dublin City Anna Livia FM, 98
Dublin City University, 3, 238, **242**
Dublin Daily, 14
Dubliner, The, 141, **150–51**
Dublin Evening Classes Guidebook, 151
Dublin Historical Record, 151
Dublin Institute of Advanced Studies, 130
Dublin Institute of Technology, 3, 237–8,
    242
    Media Production Unit, **203**
Dublin International Film Festival, 328
Dublin Lesbian and Gay Film Festival, 328
Dublin Review, 151
Dublin's Country 106.8 FM, 87
Dublin South FM, 96
Dublin University Law Journal, 151
Dublin Writers' Festival, 328
Dundalk 100 FM, 96
Dundalk Democrat, 24
Dundalk Institute of Technology, 244
Dunfermline Press, 19
Dungannon News and Tyrone Courier, 51
Dungannon Observer, 51
Dungarvan Leader, 24
Dungarvan Observer, 24
Dún Laoghaire Institute of Art, Design and
    Technology, 238, **242–3**
DVB (digital video broadcasting), 11
DVDs, 65, 193
DVM TV, 114

Early Town Films, 203
Earth Horizon Productions, 204
Eason Advertising, 271
East Antrim Gazette, 51–2
East Antrim Institute of Further and Higher
    Education, 252–3
East Antrim Times, 52
East Atlantic Productions, 204
East Coast FM, 10, **87**
East Down Institute of Further and Higher
    Education, 253

East Tyrone College of Further and Higher Education, 253
Easy Food, 151
eBay, 106
Echo, The, 24
Echo Group, 24–5
Eclipse Productions, 204
Economic and Social Review, The, 151
Edelman Public Relations, 262, **271**
Edge Films International, 204
education, 3, 236–9
Education (publication), 151
Educational Company of Ireland, 130–31
Education Matters, 151
EFE News Agency, 307
Egg Post Production, 204
Éigse: A Journal of Irish Studies, 152
Eircom, 114–15
Eircom Information Age Town competition, 105
Eircom Live, 152
Eirplay Games, 106, **115**
e-learning, 106
Element Films, 204
Element Post Production, 204
e-magazines, 143
Émail (newsletter), 152
Emap, 78
Emdee Productions 2000, 204
Emerald Rugby, 183
employment in media, 3–4, 239
Employment Law Report, 152
Empower.ie, 115
Endemol, 65–6
Energy and Environment Management, 152
Engineers Journal, 152
Enterprise Ireland, 296
Entertainment Factory, 205
Environmental Management Ireland, 152
EO Teilifís, 205
Equality News, 152
Equinox eBusiness Solutions, 115
Ergo Advertising Marketing, 271
Esperanza Productions, 205
Espresso Films, 205
Esras Films, 205
Euro Food & Drink, 152
EuroNews, 314
European Association for Viewers' Interests (EAVI), 293
European Biometrics Forum, 115
European Broadcasting Union, 314

European Foundation, 131
European Journalism Centre, 296, 314
EUROPRIX Multimedia Top Talent award, 107
Evening Echo, 16, **25**
Evening Herald, 15, 16, **25–6**
Evening News, 14
Event Guide, 152–3
Examiner Group, 16
Export and Freight, 183
Extreme Production, 234

Fáilte/Welcome, 153
Fantastic Films, 205
Farm & Plant Buyers Guide, 153
Farmers' Journal, 52
Farming Life, 52
Farm Week, 52
Farrell Grant Sparks, 296
Fastnet Films, 205
Feasta, 6, **153**
Feenish Productions, 206
Féile FM, 102
Fermanagh Herald, 183
Fermanagh News, 52
Ferndale Films, 206
festivals, 322, 323
FHM, 142
Figaro, Le, 315
film and audio-visual production, 189–94
    awards, 321–3, 325
    cinemas, 189
    digital technology, 193
    film classification, 292
    global trends, 192–4
    grants, 192, 322
    market, 191–2
    tax incentives, 190–91
    top ten films, 190
    training in, 238
Filmbase, 206
Film, Entertainment and Leisure, 206
Film Ireland, 153
Finance, 153
Financial Dynamics Ireland, 271
Financial Times, 310
    Ireland correspondent, 307
Fingal Independent, 26
Fins, 153
FireIMC, 287
Fishfilms, 206
Fish International Short Story Prize, 328

Fitzwilliam Post, 153
Flax Mill Publications, 131
Fleet Car, 153
Fleishman-Hillard, 262, **271**
Flirt FM, 96
Fluid Rock, 115
Flying in Ireland, 153
Flyleaf Press, 131
FM104, 78, **87**, 300
Focus, 154
Focus Advertising, 271
Focus on Ireland and the Wider World, 154
Foinse, 5–6, 14, **26**
Folio, 272
Food and Drink Business, 154
Food and Drink Manufacturing Solutions, 154
Food and Wine Magazine, 154
Food Ireland, 154
Food Service Ireland, 154
Footwear in Ireland, 154
Forefront Films, 206–7
Forfás, 297
Fortnight, 183
Forum, 155
Forum on Broadcasting, 9, 290
Four Courts Press, 121, **131**
Four Provinces Films, 207
Fox Broadcasting Company, 304
Fox News, 304–5
FOXTEL, 304
Foyle News, 52
Frankfurter Allgemeine, 314
Freedom of Information Act (1997), 8, 293
Fresh Film Festival, 328
Frontier Films, 207
Furrow, The, 155
Further Education Centre, 243
Fusion Films, 207
Futura, 155
Future Image, 287

Gabbro Productions, 207
Gaelcom, 207
Gaelic World, 141, **155**
Gael Media, 207
Gaffney McHugh Advertising, 272
Gallery Press, 131
Gallowglass Pictures, 207–8
Galway Advertiser, 26
Galway Bay FM, 88
Galway Film Fleadh, 328

Galway Independent, 26
Galway Magazine, 155
Galway-Mayo Institute of Technology, 243
Galway Now Magazine, 155
Game, The, 183
games industry, 106–7, 108
Gannett, 319
Garda News, 155
Garda Review, 155
Garda Times, 155
Gay Community News, 156
Gazeta, 26
Gazeta Wyborcza, 314
GCAS Group, 287
General Electric (GE), 301, 302, **319**
Generator Marketing, 272
Genesis Advertising, 287
Genuine Irish Old Moore's Almanac, 156
Geography Publications, 131
Getting Married, 183
Gibney Communications, 272
Gill & Macmillan, 121, **131**
Gillian Marsh TV Productions, 208
Ginty Films, 208
Glamour, 142
global media, 300–306
Glowworm Media, 208
GM Consultants, 287
GMTV Belfast, 73
GMTV London office, 73
Goan, Cathal, 290
Golden Spider Awards, 323, **328–9**
Goldfish Films, 208
Gold Star Media, 208
Golf Ireland, 141, **156**
Google, 263
Google Ireland, 115
Government Publications, 132
Gradireland, 156
Grafliks, 208
Granada Media Group, 8, 61, 66
Grand Pictures, 208
Graph Films, 209
Great Western Films, 209
Green Inc Productions, 234
Grey Helme, 272
Grierson 2004 awards, 323
Griffith College, 238, **243**
Grouse Lodge, 209
GSK Irish Medical Media Awards, 329
GT Media (Dublin), 272
Guardian, The (UK newspaper), 311

Guardian, The (Wexford paper), 26–7
Guerilla Films, 209
Guideline, 156
Guildhall Press, 137–8
Gúm, An, 6, **127**

H & H Productions, 209
Hallel, 156
Happy Endings Productions, 209
Harmonia, 139
HarperCollins, 302
Harvest Films, 209
Havok, 115
Hawkeye Films, 209
HBO, 302
Health, Living and Wellbeing, 156
Heartwise, 156
Heat, 142
Hello!, 142
Hell's Kitchen, 209–10
Heneghan PR, 272
Heritage Outlook, 157
Hewlett-Packard Ireland, 115–16
Hibernia Advertising, 273
Highball, 157
Highland Radio, 79, **88**
High Wire, 210
Hill and Knowlton, 273
History Channel, 302
History Ireland, 157
HMG Advertising and Marketing, 273
Hodder Headline Ireland, 122, **132**
Hofnaflús Teo, 210
Hogan Stand, 157
Hopkins Communications, 273
Horizonline Films, 210
Hospitality Ireland, 157
Hotel and Catering Review, 157
Hotel and Restaurant Times, 157
Hot Press, 141, 142, **157**
House & Home, 157
House Hunter, 158
Housing Times, 157
HRD Ireland, 158
Hummingbird Productions, 210

Ian Graham Productions, 210
IBEC (Irish Business and Employers'
    Confederation), 297
IBM Ireland, 116
ICAN Interactive, 273
Icebox Films, 210

ICE Cool, 273
IDEA, 273–4
IE Sports Review, 158
Igloo, 210
IIA (Institute of Internal Auditors) Award for
    Business Journalism, 333
IIA (Irish Internet Association) & MSN Net
    Visionary Awards, 329
Ikandi Productions, 211
Illusion Animated Productions, 211
Image, 141, 143, **158**
Imagine Ltd, 211
IMM Public Relations, 274
Imokilly People, 27
Impact Media, 274
IMPACT News, 158
Impartial Reporter, 52–3
InBusiness, 158
Independent, The, 311
Independent News and Media Group, 9, 15,
    16, 19, **27**, 61
Independent on Sunday, 311
Independent Radio and Television
    Commission (IRTC), 290
Independent Television News (ITN), 73
In Dublin, 141, **158**
Industrial and Manufacturing Engineer, 183
Industrial Relations News, 158
information, freedom of, 8, 293
Info TV, 274
Inis Films, 211
Inis Times, The, 27
Initiative, 141
Initiative Dublin, 274
In Production, 158
Inside Government Magazine, 158–9
Inside Ireland, 159
Insight Magazine, 159
Institute of Advertising Practitioners in
    Ireland, 297
Institute of Internal Auditors (IIA) Award for
    Business Journalism, 333
Institute of Public Administration, 243
    publishing, 132
Institute of Technology, Athlone, 244
Institute of Technology, Blanchardstown,
    244
Institute of Technology, Carlow, 244
Institute of Technology, Cork, 244
Institute of Technology, Dundalk, 244
Institute of Technology, Letterkenny, 245
Institute of Technology, Limerick, 245

Institute of Technology, Sligo, 245
Institute of Technology, Tallaght, 245
Institute of Technology, Waterford, 245
institutions, 289–93
Intel, 109, 110, **116**
Interactive Return, 274
Intercom, 159
International Game Developers' Association,
    107
International Herald Tribune, 314–15
International IMPAC Dublin Literary
    Award, 329
international media, 300–306
internet, 1, 106
    advertising, 10, 261, 263
    broadband, 1, 2, 108, 110, 143, 305
    companies, 106
    future trends, 108–11
    publishing and, 18, 143
    regulation, 292
    usage, 12, 105, 106
    web design, 106
Internet Advisory Board, 107, 108
Intouch, 159
Investor, The, 159
IPA Journal, 159
iPod, 111
IPU Review, 159
Ireland at Your Leisure, 159–60
Ireland International News Agency, 307
Ireland of the Welcomes, 159–60
Ireland on Sunday, 17, **27–8**
Ireland's Antiques and Period Properties, 160
Ireland's Auto Trader, 160
Ireland's Equestrian, 183–4
Ireland's Eye, 160
Ireland's Greyhound Weekly, 160
Ireland's Homes, Interiors and Living, 184
Ireland's Horse Review, 160
Ireland's Issues, 160
Ireland's Own, 160
Ireland's Pets, 184
Irish Academic Press, 132
Irish Academy of Public Relations, 245–6
Irish America Magazine, 160
Irish Angler's Digest, 161
Irish Arts Review, 161
Irish Banking Review, 161
Irish Birds, 161
Irish Brides and Homes Magazine, 161
Irish Broker, 161
Irish Building Magazine, 161

Irish Business and Employers' Confederation
    (IBEC), 297
Irish Car, 161
Irish Catholic, The, 28
Irish Christian Broadcasters (ICB), 102
Irish Commission for Communications
    Regulation (ComReg), 2, 11, 292, **296**
Irish Computer, 161
Irish Computer Directory and Diary, 162
Irish Connections Magazine, 188
Irish Construction Industry Magazine, 162
Irish Countrysports and Country Life, 184
Irish Crime, 162
Irish Criminal Law Journal, 162
Irish Current Law Monthly Digest, 162
Irish Cycling Review, 162
Irish Daily Mirror, 16, **28**
    Belfast office, **53**
Irish Daily Star, 15, 16, **28–9**
Irish Daily Star Sunday, 15, 16, 17, **29**
Irish Digital Media Awards, 107
Irish Direct Marketing Association (IDMA),
    260
Irish Economic and Social History, 162
Irish Educational Studies, 162
Irish Electrical Review Retail, 162
Irish Electrical Review Trade, 163
Irish Emigrant, The, 163
Irish Employment Law Journal, 163
Irish Engineers' Journal, 163
Irish Entrepreneur, 163
Irish Examiner, 16, **30**
    Dublin office, **31**
Irish Farmer's Journal, 14, **31**
Irish Farmers' Monthly, 163
Irish Field, The, 163
Irish Film and Television Awards (IFTA),
    321, 323, 325, **329**
Irish Film and Television Network (IFTN),
    211
Irish Film Board, 190, 192, **211–12**, 323
Irish Food, 163
Irish Forestry, 164
Irish 4x4 & Off-Road, 160
Irish Garden, 164
Irish Golf Review, 141, **188**
Irish Golf World, 141
Irish Hairdresser, 164
Irish Hardware, 164
Irish Homes Magazine, 164
Irish Independent, 15, 16, **31–3**
Irish Interiors, 164

Irish International Group, 274
Irish Internet Association, 106, 107, **116**
   IIA & MSN Net Visionary Awards, **329**
Irish Journal of Education, 164
Irish Journal of Family Law, 164
Irish Journal of Management, 164
Irish Journal of Medical Science, 165
Irish Journal of Psychological Medicine, 165
Irish Jurist, 165
Irish Language Broadcast Fund, 7
Irish language media, 4–7, 18, 97
Irish Law Reports Monthly, 165
Irish Law Times, 165
Irish Literature Exchange, 122
Irish Management Institute, 246
Irish Marketing and Advertising Journal, 165
Irish Marketing News, 165
Irish Media Contacts Directory, 165
Irish Media Guide, 133
Irish Medical Directory, 165
Irish Medical Journal, 166
Irish Medical News, 166
Irish Medical Times, 33
Irish Motor Industry, 166
Irish News, 17, **53**
Irish People, 17
Irish Pharmacist, 166
Irish Pharmacy Journal, 166
Irish Photographers' Website, 212
Irish Planning and Environmental Law
   Journal, 166
Irish Post, The, 33
Irish Practice Nurse, 166
Irish Press Group, 4, 13, 15, 239
Irish Professional Photographers Association
   (IPPA) Awards, 322, **330**
Irish Printer, 166–7
Irish Property Buyer, 167
Irish Psychologist, The, 167
Irish Racing Calendar, 167
Irish Recorded Music Association, 297
Irish Red Cross Review, 167
Irish Review, The, 167
Irish Rugby Review, 141, **167**
Irish Runner, 167
Irish Scientist Yearbook, 167–8
Irish Skipper, 168
Irish Small and Medium Enterprises
   Association (ISME), 297
Irish Soccer Magazine, 168
Irish Social Worker, 168
Irish Stock Market Annual, 168

Irish Sun, 15, 16, **33**
Irish Tatler, 140, 141, 142, 143, **168**
Irish Theological Quarterly, 168
Irish Times, 6, 15, 16, **33–5**, 239
   London office, **35**
Irish Times Books, 132
Irish Travel Trade News, 168
Irish Trucker, 168
Irish Veterinary Journal, 168–9
Irish World, 188
Irish Youthwork Scene, 169
Iris Oifigiúil, 169
ITAR Tass, 307
ITN (Independent Television News), 73
It's All about Living, 169
iTunes, 111
ITV, 60

Jam Media, 212
Javelin/Young and Rubicam, 274–5
JDM Film and Television Production, 212
Jelly Communications, 287
Jerusalem Post, 317
JH Parker and Company, 275
Jimmy Murakami Film Production, 218
Johnston Press, 19
Joint National Listenership Research
   (JNLR), 76
Joint National Readership Survey (JNRS),
   14
Jordan, Neil, 212
Journal, The, 169
Journal of Music in Ireland, 169
journalism
   awards, 321, 322, 324
   training, 3, 237
Journeyman Productions, 116, 212

Kairos Communications, 212
Kapooki Games, 107, **116**
Kathimerini, 315
Kavaleer Productions, 212
Kazaa, 111
KCLR 96FM, 88
Keating and Associates, 275
Kerry Film Festival, 330
Kerryman (book publisher), 132
Kerryman, The (newspaper), 35
Kerry's Eye, 35
Keystone, 184
Kfm, 89
Kildare Nationalist, 35

Kildare Times, 35
Kilkenny People, 36
Killarney Advertiser, 36
Killester College of Further Education, 246
Kilroy's College, 246
Kingdom, The, 36
Kiss (magazine), 169
Kiss 100 (radio station), 101
Kite Entertainment, 212–13
Kratos, 116
KT Parenting, 169

Lá, 6, 14, **54**
Lagan Press, 138
Lakeland Extra, 54
Language, 213
Laois Nationalist, 36
Lapwing Publications, 138
Larkin Partnership, 275
Larne Times, 54
LA Times, 317
Law Media Awards, 330
Law Society Gazette, 169–70
Leader, The, 54
Leader Group, 19
Legend Films, 213
Leinster Express, 36
Leinster Leader, 36
Leitrim Observer, 36
Leo Burnett Associates, 275
Letterkenny Institute of Technology, 245
Letterkenny Listener, 37
Levy McCallum Advertising Agency, 287–8
Liam Quigley Voiceovers, 213
libel, 124, 293
Libération, 315
Liberties College, 246
Liberties Press, 132
Liberty Films, 213
Liberty Media International, 11, 61
Licensed and Catering News, 184
Licensed Vintners' Association Directory and
    Diary, 170
Licensing World, 170
Lifeboats Ireland, 170
Lifejacket Media Production, 213
Lifetimes, 170
Liffey Champion, 37
Liffey Press, 132–3
Lightbox Multimedia, 116
Like It Love It Productions, 213
Lilliput Press, 133

Limavady College of Further and Higher
    Education, 253
Lime Media Solutions, 275
Limerick Institute of Technology, 245
Limerick Leader, 37
Limerick Post, 37
Limerick Regional Hospital Radio, 99
Limerick's Live 95FM, 79, **89**
Lincor Solutions, 117
Lios na Sí Teoranta, 213
Liquid Sound Radio, 103
Lisburn Echo, 54
Lisburn Institute of Further and Higher
    Education, 253
Listowel Writers' Week, 330
Little Bird, 213–14
LM FM, 10, **89**
Local Authority Times, 170
Local News, 170
Londonderry Sentinel, 54
Lon Dub Teo, 214
Longford Leader, 37
Longford News, 37
Loophead Studio, 214
Loopline Film, 214
Louis Knowles and Associates, 275
Louis Marcus Productions, 214
Lucan Gazette, 37
Lunah Productions, 214
Lurgan and Portadown Examiner, 54
Lurgan Mail, 54
Lyle Bailie International, 288
Lyric FM, 3, 75, 77, **81–2**

Macalla Teoranta, 214
Macra na Feirme Yearbook and Diary, 170
magazines and periodicals, 139–43
    advertising, 140, 142
    circulation and readership, 140–42
    Irish language, 5–6
    market, 140–42
    trends, 143
Magic 105, 101
Magill, 140, **170**
Magma Films, 214–15
Mail on Sunday, 311–12
Malone, John, 11
A Man & Ink, 196
Manufacturing Ireland, 170–71
MAPS (Media, Advertising, Promotions and
    Sponsorship), 171
Marine Times, 171

Marino College Further Education Centre, 246
marketing, 260–63
Marketing (magazine), 171
Marketing Works, 275
market research, 262
Marley Media, 275–6
Martello Press, 133
Martin, Des, 215
Mary Crotty Public Relations, 276
Mary Immaculate College of Education, 238, **251**
Mason, Hayes and Curran, 297
Mass Productions, 215
Mater Hospital Radio, Belfast, 103
Mater Hospital Radio, Dublin, 99
Maternity, 171
Matheson Ormsby Prentice, 297
Maverick House, 133
Mayo Magazine, 171
Mayo News, 37–8
McCamley Entertainment, 215
McCann Erickson
  Belfast office, 288
  Dublin office, 276
McCann Fitzgerald, 297
McChesney, Robert, 303
McConnells Advertising Service, 259, **276**
MCD, 259
McDowell, Michael, 293
McFilms, 215
McInerney, Seamus, 215
MCM Communications, 276
McNamara Films, 215
McVeigh Broadcast, 215
Mdigginphotography, 215
Meath Chronicle, 38
media, 1–12
  Irish language, 4–7, 18, 97
  market and players, 9–10
  ownership and globalisation, 291, 300–306
  regulation and policy, 7–9, 236, 289–93
  technology, 1–2, 8, 11
  trends, 11, 305–6
  see also new media
Media Access Project, 317
MEDIA Antenna Galway, 246–7
Media Bureau, 276
Mediacom, 276
MEDIA Desk Ireland, 247
mediaedge:cia Ireland, 276–7
Mediaforce, 20

MEDIA fund, 192
Media Lab Europe, 107–8, 109
Media Link, 277
Media Monitors Ireland, 298
Media Nua, 215
Media Publications, 133
Mediascapes, 216
media studies, 3, 236–9
Mediaworks, 277
Medical Missionaries of Mary Magazine, 171
Medicine Weekly, 38
Medico-Legal Journal of Ireland, 171
Meegan, Paddy, 279
Meem Productions, 216
Menswear in Ireland, 171
Mentor Publications Ltd, 133
Mercier Press, 133
Mercury Media, 277
Merlin Films Group, 216
Merlin Publishing, 133
Merrion Capital Group, 298
Messnier, Jean-Marie, 303
Meteor, 117
Meteor Ireland Music Awards, 330
Methodist Newsletter, 184
Metro Éireann (newspaper), 38
Metro Eireann Media and Multicultural Awards (MAMA), 321, **330**
Metropolitan Films, 216
MGM studios, 301, 302, 303
Michael O'Connell Productions, 216
Microsoft, 107, 260, 301, 302
  Ireland, **117**
Mid 106, 101
Midas Productions, 216
Middle East Times, 317
Midlands 103, 90
Midlands Magazine, 171–2
Midland Times, 38
Midland Tribune, 38
Midnight Movies, 216
Mid-Ulster Echo, 55
Mid-Ulster Mail, 55
Mid-Ulster Observer, 55
Mid West Radio, 79, **90**
Millar McCall Wylie, 298
Millbrook Studios, 217
Milltown Studies, 172
MindShare, 277
Mind the Gap Films, 217
Mint Productions, 217
Miramax, 302

Miss Smith Productions, 217
MMDS, 61
mobile phones
  advertising medium, 261
  games, 106–7, 109
  market, 106, 305
  Moore's Law, 109
  radio and, 11, 80
  television and, 11, 65–6
  text messaging, 104–5
  usage, 1–2, 12, 104–5
Mobile Tornado, 117
Modern Medicine, 172
Modern Woman, 140, **172**
Moiselle Casting, 298
Moments, 172
Monde, Le, 315
Mongrel, 172
Monster Animation and Design, 217
Monster Distributes, 217
Montague Communications, 277
Moondance Productions, 217–18
Moondog Productions, 234
Moore's Law, 109–11
Morrow Communications, 288
Morton Newspaper Group, 55
Moscow Times, 317
Motive, 218
Motoring & Home Life, 142
Motoring Life, 172
Motor Market, 172
Motorshow, 172
Mourne Observer and County Down News,
  55
Movie Extras, 298
Moving In, 172–3
Moving Media, 117
Moving Still Productions, 218
MR Films, 218
MRM Design, 277
MRPA Consultants, 277
MRPA Kinman, 277
MTV, 301, 302
Multi Media Arts Ireland, 218
Mundo, El, 314
Múnla, 218
Munster Express, 38
Murdoch, James, 10, 305
Murdoch, Lachlan, 305
Murdoch, Rupert, 10, 300, 303–5
Murray Consultants, 262, **277–8**
Musketeer Productions, 218

98FM, 85
Napster, 111
National College of Art and Design, 247
National College of Ireland, 247
National Enquirer, 142
National Gallery of Ireland, 133
Nationalist and Leinster Times, 38
Nationalist and Munster Advertiser, 38
National Library of Ireland Publications, 134
National Media Awards, 321, 322, 324, **330**
National Newspapers of Ireland (NNI), 17,
  298
National Training and Development
  Institute (NTDI), 247
National Union of Journalists, 239, **298**
National University of Ireland
  central office, **247**
  Cork, **247**
  Dublin, **248**
  Galway, 238, **248**
  Maynooth, 238, **248**
NBC, 302, **319**
NCBI News, 173
Near FM, 96–7
Negroponte, Nicholas, 109
Neighbourhood Retailer, 184
Nelvana International, 219
Nemeton, 219
Nenagh Guardian, 39
Nerve Centre, The, 234
Net Visionary Awards, 107
New Decade TV and Film, 219
Newgrange Pictures, 219
New Houses, 184–5
New Island Books, 134
new media, 104–11
  companies, 106–7
  'disruptive technologies', 110–11
  education and career in, 237
  penetration and use, 104–5
  policy, 107–8
  regulation, 292
  trends, 108–11, 305–6
New Media Technology College, 248
Neworld Group, 278
New Ross Standard, 39
Newry Democrat, 55
Newry Institute, 253–4
Newry Reporter, 55
News Corporation, 300, 302, 303–5, 306,
  319
News Extracts, 298

Newsfile, 219
News Letter, 17, **55–6**
News Monitoring Services, 298
News of the World, 17, 302
  Belfast office, **56**
  Dublin office, **39**
  London office, **310**
Newspaper Commission, 18
newspapers, 13–20
  advertising, 13, 17, 18, 19–20, 258
  developments, 4, 13–14
  journalism awards, 321, 322, 324
  journalism training, 3, 237
  libel laws, 293
  market, 15–17
  readership and circulation, 13, 14, 15–16
  regional, 18–20
  Sunday papers, 16–17
  trends, 17–18
Newsquest Media Group, 310
Newstalk 106FM, 10, 79, **90–91**
Newtownabbey Times, 56
Newtownards Chronicle and County Down
  Observer, 56
Newtownards Spectator, 56
New York Post, 302
New York Times, 317–18
  Dublin correspondent, 308
Niamh Lehane Design and Advertising, 278
Nickelodeon, 259, 301
Nokia, 11, 260
Nomad, 219
North Belfast News, 56
North County Leader, 39
North Down and Ards Institute (NDAI),
  254
Northern Builder Magazine, 185
Northern Ireland Arts and Business
  Creativity Awards, 323, **333**
Northern Ireland Film and Television
  Commission (NIFTC), 7, **254**
Northern Ireland Film Commission, 234
Northern Ireland Legal Quarterly, 185
Northern Ireland Press Photographers'
  Association (NIPPA), 298–9, 322
Northern Ireland Travel and Leisure News,
  185
Northern Ireland Veterinary Today, 185
Northern Ireland Visitors' Journal, 185
Northern Sound Radio (Cavan), 79, **91**
Northern Sound Radio (Monaghan), 79, **91**
Northern Standard, 39

Northern Visions, 254
Northern Woman, 142, **185**
North West Echo, 56–7
North West Institute of Further and Higher
  Education (NWIFHE), 254
North-West Radio, 79
Northwest Visitor's Guide, 173
Novell Ireland Software, 117
N Power PR International, 278
NTL, 2, 11, 61, 62, **117**
Nua, 105
Nua Media, 234–5
Nursing in the Community, 173
NvTv, 73–4

141/Red Cell, 264
O2 Ireland, 106, 109, **117**
Oak Tree Press, 134
Obair, 173
O'Brien, Denis, 10, 78
O'Brien Press, 134
Observer, The, 312
Observer Newspaper Group (N. Ireland), 57
Ocean Brand Opportunities, 278
Ocean Film Productions, 220
Ocean FM, 91–2
Octagon, 220
Ofcom, 2, 291
  Belfast office, **299**
Offaly Express, 39
Offaly Independent, 39
Official Languages Act (2003), 18
Offshore Investment Magazine, 185
Ogilvy and Mather Advertising, 278
Oireachtas na Gaeilge, 323, **330–31**
O'Leary PR and Marketing, 278
Omagh College, 255
Ombudsman, 293, **299**
One Productions, 278
OneWorld International Foundation, 310
Open University
  Belfast, 255
  Dublin, 249
Ordnance Survey Ireland, 134
O'Reilly, Tony, 9
ORF (Austrian Broadcasting Corporation),
  315
Organic Matters, 173
Oscarina Ltd, 220
O'Sullivan Public Relations, 278–9
O'Sullivan Ryan Advertising, 279
Outdoor Media Association, 258

Outhouse Advertising, 279
Outlook (missionary magazine), 173
Outlook, The (newspaper), 57
Outsider, 173
Overture, 106
Owens DDB, 279
ownership, media, 291, 300–306

Pace Entertainment Productions, 220
Pacenotes, 185
PA Consulting, 263
Padbury Advertising, 279
Paddy Meegan, 279
País, El, 314
Palomino Pictures, 220
Panos Media London, 310
Paradise Pictures, 220
Paradox Pictures, 220
Paragon Design and Image Consultants, 279
Parallel Film Productions, 220–21
Paramount, 302, 303
Park Communications, 279
Parzival Productions, 221
Patrick M. Verner Photography, 221
Paul Allen and Associates PR, 279
PC Live!, 173
Pearl and Dean, 280
Pearse College, 249
Peatland News, 174
Peer Pressure, 221
'peer-to-peer' software, 111
Pegasus Productions, 221
Pembroke Communications, 280
Penguin Ireland, 122, **134**
People, The, 312
People Newspapers, 39–40
Periodical Publishers' Association of Ireland
    (PPAI), 140
periodicals see magazines and periodicals
Peripheral Vision, 221
Phantom FM, 79, **92**
Philip Lee Solicitors, 299
Philomel Productions, 134
Phoblacht, An/Republican News, 21
Phoenix, 141, **174**
Phoenix FM, 97
Phoenix Safety, 118
Phonographic Performance Institute, 322
Photocall Ireland, 221
Pictia Productions, 221
Picture Editors' Awards, 331
Pierce Media and Advertising, 280

Pioneer, 174
Piranha Bar, 221
PixAlert International, 118
Pixel Soup, 118
Plan: The Business of Building, 174
Planet Rock Profiles, 221–2
Planet Television UK and Ireland, 222
Plantman, 174
Plumbing and Heating, 185–6
Poetry Ireland Review, 174
Poolbeg (publisher), 135
Poolbeg Productions (films), 222
Portadown Times, 57
Portfolio, 174–5
Portobello College, 249
Post IT, 222
Potter, Dennis, 305
Power of Seven, 280
Power Pictures, 222
Powertrip Productions, 222
PPA Ireland Magazine Awards, 331
PPI Radio Awards, 321, 322, 326, **331**
Practical Employment Law, 174
Prague Post, 315
Presbyterian Herald, 186
Press 22 (photographic agency), 222
Press Association
    Belfast office, 308
    Dublin office, 308
    London office, 310
Press Code of Standards, 293
Press Council, 17, 289, 293
Press Ombudsman, 293
Pricewaterhouse Coopers, 299
PrimairSites, 288
Prim-Ed Publishing, 135
Prime Productions, 222
Primus Advertising and Marketing, 280
Princes Holdings, 61
Private Research, 174–5
Prix Italia, 323
Proactive Group, 280
Proctor and Gamble, 259
Professional Insurance Broker, The, 175
Professional Ireland, 175
ProMedia, 222
Property Professional, The, 175
Property Valuer, The, 175
Province 5 Television, 71
Provincial Farmer, 40
Prudence, 175
Public Affairs Ireland, 175

Public Affairs News, 175
Public Communications Centre, 280
public relations, 262
Public Sector Times, 175
Public Service Review, 175–6
PúCán Films, 222–3
Pulse Group Ireland, 280–81
Purple, 281
Purple Productions Teoranta, 223
Puttnam, Lord, 303

Q4 Public Relations, 262, **281**
Q97.2 (Causeway Coast Radio), 101–2
Q101.2FM West (Enniskillen), 102
Q101.2FM West (Omagh), 102
Q102.9, 102
Q102FM, 92
QMP Publicis (QMP D'Arcy), 281
Quantum Advertising Group International, 281
Quantum Communications, 281
Queen's University, 3, **255**
Quin Films, 223

radio, 75–80
  advertising, 76, 78, 258
  audiences and listenership, 75–8
  awards, 321, 322, 326
  community radio, 79, 95–8
  development of, 3, 8, 75
  digital, 8, 11, 80
  hospital, 99, 103
  independent, 3, 75, 290
  Irish language, 5, 97
  licensing, 80
  local, 3, 8, 75, 79, 85–95
  market, 78–9
  regional, 77, 79
  regulation, 7–8, 289–90
  top programmes, 76–7
  trends, 77, 80
Radio and Television Act (1988), 8
Radio Corca Baiscinn, 97
Radio Craigavon, 103
Radio France Internationale, 315
Radio Kerry, 79, **92–3**
Radio Mid-Ulster, 103
Radio Moyle, 103
Radio Netherlands, 315
Radio Telefís Éireann see RTÉ
Radio Ulster, 5, 10, **100**
Radio Valley, 103

Raidió na Gaeltachta, 4, 5, 75, 77, **84–5**
Raidió na Life, 5, **97**
Raidió Pobail Inis Eoghain (ICRFM), 97
Random House, 303
Rapid Film, 223
Rapport Marketing Communications, 281
Rathbane Publishing, 135
Rathmines College, 237, **249**
Rational Decisions, 281
Ravel Productions, 223
Raw Nerve Productions, 235
Reach: Journal of Special Needs Education in Ireland, 176
Reality Design and Marketing Consultants, 282
Reality Magazine, 176
Realt Entertainment, 223
Recruit Ireland, 118
Recruitment, 186
Red Cell, 264
Red FM 104–106, 93
Red Lemonade Productions, 223
Red Pepper Productions, 223
Reel Fishy, 223
Regional Advertising Associates, 282
Regional Film and Video, 186
Regional Newspapers Association of Ireland (RNAI), 19, **299**
regulation, 7–9, 289–93
Relay Books, 135
Religious Life Review, 176
Renovate Your House and Home, 176
Repubblica, La, 315
Research and Markets, 299
Retail Grocer, 186
Retail News, 176
Reuters, 310
  Dublin office, 308
  Foundation, 310
Reverse Perspective, 118
Ringsend Technical Institute, 249
Rí Productions, 118
River Films, 224
RLA Group, 288
Rocket Animation, 224
Roe Valley Sentinel, 57
Ronan O'Leary Productions, 224
Room, 176
Rooney Prize for Irish Literature, 331
Roscommon Champion, 40
Roscommon Herald, 40
Rosg, 224

Rothco, 282
Rough Magic Film Productions, 224
Royal Irish Academy, 135
Royal Television Society (RTS), 322, **333**
RTBF, 316
RTÉ (Radio Telefís Éireann)
  awards, **331**
  complaints process, 293
  development of, 1, 3, 9, 60–62, 75
  digital broadcasting and, 62
  financial base, 9, 61, 62
  policy and regulation, 7–8, 9, 236, 289–90
  radio, 76–8, **81–5**
  Lyric FM, 3, 75, 77, **81–2**
  Radio 1, 75, 76, 77, **82–3**
  Radio 2FM, 75, 76, 77, **83–4**
  Raidió na Gaeltachta, 4, 5, 75, 77, **84–5**
  RTÉ 1, 60
  RTÉ 2, 60, 63
  television, 60, 62–5, **67–8**
  TG4, 4–5, 7, 61, 63, **69**, 323
RTÉ Authority, 9, 289, 293
RTÉ Charter, 9
RTÉ Guide, 141, 142, **176**
RTL, 303
Rubicon Advertising, 282
Running Your Business, 176
Runway Airports, 177
Russell Avis Productions, 224
Ryanair, 259

Sacred Heart Messenger, 177
Saffron Pictures, 224
Safinia Productions, 224
Sagasnet, 316
St Ita's Hospital Radio, 99
St John's Central College of Further
  Education, 250
St Kevin's College, 250
St Leger, Joe, 225
Salesian Bulletin, 177
Salmon Publishing, 135
Samson Films, 225
Saoirse, 177
Saol na nOileán, 177
Saor-Oilscoil na hÉireann (Free University
  of Ireland), 249
Saothar, 177
Scannáin Dobharchú, 225
Scannáin Lugh, 225
School of Celtic Studies, 130
Science, 177

Science Spin, 177
Scottish Radio Holdings (SRH), 10, 19, **40**,
  78–9, 300
Screen Directors' Guild of Ireland, 225
Screen Producers Ireland (SPI), 192, **225**
Screen Scene, 225
Screentime ShinAwiL, 118, 225–6
Screen Training Ireland, 192, **249–50**
Scripture in Church, 177–8
Scun Scan, 226
Seagate Foyle Film Festival, 333
Search, 178
Selatra, 106, **118**
Self Building, Extending and Renovating
  Homes, 186
Senior College Dún Laoghaire (SCD), 250
Senior Times, 178
Services, Industrial, Professional and
  Technical Union (SIPTU), 299
Setanta Communications, 282
Setanta Sport, 69–70
SháineFilms, 226
Shannon Region Visitor's Guide, 178
Shannonside 104FM, 79, **93**
Shelflife, 178
Sheridan, Jim, 191
Shine FM, 102
Shine On Productions, 226
ShopAD, 119
Shortt Comedy Theatre Co/Warehouse TV,
  226
Siemens, 119
Signal, 178
Simon and Schuster, 302
Simpson Financial and Technology PR, 282
Sin Sin! Teo, 226
Síocháin, 178
SIPTU, 299
Sites Media, 282
Sitric Books, 135
Sky (BSkyB), 8, 10, 11, 60, 61, 259, 303,
  304
  Sky News (Belfast Bureau), **74**
  Sky News (Ireland), **70**
Skype, 111
Sláinte, 178
Slattery Communications, 282
Sligo Champion, 40
Sligo Institute of Technology, 245
Sligo Weekender, 40–41
SLS Legal Publications (NI), 138
Smart Company, 178

SMIRSH Films, 226
SMS text messaging, 104–5
Smurfit Communications, 139, 140
Social & Personal, 140, **178**
Socialist Voice, 179
Solo Too, 226–7
SOL Productions, 227
Sonas Innovation (Sonasi), 119
Sony, 105, 111, 300, 301, 302, 303, **320**
  Radio Academy Awards, 322, **333**
Sorrento Pictures, 227
Source, 186
South African Broadcasting Corporation
  (SABC), 318
South Belfast News, 57
South China Morning Post, 318
South City Express, 41
SouthCoast TV (SCTV), 71
South East Radio, 93–4
Southern Advertising and Marketing (Cork),
  282–3
Southern Advertising and Marketing
  (Limerick), 283
Southern Star, 41
South Tipperary General Hospital Radio, 99
South West Clare Community Radio, 97
Space Synapse, 119
Spark Marketing Communications, 283
Specify, 186
Speers Films, 227
SP Films, 227
Spin 1038 FM, 10, **94**
Spirituality, 179
Spokesman Advertising Company, 283
sponsorship, 260
Sporting Press, 179
Sportsbrand Media, 119
Stacey Marketing Services, 283
Standard, Der, 313
STAR (satellite network), 304, 305
Starcom-MediaVest Group, 283
Starfish, 283
Stars on Sunday, 14
Stationery Office (TSO Ireland), 138
Stillorgan College of Further Education, 250
Stirling Film and Television Productions, 235
Stoney Road Films, 227
stop.watch television, 227
Strabane Chronicle, 57
Strabane Weekly News, 57
Straight Forward Film and Television
  Productions, 235

Stranger Than Fiction Documentary Festival
  and Market, 331
Stratus Marketing and Development, 283
Stray Dog Films, 227
Strokestown Poetry Competition, 332
Stuart Kenny Associates, 283
Student Link, 283–4
Studia Hibernica, 179
Studies, 179
Subotica Entertainment, 228
Subsea Magazine, 179–80
Süddeutsche Zeitung, 316
Sugar, 142
Sumner Redstone, 301
Sun, The, 302, **312**
Sunday Business Post, 4, 17, **41**
Sunday Express, 312
Sunday Independent, 15, 16, 17, **41–2**
Sunday Journal, 57–8
Sunday Life, 17, **58**
Sunday Mirror, 17
  Belfast office, **58**
  Dublin office, **42**
  London office, **311**
Sunday Telegraph, 311
Sunday Times, 17, 259, 302
  Dublin office, **42**
  London office, **312**
Sunday Tribune, 15, 17, **43**
Sunday World, 15, 16, 17, **43**
  Northern Ireland Edition, **58**
Swift Agency, 284
Sydney Morning Herald, 318
Synergy Learning, 255

2FM, 75, 76, 77, **83–4**
2RN, 75
2000 AD Productions, 195
3C (Continuous Cool Country), 100
3G phones, 11, 109
Taisce, An, 145
Tallaght FM, 97–8
Tallaght Institute of Technology, 245
TDP Advertising, 288
Teacher Magazine, 179
Technology Ireland, 179
Telegael Media Group, 228
Telegraaf, De, 313
television, 60–66
  advertising, 10, 62, 66, 258, 290–91
  awards, 321–3, 325
  development of, 1, 3, 8, 9, 60–62

digital, 1, 8, 10, 11, 60, 61–2, 289
independent, 3–4, 8, 61, 290
Irish language, 4–5, 7
licence fees, 9, 61
market, 60, 62–5
mobile television, 65–6
regional and community, 9, 62, 71
regulation, 7–8, 9, 61–2, 289–90
satellite, 8, 10, 11, 60, 61, 289, 304, 305
top programmes, 64–5
trends, 11, 65–6
Telwell Productions, 228
Temple Bar Music Centre, 228
Terraglyph Productions, 228
Text 100 International, 284
text messaging, 104–5
TG4, 4–5, 7, 61, 63, **69**, 323
Thomas Crosbie Holdings, 19, **43**
Tiernan MacBride International
    Screenwriting Award, 332
Tile Films, 228
Time Horizon Productions, 228
Times, The, 312
Time Warner, 301, 302, **320**
Tipp FM, 94
Tipperary Institute, 250–51
Tipperary Mid West Community Radio, 98
Tipperary Star, 44
Tirconaill Tribune, 44
Tír Eolas, 135
Tish Barry Productions, 198
TKO Software, 106, **119**
TMP Worldwide Advertising and
    Communications
  Cork, 284
  Dublin, 284
Today FM, 3, 75, 76, 77, 78, **85**, 300
Today's Farm, 179
Today's Grocery Magazine, 180
Topic Newspapers Ltd, 44
Torc Interactive, 107, **119**
Totally Dublin, 180
Touchstone, 302
Townhouse, 135–6
Toytown Films, 229
training, 3, 236–9
Tralee Advertiser, 44
Translucid Media Ireland, 229
Travel Extra, 180
Treasure Films, 229
Trigger Productions, 229
Trinity College, Dublin, 3, **251**

TSO Ireland, 138
Tuam Herald, 44
Tullamore Tribune, 44
TV3, **70–71**
  development of, 3, 8, 61, 66
  market share, 60, 62, 63, 64
TVD, 235
TV-DVD, 65
TV Now!, 141, **180**
TV Times, 142
Twelve Horses, 119
Tyrone Constitution, 58
Tyrone Herald, 58
Tyrone Productions, 229
Tyrone Times, 58

U Magazine, 140, 142, 143, **180**
U2, 111
Ulster Architect Magazine, 186–7
Ulster Bride, 187
Ulster Business, 142, **187**
Ulster Farmer, 187
Ulster Gazette and Armagh Standard, 58
Ulster Grocer, 187
Ulster Herald, 59
Ulster Historical Foundation, 138
Ulster Hospital Radio, 103
Ulster Star, 59
Ulster Tatler, 142, **187**
Ulster Tatler Interiors, 187
Ulster Tatler Wine and Dine Guide, 187
Ulster Television see UTV
Unique Perspectives Advertising, 284
United Global Com (UGC), 2, 11, 61
United News, 187
Unity, 180
Universal McCann, 284
Universal Pictures, 303
University College Dublin Press, 122, **136**
University of Limerick, 3, **251**, 263
  Mary Immaculate College, 238, **251**
University of Ulster, **255**
  Coleraine, 237, **255–6**
Upper Bann Institute, 256
Upstart Games, 106, **120**
UTV (Ulster Television), 10, 60, 61
  Belfast office, **74**
  Dublin office, **71**
  radio, 78, 79

Vale Star/Mallow Star, 44
Vedanta Productions, 229–30

Venus Film and Television Productions, 230
Veritas, 136
Viacom, 301–2, 303, 306, **320**
Vico Films, 230
video games, 104, 105, 107
Village, The, 140, 141, **180**
Vinegar Hill Productions, 230
VIP Magazine, 140, **180**
Vision Advertising, 284
Visitor Magazine, 180
Vitel Productions, 230
Vivendi, 107, 303, **320**
Vocational Education Committees, 238
Vodafone Ireland, 106, **120**, 259
Voice, The, 180
Voicebank, 230
VoIP (voice ver IP), 110
VRT, 316

Walker Communications, 288
Walking Matters, 181
Walking World Ireland, 181
Wallslough Studios, 230
Wall Street Journal, 318
WalshCreative, 230
Walsh Public Relations, 284
Walt Disney Company, 191, 302, **320**
Warner Brothers, 300, 320
Washington Post, 318
Waterford Institute of Technology, 245
Waterford News and Star, 44
Waterford Today, 44
Web4mations, 231
web design, 106
Weber Shandwick Ireland, 262, **285**
Weber Shandwick Northern Ireland, 288
Wedding Journal, 181
Weddings Irish Style, 181
Weekender Newspaper, 45
Weekly Observer, 45
West Cork Literary Festival, 332
West Dublin Access Radio, 98
Western People, 45
Westinghouse, 301
West Limerick 102, 94
Westmeath Examiner, 45
Westmeath Independent, 45
Westmoreland College of Management and
    Business, 251
Wexford Book Festival, 332
Wexford People, 45
White Book, The, 181

Whytes, 136
Wicklow People, 45
Wicklow Times, 45
Wide Eye Films, 231
Wider Vision Productions, 231
wi-fi, 110
Wildfire Films and Television Production,
    231
Wilson Hartnell Public Relations, 285
WiMAX, 110
Wine Ireland, 181
Wired FM, 98
WLR FM, 79, **94–5**
Woman, 142
Woman's Own, 142
Woman's Way, 140, 142, **181**
Women's News, 187
Wonderland, 231
Woodend Films Teo, 231
Woodtown Music Publications, 136
Word, The, 181
World 2000 Entertainment, 231
World of Irish Nursing, 181
Wynkin deWorde, 136

X:Stream Pictures, 232
Xwerx, 120

Yellow Asylum Films, 232
YLE, 316
Young Euro RSCG, 285
Young Irish Film Makers, 232

Zamano, 120
Zanita Films, 232
Zanzibar Productions, 232
Zebedee Marketing, 285
Zenark, 120
ZenithOptimedia Ireland, 285
Zink Films, 232